INCREDIBLE ENGLISH KIT

Teacher's Book 3

Nick Beare

OXFORD
UNIVERSITY PRESS

Syllabus

Unit	Main topic and core language	'Learning through English' topic and language (CLIL)*	Other language (stories, songs, etc.)	Skills	Cognitive skills Learning for life Mini project
0	<u>Personal information questions:</u> **When's your birthday?** **It's on the twenty-third of October.** **What's your phone number?** **What's your surname?** <u>**Ordinal numbers:**</u> **first, second, third (etc.)** <u>**Months of the year:**</u> **January, February, March, April, May, June, July, August, September, October, November, December** <u>RECYCLED</u> numbers 1–30 (figures only) What's your name? How old are you? I'm …	(No CLIL topic)	(No songs or stories in this unit)	<u>Reading:</u> • Read ordinal numbers and months • Read personal information questions <u>Listening:</u> • Listen to personal information <u>Speaking:</u> • Ask and answer about personal information (name, age, address, phone number, birth date) • Act out a role play <u>Writing:</u> • Complete a crossword with months	<u>Cognitive skills:</u> • Act out dialogues with finger puppets, matching intonation on CD • Match ordinal number words to figures • Find information in membership forms <u>Cut and make:</u> • Finger puppets of the course characters
1	<u>**Personal possessions:**</u> **sweets, glasses, rollerblades, magazine, watch, umbrella, cards, bag, football** <u>**Prepositions:**</u> **behind, in front of, next to** <u>**is / are:**</u> **The glasses are next to the bag.** **Where are my …?** **They're …** **They aren't …** **Are they …?** <u>RECYCLED</u> cat in, on, under It's … The cat's in the bag. I've got (sweets and a magazine). Days of the week	***Maths: Telling the time*** <u>**Time phrases:**</u> **What's the time?** **It's seven o'clock.** **It's quarter past seven.** **It's half past seven.** **It's quarter to eight.** **morning** **night** **afternoon** **evening** digital clock face (clock) big / small hand (clock) minute, hour, second at school in bed on the bus <u>**Optional extension:**</u> digital time (twelve-fifteen, twelve forty-five, etc.)	wear carry I like your watch. I love your umbrella. Can you spell that, please? Go away! Scat! What a mess! poor cat member mess club welcome board games have fun place everyone outing trip join drink (n) mint frog	<u>Reading:</u> • Read a story • Read the personal possessions words and time words • Read and draw items in the correct location • Read a leaflet about club activities <u>Listening:</u> • Listen to a story • Recognize the personal possessions words and time phrases • Listen and write surnames • Listen and identify location <u>Speaking:</u> • Sing a song • Say a pronunciation chant • Talk about what you have got with you • Talk about where things are • Act out a story • Tell the time <u>Writing:</u> • Write the words for personal possessions • Write about where things are • Write part of a story • Write a leaflet about a club	<u>Cognitive skills:</u> • Create your own version of a story • Remember increasingly long sequences of items • Categorize words • Construct sentences using word tiles • Find out information from a leaflet • Think about the advantages of joining clubs • Tell the time (reading digital and analogue clocks) • Match words to pictures • Match words that have the same vowel sound • Solve a wordsearch • Solve a crossword (optional) • Solve a puzzle (optional) • Evaluate your progress in class <u>Learning for life:</u> • Joining clubs and doing things with friends <u>Mini project:</u> • Make a clock

* 'CLIL' = Content and Language Integrated Learning   Words and phrases in **bold** are the core language syllabus.

Unit	Main topic and core language	'Learning through English' topic and language (CLIL)	Other language (stories, songs, etc.)	Skills	Cognitive skills Learning for life Mini project
2	<u>Clothes:</u> **belt, coat, gloves, scarf, shirt, tights, tracksuit, trainers, cap** <u>Possessive adjectives:</u> **his / her** **What colour's his jacket?** **What colour are her shoes?** <u>***this / these*, possessive 's:**</u> **This is Luke's CD.** **These are Molly's shoes.** <u>RECYCLED:</u> dress, trousers, shoes <u>Present continuous with *wearing*:</u> What's he / she / Finn wearing? He's / She's wearing …	*Art: Portraits* <u>Adjectives to describe people:</u> **rich, poor, serious, angry, happy, sad** portrait painting drawing realistic abstract I think (he's poor). <u>Optional extension:</u> eyebrows, forehead, chin	top half bottom half team autograph manager Brilliant! Me too! Here you are. amazing fantastic menu snack bar coffee tea milkshake vanilla eighty pence one pound fifty energy	<u>Reading:</u> • Read a story • Read the words for clothes and adjectives to describe people • Read menus <u>Listening:</u> • Listen to a story • Recognize words for clothes and adjectives to describe people <u>Speaking:</u> • Sing a song • Say a pronunciation chant • Say what someone is wearing • Ask and answer about colour • Act out a story • Talk about portraits <u>Writing:</u> • Write the words for clothes and adjectives to describe people • Write about who things belong to • Write part of a story • Write a menu	<u>Cognitive skills:</u> • Create your own version of a story • Play an elimination game • Categorize words • Understand the link between spelling and pronunciation • Construct sentences using word tiles • Do mental arithmetic with small sums (adding up prices) • Think about healthy eating • Look at and talk about portraits (different types – painting, photo, drawing, etc.) • Talk about the differences between abstract and realistic portraits • Match descriptions to pictures • Match words that have the same vowel sound • Match patterns (optional) • Evaluate your progress in class <u>Learning for life:</u> • Eating for energy <u>Mini project:</u> • Make a portrait
3	<u>Camping things:</u> **blanket, comb, mat, pillow, pyjamas, sleeping bag, toothbrush, torch, towel, sunglasses** <u>***have got*:**</u> **Have you got a torch?** **Have you got any brothers?** **I haven't got a / any …** <u>RECYCLED:</u> book, teddy <u>***is / are*, prepositions:**</u> Is the comb on the bed? No, it's on the chair. Are the pyjamas under the table? No, they're on the bed.	*Music: Describing pitch, dynamics and tempo* <u>Adjectives to describe music:</u> **high, low, fast, slow, loud, quiet** pitch tempo dynamics It's fast and high. I think it sounds like a hen. I think the cow's music is slow and low. <u>Optional extension:</u> CD, cover, back, front, spine	What else? spotty I can't find my sunglasses. Don't forget your pillow! clubhouse ready scared (of) the dark scaredy cat owl bear everything Look, here's my sports bag. Let's check it. certificate tidy congratulations I'm happy to be me! hook	<u>Reading:</u> • Read a story • Read the words for camping things and adjectives to describe music • Read a certificate <u>Listening:</u> • Listen to a story • Recognize the words for camping things and adjectives to describe music <u>Speaking:</u> • Sing a song • Say a pronunciation chant • Ask and answer about what you have / haven't got • Act out a story • Describe music <u>Writing:</u> • Write the words for camping things and adjectives to describe music • Write about what you have / haven't got • Write part of a story • Write a certificate	<u>Cognitive skills:</u> • Create your own version of a story • Think about putting things into categories • Categorize words • Construct sentences using word tiles • Find information in certificates • Think about how people have different abilities and skills • Talk about music (pitch, tempo, dynamics) • Think about how different types of music can represent different animals • Match words that have the same vowel sound • Solve a wordsearch • Solve puzzles (optional) • Evaluate your progress in class <u>Learning for life:</u> • Being positive about ourselves Mini project: • Make animal music

Unit	Main topic and core language	'Learning through English' topic and language (CLIL)	Other language (stories, songs, etc.)	Skills	Cognitive skills Learning for life Mini project
4	<u>Animals:</u> **ant, guinea pig, lizard, stick insect, tortoise, butterfly, canary, snail** ***<u>has got:</u>*** **Has he got a guinea pig?** **Has she got a lizard?** **He / She hasn't got …** <u>RECYCLED:</u> rabbit, parrot, snake, fish He / She's got … Do you like guinea pigs? I like / don't like snails.	*Science: Insects* <u>Insects:</u> **fly, bee, ladybird, grasshopper, dragonfly** head, thorax, abdomen antennae lay eggs queen bee, spider It's brown. It's got big wings. It's got long legs. It can't fly. It can sting. <u>Optional extension:</u> fins, salmon, cod, goldfish	beautiful Who's Mrs Ripley? reptile, owner, python, chameleon Shame! Too bad! What's the matter? I can't find Camilla. Can I hold her? stripy postcard, address, teeth change colour fun, boring jungle, sea, grass, mountain, field, world crawl stamp (v)	<u>Reading:</u> • Read a story • Read the animal and insect words • Read postcards • Read descriptions of insects <u>Listening:</u> • Listen to a story • Recognize the animal and insect words • Listen and identify insects <u>Speaking:</u> • Sing a song • Say a pronunciation chant • Ask and answer about what animals people have got • Act out a story • Describe insects <u>Writing:</u> • Write the animal and insect words • Write part of a story • Write a postcard	<u>Cognitive skills:</u> • Create your own version of a story • Play an elimination game • Categorize words • Understand symbols to express likes and dislikes • Understand spelling patterns • Construct sentences using word tiles • Find information in postcards • Think about respecting animals' habitats • Talk about the parts of an insect's body • Match words that have the same vowel sound • Evaluate your progress in class <u>Learning for life:</u> • Respecting animals' habitats <u>Mini project:</u> • Invent an insect
5	<u>Food:</u> **broccoli, butter, cocoa, coconut, flour, spinach, asparagus, strawberries** **He likes / doesn't like …** **Does he / she like?** <u>RECYCLED:</u> biscuits, sugar, cheese, eggs *<u>is / are:</u>* How much is flour? It's … How much are strawberries? They're …	*Science: Parts of a plant* <u>Parts of a plant:</u> flower, fruit, leaf, stem, root, seed Chocolate is made from … cocoa beans, vanilla, pod, candle, salad soup, sauce, melon, maize, cane, tea leaves We use maize seeds to make cereals for breakfast. <u>Optional extension:</u> come out of, turn into, get bigger	We need flour. Let's buy some biscuits. mouse / mice, birthday What are you doing? We're making a cake. Let's buy a present. Off you go! Ready, steady, go! Look out! This cake is delicious! plate, tray recipe, glass, scoop, sprinkles, bowl, fork, jar, mash, shake, salad, mayonnaise chop, stop, top, teatime, pizza paper, ruler, pasta, scissors, rubber	<u>Reading:</u> • Read a story • Read the words for food and parts of plants • Read a recipe <u>Listening:</u> • Listen to a story • Recognize words for food and parts of plants • Listen and write prices <u>Speaking:</u> • Sing a song • Say a pronunciation chant • Act out a story • Ask and answer about prices • Ask and answer about what parts of the plant different foods are <u>Writing:</u> • Write the words for food and parts of plants • Write part of a story • Write a recipe	<u>Cognitive skills:</u> • Create your own version of a story • Play an elimination game • Categorize words • Do mental arithmetic with small sums (adding up prices) • Construct sentences using word tiles • Use codes • Think about working collaboratively • Talk about parts of plants which give us food • Think about the life cycle of a plant (optional) • Match words to pictures • Evaluate your progress in class <u>Learning for life:</u> • Working together <u>Mini project:</u> • Make a fruit and vegetable book

Unit	Main topic and core language	'Learning through English' topic and language (CLIL)	Other language (stories, songs, etc.)	Skills	Cognitive skills Learning for life Mini project
6	<u>Places in a town:</u> **bus station, car park, library, post office, restaurant, supermarket, shopping centre, swimming pool** **opposite** **There's a slide.** **There are eight swings.** **Is there a …?** **Are there any …?** <u>RECYCLED:</u> cinema, park, school Where's the shopping centre? It's next to the park.	*Geography: Map co-ordinates* <u>**Places in the country:**</u> **path, bridge, river, picnic area, wood, beach, shop** map, adventure, island, key, symbol cross (v), drive, return Here is the symbol for a picnic area. Can you find the picnic area on the map? Start at the shop. Walk to the wood. Cross the river. Return to the shop. <u>**Optional extension:**</u> north, south, east, west	Excuse me? Where's …? It's over there. I can see my favourite restaurant. Where are the visitors? Come and see our town. It's great! This is the park. late, enormous, slide, swing It's mine! Me first! bus station, train station opening times, adults, babies Don't drop rubbish. Put your rubbish in a bin. banana skin, street	<u>**Reading:**</u> • Read a story • Read the words for places in the town and the country • Read about places and identify them • Read a web page <u>**Listening:**</u> • Listen to a story • Recognize words for places in the town and the country • Listen to descriptions of streets and identify them <u>**Speaking:**</u> • Sing a song • Say a pronunciation chant • Ask and answer about where places are • Act out a story <u>**Writing:**</u> • Write the words for places in the town and the country • Write descriptions of places • Write part of a story • Write a web page	<u>**Cognitive skills:**</u> • Create your own version of a story • Play an elimination game • Categorize words • Construct sentences using word tiles • Find information in a web page • Think about why we shouldn't leave litter • Use symbols to locate places in a map grid • Use map co-ordinates • Draw a map and create a key of place symbols • Use compass points (optional) • Match words to pictures • Match words that have the same vowel sound • Evaluate your progress in class <u>**Learning for life:**</u> • Keeping public places tidy <u>**Mini project**</u> • Make a map and a leaflet
7	<u>Sports:</u> **badminton, baseball, basketball, chess, gymnastics, hockey, judo, table tennis, tennis, volleyball** **Do you play chess?** **Do you do judo?** **I play tennis.** **I don't do judo.** <u>RECYCLED:</u> football Is there a tennis class on Monday? There's football on Monday.	*Maths: Fractions* <u>**Football things:**</u> **wig, drum, flag** **half, quarter, three quarters** Half of the fans have got drums. A quarter of the boys are wearing T-shirts. Three quarters of the children are girls. <u>RECYCLED</u> hat, scarf, T-shirt	I want to do judo / play tennis. timetable, with, without Can I help you? Let me see. pass (a ball), ladder, over, hedge, hole Come on! We can play basketball. I prefer tennis. What about me? You're too small. What are you doing? On the other side. Come and play basketball. special offer, souvenir, pencil sharpener, farm, free, feed, tractor signs, square Don't feed the animals. Don't run in the hall.	<u>**Reading:**</u> • Read a story • Read the words for sports and football things • Read signs and notices <u>**Listening:**</u> • Listen to a story • Recognize words for sports and football things • Listen to a description of a picture and say true or false <u>**Speaking:**</u> • Sing a song • Say a pronunciation chant • Ask and answer about activities • Act out a story • Describe a picture **Writing:** • Write the words for sports and football things • Write about activities you do • Write descriptions of football fans • Write part of a story • Write a notice	<u>**Cognitive skills:**</u> • Create your own version of a story • Categorize words • Construct sentences using word tiles • Find information in a timetable • Use codes • Find information in signs and notices • Think about signs and notices, and why it is important to obey them • Find fractions of a number • Match words to pictures • Match words that have the same vowel sound • Solve a puzzle (optional) • Evaluate your progress in class <u>**Learning for life:**</u> • Obeying signs <u>**Mini project:**</u> • Make a picture of football fans

Unit	Main topic and core language	'Learning through English' topic and language (CLIL)	Other language (stories, songs, etc.)	Skills	Cognitive skills Learning for life Mini project
8	<u>Daily routines:</u> **get up, have breakfast, go to work, go to school, have lunch, leave work, leave school, have dinner, go to bed** **What time does he have breakfast?** **What time does he leave work?** **He has / leaves / gets / goes …** **He works in Middleton.** **He doesn't work in Middleton.** <u>RECYCLED:</u> have a shower Do you get up at eight o'clock? No, I get up at seven o'clock.	***Science: Electrical components*** **<u>Electrical components:</u>** **bulb, battery, wire, motor, switch** plug, circuit, mains electricity dangerous sometimes Never touch plugs with wet hands. Batteries make electricity. Circuits need batteries and wires. Tell me about this circuit. It's got a motor. It doesn't work! **<u>Optional extension:</u>** I think the light is dim / bright / very bright.	inventor, robot, workshop, machine My robot makes dinner. Where does he work? Not far away. There's a traffic jam! At last! Help me set up my machine. plug it in, switch it on Not too quick! Be careful! advert, today, electronics around, decide, cheap What shall I buy? It's really cool. I just can't wait! Wait a minute. What's it like? Stop and think before you buy!	**<u>Reading:</u>** • Read a story • Read the words for daily routines and electrical components • Read an advert **<u>Listening:</u>** • Listen to a story • Recognize words for daily routines and electrical components • Listen and identify circuits **<u>Speaking:</u>** • Sing a song • Say a pronunciation chant • Ask and answer about daily routines and circuits • Act out a story **<u>Writing:</u>** • Write the words for daily routines and electrical components • Write questions about daily routines • Write part of a story • Write an advert	**<u>Cognitive skills:</u>** • Create your own version of a story • Play an elimination game • Categorize words • Put activities in chronological order • Construct sentences using word tiles • Find an odd one out • Find information in adverts • Think about how adverts influence us • Think about what makes up an electrical circuit • Match words to pictures • Match words that have the same vowel sound • Make word spidergrams (optional) • Solve a puzzle • Evaluate your progress in class **<u>Learning for life:</u>** • Making informed choices **<u>Mini project:</u>** • Write about things that use electricity
9	<u>Circus actions:</u> **do a cartwheel, swing on a trapeze, do a somersault, walk on stilts, do a handstand, walk on your hands, do a headstand, ride a horse** **Is she walking on stilts?** **Is he riding a bike?** **We're walking.** **They're swimming.** <u>RECYCLED:</u> ride a bike, juggle I'm jumping. I can do a somersault. I can't walk on my hands. Can you juggle?	***Art: Drawing figures using ovals*** **<u>Parts of the body</u>** **neck, hip, shoulder, elbow, knee, foot** Draw three ovals for the head, neck and body. A leg is two ovals. The ovals overlap at the knees. The shoulders are one long oval. What do you think of this picture? I think the arms are too long. I think it's fine. <u>RECYCLED:</u> head, hand	There's a circus. I love circuses! circus tent fall I like trapeze artists best. Coco's a star! I can do that, too. poster sports day laugh races lose Do your best. Try again. Everyone's a winner! fun	**<u>Reading:</u>** • Read a story • Read the words for circus actions and parts of the body • Read a poster **<u>Listening:</u>** • Listen to a story • Recognize words for circus actions and parts of the body • Listen and identify pictures of actions **<u>Speaking:</u>** • Sing a song • Say a pronunciation chant • Ask and answer about what circus actions you can do • Act out a story **<u>Writing:</u>** • Write the words for circus actions and parts of the body • Write part of a story • Write questions about and descriptions of what people are doing • Write a poster	**<u>Cognitive skills:</u>** • Create your own version of a story • Play an elimination game • Categorize words • Use codes • Construct sentences using word tiles • Find information in a poster • Think about how to be a good loser and a good winner • Think about how it's not just winning but taking part that counts • Think about how to draw figures using ovals • Match words to pictures • Match words that have the same vowel sound • Evaluate your progress in class **<u>Learning for life:</u>** • Being a good loser and a good winner **<u>Mini project:</u>** • Draw a circus figure

Festivals	Language	Objectives
Christmas	**Father Christmas, reindeer, paper, ribbon, bow, label**	• Find out about Christmas in English-speaking countries • Sing a Christmas song • Make a Christmas gift box
Valentine's Day	coupon	• Find out about Valentine's Day in English-speaking countries • Think about being generous to our friends and family • Make gift coupons
Environment Day	recycle, reuse, reduce Save old wrapping paper! Pass on your clothes! Use less water! Use plastic bags again! Put glass in the glass bin!	• Find out about World Environment Day • Think about recycling • Make a recycling chart

Children around the world	Language	Objectives
My country	stripe, cross, dragon, moon **Morocco, Wales, Norway, Japan** **Arabic, Welsh, Norwegian, Japanese**	• Find out about and compare the lives of children in four countries around the world • Find out about and compare different countries' flags • Draw and write about your national flag
My town	**market, castle, square, building**	• Find out about and compare towns in different countries • Draw and write about your perfect town
Sport in my country	**running, dog sledding, rugby** player, stadium, sled, race, winter	• Find out about sport in different countries • Draw and write about sport in your own country

Key Competences

The inclusion of the key competences in the curriculum is part of an attempt to integrate the formal learning specific to each subject area with less formal learning, allowing pupils to see the relationship between the different subjects and use skills learned in one area in different contexts.

Based on those outlined by the Council of Europe, the *Real Decreto de Enseñanzas Mínimas de Educación Primaria* defines eight key competences:

- Competence in linguistic communication
- Competence in social skills and citizenship
- Artistic and cultural competence
- Learning to learn
- Autonomy and personal initiative
- Competence in processing information and the use of ICT
- Mathematical competence
- Competence in interaction with the physical environment

Foreign language learning contributes directly to the development of competence in linguistic communication as it increases, enriches and complements the pupil's communicative capacity. When language learning is based on the development of the four communicative skills (speaking, listening, reading, and writing), it helps develop this competence in the same way as the study of the pupil's native language. However, the development of the key competences can be achieved in all subject areas of the curriculum.

Incredible English Kit Key Competences Book 1-6 looks at the aspects of the eight competences which can most easily be developed within the subject area of foreign languages, and specifically in English. It describes how the competences are included and developed in *Incredible English Kit*. It also offers a bank of worksheets designed to complement the *Incredible English Kit* material.

Introduction

Welcome to the course

This is the third level of a six-level primary course. The course provides teachers with a very rich and flexible set of teaching materials, allowing them to expand the language syllabus into other areas of the curriculum, and providing a wide range of optional additional materials to cater for different timetabling needs.
The context is fresh, light-hearted, and fun while the underlying methodology is sound and well-established.

Level 3 components

Class Book

This is an 88-page colour book containing all the presentation material you will need for your lessons, including stories, songs, games, reading texts, and other activities.

The nine main units are eight pages long and are based on topics familiar to children of this age group.

New at this level is a focus on different **text types** – leaflets, menus, certificates, postcards, recipes, web pages, notices, adverts, and posters. A model of the text type is presented in each unit of the Class Book. Pupils then do a supported writing activity in the Activity Book (e.g. a listening gap-fill) and finally do more open work on a photocopiable template, producing their own version of the text type.

After the main units there are three festivals (Christmas, Valentine's Day, and World Environment Day) and three culture sections focusing on the lives of four children around the world.

At the back of the book you will find a syllabus summary and a comprehensive wordlist.

Activity Book

This is a 104-page black-and-white book full of challenging puzzle-type tasks to practise the language. The activities include matching, sorting, labelling, crosswords, and mazes, and are designed to motivate and challenge the pupils.

The Activity Book contains a bank of extra grammar worksheets on pages 97–104 to further consolidate the structure presented in each unit. The worksheets can be used after Lesson 5 of each unit.

Each unit includes a playscript activity, where pupils are able to manipulate the language from the Class Book story, and create their own version to act out in class.

The course structure integrates the Activity Book fully with the Class Book in the lessons. The Activity Book is designed mainly for use in the class, although some activities can be done for homework, such as the writing activities. A separate list of suggestions for homework activities is included in this Introduction on page 13.

The Activity Book includes a self-evaluation feature at the end of each unit, designed to make pupils aware of their own learning (see the Lesson 12 section on page 17 for further details).

Teacher's Book

The Teacher's Book serves as a clear and flexible guide for the teacher. It contains the following:

- The course syllabus;
- This introduction, setting out the overall objectives and principles of the course, and giving an outline of how the course works;
- A resource bank of games and activities (pp19–22);
- A list of sample classroom language (pp23–24);
- Step-by-step teaching notes for every lesson in the book, including 'Teaching tip' boxes with extra teaching ideas or suggestions for classroom management;
- Transcripts for all the recordings;
- Answers for all the activities (unless these are included in the transcripts);
- Teaching notes for the three festivals, including cultural information;
- Photocopiable test pages (see below);
- Photocopiable portfolio pages (see below);
- A wordlist containing the core vocabulary and other key language.

Test/Portofolio Section

This section includes flexible test material to reflect the course objectives. It contains nine unit tests for each unit and three term tests (with optional listening sections) to be used after Units 3, 6, and 9. These tests use a mixture of exercises similar to those found in pupils' Activity Books and formats which offer practice for the Cambridge Young Learners English Tests (Starter level).

For flexibility, there are two tiers for each unit test (Standard and Higher). The Higher Test is more demanding of the pupil and the teacher can differentiate to suit each pupil's ability. There are also parallel tests for the term tests (Tests A and B). Both tests are at the same level but the teacher can set these tests at the same time to avoid cheating, i.e. in pairs one pupil has Test A and the other, Test B. The teacher could also set one test and use the other later on.

A photocopiable record card on page 215 allows you to keep a record of pupils' achievements in reaching linguistic objectives.

In addition to the test material there are five photocopiable pages for pupils to create their own *Language Portfolio*, to which they can add examples of their work, exam certificates, materials from abroad etc. (For further information on portfolios, see page 216.)
A photocopiable record card is included to allow you to keep a unit-by-unit record of pupils' achievements in reaching linguistic objectives.

CDs

For Level 3 of the course there are three CDs to support teaching in class. These contain recordings of all the songs, chants, stories, and other listening activities, as well as the unit and term tests.

Songs and chants can be used to change the pace of the lesson and to help manage the transition from one stage to another. In Level 3 the songs also carry the 'Learning for life' message (see list of topics on page 11).

Teacher's Resource Pack

The Teacher's Resource Pack contains material for Levels 3 and 4 of the course. The Level 3 components are described below.

Flashcards

There are 152 picture cards for Level 3. These include the main unit vocabulary for Units 1–9 (10–12 new words in most units), the additional vocabulary input from the 'Learning through English' lessons (normally around 6 words), and the course characters.

Flashcard list

The flashcards are double-sided, so each card has two images.

1 Eve / strawberries
2 Luke / biscuits
3 Molly / sugar
4 Finn / eggs
5 Archie / cheese
6 Jazmin / stem
7 Coco the cat / root
8 magazine / leaf
9 sweets / flower
10 watch / seed
11 glasses / fruit
12 rollerblades / bus station
13 cards / swimming pool
14 umbrella / shopping centre
15 bag / car park
16 football / restaurant
17 belt / supermarket
18 coat / library
19 gloves / post office
20 scarf / cinema
21 shirt / park
22 tights / school
23 tracksuit / wood
24 trainers / path
25 cap / river
26 dress / bridge
27 shoes / picnic area
28 trousers / beach
29 serious / shop
30 angry / tennis
31 rich / basketball
32 poor / table tennis
33 happy / hockey
34 sad / badminton
35 comb / chess
36 sunglasses / judo
37 blanket / gymnastics
38 mat / volleyball
39 pillow / baseball
40 pyjamas / football
41 sleeping bag / wig
42 toothbrush / drum
43 torch / flag
44 towel / hat
45 book / T-shirt
46 teddy / get up
47 high / have breakfast
48 low / go to school
49 fast / have lunch
50 slow / leave school
51 loud / have dinner
52 quiet / go to bed
53 rabbit / have a shower
54 parrot / bulb
55 canary / battery
56 fish / wire
57 guinea pig / motor
58 lizard / switch
59 snail / ride a horse
60 tortoise / swing on a trapeze
61 snake / do a somersault
62 ant / walk on stilts
63 butterfly / do a handstand
64 stick insect / walk on your hands
65 grasshopper / do a cartwheel
66 ladybird / do a headstand
67 fly / juggle
68 bee / ride a bike
69 dragonfly / shoulder
70 broccoli / hip
71 butter / elbow
72 cocoa / knee
73 coconut / neck
74 flour / head
75 spinach / hand
76 asparagus / foot

Photocopy Masters Book (PMB)

The PMB has 56 pages of material:

- finger puppets of the course characters (for use in play acting in each unit);
- pupil picture cards for each unit;
- a template of blank pupil word cards (optional use);
- cut-out 'grammar tiles' for the 'Language focus' lessons (Lessons 4 and 5 of each unit);
- a template for the 'Reading and Writing' page (Lesson 7 of each unit);
- a template for the third 'Learning through English' lesson (Lesson 11 of each unit);
- an optional extra lesson for each unit ('Learning through English' extension – Lesson 11a);
- a page for each of the three 'Festivals' lessons;
- a page for each of the 'Children around the world' sections;
- a template for a Picture Dictionary (optional use).

Finger puppets

These are made in the Starter unit, and used in each unit to act out the stories. As well as the main course characters, a blank puppet template is included for pupils to make the extra characters who occasionally appear in the stories. (For further details of how to use the puppets in class, see the 'Activities and games' section at the end of this Introduction.)

Picture cards

The cards for the main vocabulary input are prepared by the pupils in Lesson 2 and used by them in the activities and games throughout the unit.

Photocopying onto card rather than paper is recommended in order to make the cards last longer.

If timing is an issue when preparing the cards, pupils could take the picture cards home and colour them in preparation for the next lesson.

Once the cards are prepared they should be kept in the classroom in separate sets, e.g. in envelopes (with the pupils' names on) so that pupils can use them many times for games and revision.

Blank word cards

These are card shapes for the pupils to cut out and write words from a vocabulary set on. They can be used for a variety of activities such as games (see p30). Their use is optional, but it is suggested that, if used, they are made at the same time as the corresponding picture cards in Lesson 2.

Grammar tiles

These are cut-out word and phrase cards, which are used in Lessons 4 and 5 by pupils to create different sentences using the target structures of the unit. Blank tiles are included so that pupils can add their own vocabulary to make additional sentences.

Templates

These provide the pupils with page layouts which include a space or spaces for drawings, and a space for the text they are going to write. The templates for the Reading and Writing page (Lesson 7) follow the style and layout of the example text which the pupils have just read, which they can use as a model for their writing. The templates for the third 'Learning through English' lesson (Lesson 11 – mini project) expand on the CLIL theme, and in this case the pupils use an activity in their Activity Books as a model for their writing. The templates for the optional 'Learning through English' extension lesson (Lesson 11a) follow on from the main CLIL topic, giving you the opportunity to further develop the themes explored in the content areas of each unit. The activities aim to extend the pupils' interest in the topic, and add to their enjoyment of learning through active participation.

Festivals
The Photocopy Masters for the three festival pages (pp50–52) are objects for the pupils to cut out and make, and use either in the class or at home. In all three cases the object they make relates to a values theme (being generous – making a gift box, being helpful – making coupons for helping round the house, and recycling – making a recycling chart).

Children around the word
These three pages (pp53–55) are based on the themes of the corresponding two-lesson mini-unit. They allow pupils to describe their lives in the context of children around the world, and highlight similarities and differences in children's lifestyles in different countries.

The Rollercoaster Game poster

This poster is used to make pupils aware of their learning throughout the unit, and to play a game at the end of the unit. It is used in three specific lessons (though it can be kept on the wall and referred to at any point):

Lesson 1 – Unit overview
In Lesson 1 the poster is used to give an overview of what is to come. Pupils are asked to look through the new unit in the Class Book, and to tell the teacher what activities they think they will be doing. The teacher writes a quick summary on the board, relating the activities to the shapes on the poster.

Lesson 8 – Unit review
In Lesson 8 the poster is used to revise the language of the unit so far. At this point in the unit there is the opportunity for reflection and re-evaluation. When you take out the poster you can ask the pupils to recall the vocabulary and talk to them about the activities they have been doing. This can encourage and motivate the pupils to continue to participate in the lessons as they recognize and remember what they have done.

Lesson 12 – End of unit review
In Lesson 12 the poster is used to recall the activities and related language and to prepare the pupils for self-evaluation. As in Lesson 8 there is opportunity for reflection. Pupils can discuss their personal learning, saying what they like, and what they find difficult / easy. Pupils then use the poster to play a game in groups, to see how much they have done.

The Rollercoaster Game
The Rollercoaster Game is played in groups. Each group has a story character counter which is moved around the poster along the rollercoaster route. The groups take turns to throw the dice (either one or two) and move. If they land on an arrow, they stay where they are until their next turn. If they land on an exclamation mark, they take a 'chance' card, which will tell them to move forward or back by a number of places. If they land on a shape (corresponding to the different sections / activity types in the unit), then they take a card which has the same shape on the front of it. They read out the card to the class and do the challenge. If they get it right, they move on two places. If they get it wrong, they stay where they are. The game is finished when all characters have arrived at the Finish.

There are two chants printed on the poster, which pupils will chant each time a group gets a question right or wrong:

You got it right!
Well done to you!
You're now allowed
To move on two!

If you're not sure,
Then open your book.
You'll find the answer
If you look!

'Learning through English' posters

There are six posters which aim to help teachers who would like more materials to develop the 'Learning through English' topics that are taught in the Class Book and on the *Incredible English* DVD (see below). They develop the subject from a different angle to the one on the DVD or in the Class Book but use the same subject so pupils already have the language for that topic. They give pupils extra information and also extra practice in using the Class Book language. The posters include interactive questions to engage pupils' interest, and offer scope for personalization through a 'Show and tell' activity. There are many activities and suggestions for how to use each individual poster which can be found on the back of the posters themselves.

DVD and DVD Activity Book (Levels 3 and 4)

An optional DVD (covering Levels 3 and 4) and an accompanying Activity Book are available to support the 'Learning through English' aspect of the course, which aims to connect English with other areas of the curriculum. The DVD provides exciting reports on cultural and educational topics, and features a distinctive interactive format. The DVD Activity Book provides activities for pupils and notes for teachers so that these components form a stand-alone easy-to-teach thinking skills course as well as offering an extension of the book material.

Course principles

The learning objectives

The learning objectives of this course are based on fundamental educational aims. They recognize the importance of helping pupils to apply their learning and develop interpersonal and intrapersonal skills. Six threads run through the course:

1 Language
2 Strategies for learning
3 Learning for life
4 Understanding myself and others
5 Learning through English
6 Assessment

These strands are further explained below.

1 Language

Language in context
Children are likely to learn a second language more effectively if they hear and see the language used in meaningful contexts before they use it and if they are involved in enjoyable activities. In line with this approach it is hoped that the teacher will:

- make connections with the pupils' developing sense of the world;
- use the pupils' mother tongue as a bridge to their learning of English;
- take as many opportunities as possible to speak in English;
- be aware of the potential for absorbing English when organizing and preparing activities and talking to pupils about their immediate surroundings.

In Level 3, language is presented and practised in a clear context through the four skills:

- New vocabulary is presented in a story-related context or a CLIL context (CLIL stands for Content and Language Integrated Learning, and in this course takes the form of the 'Learning through English' lessons). The pupils become more familiar with the vocabulary through reading and listening activities. They are encouraged to use the new vocabulary in speaking and writing tasks.
- New language structures are presented through the story. The pupils are then shown the structure arranged as grammar tiles and encouraged to experiment with it. The emphasis is always on using the new structure in a meaningful context.

The vocabulary and structures listed in the Syllabus on Class Book pp84–85 are the 'core' language from Units 1–9. This is what the pupils should be able to understand and use by the end of the book.

In addition to this core language, pupils will also absorb language from a range of sources such as:

- the festivals and culture sections;
- language for setting up and doing activities;
- the many classroom situations that offer opportunities for meaningful use of English.

The language focus

In Level 3 the focus is on the acquisition of vocabulary and structures in meaningful contexts such as stories and conversations. Pupils are encouraged to adapt the example stories and conversations with alternative vocabulary to express what they want to say or write.

The 'grammar tiles' approach in the 'Language focus' lessons (Lesson 4 and Lesson 5 of each unit) helps the pupils to understand the ways in which words can be linked to make sentences and questions. This is a 'hands on' approach to grammar; the pupils are encouraged to arrange their own grammar tiles (made with PMB photocopies) to make sentences on their desks or on the board. Grammatical terminology is not used.

The skills-based syllabus

Language is practised through the four skills – moving from the recognition skills of listening and reading to the production skills of writing and speaking. In addition to using the skills as a means of acquiring, reinforcing, and recycling language, the pupils are also guided through a skills development programme:

Reading – the pupils read texts from different sources such as recipes, leaflets, and menus. They learn how to recognize these sources and how to understand and use the information in them.

Listening – the pupils practise listening for specific information in a variety of listening contexts. They also listen to the stories before they read them (during the second listening); in this way they develop a better understanding of the sometimes complex links between spoken English and its written form.

Writing – the pupils learn how to write texts in a variety of different styles and presentations, based on the reading texts.

Speaking – the pupils practise meaningful dialogues which reflect the conversations they may later have in 'the real world'.

2 Strategies for learning

Pupils need to:

- become effective and independent learners;
- develop an awareness of their own learning strategies;
- do activities to suit their diverse learning styles;
- have opportunities to reflect on how they learn best.

This course upholds these objectives by providing material to support a range of different learning styles:

- Linguistic: stories, teacher talk
- Musical: songs and chants
- Kinaesthetic: action games, tracing and joining activities, 'make and do' activities
- Visual: artwork, diagrams, flashcards, 'cutting and sticking', observation such as 'look and find' activities
- Mathematical: activities that call on the pupils to sequence and order items
- Natural: activities based on the natural world, including observation, categorizing, cycles
- Interpersonal: pair and group games, pair and group work
- Intrapersonal: personal word collection (optional Picture Dictionary), reflecting and talking about own styles and abilities, target and goal setting

The course also offers a rich visual and auditory context, which encourages pupils to become visually and aurally literate through:

- predicting, listening to and reading stories;
- meeting familiar characters in pre- and post-story activities;
- using finger puppets to act out playscripts;
- using visual supports (Class Book / Activity Book pictures, flashcards, PMB picture cards, the posters, and all the visual material that individual pupils make in class).

3 Learning for life

A focus on personal, social, and health education is introduced in songs and through stories and follow-up activities. In particular, the songs are an opportunity for class discussions on the theme of the song.

Song topics

Unit 1 – Joining clubs
Unit 2 – Eating for energy
Unit 3 – Being positive about ourselves
Unit 4 – Respecting animals' habitats
Unit 5 – Working together
Unit 6 – Keeping public places tidy
Unit 7 – Obeying signs
Unit 8 – Making informed choices
Unit 9 – Being a good loser and a good winner

Elsewhere in the course every opportunity is taken to encourage appropriate behaviour, community feeling, caring for others, and developing good relationships.

4 Understanding myself and others

Cultural awareness and intercultural learning are part of language education.

It is important for children to:

- develop an awareness of the people around them;
- learn about people who live in other countries;
- understand and reflect on the difference and similarities between their own and other cultures.

The intercultural learning objectives are based on the pupils' immediate experiences, and include:

learning about celebrations around the world and comparing them to their own

- Christmas, Valentine's Day, Environment Day (see pp75–77 of the Class Book)

becoming aware of children's lives in other countries

- 'Children around the world' (see pp78–83 of the Class Book)

These sections include topics which allow for comparison: languages, flags, towns, and sports.

5 Learning through English

This key element of the course links directly to subjects such as Maths, Science, Art, Music, and PSHE (Personal, Social, and Health Education).

All nine units contain a specific section which aims to connect with a subject topic and act as a starting point for teachers who wish to explore it further with their classes.

This section includes:

- new vocabulary;
- listening and reading activities which develop the pupils' understanding of the subject and practise subject-specific skills;
- a writing activity which allows pupils to become personally involved with the topic;
- a photocopiable worksheet for teachers who wish to pursue the topic further (this is the extra optional Lesson 11a).

In this section the focus is as much on the content as the language used to convey it.

Content topics

Unit 1 – Maths / Telling the time
Unit 2 – Art / Portraits
Unit 3 – Music / Describing music
Unit 4 – Science / Insects
Unit 5 – Science / Fruit and vegetables
Unit 6 – Geography / Maps
Unit 7 – Maths / Fractions
Unit 8 – Science / Electrical circuits
Unit 9 – Art / Drawing figures

At this stage in the children's learning, many of the class teacher's and the English teacher's objectives may coincide. The course will assist development in many of these areas and complement the work done in other subject areas, e.g. developing sound / letter recognition which is supported by activities from Lesson 12 in any unit.

The optional DVD and accompanying Activity Book (see page 22) can be used to support these lessons and really bring the subject to life.

6 Assessment

Three lessons in every unit have specific sections that are part of ongoing assessment (see notes on the Rollercoaster Game poster on page 10). These aim to:

- focus the pupils on the activities they are going to do in the unit they have just started (Lesson 1);
- help pupils understand the purpose and aim of the lessons and their own learning (Lesson 8);
- increase their feelings of achievement (Lesson 12).

There is a simple self-evaluation activity in Lesson 12 (in the Activity Book). This activity encourages the pupils to reflect on the activities they have done in the unit they have just finished. The focus is on becoming aware of the progress they are making and of areas that need more attention, not on 'how well' they are doing.

To support teacher observation and to help teachers chart what pupils can do there is a **photocopiable record card** (see page 215) which can be used to keep a unit-by-unit record of pupils' achievements in reaching linguistic objectives.

The **Test section** in this Teacher's Book includes flexible test material that reflects the objectives of the course. It contains nine end-of-unit tests at two levels that review what pupils have done in each unit and three end-of-term tests (parallel tests A and B for the written sections) that can be used after Units 3, 6, and 9.

Teaching and learning a new language

Children learn a new language when they have sufficient exposure to it and they experience the new language in meaningful situations which engage their attention. They need to see that English is a normal means of communication, like their own language, and they will begin to use it when they can.

Exposure

The main task for a teacher of English is to provide learners with a lot of exposure to the language by talking about what pupils can see and understand. Whatever you say in English has to be made understandable for the pupils by:

- building on routines they already know;
- giving instructions to them in English;
- using gesture and body language;
- modelling what they are going to do.

When pupils see that you enjoy speaking and reading in English, and that you encourage and praise their efforts, they will develop confidence and be motivated to do the same. There are many situations in class when we have opportunities to vary what we say and increase pupils' exposure. Some suggestions arising from basic classroom situations are given in the language grid on pages 23–24 of this Teacher's Book.

Mother tongue

The abbreviations **L1** and **L2** stand for 'first language' and 'second language' and are used in this course to refer to the pupils' mother tongue (L1) and English (L2).

Mother tongue (L1) plays a very important role in the language learning process. Children need:

- to be understood;
- to be able to respond freely and naturally in their mother tongue.

It will be a long time before they can do this in English (L2). When they respond in their mother tongue they are showing their understanding and this should be acknowledged. The teacher can:

- respond in English while making the meaning clear to the pupils;
- 'recast' (what the child has said) in English (see below).

Recasting

Recasting is repeating what the pupils have said to you in their mother tongue, but expressing it in English. It may involve anything from individual words to phrases and whole sentences. By using recasting the mother tongue can be used as a bridge to learning English. Recasting shows pupils that they are understood and that all languages have the same communicative function. Throughout the lesson notes opportunities for recasting have been mentioned. When recasting, use gesture and mime to support your meaning, e.g. *Yes, it's big!* (open your arms wide).

Homework

One aspect of encouraging learner independence and developing learner training is homework. By asking the pupils to make a note of their homework, do it at home, and bring it to class you are encouraging good study skills. However, not all schools allow homework at this level, so there are no specific homework activities in the course. If you are allowed to set homework, here are some suggestions for homework activities:

- colouring and cutting out picture cards
- writing and cutting out word cards
- colouring, cutting out, and making puppets
- studying vocabulary for dictations
- doing the final version of the Photocopy Masters for Lessons 7, 11, and 11a of each unit, and the Festivals and 'Children around the world' PMB activities
- preparing cut-outs from magazines and newspapers for use in the next lesson
- preparing the final versions of portfolio work
- preparing questions about vocabulary and language structure for pre-test / exam revision classes

In addition, many of the written activities in the Class Book and Activity Book are suitable for homework.

Classroom management

As a teacher, you are the organizer of all the activities in the class. In many ways you are similar to the manager of an office or a shop. Just as the manager is responsible for the smooth running of the workplace, so you are responsible for the smooth running of the class. And just as the atmosphere in the office and the amount of work done in it depends on the manager, so the atmosphere in the class and the amount of language learnt in it depends on you.

Here are some suggestions for effective class management:

1 Discipline: Make sure your pupils understand the rules of your class and follow them. Write the rules on a large card and stick it on the classroom wall; when a rule is broken, point to the relevant rule on the card and explain what the problem is. Be consistent in the way you apply the rules; they apply to all pupils, at all times.

Discipline is also about how your pupils should approach each activity. In this Teacher's Book, for example, there are suggestions for how to act out the playscripts effectively. Your pupils may need suggestions for other activities, such as

- listening – look at the speaker, concentrate on what is said, use expressions such as *Could you say that again, please?* if you didn't understand
- writing texts – plan what you are going to write, check what you have written for grammar and spelling
- speaking – look at the person you are speaking to, speak clearly, be aware if the person has understood you or not

2 Variety: Even the most interesting activities become boring after a time. Each lesson needs a variety of activities covering, if possible, all four skills. Use songs, chants, and games to make the lessons more enjoyable, but mix these with quieter listening, reading, and writing activities.

3 Clarity: The more words you use to explain an activity, the more confusing it is. Model activities with a pupil as an example; this is much clearer than trying to explain an activity again and again.

4 Motivation: Be encouraging and positive with your pupils. Criticism and negative attitudes are often counter-productive. Instead, encourage your pupils to reflect honestly on what they are doing well, and how they can improve.

Pupils will not learn effectively in an environment which is undisciplined, boring, confusing, or un-motivating. As the teacher, it is up to you to provide a disciplined, interesting, clear, and motivating environment in which your pupils will work to the best of their ability.

Course structure

There are nine main units. Each unit is made up of twelve core lessons and an optional lesson (for teachers with more time) The lessons are split between the Class Book, Activity Book, and Photocopy Masters Book. Activities consist of presentation, practice and practical activities to give pupils the variety of activity types they need to keep them engaged.

There is also a bank of extra grammar activities in the Activity Book to be used after Lessons 5.

In addition to the nine main units, there is a Festivals section comprising three lessons, and a Culture section ('Children around the world') comprising three mini-units of two lessons each. There is also an optional 'Show what you know!' page in each of the main units, focusing on vocabulary. These pages are designed to be used flexibly. They can be used as follows:

- to provide extra whole-class teaching material
- to provide extra material for fast finishers
- for homework

The core material provides for approximately 100 hours of material for the year. Teachers with more teaching time than this may choose to teach the optional lessons 11a (extension of the 'Learning through English' topic) and also use the 'Show what you know!' activities in each unit. These, together with the tests, provide a total of approximately 30 extra teaching hours.

Unit structure

Each unit in Level 3 follows the same sequence. This makes it easier for both the pupils and the teacher to use the book (see the grid on p18 for an overview of the unit structure and the components used in each lesson).

Lesson 1 – Introducing vocabulary

Rollercoaster Game poster

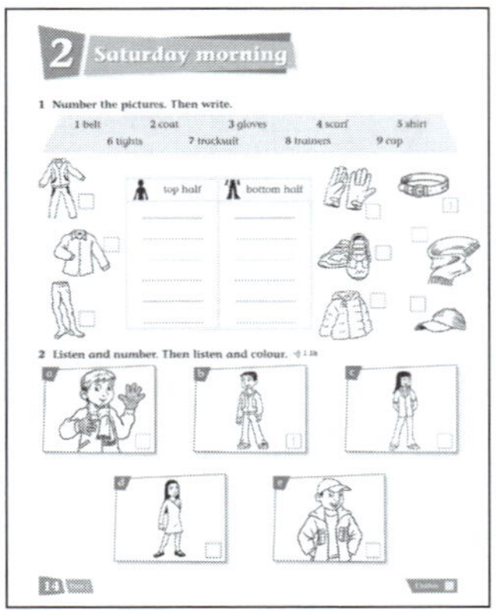

Class Book page 11 **Activity Book page 14**

This lesson introduces the topic and the first set of new vocabulary.

At the start of this lesson the Rollercoaster Game poster is used to give the pupils an overview of what they are going to learn in the unit. Pupils look through the unit in their Class Books and the teacher quickly writes the topics and activities they will be doing on the board, relating them to the relevant shapes on the poster (which the pupils will use again in Lessons 8 and 12).

The new vocabulary is first presented by the teacher using the flashcards. The unit-opener page in the Class Book is then used to introduce the new vocabulary in context, via a listening activity. The unit-opener picture always links with the story, but it is not part of the story. The pupils then practise a conversation or play a game using the new vocabulary. After this, they focus on the spelling of the new words, and finally they group the new words in meaningful categories.

Lesson 2 – Practising vocabulary

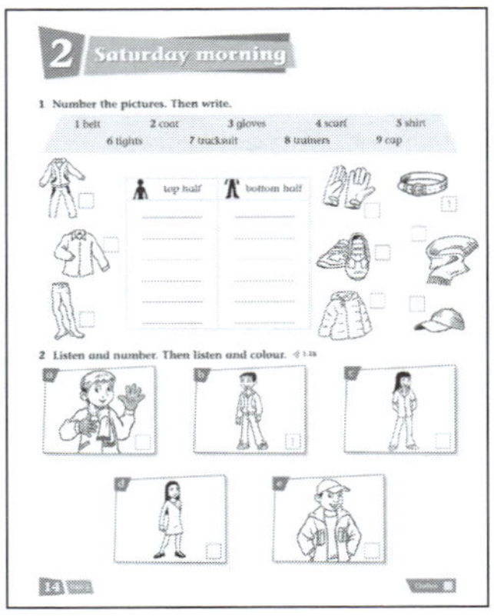

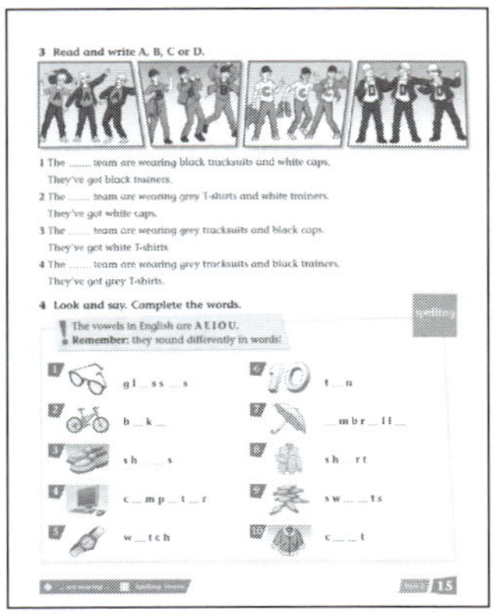

Activity Book pages 14 and 15

In this lesson, the pupils review the vocabulary from the previous lesson, and practise it in a meaningful way. First they listen to conversations which include the new vocabulary and match each conversation with a picture. Then they use the vocabulary in a written exercise, in conjunction with other vocabulary they have seen. After this, they focus on the spelling of the new words. Finally they cut out and colour the PMB picture cards for the vocabulary set, and use them in a game.

Lesson 3 – Story

Class Book pages 12 and 13

This is the story lesson. First the pupils review the new vocabulary with a game. After this, they close their books and listen to the story (with a question to answer), and then open their Class Books and listen again, at the same time as reading it in their Class Books. After the two listenings, the pupils' comprehension is checked with matching activities, such as matching sentences from the story with the pictures in the story. Finally, some 'fun expressions' from the story are highlighted.

The story includes examples of the new language structure that will be formally presented and practised in Lesson 4 and Lesson 5. However, the pupils are not expected to produce the new language structure in this lesson: the idea is to become familiar with the structure and its meaning before the formal presentation and practice.

Lesson 4 – Language focus 1

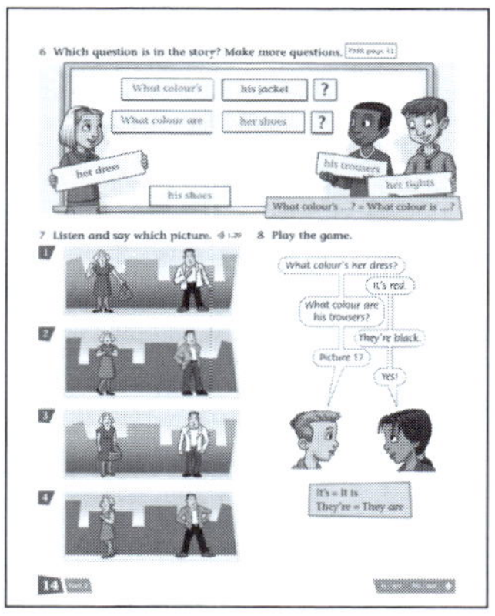

Class Book page 14

Activity Book page 16

This lesson gives the pupils the opportunity to practise the first language point that they saw in the story in the previous lesson. The language point is introduced with the grammar tiles in the Class Book, which show two sentences or questions. The pupils read the sentences / questions and identify which one was in the story. Then they make more sentences / questions using the first set of grammar tiles (they can either do this from the Class Book page, or they can use the cut-out grammar tiles from the Photocopy Masters Book for a more hands-on approach).

After this, the pupils listen to conversations featuring the language point. They listen and match each conversation with a picture. In the last part of the lesson the pupils do speaking and writing practice of the new structure.

Lesson 5 – Language focus 2

Activity Book pages 16 and 17

In this lesson the pupils see the second language point, which is usually related to the first language point. For example, the first language point may be the question form of the present simple, and the second language point is the negative form of the present simple.

This lesson uses grammar tiles to show the structure, as in Lesson 4. However, the sequence of activities is slightly different. Firstly, the instructions normally suggest a way of presenting the new language to the pupils before they use the grammar tiles on the page. This is because several days will have passed since the pupils first saw the structure in the story. The next part of the sequence is the same as in Lesson 4: the pupils read the grammar tiles and identify the sentence / question which was in the story. However, after this comes the second difference. There is a second set of cut-out PMB grammar tiles for this lesson, which this time includes blank tiles for pupils to fill in with their own choice of language. Pupils can then make a range of sentences using the second set, and can also often combine the tiles with the first set to extend the vocabulary possibilities.

Then pupils listen to conversations with the language point, and do a written exercise for further practice. Lastly pupils can do the extra grammar practice at the end of the Activity Book.

Lesson 6 – Playscript

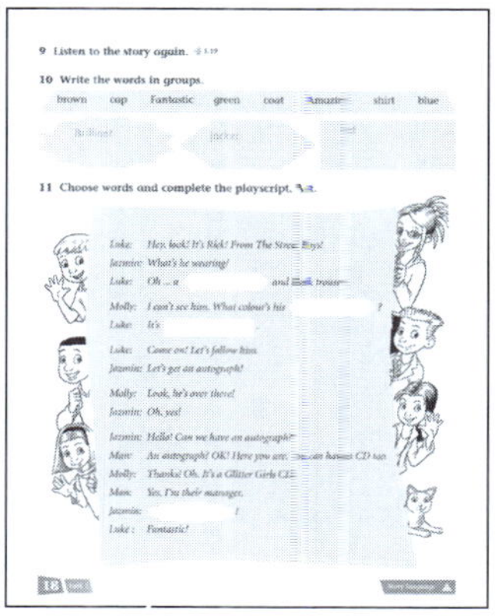

Activity Book page 18

In this lesson the pupils complete and read a playscript. The playscript is a shortened version of the story in the unit. First the pupils group words in categories, then they choose words from the categories to complete the playscript. Each pupil takes the role of one (or sometimes more than one) character in the playscript. They use their finger puppets while they read the playscript in their groups.

Lesson 7 – Reading and writing

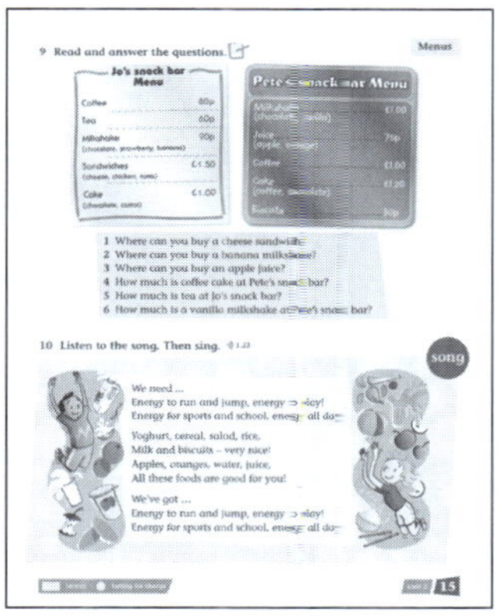

Class Book page 15

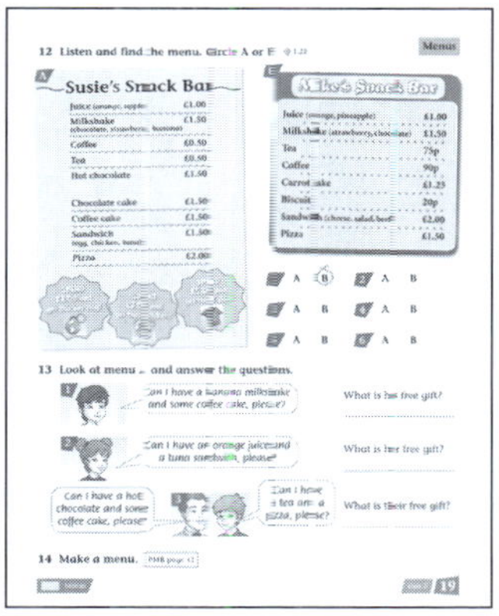

Activity Book page 19

This lesson focuses on writing styles and sources. In each lesson the pupils see an example of written material, for example a leaflet or a recipe. They read the example and the teacher has an opportunity to point out the features of the style, such as the way quantities are written in a recipe, and the way they are said. After this they answer questions about the example as an aid to comprehension and appreciation.

After the comprehension exercise, the pupils are given a PMB photocopy on which to write a parallel piece of writing. It is always suggested that the pupils plan their piece of writing before they write on the PMB photocopy, and do a first version on rough paper or in their notebooks. This gives the teacher a chance to correct any mistakes in style, vocabulary, or grammar. The pupils then do their final version on the PMB photocopy.

The finished PMB photocopies are ideal for inclusion in the pupils' portfolios. Each pupil should be encouraged to look critically at the work he / she produces in this lesson, and to decide for themselves if the standard is high enough to include in his / her portfolio.

Lesson 8 – Learning for life (song)

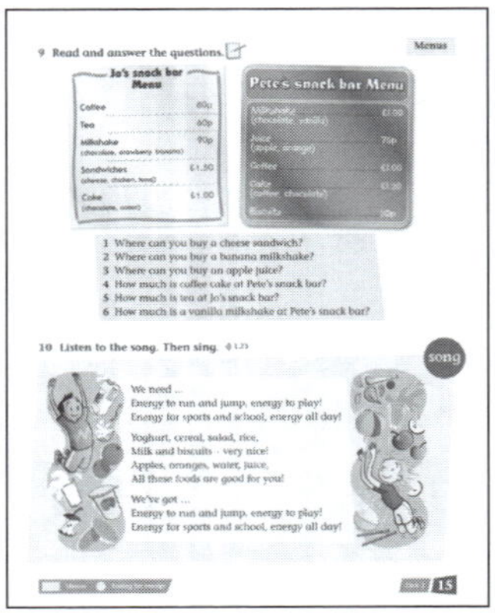

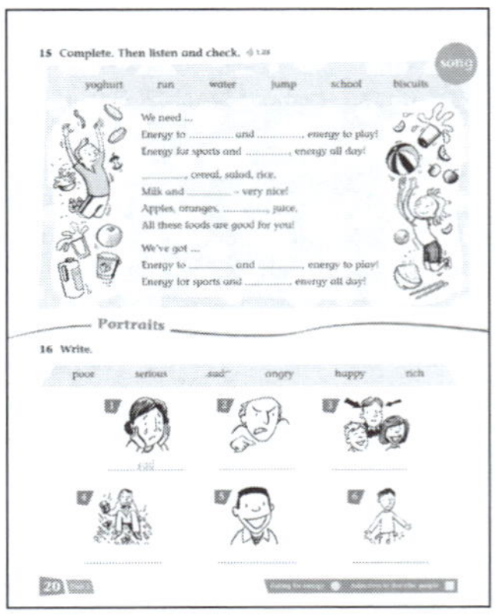

Class Book page 15 **Activity Book page 20**

This lesson has a double purpose: to make the pupils aware of the language they have seen and practised in the unit, and to introduce a values theme, such as doing your best or protecting the environment.

At the beginning of the lesson the pupils review the work they have done so far in the unit, using the Rollercoaster Game poster.

After this, the teacher introduces the values theme and encourages discussion of it in the class. Finally, the pupils sing a song about the values theme.

Lesson 9 – Learning through English

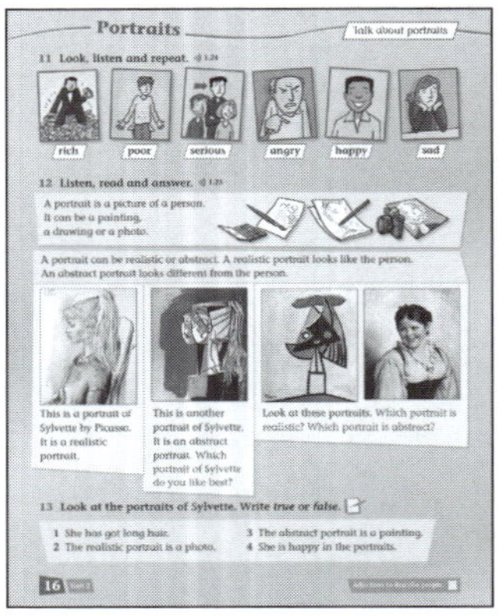

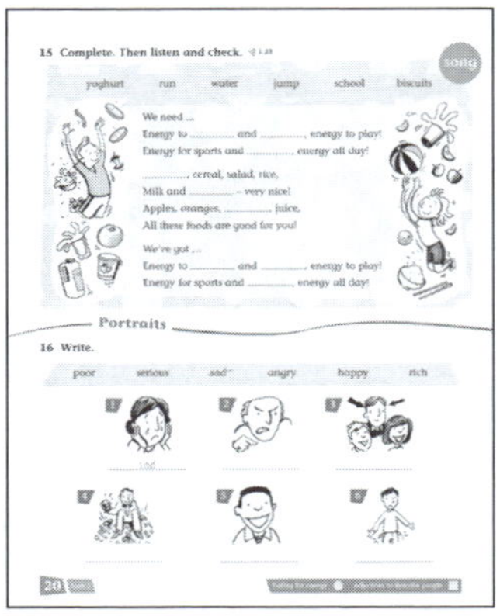

Class Book page 16 **Activity Book page 20**

This is the first lesson of the three-part CLIL (*Content and Language Integrated Learning*) section. At the beginning of the lesson, the teacher introduces the CLIL topic with a class discussion. This is followed by the presentation of a new set of vocabulary with flashcards. This vocabulary set is based on words which the pupils will need for the CLIL topic. The pupils practise this new vocabulary, and then have a listening on the CLIL topic, featuring the new vocabulary. For example, in the CLIL section on music (Unit 3) they listen to a person describing different pieces of music using the new vocabulary, which is words to describe music. This is followed by further activities in which the pupils make use of the new vocabulary in the CLIL context.

At the end of the lesson, the pupils cut out and colour the picture cards for the new vocabulary. They do one of the games suggested to consolidate their knowledge of the new words.

Lesson 10 – Learning through English

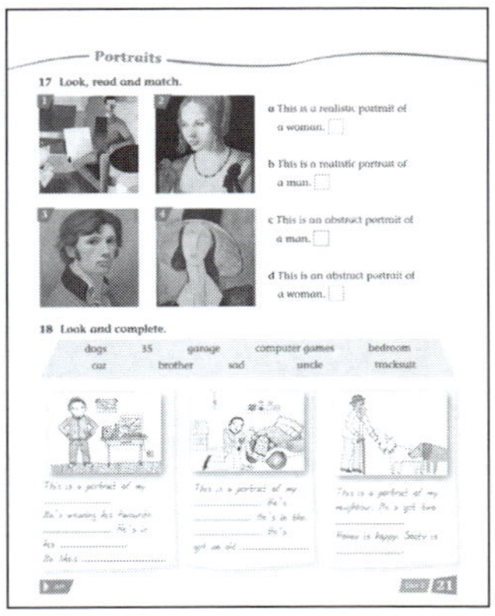

Class Book page 17 **Activity Book page 21**

This is the second lesson of the three-part CLIL section. First the pupils review the new vocabulary. After this, the pupils listen to conversations that continue with the CLIL topic. For example, in the CLIL sequence on music, the pupils listen to people talking about which animals different pieces of music make them think of. After this, the pupils listen to other pieces of music and discuss the animals the music could be about. Finally, the pupils do a vocabulary activity relating the new vocabulary from the previous lesson to the CLIL theme.

Lesson 11 – Learning through English

Class Book page 18

This is the final lesson of the three-part CLIL section. The pupils review the second set of vocabulary (which they saw in the first CLIL lesson, Lesson 9). After this, the pupils do a project using a Photocopy Master. For example, in the CLIL music sequence (Unit 3), they draw animals, describe suitable music for that animal, and attempt to make the music themselves using classroom objects. As with the writing styles work with Photocopy Masters, it is suggested that the pupils do their first version on rough paper or in their notebooks. They then transfer this, after correction and suggestions from the teacher, to their PMB photocopy.

An important part of this lesson comes at the end, with the display of project work around the class. This gives the pupils a chance to compare their work with their classmates' work, to get ideas for future work, and to praise their classmates' work where appropriate.

Lesson 11a – Learning through English (optional extension lesson)

PMB page 14

This is an optional extra lesson in the CLIL section. The pupils use a PMB photocopy to expand their knowledge of the CLIL theme. There are no activities in the Class Book or the Activity Book, but the teacher's notes for this lesson include a range of activities for before, during, and after using the PMB photocopy to make a complete lesson.

These lessons do not include new language structures, and only a small amount of new vocabulary, if any. However, they serve as a valuable source of extra practice for the unit vocabulary and language, as well as widening the scope of the CLIL theme.

Lesson 12 – Review and self-evaluation

Class Book page 18

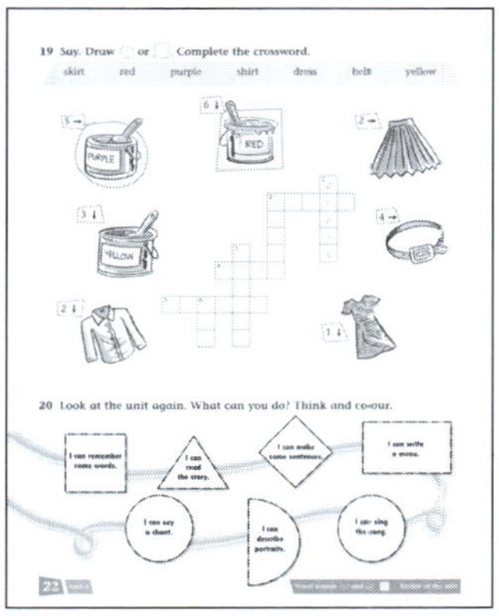

Activity Book page 22

This lesson has three purposes: to make the pupils aware of all the vocabulary, language structures, and other work they have done in the unit; to focus on the pronunciation of specific vowel sounds, usually comparing one vowel sound with another; and to encourage the pupils' awareness of the progress they are making, the areas in which they are doing well, and the areas in which they need to do more work.

First, the pupils use the Rollercoaster Game poster to recall the new vocabulary and language they have seen in the unit, by playing a game.

After this, the pupil listen to words with contrasting vowel sounds and practise distinguishing them and saying them. They then say a chant which features the contrasting vowel sounds to reinforce the pronunciation differences, and follow this with a crossword or wordsearch featuring words containing the target sound(s).

Finally, the pupils do a self-evaluation activity in their Activity Books.

Lesson 12a – Show what you know!

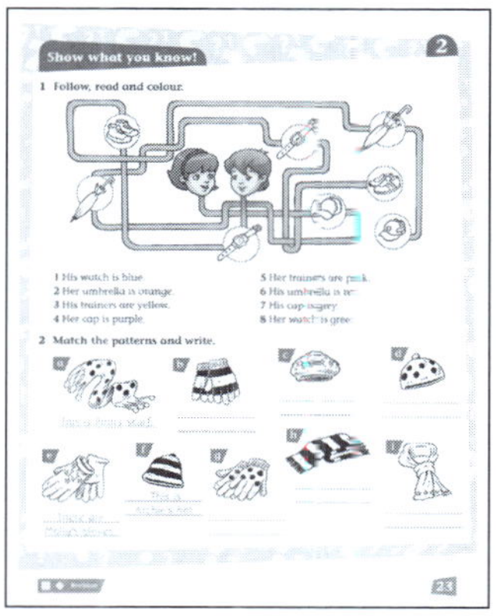

Activity Book page 23

This optional lesson focuses on consolidating the pupils' knowledge of vocabulary through simple activities and puzzles. These activities can be done as a whole-class lesson, using the notes in this Teacher's Book. Alternatively, one or more activities can be given to early finishers for them to complete individually, or activities can be set as homework.

Festivals lessons

There are three festivals lessons (see Class Book pp75–77):

- One lesson on the celebration of Christmas;
- One lesson for Valentine's Day (February 14th);
- One lesson for Environment Day (June 5th).

The choice of festivals means that you can divide the lessons throughout the school year from autumn to summer. The language demands of the activities are based on what pupils are already familiar with. In addition to recycling, these three lessons offer opportunities for extension (extending the list of ideas for the Valentine's Day coupons, listing items for recycling, etc.).

Culture lessons ('Children around the world')

There are six culture lessons (see Class Book pp78–83). These lessons:

- focus on the lives of four children from Morocco, Norway, Japan, and Wales;
- deal with topics your class will already know from their main lessons (sports, places in a town);
- have been structured to allow pupils to recycle the language they will have covered in the main units.

The aim of the culture lessons is to:

- allow your class to get to know about the similarities and differences in other children's lives around the world;
- help pupils develop an awareness of being part of a global community through fostering a sense of their own identity;
- help pupils understand the ways of life of peoples throughout the world, and respect the cultural differences.

The culture lessons are intended to be taught as follows:

- the 'My country' lessons should be taught after Unit 3;
- the 'My town' lessons should be taught after Unit 6;
- the 'Sport in my country' lessons should be taught after Unit 9.

The lesson topics:

- demand natural recycling of the vocabulary and language that the pupils are already familiar with;
- are personalized, as pupils take the theme of each lesson and relate it to their countries (see PMB pp53–55).

Unit structure overview

Lesson	Focus	Description	CB	AB	Other materials
1	Introducing vocabulary	• Presenting new core vocabulary for the topic of this unit	*Page 1 of the unit:* Vocabulary presentation page		Rollercoaster Game poster (unit overview)
2	Practising vocabulary	• Practising the core vocabulary from Lesson 1		*Pages 1 and 2 of the unit*	PMB picture cards
3	Story	• Listening to and working with the story	*Pages 2 and 3 of the unit*		
4	Language focus 1	• Practising the first structure introduced in the story	*Page 4 of the unit*	*Page 3 of the unit*	PMB grammar tiles
5	Language focus 2	• Practising the second structure introduced in the story		*Pages 4 and 5 of the unit*	PMB grammar tiles
6	Playscript	• Modifying and acting out a playscript based on the story		*Page 6 of the unit*	PMB finger puppets
7	Reading and writing	• Learning about a writing style / source • Writing a parallel text	*Page 5 of the unit*	*Page 7 of the unit*	PMB template
8	Learning for life	• Personal, social and health education	*Page 6 of the unit*	*Page 8 of the unit*	Rollercoaster Game poster (unit review)
9	Learning through English	• Part 1 of the CLIL section: introducing the topic and vocabulary	*Pages 7 and 8 of the unit*	*Page 9 of the unit*	PMB picture cards
10	Learning through English	• Part 2 of the CLIL section: learning more about the topic	*Pages 9 and 10 of the unit*	*Page 11 of the unit*	
11	Learning through English	• Part 3 of the CLIL section: doing project work	*Page 11 of the unit*		PMB template
11a	Learning through English (optional)	• Optional part 4 of the CLIL section: further work on the topic			PMB page
12	Review and self-evaluation	• Pronunciation work • Review of the unit • Self-evaluation	*Page 12 of the unit*	*Page 12 of the unit*	Rollercoaster Game poster (end-of-unit review and game)
12a	Show what you know!	• Vocabulary extension	*Page 13 of the unit*		

Activities and games

The following activities and games are suggested in the lesson notes. As with all material it is up to you to choose what best suits your teaching situation. These games all have a linguistic focus but are also active and enjoyable. Some of the games mention *Total Physical Response* (TPR) which is deservedly popular. At its simplest TPR looks for a response from the child that shows an understanding of language and as such is of constant use in the classroom.

Some of the activities require the flashcards to be turned over so that the image is hidden. The flashcards in this course are double-sided, and so it is recommended that when you start to work with a new flashcard set, you temporarily cover the back of each card with paper (e.g. using a reusable adhesive such as Blu-Tack) to hide the other image on the reverse. Alternatively you can slot the flashcards into A5 plastic wallets with paper or cardboard at the back to hide the image you are not using.

Introducing new vocabulary

There can be up to 12 words in the first lesson of a unit. Many teachers have a routine when using flashcards to introduce new vocabulary. For example you could:

- show the pupils two or three flashcards and say what each one is;
- continue to show them new flashcards in groups of two or three;
- repeat earlier words as you continue to show them new words (this will help them remember all the words);
- give the flashcards to 12 pupils (use different pupils each time you do this);
- ask the pupils to help you put the 12 flashcards on the board;
- call out different words and ask the whole class to point to the cards (every time you say and identify a new word the meaning becomes more established and the pupils absorb more pronunciation);
- ask the pupils to point and repeat the words.

Dictation

This is one of the most useful tools in the classroom. Use dictations to:

- encourage pupils to focus on spelling;
- reinforce vocabulary;
- change the tempo of the lesson;
- encourage study skills;
- encourage listening skills;
- make good use of a few minutes free at the end of a lesson.

There are many different types of dictation; here are some of the most useful:

Single word dictation

standard	say a list of six to ten words; the pupils write each word after you say it
opposites	say a list of words with obvious opposites; the pupils write the opposite word. For example, you say *happy*, the pupils write *sad*
letter by letter	spell each word of the set letter by letter, for example *S – H – O – E – S*

Sentence dictation

standard	say five or six sentences; the pupils write each sentence after you say it
missing words	say sentences with a missing word; the pupils write the missing word after each sentence. The missing word must be obvious, for example, the pupils write *don't* or *doesn't* in sentences such as *I ______ like fish* and *My mother ______ like loud music.*
Picture dictation	describe a picture; the pupils draw the picture (and possibly colour it as well) as you describe it. This works well with prepositions (*There's a chair. There's a book on the chair*, etc.) and colours (*The chair is red*, etc.).

Word and sentence dictations are ideal for mini-competitions within a class; they can run over a month or so and winners can be highlighted on the class noticeboard.

Regarding the importance and usefulness of dictation, it's worth noting that most upper primary school children in England have weekly dictation-style spelling tests. These tests are seen as a necessary part of learning to read and write for young speakers of English as a mother tongue; the same is just as true for speakers of English as a foreign language.

Just a little bit

- Hold the flashcards facing you so that the pupils cannot see them.
- Cover the first flashcard with a piece of card, then turn it round so that the pupils can see it.
- Pull down the card bit by bit; the pupils make guesses about what it is as soon as they can.
- As a variation, pull the card away to reveal the bottom of the picture, or one of the sides.
- Alternatively, turn the card round for just a short moment so that the pupils can only just see it.
- Repeat with the other flashcards.

Pass the ball

- Ask the pupils to make a big circle.
- Put on a cassette or CD with lively music.
- Pass around a ball and stop the music at random.
- When the music stops the child with the ball has to choose a flashcard (e.g. from a fan held in your hand so the pupils cannot see the pictures) and say what it is.
- If any pupils are worried about doing this, let the child who has the ball ask the rest of the class to say what is on the flashcard.

What's missing?

- Stick the set of flashcards on the board and ask the pupils to say the words.
- Take the flashcards down, remove one, and put them up again.
- The pupils identify which flashcard is missing.
- Call individual pupils up to the front to remove a card and put the others back up on the board.
- This game can also be played in pairs using the pupils' PMB picture cards.

Memory (pairs)
This game can be played in pairs or small groups. Each pair or group will need a set of picture cards and the optional word cards, made from the Photocopy Masters.

- The pupils mix up the cards and put them face down on their desks. One pupil picks up and shows two cards to his partner(s).
- If the cards are a matching picture and word pair the pupil keeps them.
- If the two cards do not match, he puts them back face down on the desk.
- The pupils take turns to pick up two cards, until all the cards have been matched.
- The winner is the pupil with the most pairs.
- An alternative version is to play with two sets of picture cards – pupils match the pictures, and say the words.

Get moving!
- Stick the flashcards on the board. Ask the pupils to suggest simple mime gestures for each word (for example, *supermarket* – pushing a shopping trolley, *swimming pool* – swimming, etc.).
- Take the cards down, and do one of the gestures. The pupils say the word. Repeat with the other words.
- Ask individual pupils to do the mime gestures, for the other pupils to guess.

Around the class
This activity works well with large vocabulary sets – ten or more.

- Place the flashcards all around the classroom: some on the walls, some on the windows, some on the desks, etc.
- Say one of the vocabulary words; the pupils must find the flashcard and point to it.
- Repeat several times, then ask individual pupils to say words for the other pupils to point to.

For extra fun, put some in places that are difficult to see, such as on the floor in the corner of the room, or even inside a bag.

As a variation, you can choose six pupils around the room and give a flashcard to each. First each pupil with a flashcard stands up, says the word, and shows the card. Then these pupils sit down and turn the cards round so that the other pupils can't see them. Say words and ask the other pupils to point as before, but now they have to remember where each card is.

Where is it?
This game works best with connected vocabulary sets, such as pairs of opposite adjectives – *good / bad, happy / sad*, etc., or with pairs of words, for example a set with two colours, two animals, two clothes, etc.

Note: to do this game, make a small mark on the back of each flashcard so that you know which flashcard it is. Obviously, the pupils should not be able to see these marks.

- Put all the cards on the board and ask the pupils to say the words.
- Stick the cards in pairs, face down on the board.
- Ask, for example, *Where is 'happy'?* Select individual pupils to guess; turn the card over when a pupil guesses correctly.
- Repeat with the other words in the set: the pupils will have to guess some, but they will be able to work out where the second word in each pair is.

Where is it? (ordinals)
This game is a good way of practising ordinal numbers in addition to the vocabulary set.

- Arrange the flashcards in three or four rows on the board. Review the vocabulary with the pupils, then turn all the cards face down on the board.
- Say for example, *Where's the parrot?* The pupils must say which row the flashcard is in (for example, *It's in the second row*).
- Point to one of the flashcards and ask *Is this the parrot?* The pupils say either *Yes* or *No, it's the first / second / third / fourth card.*

That's my word!
This game is ideal for smaller vocabulary sets (about six words).

- Put the flashcards on the board and write a number from one to six next to each.
- Then assign a number from one to six to each pupil.
- Point to the numbers on the board and say each one; the pupils who have that number say the word chorally.
- Then take the cards off the board, mix them up, and show them to the pupils one by one. Suppose, for example, you give the number 3 to the flashcard *torch*; when you show that card to the pupils, all the pupils whose number is 3 say *That's my word! Torch!*

To add a TPR element, the pupils can put their hands up as well, or stand up to say *That's my word!* Pupils can also play this game using their PMB picture cards or word cards – when they hear their word, as well as saying *That's my word! (Torch!)*, they quickly find and hold up the correct card.

Hangman
This is a traditional spelling guessing game. It can be played with the whole class, or in small groups.

- Think of a word.
- On the board, write a dash to represent each letter in the word.
- Pupils guess the letters.
- Each time they guess correctly, write the letter on the appropriate line.
- Each time they guess incorrectly add a line to the 'hanging man' and write the letter underneath.

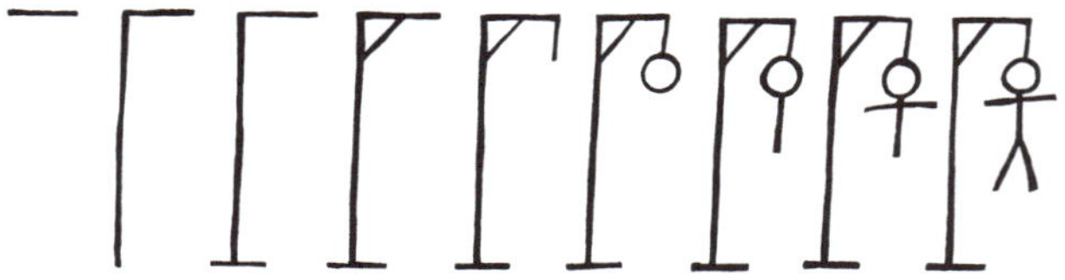

Guess the word
This activity works well with words that have distinctive spelling patterns such as double letters.

- Draw a line for each word in the vocabulary item, for example __________ for *restaurant* or _________ ____ for *swimming pool.*
- Add one distinctive spelling pattern for each vocabulary item, in approximately the right positions, such as ___*st*______ for *restaurant* and ___*mm*___ ____ for swimming pool.
- The pupils try to guess each vocabulary item.

- If necessary, add more than one spelling pattern.
- Avoid using the first or final letter of each word so that the pupils focus on the spelling patterns.

Colours

This game needs objects with a definite colour, so it works best with food, animals, etc.

- Choose a set of flashcards and show each one to the pupils.
- The pupils say the colour and word, for example *a red tomato.*
- Allocate a colour to each of the pupils.
- Show the pupils the cards again: this time only the pupils whose colour is the same should say the word and the colour.

Cards and letters

This game is for vocabulary sets where each word begins with a different letter.

- Write the first letter of each word in the vocabulary set on pieces of card.
- Review the flashcards with the pupils and stick them on the board.
- Ask a pupil to choose one of your letter cards. Show the card to the group and say the sound of the letter.
- The pupils say the word and point to the flashcard.
- Repeat with the other letter cards.

First sounds

This is basically the same as *Cards and letters*, but without the letters. Just say the first sound of each word: the pupils point to the corresponding flashcard.

Memory words

This game works best when the pupils can touch or point to the vocabulary items, for example with parts of the body.

- Say each word; the pupils point to the object.
- Then say sets of three or four words; the pupils point to the objects in the same order.
- See how far you can go, making longer sequences of objects.
- Ask individual pupils to say sequences for the other pupils to follow.

Memory numbers

Note: to do this game, make a small mark on the back of each flashcard so that you know which flashcard it is. Obviously, the pupils should not be able to see these marks.

- Stick the set of flashcards on the board and ask the pupils to say the words.
- Write a number under each of the flashcards, then turn them so that they are face down on the board.
- Say a number; the pupils say which flashcard it is. Repeat with other numbers, then try with sequences of two or three numbers.
- Choose individual pupils to say single numbers or sequences; the other pupils say the flashcards.

Bingo

This works best with large sets of words, for example three or more vocabulary sets, or numbers from twenty to fifty.

- Ask the pupils to choose six words from the set(s) and write them in their notebooks. Then say the words from the vocabulary set in random order.
- Each time a pupil hears a word in his list he crosses it out. The first pupil to cross out all the words on his card is the winner.
- To add an appealing visual element to the game, show the pupils how to draw a small bingo card in their notebooks, with a grid for the words they choose, and with the title *Bingo!*
- An alternative way to play the game is to use the PMB picture cards or optional word cards. Ask pupils to choose six cards and place them in a grid layout. Each time a pupil hears a word in his grid, he turns that card over. The first pupil to turn all their cards over is the winner.

Note: <u>Always</u> write down each word as you say it. It's very difficult to remember which words you have said, and you will need the list to check the winner's bingo card.

Musical flashcards

For this game you will need music with a strong, easy-to-follow beat.

- Put the flashcards on the board. Call a pupil to the front of the class and make sure he knows how to pause the CD player. This pupil should face the class and not be able to see the board.
- Start the music and point to the flashcards in time with the beat.
- The pupil pauses the music at random points; the other pupils say the flashcard that your finger is pointing to.
- Repeat with other pupils pausing the CD or pointing to the flashcards in time with the music.

Show me!

For this game, the pupils will need a set of PMB picture cards for the vocabulary set.

- Stick the set of flashcards on the board and ask the pupils to say the words. Take the flashcards down.
- Say words from the set; the pupils hold up the correct picture cards.
- As a variation, use mime gestures instead of words, or letter by letter dictation. You can also say sequences of two or three words; the pupils hold up their picture cards in the same order.

Who's got ...?

For this game, the pupils will need a set of <u>coloured</u> PMB picture cards for the vocabulary set.

- This game is similar to *Show me!*, but you are looking for specific colours. For example, ask *Who's got red trousers?* Only the pupils who have coloured the trousers in the PMB picture card red show you their cards.
- As a variation, you can ask about real objects in the classroom; *Who's got a blue bag? Who's got two rulers?*, etc.

Wordsearch puzzles

Pupils should be familiar with this puzzle format from the Lesson 12 activities in the Activity Book. Writing their own puzzles is a useful exercise in copying and spelling, and creating learning materials for their classmates in this way will give a sense of pride and achievement.

- Ask the pupils to make a grid of 10 x 10 (100 squares in total). Alternatively, you can prepare photocopied grids in advance.
- The pupils choose approximately eight words from the vocabulary set (or multiple vocabulary sets) and write these horizontally and vertically into the grid. They then fill in the other grid squares with random letters.

- The pupils write a list of the words to be found (or draw pictures of the items) next to the grid.
- The completed puzzles can be stored in photocopied sets in class and used by fast finishers, or by pupils who want / need extra practice in class or at home.

Finger puppets

Pupils should make their finger puppets when they do the Starter Unit of the course. After this, they should keep their finger puppets in a safe place, such as:

- a plastic wallet or large envelope (this can be stuck inside the Activity Book);
- a cupboard in the classroom.

If the pupils keep their own puppets, you will have to remind them at the end of Lesson 5 to bring them to the next lesson. Establish a firm policy about pupils who forget to bring their puppets: this can either be:

- no borrowing – pupils must make a new puppet each time they forget theirs. This means that you will always have to keep extra copies of the Photocopy Master for the finger puppets;
- limited borrowing – pupils can borrow puppets from their classmates a limited number of times (for example, 3 times a term). This means that you will have to keep a record of when pupils have to borrow;
- unlimited borrowing – pupils can borrow puppets from their classmates whenever they forget their own. This is the easiest solution to begin with, but expect more and more pupils to 'forget' their puppets each time.

Whichever policy you choose, it's important to apply it consistently.

Multimedia extension

Learning other subjects through English

The course includes an optional multimedia component (one interactive DVD and accompanying Activity Book per cycle) to support the 'Learning through English' strand of the syllabus. The DVD aims to support teachers who wish to extend the range of teaching materials, and give their pupils exposure to live action and dialogue, in an interactive format. The Activity Book contains creative and practical activities, linked with the content of the DVD, as well as full teaching notes.

The DVD for Levels 3 and 4 is divided into eight sections: Art, Science 1 and 2, Geography 1 and 2, Maths 1 and 2, and History. The table opposite shows how these sections connect with the topic areas of Levels 3 and 4 of the course, and gives a brief summary of contents:

Section	Content	Task	Topic area link
Art	Report on the process of creating a portrait	Making a realistic picture	Level 3, Unit 2 (Portraits) and Unit 9 (Drawing figures)
Science 1	Report on how pizza is made	Inventing a pizza topping	Level 3, Unit 5 (Food)
Geography 1	Report from the Isle of Wight showing places on a map	Matching photos with map symbols	Level 3, Unit 6 (Places in a town / Map co-ordinates)
Maths 1	Report on match day at Oxford United football ground	Doing calculations with fractions	Level 3, Unit 7 (Fractions / Football things)
Geography 2	Report on the water cycle in the Amazon rainforest	Doing a water cycle experiment	Level 4, Unit 1 (Weather / The water cycle)
Maths 2	Report on cars in a Motor Museum	Working out how far different cars can travel	Level 4, Unit 6 (Road safety)
History	Footage showing typical Ancient Egyptian features	Using reference material to match pictures, objects and people	Level 4, Unit 7 (Ancient Egypt)
Science 2	Footage of sea life	Completing a sea picture	Level 4, Unit 8 (Aquatic life)

Classroom language

Saying what you are going to do

Maria's going to …	*show us the picture.* *hold the flashcards.* *find the photocopies.*
In this unit we're going to …	*listen to a story.* *play some games.* *make a fruit and vegetable book.* *talk about keeping public places tidy.* *get to know some names.* *learn a rhyme / chant.*
Today we're going to …	*look at our poster.* *do some colouring / drawing / painting.* *listen and colour.* *listen and identify.*
Now we're going to … *Let's …*	*sing a song.* *play a game.* *draw a circus figure.* *listen carefully.* *draw a circle / square around the picture.*

Showing pupils how to do something

We'll … *We can …*	*start like this.* *do it like this.*
Let's do some together first so you'll see … *I'm going to show you …*	*what I mean.* *how to do it.* *how to do it.*
This is … *Here's …*	*one I made.* *what it looks like when it's finished.* *how you do it.*
Watch carefully …	*then you can try.* *and try to do it the same way.*

Giving instructions for moving around and helping in class

Okay everybody, … *Now everyone, …*	*stand up, please.* *come out here to the front, please.* *come and stand around the board.* *move a bit further apart.* *step back a bit, please … that's good!*
I want you to …	*make a circle.* *make (four) lines of five.* *stand in a line here.* *stand next to your desks / tables.* *move forward a bit.* *turn around and not look at the board.* *look carefully and tell me what's missing.* *go back to your places.*
(name / names) Can you … *(name / names) Would you …*	*move over here?* *hold this flashcard?* *put this text card next to the flashcard?* *pass me the card?* *give out the photocopies?* *collect the word cards / picture cards / photocopies?*
I need … *Can I have …*	*four helpers, please.* *nine children to hold the flashcards.*
Who'd like to …	*help?* *put away the cards?* *give out the sheets of paper?*
Let's …	*clear everything up nicely.* *pick up all the papers.*

Setting up pairs and groups	
Are you ready? You're going to do this …	*in pairs / in twos.* *in threes / in small groups.* *in groups of three / four.*
Here are two pictures, but …	*don't colour them now.* *don't show them to anyone else.*
We're going to …	*play this together.* *divide the class in two.* *make four groups.*
You can look at them … *You can practise it …*	*now.* *together.*

Encouraging good work / behaviour	
Well done (name), … *That's very good (name), …* *Excellent (name), …*	*you're really good at this.* *that's / it's a lovely picture.* *you've done a really good job.*
That's …	*very nice / lovely! / wonderful! / fantastic! / really good!*
Quiet everyone now, …	*settle down.* *calm down.*
(name / s), could you …	*sit down like the others, please?* *do it the way we practised?*
Okay, …	*does everyone remember how to prepare …?* *let's listen …* *lots of hands up … That's very good.* *everyone is sitting down … That's excellent.*
That was really good, now …	*let's do it again.* *do the actions.* *sing it again and do the actions at the same time.*

Asking for recall of words, phrases, activities	
Now, who can …	*show me the kitten?* *tell me what this is?*
Let's see. Can you remember …	*what Molly says?* *what's in Eve's bag?* *what comes next?*
What's …	*this?* *his favourite (food)?*
Can you …	*do the actions and sing the song?* *see Molly climbing the wall?* *find the hen?* *remember what this is called?* *say all the names?* *help me tell the story?* *remember six things?*

Ending an activity / a lesson	
Okay, …	*we're going to stop now.* *that's all for now.* *just one more time before we finish.* *just one more time – and that's it.*
Now let's …	*pick up all our things.* *put the flashcards away.* *leave the Picture Dictionaries over here.*
We've no time …	*now.* *for anything else.* *today but we'll do it tomorrow.*
That's all …	*you can do now.* *for today.*
We'll do …	*more tomorrow.* *it again on Monday.* *it first thing tomorrow.*

0 The Incredible Club

Lesson 1

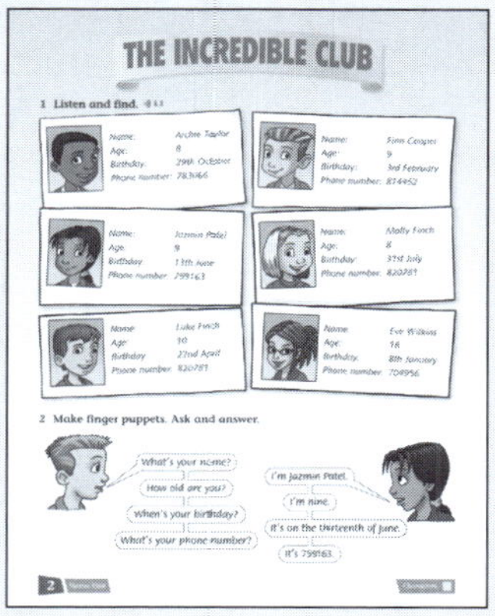

CB page 2

Objectives

- Review numbers 1–30
- Become familiar with the story characters in Level 3
- Make finger puppets of the story characters in Level 3
- Practise talking about yourself and asking about other people

Core language

Names (*Eve, Luke, Molly, Finn, Archie, Jazmin, Coco*)
What's your surname?; What's your phone number?

Review of

- numbers 1–30
- *What's your name?; How old are you?*
- language used in Level 1 and Level 2

Other language

When's your birthday?; It's on the twenty-ninth of October.

Materials

Character flashcards (Eve, Luke, Molly, Finn, Archie, Jazmin, Coco – the cat); Finger puppets (PMB p3) – one photocopy per pupil; Scissors; Glue; Crayons; CD 1

Recall numbers

- Write the numbers 1–10 on the board. Point to each one and ask the pupils to say them chorally and individually. Repeat with numbers 11 to 20 and then 21 to 31.
- Play numbers Bingo with the pupils (see p21); the pupils choose six numbers for their Bingo card and circle each one as you say it. (For the pupils, this activity is an opportunity to become familiar with your voice and teaching style. For the teacher, it's an opportunity to develop a positive and friendly atmosphere in the classroom right from the beginning of the course.)

Introducing the characters

- Show the character flashcards one by one. Say the names. The pupils repeat the names chorally and individually.

Teaching tip

This aim of this activity is to make the pupils familiar with the names of the characters. Accurate pronunciation isn't important at this stage.

PMB p3 Make finger puppets

- Say *We're going to make puppets of Eve, the children, and Coco.* Give a photocopy of the finger puppets sheet to each pupil. Point to each puppet and ask *Who is it?* The pupils identify the puppets.
- The pupils colour, cut out, and stick the puppets.
- Show some examples of the completed puppets to the class and ask *Who is it?* about each one.
- Explain that the pupils will use the puppets to act out conversations and mini-plays in class. They need to keep their puppets in a safe place. There are suggestions for how to store the puppets on p21.

CB p2 Activity 1 Listen and find.

- Point to the picture of Archie and ask *What's his name?* The pupils answer *Archie*. Repeat with the other pictures.
- Play the first conversation on the CD. The pupils point to the correct picture (Molly).
- Ask the pupils if they can tell you the meaning of *What's your surname?* Make sure the pupils understand the difference between *name* and *surname*; write some pupils' names on the board and point to each part as you say, for example: *Maria … Hernández … Look, Maria is the name, and Hernández is the surname.*
- Play the other conversations; the pupils point to the correct picture for each one.

1.1

Eve:	Hello, what's your name?
Molly:	I'm Molly.
Eve:	What's your surname?
Molly:	Finch. I'm Molly Finch.
Jazmin:	Hello, I'm Jazmin Patel.
Eve:	Hello! How old are you, Jazmin?
Jazmin:	I'm nine.
Eve:	Hello, what's your name?
Archie:	I'm Archie.
Eve:	What's your surname?
Archie:	Taylor. I'm Archie Taylor.
Eve:	When's your birthday, Archie?
Archie:	It's on the 29th of October.
Luke:	Hello. I'm Luke. I'm Molly's brother.
Eve:	Oh! So your surname is Finch?
Luke:	Yes. I'm Luke Finch.
Eve:	What's your phone number?
Luke:	It's 820787.
Finn:	Hello. I'm Finn. Finn Cooper.
Eve:	Hello! How old are you, Finn?
Finn:	I'm nine.
Eve:	When's your birthday?
Finn:	It's on the 3rd of February. And what's your name?
Eve:	Oh! I'm Eve. Eve Wilkins.
Everyone:	Hello, Eve!

- Write these three questions on the board: *What's your name? How old are you? What's your phone number?* Ask the pupils to say these questions in their own language.
- Say each question clearly and ask the pupils to repeat it chorally. Ask each question to individual pupils, then ask other pupils to ask the question to you. Finally, choose pupils to ask the questions to other pupils.

Teaching tip

We say telephone numbers in English as sets of individual numbers, so 820781 is *eight two oh, seven eight one*. We don't say *eighty-two, zero seven, eighty-one*. We can say 0 as *o* or *zero*. For double numbers, such as 44, we say *double four.*

Role-play

- Put the puppets of Finn and Jazmin on your fingers: use them to ask and answer the questions on the board from Activity 1. Move each puppet to indicate when it is speaking, and if you like, use different voices.
- Take two other puppets, e.g. Archie and Molly, and act out the questions.
- Call a pupil to the front of the class and give him / her one of the puppets. Act out the questions with the puppets. Repeat with other pupils and other puppets.
- Say *Choose one of your puppets and put it on your finger.* When the pupils are ready, ask them the questions on the board. The pupils answer for their puppets.

Game

- Finish the lesson with a game to review numbers 1–30. Divide the class into two teams and write ten of the numbers on the board.
- Call one pupil from each team up to the front and say one of the numbers. The first pupil to put his / her hand on the correct number (or point to it) gets a point for his / her team.
- Repeat with other pupils and other numbers, until all the pupils have had a turn. Announce the winning team.

Lesson 2

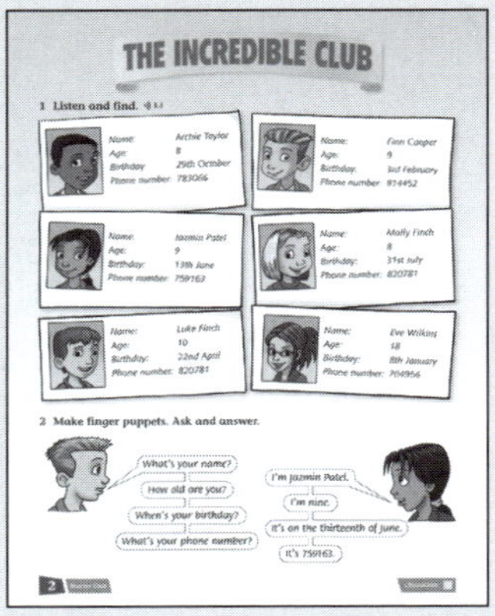

CB page 2

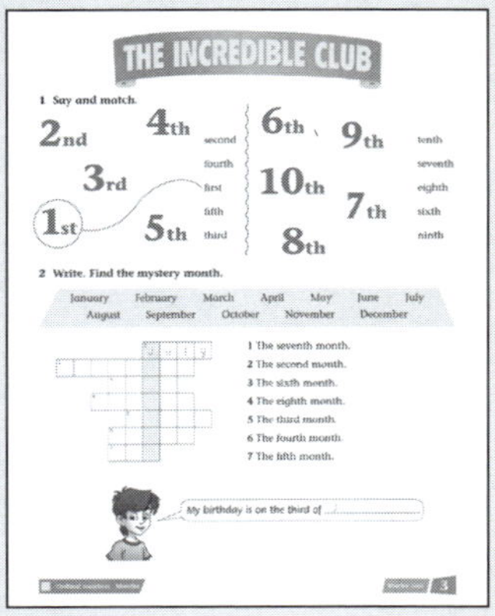

AB page 3

Objectives

- Review numbers 1–30
- Become familiar with ordinal numbers and months
- Say and understand dates
- Practise asking about birthdays

Core language

Ordinal numbers (*first, second, third … thirtieth, thirty-first*)

Months (*January, February, March, April, May, June, July, August, September, October, November, December*)

Dates (*on the 3rd of February*)

When's your birthday?; It's on the twenty-ninth of October.

Review of

- numbers 1–30
- language used so far

Materials

Flashcards (prepared by the teacher) for numbers 1 to 31; Blank word cards (PMB p4) – one photocopy per pupil; Character flashcards (x7); Finger puppets (from Lesson 1)

Review vocabulary

- Review numbers 1 to 31 with the pupils. Show the pupils the number flashcards you have made one by one; the pupils say the numbers chorally.
- Divide the class into three groups, one group for numbers 1 to 10, one group for numbers 11 to 20, and one group for numbers 21 to 31. Show the pupils the number flashcards again, but this time only the pupils in the corresponding group say the numbers.
- Change the groups so that all the pupils practise saying all the numbers.

Introduce ordinal numbers

- Point to the membership forms on page 2 of the Class Book. Say *Look at the dates* and read the dates (*the twenty-ninth of October, the third of February*, etc.). Write the dates on the board: *29th October, 3rd February*, etc.
- Point to the numbers on the board and say *We use special numbers for dates.* Write *1* on the board and next to it write *1st*. Say the two numbers (*one … first*). Repeat with other pairs up to ten (*2 – 2nd, 3 – 3rd … 10 – 10th*).
- Make sure the pupils understand that only numbers 1–3 are irregular; the other numbers just add *-th* (with the exception of number 5, which has a slight change in spelling, and pronunciation of the vowel sound, i.e. *five* /fʌɪv/ – *fifth* /fɪfθ/).

- Say cardinal numbers between 1 and 10 (*five, ten, three*, etc.) and ask pupils to say the ordinal number (*fifth, tenth, third*, etc.).

AB p3 Activity 1 Say and match.

- Point to *1st* in the activity. Ask the pupils to say it chorally. Repeat with the other numbers.
- Show the line from *1st* to *first*. The pupils draw the other lines.

Answers: 1st – first, 2nd – second, 3rd – third, 4th – fourth, 5th – fifth, 6th – sixth, 7th – seventh, 8th – eighth, 9th – ninth, 10th – tenth

PMB p4 Make number cards

- Show the pupils how to make ordinal numbers from *11th* to *31st*. Write ordinal numbers between 11th and 31st on the board; the pupils say the numbers chorally and individually. Point out the endings of ordinal numbers (*st* for *1*, *nd* for *2*, *rd* for *3*, *th* for all the other numbers).
- Give each pair of pupils a photocopy of the blank word cards sheet (PMB p4). Each pupil cuts out ten blank word cards and writes a different ordinal number (*3rd, 8th, 22nd*, etc.) on each one. In pairs, one pupil takes a card and shows it to the other pupil, who says the number.
- After this activity, the pupils put the word cards in a pile face down on the desk. They will use them again later in the lesson.

Introduce months and dates

- Draw twelve lines in a column on the board and number them from 1 to 12: these are for writing the months of the year on.
- Ask the pupils to find the months in the membership forms on Class Book page 2. Write the months on the appropriate lines.
- Ask the pupils *What are the other months?* Write any correct suggestions on the lines and complete the list.
- Point to each of the months and say the word clearly. The pupils repeat chorally and invidually.

AB p3 Activity 2 Write. Find the mystery month.

- Read the months with the pupils. Point to number 1 and read the clue (*The seventh month*). Count the months on the fingers of your hand. Show the pupils how the seventh month is *July*.
- Point out the example answer *July* in the crossword; pupils then complete the rest of the crossword individually.

Answers: 1 July **2** February **3** June **4** August **5** March **6** April **7** May

- Ask the pupils to read the shaded column to find the 'mystery month' (*January*). The pupils write the 'mystery month' on the line.

PMB p4 Make months cards

- Give each pair of pupils another photocopy of the blank word cards sheet (PMB p4). The pupils write the months of the year on them; they can repeat some months to use up all the cards. They cut them out and put them in a pile face down on their desks.

Saying dates

- Write the date on the board, for example *16th September*. Point to each part and focus on how to say it in English (*the sixteenth of September*). The pupils repeat chorally and individually.
- Repeat with other dates.
- Take one of the pupils' number cards and one of the month cards. Show them to the class and ask *What's the date?* The pupils reply chorally and individually. Repeat with other combinations of cards.
- In pairs, the pupils use the months word cards and the number word cards they made earlier in the lesson to make and say dates.
- After the activity, make sure the pupils store the word cards they have made in a safe place.

CB p2 Finger puppets. Ask and answer. *see p22*

- Point to each of the characters on Class Book page 2 and ask *When is his / her birthday?* The pupils say the date for each character.
- Put the Jazmin puppet on your finger. Model the conversation in Activity 2 between yourself and the puppet. Repeat the conversation with another puppet.
- Say *Get out your finger puppets. Put one of the puppets on your finger.* Repeat the conversation with pupils answering the question for their puppets, or asking your puppet the question.
- Say *Now talk in pairs. Use all your puppets.* The pupils act the conversations in pairs with their puppets.

Teaching tip

To help the pupils understand the story in Units 1–9 and talk about it, they need to remember the names of the characters in the story. During the first weeks of the course, check the names regularly, like this:
either – Point to the pictures on Class Book page 2 and ask *Who is it?* The pupils say the name of the character.
or – Ask pupils to open their Class Books at page 2, and ask *Who is Jazmin?* The pupils point to the correct picture in their books.

Pupils' birthdays

- Say *Put your finger puppets away* and make sure the pupils put their puppets in a safe place.
- Point to individual pupils and ask *When's your birthday?* The pupils answer, for example, *the 12th of May*.
- Select individual pupils to ask other pupils in the class. For pupils who had a birthday recently, you can teach the whole class to say *Happy Birthday!*

1 Hello, kids!

Lesson 1 ■ = Words

Introducing vocabulary

CB page 3

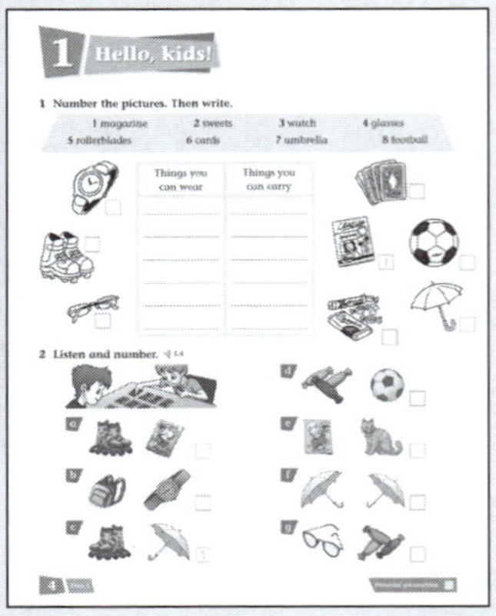

AB page 4

Objectives

- Understand the theme of the unit
- Become familiar with vocabulary for personal possessions
- Practise talking about your possessions
- Focus on spelling

Core language

Personal possessions: *magazine, sweets, watch, glasses, rollerblades, cards, umbrella, football, bag*

Review of

- animal vocabulary: *cat*
- language used so far

Other language

wear, carry

Materials

Rollercoaster Game poster; Personal possessions flashcards (*magazine, football, sweets, watch, glasses, rollerblades, umbrella, cards, bag*); Flashcard for *cat* (use the flashcard of Coco from the Starter Unit); CD 1

Unit overview

- Put up the Rollercoaster Game poster where pupils can see it.
- Tell the pupils they are going to learn about personal possessions in this unit. Ask them what things they carry in their bags, and what games and snacks they bring to school. Recast their answers if necessary, and write them on the board.
- Ask the pupils to look through Unit 1 in their Class Books. Talk with them about the unit and quickly write the different topics and activities on the board, relating them to the shapes on the poster:
  - ■ Words – personal possessions
  - ▲ Story – *Scat, cat!*
  - ◆ Sentences – *Where are my glasses? They're on the table.*
  - ▬ Text work – leaflets
  - ● Song – *Join our club!* / Chant – *He's got a kitten*
  - ◗ Other subjects – Maths (telling the time)
- Tell the pupils that at the end of the unit they will use the poster to play a game to see how much they have remembered.

Introduce new vocabulary *see p19*

- Use the personal possessions flashcards to teach the new vocabulary. Also use the Coco flashcard to revise the word *cat*. The pupils say the words chorally and individually.
- With the pupils, work out a gesture for each object (for example, reading for *magazine*, chewing for *sweets*, etc.).
- Play *Get moving!* (see p20) with the pupils. First do the gestures and ask the pupils to say the object. Then ask individual pupils to do the gestures for the other pupils to guess.

CB p3 Activity 1 Look, listen and repeat.

- The pupils listen to the recording. They repeat each word chorally and point to the correct flashcard on the board.

1.2

1 watch, **2** cards, **3** football, **4** magazine, **5** umbrella, **6** sweets, **7** glasses, **8** cat, **9** rollerblades, **10** bag

CB p3 Activity 2 Listen and find.

- Play the dialogue.
- The pupils listen for the vocabulary words and point to each one in their Class Books.
- Play the dialogue again, pausing after each new vocabulary item to check pupils have found it in the picture: *Some cards. Where are they? Yes, number two.*

1.3

Luke:	Hi, Finn!
Finn:	Hi, Luke! Look, I've got some cards.
Luke:	And I've got a football.
Finn:	Great! Let's play!
Jazmin:	Hi, Molly!
Molly:	Hello, Jazmin. I like your bag.
Jazmin:	Thanks. Look. I've got a magazine.
Molly:	Oh, that's my favourite magazine!
Jazmin:	I love your umbrella!
Jazmin:	Hello, Archie!
Archie:	Hi, Molly. Hi, Jazmin. Look, I've got rollerblades!
Jazmin:	Very nice! I like rollerblades.
Archie:	And I've got some sweets.
Molly:	Ooh, sweets!
Archie:	Do you want one?
M & J:	Yes, please!
Eve:	Hello, kids!
Finn:	Hello, Eve! I like your glasses.
Eve:	Thanks, Finn! And I like your watch! What's the time?
Finn:	It's four o'clock. Hey, look! A cat!
Coco:	Miaow!,

Teaching tip: using 'bookmarks'

In previous levels, pupils used an Incredible English 'bookmark' to focus on individual vocabulary items within a picture. If you wish to continue using this technique in this level, ask pupils to make a new bookmark, either in class or at home (or they can use their bookmarks from Level 2, if they still have them). The bookmark should incorporate a hole 5cm in diameter. Pupils place the bookmark on a picture so that the vocabulary item in question is visible through the hole. Pupils can use their bookmarks throughout the year to find the items in the Class Book 'Listen and find' vocabulary presentation activities, rather than pointing at the pictures.

CB p3 Activity 3 Ask and answer.

- Demonstrate the game to the pupils like this:
  1 Point to one pupil and say the first sentence (*I've got sweets*).
  2 Point to another pupil and say the second sentence (*I've got sweets and a magazine*). Emphasize the new object (*and a magazine*).
  3 Point to another pupil and say the third sentence (*I've got sweets and a magazine and a cat*). Emphasize the new object (*and a cat*).
  4 Point to another pupil and elicit a suitable sentence, with a new object (for example, *I've got sweets and a magazine and a cat and an umbrella*).
  5 Repeat with other pupils, each one adding an object (pupils can look at their books to remind themselves of the new vocabulary items).
  6 The pupils play the game in groups of four or five.

Teaching tip

If any group is able to keep the sentence going for all ten new objects, encourage them to continue with any other words they can think of, e.g. *I've got … a pencil, a dog, a yoghurt, …*

Spelling

- Ask the pupils to identify:
  1 words that are similar in their language (highlight the differences in spelling)
  2 words that are plural (for example, *sweets*)
  3 words that end with a vowel (for example, *magazine*)
  4 words with double letters (for example, *glasses*)

AB p4 Activity 1 Number the pictures. Then write.

- Point to the picture of the magazine and ask *What is it?* Point out the example answer *1* (for *magazine*) next to the picture.
- The pupils identify the other pictures and write the numbers from the word pool.
- Read the two headings (*Things you can wear* and *Things you can carry*) to the pupils. Use mime gestures to show the difference between *wear* (for clothes on your body) and *carry* (for things in your hand).

Answers: Things you can wear: watch, glasses, rollerblades
Things you can carry: magazine, sweets, cards, umbrella, football

Lesson 2 = Words

Practising vocabulary

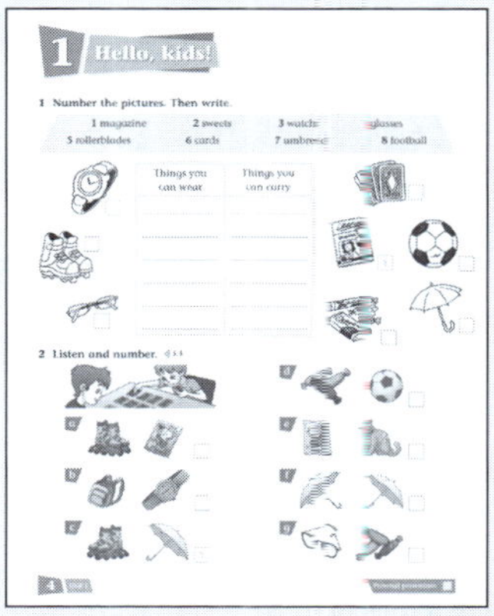

AB page 4

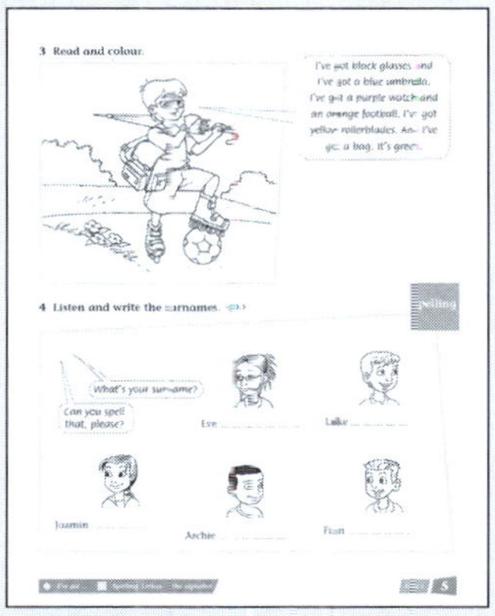

AB page 5

Objectives
- Review vocabulary for personal possessions
- Practise listening and talking about possessions
- Practise listening to and writing surnames

Core language
Review of
- personal possessions vocabulary
- language used so far

Other language
surname; Can you spell that, please?

Materials
Personal possessions flashcards (x10, including Coco the cat from the Starter Unit); CD 1; Personal possessions picture cards (PMB p5) – one photocopied set per pupil; Word card template (PMB p4) – one photocopy per pupil (optional)

Review vocabulary

- Put the personal possessions flashcards on the board. The pupils say the words chorally and individually.
- Play *Bingo* with the pupils: they choose four of the words and write them in their notebooks to use as their Bingo cards.

AB p4 Activity 2 Listen and number.

- Point to each of the pictures and ask *What can you see?* The pupils describe each picture (*rollerblades and a magazine*, etc.).
- Play the CD. Explain that the children are playing the game 'Pairs', and teach the word *pair*. The pupils match each conversation with a picture. They number the pictures in the order they hear about them.

1.4

1 Child 1: What have you got?
Child 2: I've got rollerblades and an umbrella.

2 Child 1: My turn.
Child 2: What have you got?
Child 1: I've got a magazine and a cat.

3 Child 2: My turn …
I've got a bag and a watch.

4 Child 1: My turn.
Child 2: What have you got?
Child 1: I've got sweets and glasses.

5 Child 1: My turn.
Child 2: What have you got?
Child 1: I've got sweets and a football.

6 Child 1: My turn.
I've got rollerblades and a magazine.

7 Child 2: My turn.
Child 1: What have you got?
Child 2: I've got an umbrella … and an umbrella. I've got a pair!
Child 1: Well done!

Answers: a 6 b 3 c 1 d 5 e 2 f 7 g 4

AB p5 Activity 3 Read and colour.

- Read the first sentence. Show the pupils how the glasses are black in the picture.
- Read the other sentences. After each one, the pupils colour the appropriate objects.

Answers: rollerblades – yellow, bag – green, watch – purple, umbrella – blue, football – orange

AB p5 Activity 4 Listen and write the surnames.

- Point to each of the pictures. Ask the pupils to read the names.
- Remind the pupils of the meaning of *surname*. Say your surname, and ask individual pupils to say their surname.
- Play the first dialogue on the CD. Ask the pupils to say and spell the surname (*Wilkins, W-I-L-K-I-N-S*).
- The pupils complete the first line with the surname.
- Repeat with the other conversations.

1.5

Luke: Eve, what's your surname?
Eve: Wilkins.
Luke: Can you spell that, please?
Eve: W-I-L-K-I-N-S.

Eve: Luke, what's your surname?
Luke: Finch.
Eve: Can you spell that, please?
Luke: F-I-N-C-H.

Eve: Jazmin, what's your surname?
Jazmin: Patel.
Eve: Can you spell that, please?
Jazmin: P-A-T-E-L.

Eve: Archie, what's your surname?
Archie: Taylor.
Eve: Can you spell that, please?
Archie: T-A-Y-L-O-R.

Eve: Finn, what's your surname?
Finn: Cooper.
Eve: Can you spell that, please?
Finn: C-double O-P-E-R

Answers: Wilkins, Finch, Patel, Taylor, Cooper

- Practise the dialogue with the pupils. Point out how Finn spells out the double letter in his name: *double O*.
- In pairs, the pupils ask each other to say and spell their surnames.

Spelling game

- The pupils make a wordsearch using the personal possessions vocabulary (see p21).

PMB p5 Make the picture cards

- Give out the photocopies of the personal possessions cards. The pupils colour and cut out the picture cards.
- They can use their cards to play a game, for example *Show me!* (see p21).
- Remind the pupils to keep the cards in a safe place.

Teaching tip

Page 4 of the Photocopy Masters Book contains a blank template for pupil word cards, for teachers who wish to continue using word cards in combination with the picture cards, as in previous levels. Pupils can make the word cards at the same time as the picture cards, or in later lessons, and then use them to do matching activities, or any of the relevant games suggested in Levels 1 and 2. Give out a copy of the blank template (or as many cards from it as are necessary) and ask pupils to copy the words from the board.

Lesson 3 ▲ = Story

Story

CB page 4

CB page 5

Objectives

- Listen to a story
- Read a story
- Listen for words and phrases in a story
- Practise story language

Core language

Where are my …?; Are they …?; They aren't …
in, on, under, next to
Review of
- language used so far

Other language

Go away!, Scat!, poor cat, flying, What a mess!, member, mess, welcome

Materials

CD 1; Personal possessions flashcards (x10, including Coco the cat)

Review vocabulary

- Put the personal possessions flashcards on the board. The pupils say the words chorally and individually.

- Play *Cards and letters* with the pupils (see p21): start spelling words and encourage the pupils to identify them.

Introduce the story

- Explain that the pupils are going to meet a new member of the club.

CB pp4–5 Activity 4 First listening with the books closed

- Tell the pupils to listen and tell you what animal the story is about. What other animal can they hear?
- Play the CD. The pupils listen with their books closed.

1.6

[1] At the clubhouse …
Eve: Hello, kids! Come in.
Archie: Can the cat come in too?

[2] Eve: No! Go away!
Jazmin: Scat, cat!
Archie: Poor cat.

[3] Eve: Where are my glasses? Are they under the table?
Luke: No.

[4] Jazmin: They aren't on the chair.

[5] Eve: And can you see my bag?

[6] Luke: Yes! It's next to the door.

[7] Archie: Look! A flying cat!

[8] Jazmin: Oh! The cat's in the bag!
Eve: And she's wearing my glasses!

[9] Jazmin: What a mess!
Archie: Look!

[10] Luke: Now the cat is a member of the club!
Archie: Let's call her Coco! Coco the cat.
All: Welcome to the club, Coco!

- Check the answer to the questions (*a cat, and a dog*) and ask other questions such as *What is Eve looking for? What is the cat wearing at the end?* Recast the pupils' answers as necessary.
- Demonstrate the meaning of *next to*: put a book next to a bag on your table and say *The book is next to the bag.* Show the space between the two objects to make the meaning clear. Repeat with other combinations of classroom objects.

CB pp4–5 Activity 4 Second listening with the books open

- Tell the pupils to open their books and look at the story.
- Ask questions about the story such as *Who is the new member of the club?*
- Play the recording again while the pupils follow in their Class Books.
- Go through any vocabulary queries with the class.

CB p5 Activity 5 Read and find the picture.

- Explain that each sentence refers to a picture in the story.
- Ask the pupils to identify the frame for the first sentence (Frame 8).
- The pupils read each sentence and match it with a frame. This can be done as a whole-class activity or working in pairs.
- The pupils write the answers in their notebooks.

Answers: a 8 b 5 c 1 d 10 e 3 f 6

Fun expressions

- Write these 'fun expressions' from the story on the board:
  Go away!
  Scat, cat!
  What a mess!
- Play the story again: the pupils put up their hands when they hear one of the phrases.
- Pause the recording. The pupils repeat the phrase chorally and individually. Encourage the pupils to copy the intonation on the CD.

Lesson 4 ◆ = Sentences

Language focus 1

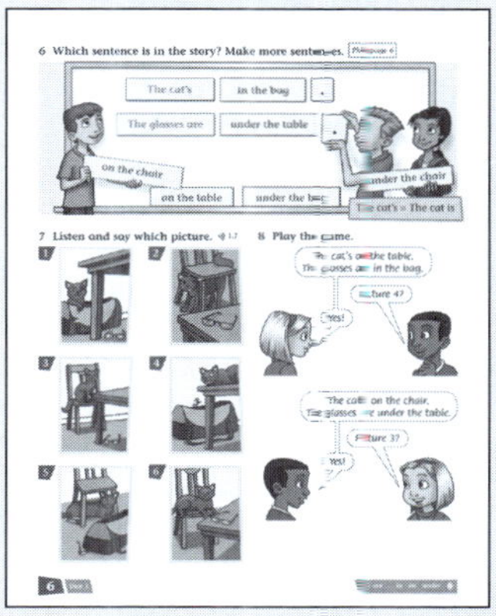

CB page 6

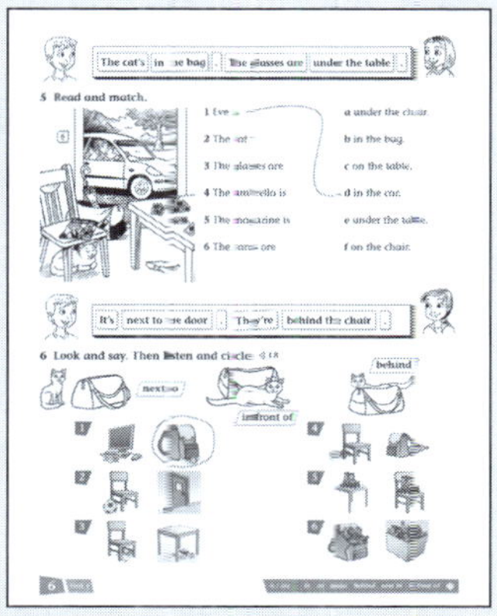

AB page 6

Objectives

- Understand the use of *They're in / on / under …*
- Review *It's in / on / under …*
- Practise using the new language

Core language

They're in / on / under …

Review of

- language used so far

Materials

Grammar tiles (PMB p6) – one photocopy of Set 1 per pupil (optional); CD 1

Recall the story

- Ask the pupils to remember as much as they can from the story.
- Say the following sentences from the story, and ask the pupils to identify who says each one:
  Where are my glasses? (Eve)
  They aren't on the chair. (Jazmin)
  The cat's in the bag. (Jazmin)
  Now the cat is a member of the club! (Luke)
  Welcome to the club, Coco! (all)

Revise prepositions

- Use classroom objects to revise the prepositions *in, on, under*, and *next to* with the pupils (*next to* is new at this level – see the Lesson 3 story, but pupils should remember the other prepositions from Level 2). For example, hold a pencil in, on, under, and next to other items in the classroom and ask pupils to tell you where it is: *Where's the pencil? That's right, it's on the table / in the bag / under the table / next to the ruler.*

PMB p6 CB p6 Activity 6 Which sentence is in the story? Make more sentences.

- Read the sentences in the grammar tiles.
- Ask the pupils to say which sentence is in the story. (*The cat's in the bag.*)
- Focus on the singular and plural forms (*is* and *are*). Write *is* and *are* in big letters on the board, and in a separate area of the board write these words / phrases: *Molly, Molly and Luke, the cat, the cat and the dog, the cats, Jazmin and the cat.* Call individual pupils up to the front to write one of the words / phrases above *is* or *are* as appropriate.
- Point out to pupils the reminder box: *The cat's = The cat is.* You can explain that *is* is often elided (run together) with the previous word to make it quicker and easier to say. In writing, the apostrophe stands in for the missing letter; it is important to include it so that the word doesn't look like a plural word, i.e. *cats.*
- The pupils say the sentences in the grammar tiles chorally and individually.
- The pupils make more sentences using the other tiles in the picture. Alternatively, give each pupil a copy of Set 1 of the grammar tiles from the PMB: the pupils cut out the tiles and arrange them in sentences on their desks. Ask individual pupils to read out their sentences for the class.

CB p6 Activity 7 Listen and say which picture.

- Show the pupils the pictures.
- Play the first sentence on the CD. The pupils match it with the correct picture.
- Repeat with the other sentences.

1.7

Molly:	The cat's under the chair. The glasses are on the table.
Presenter:	Which picture is it?
Archie:	The cat's on the chair. The glasses are on the table.
Presenter:	Which picture is it?
Molly:	The cat's under the chair. The glasses are under the bag.
Presenter:	Which picture is it?
Archie:	The cat's in the bag. The glasses are under the table.
Presenter:	Which picture is it?

Answers: picture 2, picture 6, picture 5, picture 1

CB p6 Activity 8 Play the game.

- Read the conversation to the pupils.
- Say you are thinking of a picture. Say two sentences about it.
- The pupils identify the picture you are thinking of.
- The pupils play the game in pairs.

AB p6 Activity 5 Read and match.

- Show the picture to the pupils. Ask questions such as *Where are Eve's glasses? Where's the umbrella?* The pupils find each item and say where it is: *(They're) under the table. (It's) in the bag.* Encourage pupils to use the full sentences, including pronouns, but do not make a point of this – simply recast their answers correctly: *On the chair? Yes, it's on the chair.*
- You might like to point out to pupils at this point that you used *Where's …?* to ask about single items, and *Where are …?* to ask about plural things.
- Look at the example with the pupils.
- Read the second sentence beginning to the pupils (*The cat is …*). The pupils complete the sentence with the correct ending (*… under the chair*). The pupils draw a line to connect the beginning and the ending (in this case, from Number 1 to e).
- Repeat with the other sentences.

Answers: 1 d 2 a 3 e 4 b 5f 6 c

Further question practice (optional)

- Write up the questions *Where's …?* and *Where are …?* on the board. Draw a single pen next to the first question, and several pens next to the second question.
- Write the corresponding answers next to each question: *It's … / They're …*
- Help pupils again to understand that different questions and answers are used for singular and plural objects.
- Play a game with pupils. Pupils take turns to choose an item or items from their pencil case, hold it up, then position it somewhere, and ask the class about it, e.g. *Where's my pencil? It's on the table. Where are my pens? They're in the bag.* Help and encourage pupils to use the correct question and answer forms.

Lesson 5 ◆ = Sentences

Language focus 2

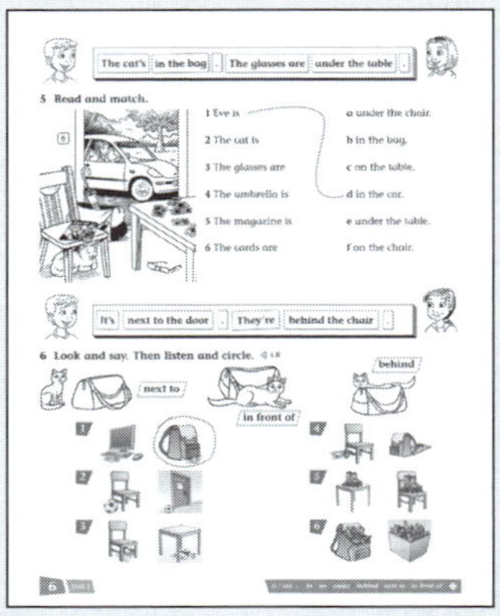

AB page 6

AB page 7

Objectives

- Understand the use of *behind, next to, in front of*
- Review the use of *It's … / They're …*
- Review sentences and questions about where things are
- Practise the question forms
- Practise asking and answering questions about where things are

Core language

It's … / They're … behind / next to / in front of …

Review of language used so far

Materials

Grammar tiles (PMB p6) – one photocopy of Set 2 per pupil; Pupils' grammar tiles (Set 1) from Lesson 4 (optional); CD 1

Recall prepositions of place

- Put a bag and a book on your desk. Arrange the two objects to show these positions:
  the book is in the bag
  the book is under the bag
  the book is on the bag
- The pupils say the corresponding sentence for each position (*The book is in the bag*, etc.).
- Repeat with a variety of objects (*The pencil is under the book*, etc.).
- Remind pupils that we can also say *It's in / on / under the bag*.

PMB p6 / AB p6 Focus on language

- Point to the second set of grammar tiles on the Activity Book page. Read the sentences to the pupils (*It's next to the door. / They're behind the chair.*)
- Ask the pupils *Which sentence is in the story?* (*It's next to the door.*)
- The pupils say the sentences in the grammar tiles chorally and individually.
- Point to the pictures of *next to*, *in front of*, and *behind*. Use combinations of classroom objects to show the meaning and say a sentence about each one. For example, put a pencil behind a book and say *The pencil is behind the book.*
- Give each pupil a copy of Set 2 of the grammar tiles from the PMB. Ask the pupils to suggest phrases to put in the blank tiles (*next to the table, behind the door*, etc.). Write the suggestions on the board. The pupils can choose phrases to copy in the blank tiles.
- The pupils cut out all the tiles and use them to make sentences on their desks. Ask pupils to read out their sentences for the class.
- Pupils can combine the Set 2 tiles with some of the Set 1 tiles to make more sentences, for example *It's in the bag. They're under the chair*, etc.

Practice

- Point to the pictures (on Activity Book p6) of *next to, in front of*, and *behind* again. Ask the pupils to say the words *next to, in front of, behind* chorally.
- Show the pupils a book and a pen, then put the pen in front of the book and say *The pen is in front of the book.* Repeat with the pen behind the book (*The pen is behind the book*), and next to the book (*The pen is next to the book*).
- Repeat with a set of three pens. The pupils say, for example, *The pens are behind the book.*
- Repeat with different objects: the pupils make a sentence with *next to, behind*, or *in front of* for each position you show.
- Repeat the activity again, but this time get pupils to make sentences using *It's …* and *They're …* instead of the nouns.

AB p6 Activity 6 Look and say. Then listen and circle.

- Play the first conversation. Point to the first pair of pictures and ask the pupils *Which picture is it?* The pupils point to the correct picture and circle it.
- Repeat with the other conversations on the CD.

1.8

1 Child: Where's my watch?
Woman: It's in front of the bag.

2 Child: Where's my football?
Woman: It's next to the chair.

3 Child: Where are my cards?
Woman: They're under the table.

4 Child: Where's my magazine?
Woman: It's behind the chair.

5 Child: Where are my rollerblades?
Woman: They're on the table.

6 Child: Where are my sweets?
Woman: They're in the bag.

Answers: 1 2nd picture **2** 1st picture **3** 2nd picture **4** 1st picture **5** 1st picture **6** 1st picture

- When you have checked the answers with the class, pupils can use the pictures to do a speaking activity in pairs. Pupils take it in turns to ask and answer about the objects in the pictures: *Where's the watch? It's in front of the bag*, etc.

AB p7 Activity 7 Read and draw.

- Copy the picture of the display case with the items on the board. Point to each item and ask *What is it? / What are they?* The pupils identify the objects (*an umbrella, glasses, rollerblades*).
- Read the first sentence to the pupils. Show the pupils how the rollerblades are next to the glasses.
- Read the second sentence to the pupils. Call a pupil up to the front to draw the watch in the correct position (behind the glasses).
- The pupils read the rest of the sentences and complete the picture individually.
- Call individual pupils up to the front to draw one item each on the picture on the board.

Answers:

AB p7 Activity 8 Write the questions and answers.

- Point to the box with contractions and full forms (*Where's = Where is*, etc.). Read each one to the pupils, using hand movements to suggest the ideas of contractions and expansion.
- Point to the items in the picture. The pupils say a sentence about each item, for example: the bag – *It's under the table.*
- Read the first question and answer to the pupils. Relate the question and answer to the objects in the picture. Repeat with the second question and answer.
- Read the next question. The pupils answer *It's behind the computer* and write the sentence on the line.
- Repeat with the other questions and answers.

Answers: **3** It's behind the computer. **4** They're in the bag. **5** Where are my sweets? **6** Where's my cat?

A guessing game

- Tell the pupils you are thinking of an object in the classroom. Say *Ask me a question with 'where'*. The pupils ask *Where is it?*
- Say answers with prepositions (*in, on, under, next to, behind, in front of*), for example *It's next to the table.* The pupils guess what it is.
- Repeat with different classroom objects, then ask individual pupils to think of objects and answer the other pupils' questions.
- With more confident groups, the pupils can play the game in pairs.

For extra grammar practice, see AB page 97.

Activity 1 Look and write.

Answers: **2** The rollerblades are under the table. **3** The watch is on the table. **4** The glasses are next to the watch. **5** The bag's in front of the chair. **6** The magazine's in the bag. **7** The umbrella's behind the table.

Activity 2 Read and write.

Answers: **2** They're under the table. **3** They're on the table. **4** It's behind the bag. **5** It's next to the chair. **6** They're in the box.

Lesson 6 ▲ = Story

Playscript

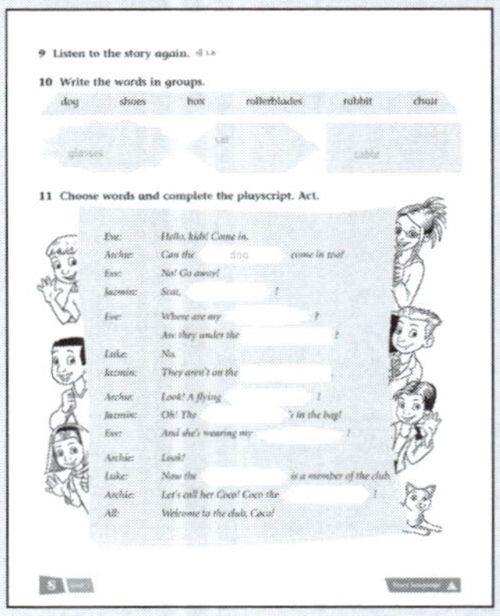
9 Listen to the story again.
10 Write the words in groups.
dog shoes box rollerblades rabbit chair
11 Choose words and complete the playscript. Act.

AB page 8

Objectives

- Read and complete a playscript
- Use finger puppets to act out a playscript
- Act out the play

Core language

Review of language used so far

Materials

CD 1; Character finger puppets (that pupils made in the Starter Unit); Spare photocopies of the finger puppets (PMB p3)

AB p8 Activity 9 Listen to the story again.

- Tell the pupils to look at pages 4–5 in the Class Book again.
- Play the CD while the pupils listen and read.
- Alternatively, the pupils can read the story aloud in groups of four. Each pupil should read one character's lines.

AB p8 Activity 10 Write the words in groups.

- Read the words in the word pool to the pupils.
- Point to each of the boxes and read the word in each one. Ask the pupils to suggest words from the word pool to go in each box.
- The pupils write the words from the word pool in the correct category.
- Ask pupils to talk about how they grouped the words, and to describe the categories, i.e. the first group is things you wear, the second group is animals, and the third group is items of furniture / things made of wood.

Answers: set 1 – glasses, shoes, rollerblades; set 2 – cat, rabbit, dog; set 3 – table, box, chair

- Ask the pupils to suggest new words for each category.

AB p8 Activity 11 Choose words and complete the playscript. Act.

- Read the playscript to the pupils. When you come to a blank, ask *Which word was in the story?* The pupils say the words from the story.
- Read the playscript again. Ask the pupils to suggest alternative words from Activity 10 to complete the blanks.
- Divide the pupils into groups of four. In their groups, the pupils decide which words to use when they read the playscript.

Finger puppets *see p22*

- Ask the pupils *How many characters are there in the story?* (four, plus the cat). The pupils identify the four characters (Eve, Archie, Jazmin, and Luke).
- In their groups, the pupils decide who is going to take each part. One pupil can also take the part of Coco the cat.
- If the pupils have got their finger puppets with them, tell them to get out the puppet for the character(s) they are going to play.
- If the pupils haven't got their finger puppets, they will have to make them now. Give each pupil a photocopy of the finger puppets. The pupils cut out, colour and stick the photocopy of the character they are going to play.

Practice

- Talk with the pupils about the five points of successful play acting:
  1 Listen to the other actors.
  2 Wait for your turn.
  3 Speak clearly.
  4 When the puppets are speaking to each other, they should face each other.
  5 Don't move your puppets unnecessarily.
- The pupils act out the play with their puppets. While they are doing this, circulate around the classroom. Make a note of the points the pupils should improve on next time.
- Ask one or two groups to come to the front to act out the play with their puppets.

Lesson 7 ▬ = Text work

Reading and writing

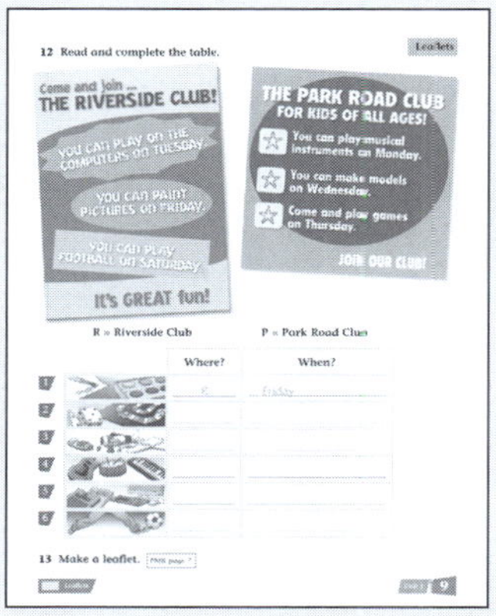

CB page 7 AB page 9

Objectives

- Review days of the week
- Read and understand a leaflet about activities
- Write a leaflet about activities

Core language

Review of

- days of the week
- language used so far

Other language

leaflet, board games

Materials

Leaflet template (PMB p7) – one photocopy per pupil

Review vocabulary

- Write the days of the week in random order on the board and read them with the pupils.
- Tell the pupils *Say the days of the week again in the correct order.*
- Erase the words from the board, but write the first letter of each day in the correct order, like this: *M______ T______ W______*, etc. Repeat the instruction.
- Erase the first letters and repeat the instruction.

CB p7 Activity 9 Read and write the missing words.

- Talk to the pupils about the activities they do on different days of the week.
- Explain that the pupils are going to look at a leaflet. The leaflet shows the activities at The Incredible Club on each day of the week.
- Read the first sentence. Ask the pupils what Luke's favourite day is (*Wednesday*).
- The pupils read the other sentences and write all the answers in their notebooks.

Answers: **1** Wednesday **2** Saturday **3** Monday **4** Friday **5** Tuesday

- As a follow-up activity, ask individual pupils *What's your favourite day at the Incredible Club?*

AB p9 Activity 12 Read and complete the table.

- Point to the first leaflet and ask *Where is it?* The pupils answer *the Riverside Club*. Repeat the question about the second leaflet (*the Park Road Club*).
- Read the sentences about the Riverside Club to the pupils.
- Ask questions about the Riverside Club, such as *What can you do at the Riverside Club on Saturday?* The pupils answer the questions (*You can play football*).
- Repeat with the sentences about the Park Road Club.
- Show the pupils the first cue picture and ask them *What is it?* The pupils answer *painting / paint pictures*. Show the pupils how the two columns are answered with *R* for *Riverside Club* and the day (*Friday*).
- Ask the pupils to identify the second cue picture (*board games*) and ask them to identify the place and the day (*Park Road Club, Thursday*). Show the pupils how to write the answers. Repeat with the other cues.

Answers: **1** R, Friday **2** P, Thursday **3** P, Wednesday **4** P, Monday **5** R, Tuesday **6** R, Saturday

PMB p7 / AB p9 Activity 13 Make a leaflet.

- Explain to the pupils that they are going to write a leaflet about a club.
- Remind pupils that they have to choose work for their portfolio during the course (see p198). Point out that this piece of work would be a suitable piece to include.
- Brainstorm ideas for names for the club and activities at the club. Write some of the suggestions on the board.
- Give out the photocopies of the writing template. Show the pupils how to write the leaflet, using the texts in Activity 12 as a model.
- The pupils write a rough copy of the leaflet in their notebooks for you to correct. After you have checked the rough copy, they write their final copy on the photocopied template.

Lesson 8 ● = Song / chant

Learning for life

CB page 7 AB page 10

Objectives

- Review the unit so far
- Understand why it's important to do activities with groups of friends
- Talk about the activities you do outside school
- Sing a song about activities

Core language

Review of language used so far

Other language

join, have fun, place, everyone, outings, trips

Materials

Rollercoaster poster Personal possessions flashcards (x10, including Coco the cat from the Starter Unit): CD 1

Unit review

- Use the Rollercoaster Game poster to review the unit so far. Talk with the pupils about the activities they have done, and relate these to the shapes on the poster.
- The pupils give examples of the language they used in each activity.

Review vocabulary (categorizing)

- Ask the pupils to tell you all the new words they remember from the unit.
- Put all the flashcards on the board and ask the pupils to arrange them in these two categories: *things we need* and *things we don't need*
- Repeat with other categories, such as:
  things which are made of metal / things which are not made of metal
  things which move / things which don't move
  things I have / things I don't have

Introduce the topic

- Talk with the pupils about joining in activities: What activities do you join in? Do you enjoy joining in activities? Why is it more fun doing activities in a group? Do you learn better in a group? (Use the pupils' own language if necessary.)
- Encourage the pupils to talk about some or all of these ideas in their answers:
  – making friends
  – learning from other people
  – helping other people
  – learning to cooperate
- The pupils can express their ideas in their own language. If they do, recast their answers in English.

CB p7 Activity 10 Listen to the song. Then sing.

- Read the song with the pupils. Explain any new words.
- Play the song on the CD.

1.9

Join our club and have some fun.
It's a place for everyone!

Do you like reading?
Yes, we do!
Do you like playing?
Yes, we do!
We've got books and games for you!

Do you like music?
Yes, we do!
Do you like outings?
Yes, we do!
We've got songs and trips for you!

Join our club and have some fun.
It's a place for everyone! *(repeated)*

- Work out simple mime gestures for these words in the song: *reading, playing, music, outings*. Work out another mime gesture for *It's a place for everyone!*
- Read through the song again and ask the pupils to use the mime gestures as you read.
- Play the song again and encourage the pupils to join in, singing and miming.

AB p10 Activity 14 Number the lines. Then listen and check.

- Tell the pupils to close their Class Books. Show them the lines of the song in the Activity Book. Ask the pupils to find the first line of the song (*Do you like reading? Yes, I do*). Point out the example answer *1* in the box next to this.
- Ask them to find the next line (*Do you like playing? We do, too!*) and to write *2* in the box.
- Repeat until they have numbered all the lines of the song.
- Play the song again; the pupils check the order they suggested.

Teaching tip

Pupils can write the answers in pencil first, and then write them in pen once they have listened and checked their answers.

Answers: 4, 1, 5, 3, 2; 8, 6, 10, 9, 7

- To finish the lesson, divide the pupils into five groups. Give each group a number from 1 to 5. Each group reads the corresponding line of the song chorally in the first verse and the second verse. (Pupils can quickly renumber the second verse in the Activity Book 1–5 rather than 6–10, in pencil, to help them.)

Lesson 9

= Words = Other subjects

Learning through English

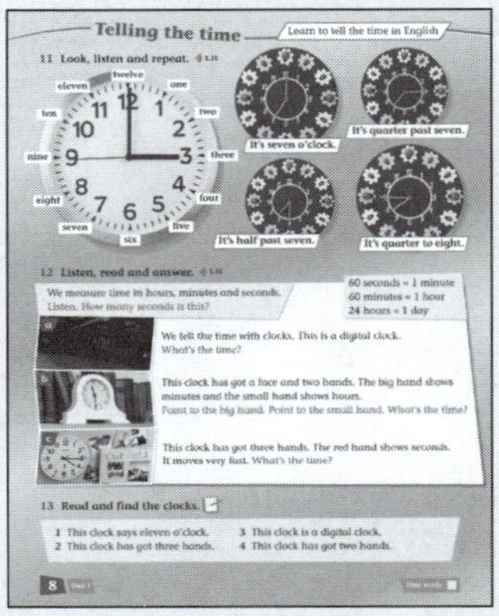

CB page 8

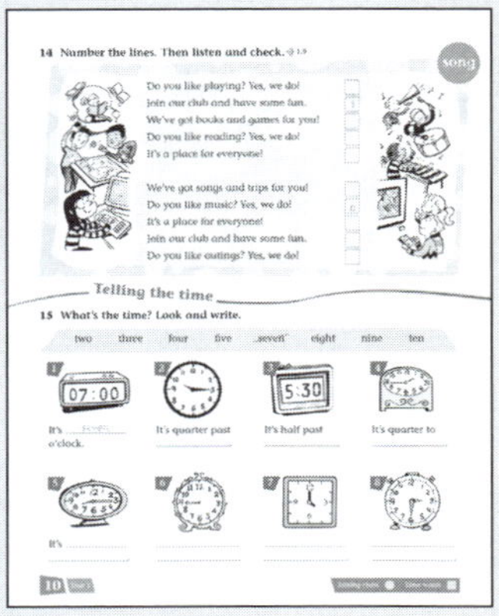

AB page 10

Objectives

- Learn to tell the time in English
- Learn about the units of time

Core language

Time words: *o'clock, quarter past, quarter to, half past*
Review of language used so far

Other language

clock, hour, minute, second, digital, face, big hand / small hand

Materials

A clock / watch (or several clocks / watches of different types, if possible, e.g. digital, analogue, with alarms, stopwatches, etc.); CD 1; Clock time picture cards (PMB p5) – one photocopied set per pupil; Blank word cards for clock times (PMB p4) (optional)

Introduce the topic

- Show the pupils a clock and say *This is a clock*. Ask what it is used for.

- Discuss the different ways you use a clock each day. Encourage the pupils to say these ideas:
  – To see when it's time for a programme on television.
  – To wake you up in the morning.
  – To see how long something takes.
- Recast their sentences if necessary.
- If possible, show the pupils a variety of clocks (digital, analogue, with alarms, stopwatches, etc.) and talk about the different types.
- Tell the pupils they're going to learn how to tell the time in English.

CB p8 Activity 11 Look, listen and repeat.

- Talk about the pictures with the pupils. Ask the pupils what they can see.
- Play the CD. The pupils repeat each sentence chorally and point to the correct picture.

1.10

It's seven o'clock.
It's quarter past seven.
It's half past seven.
It's quarter to eight.

- Point to the first clock and model the sentence. The pupils repeat chorally and individually.
- Repeat with the other clocks.
- Draw a clock on the board. Draw the hands at nine o'clock and ask *What's the time?* The pupils say *Nine o'clock.*
- Change the clock hands to quarter past nine, half past nine and quarter to ten. For each time, ask the pupils *What's the time?*
- Focus on the phrases *quarter past*, *half past*, and *quarter to.* Draw arrows around the circumference of the clock to make sure the pupils understand.
- Focus on the change in the hour with *quarter to.* Draw clock faces at quarter past six and quarter to seven; ask the pupils *What's the time?* Repeat with other times, contrasting *quarter past* and *quarter to.*

CB p8 Activity 12 Listen, read and answer.

- Quickly teach the meaning of *hour*, *minute*, and *second.*
- Play the first section on the CD to the pupils.
- The pupils guess how many seconds the sound was.
- Play the second section to the pupils. The pupils say the time on the clock (eleven o'clock).
- Play the third section. Make sure they understand the difference between the big hand and the small hand.
- The pupils say the time on the clock.
- Play the fourth section. Make sure they see which hand is the second hand.

1.11

We measure time in hours, minutes and seconds.
Listen. How many seconds is this?
(A five second peep or buzz.)

We tell the time with clocks. This is a digital clock. What's the time?

This clock has got a face and two hands. The big hand shows minutes and the small hand shows hours.
Point to the big hand. Point to the small hand. What's the time?

This clock has got three hands. The red hand shows seconds. It moves very fast. What's the time?

CB p8 Activity 13 Read and find the clocks.

- Read the first sentence to the pupils. Ask the pupils to match the sentence with the clocks in Activity 12 (*clock a*).
- The pupils read the other sentences and write the answers in their notebooks.

Answers: 1 a 2 c 3 a 4 b

AB p10 Activity 15 What's the time? Look and write.

- Read the words in the word pool to the pupils.
- Point to the first clock and read the sentence (*It's seven o'clock*).
- Point to the second clock and ask the pupils to say the time (*It's quarter past ten*).
- Repeat with the other clocks. The pupils complete the sentences in their Activity Books.

Answers: 1 It's seven o'clock. 2 It's quarter past ten. 3 It's half past five. 4 It's quarter to two. 5 It's quarter past eight. 6 It's quarter to nine. 7 It's four o'clock. 8 It's half past three.

PMB p5 Make the picture cards

- Give out the photocopies of the time words picture cards. The pupils colour and cut out the picture cards.
- Check the times on the picture cards with the pupils: *four o'clock, quarter past eight, half past ten, quarter to two.*
- They can use their cards to play a game, for example *What's missing?* (pairs version) (see p19).
- If your pupils are using word cards, they can prepare them now (see p30). Pupils cut them out and match them with the picture cards.
- Remind the pupils to keep all the cards in a safe place.

Lesson 10 ■ = Words ◗ = Other subjects

Learning through English

CB page 9

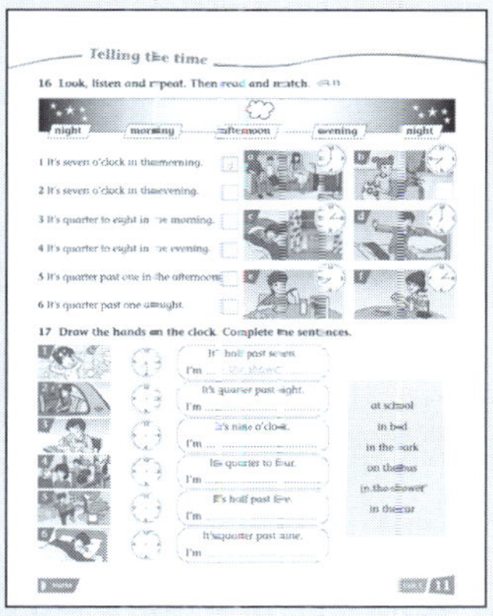

AB page 11

Objectives

- Practise listening to and saying the time
- Become familiar with expressions for different times of day

Core language

Times of day: *morning, night, afternoon, evening*
Review of language used so far

Other language

at school, in bed, on the bus

Materials

Personal possessions flashcards (x10); CD 1

Review language

- Draw a clock face on the board. Draw the hands at four o'clock. Ask *What's the time?* The pupils answer chorally.
- Repeat with other times, such as quarter past five, half past seven, quarter to eleven.

CB p9 Activity 14 Listen and say which clock.

- Point to the first picture and ask *What's the time?* The pupils answer chorally.
- Repeat with the other pictures.
- Play the first conversation on the CD. The pupils identify the picture it refers to.
- Repeat with the other conversations.
- After each conversation, ask follow-up questions about the conversations, such as *What are they going to do?*

1.12

	(Alarm clock rings.)
Mum:	Good morning! Time to get up!
Boy:	Why? What's the time?
Mum:	It's half past seven.
Boy:	*(groan)*
Man 1:	Excuse me. What's the time?
Man 2:	I'm sorry. I don't know.
	(Clock strikes.)
Man 1:	Oh, it's quarter to two.
Man 2:	And here's the bus.
Teacher:	What's the time?
Boy:	It's half past ten.
Girl:	It's break time!
	(Bell rings.)
Boy:	Hurry up!
Girl:	Wait a minute.
Boy:	Come on! It's half past three. We're late!
Boy:	What's the time?
Girl:	It's five o'clock.
Boy:	Great! Time for my favourite programme.
Man:	Come on, kids! Breakfast time!
Boy:	Good. I'm hungry!
Girl:	What's the time?
Man:	It's quarter past eight.

Answers: 5, 4, 2, 6, 1

CB p9 Activity 15 Point to the clocks. Ask and answer.

- Point to one of the pictures in Activity 14. Select a pupil to ask the question *What's the time?*
- Select another pupil to answer.
- Point out how the *Talk about it!* box gives them all the language they need.
- Repeat with other pictures and other pairs of pupils.
- The pupils practise the questions and answers in pairs.

AB p11 Activity 16 Look, listen and repeat. Then read and match.

- Point to each of the pictures at the top of the page and say the words (*night, morning, afternoon, evening*). The pupils repeat the words chorally and individually.
- Play the CD, for pupils to listen and repeat again.

1.13

night – morning – afternoon – evening – night

- Point to each of pictures a–f and ask the pupils to say the time (*seven o'clock*, etc.).
- Read the first sentence to the pupils (*It's seven o'clock in the morning*). The pupils match it to the correct picture (*d*).
- Repeat with the other sentences.

Answers: 1 d 2 a 3 e 4 b 5 f 6 c

AB p11 Activity 17 Draw the hands on the clocks. Complete the sentences.

- Read the words in the word bank with the pupils.
- Look at the first picture with the pupils. Read the first sentence opener *It's half past seven. I'm …* Pupils answer *in the shower*. Show them how the clock is completed with the correct time.
- Repeat for the second picture. The pupils write the answer on the line, and draw the hands on the clock.
- Repeat with the other sentences.

Answers:

1  – in the shower

2  – in the car

3  – at school

4  – on the bus

5  – in the park

6  – in bed

Lesson 11 = Other subjects

Learning through English (Project)

CB page 10

Objectives

- Review how to tell the time
- Make a clock and use it to practise saying the time
- Practise talking about daily routines

Core language

Review of language used so far

Materials

Clock template (PMB p8) – one photocopy per pupil (copy or stick onto cardboard to make a sturdier version); Split pins – one per pupil; Scissors

Review language

- Draw a clock face on the board. Draw the hands at seven o'clock. Ask *What's the time?* The pupils answer chorally.
- Repeat with other times, such as quarter past three, half past eleven, quarter to five.

Present the project

- Tell the pupils they are going to make a clock. They are going to use the clock to tell the time. Then they are going to write about their daily routine.

PMB p8 / CB p10 Activity 16 Make a clock.

- Give out copies of the clock template, plus scissors and a split pin for each pupil.
- Show the pupils how to cut out the hands and attach them with a split pin.
- The pupils make their clocks.
- Read the sentences from Activity Book page 11, Activity 17 again with the pupils.
- Write up the *I'm …* statements on the board, and elicit other ideas from the pupils about where they might be at certain times of the day, e.g. *I'm in the garden, I'm at home, I'm in the living room.*
- Tell the pupils about your daily routine. Show the time on the clock and say a sentence. For example: *It's seven o'clock. I'm in bed.* Use mime to help pupils understand the meaning of what you are saying.
- The pupils write sentences in rough about their daily routine, using the sentences from Activity 17 as a model.
- Check the pupils' sentences and tick them when they are adequate. The pupils can then copy them onto their sheets, and draw the times in on the mini clocks.
- Select individual pupils to talk about their daily routine, showing the time on their clocks.

Display

- Display the clocks in the classroom.
- Allow the pupils to move around the classroom, look at the clocks and read the daily routines.
- Have a feedback session in which the pupils discuss their different daily routines. For example: *At half past seven, Carl is in bed, but I'm on the bus!*

Lesson 11a (optional)

Learning through English (Extension)

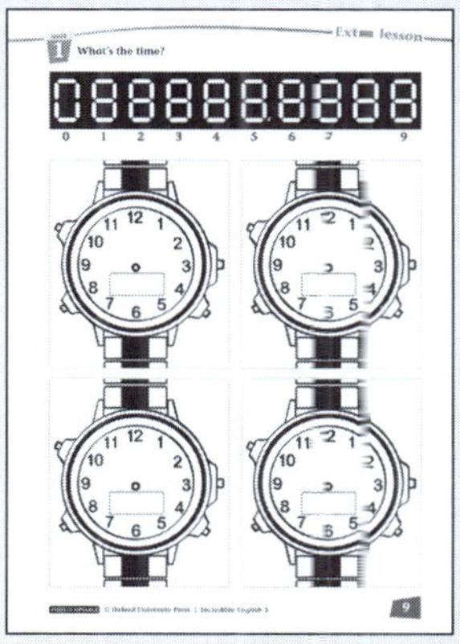

PMB page 9

Objectives

- Understand different ways of saying the time
- Write and show the time in different ways
- Learn a simple trick with numbers

Core language

Review of

- telling the time
- language used so far

Other language

Telling the time with digital clocks (*twelve fifteen / thirty / forty-five*), *zero*

Materials

An analogue watch and a digital watch (optional); One or more electronic calculators (optional); 'What's the time?' sheet (PMB p9) – one photocopy per pupil and three copies for yourself

Review language

- Draw a clock on the board showing e.g. quarter past seven. Ask *What's the time?* The pupils answer *Quarter past seven.*
- Repeat with the clock showing other times.
- Review numbers 15 and 30, and present the number 45 (*forty-five*); write the numbers on the board and ask the pupils to say them chorally and individually.

Preparation

- Draw a digital clock next to the analogue clock on the board.
- If possible, show the pupils an analogue watch and a digital watch, both with the same time. Explain that in this lesson they are going to use two ways of the saying the time.
- Show the time on the analogue watch and draw the hands on the clock on the board.
- Show the time on the digital watch and write the numbers on the digital clock on the board. Explain that when reading the time on a digital watch or clock we don't usually use *quarter* and *half*. We say the times as, for example, *four fifteen, four thirty, four forty-five.*
- Talk about how pupils say the time in their own language – do they use words for quarter and half past to or from the hour, or do they talk about the number of minutes? Or both?

- Erase the times on the clock faces, then draw in the hands on the analogue clock face at, for example, quarter past six.
- Call individual pupils up to the front to draw the time on the digital clock face and say the time in digital format (*six fifteen*). Repeat with other times.
- Make sure pupils understand that in the digital system you count the number of minutes on from the previous hour. So, for a quarter to six, they need to say *five forty-five* rather than *six forty-five*. Practise this with several examples.

Teaching tip: 24 hour clock

You might also like to talk about the 24 hour clock with pupils at this point, particularly if it is widely used in their country. Explain that with this system of timekeeping, the 'hour' numbers do not start again at one after midday, but carry on from twelve, e.g. quarter past one is said as 13.15 (*thirteen fifteen*). Digital clocks and watches usually display time according to the 24 hour clock, so quarter past five in the evening would be displayed as 17.15, which can either be said as *seventeen fifteen*, *five fifteen* or *quarter past five*.

PMB p9 Using the Photocopy Master

- Give each pupil a photocopy of the 'What's the time?' sheet.
- Point to the digital number outlines at the top of the page. Explain that the pupils can colour in these outlines to make numbers, like the numbers on a digital clock or a calculator.
- Show the pupils how to colour in the outlines to make numbers 0 and 1. Show the pupils how these are like the numbers 0 and 1 on the screen of an electronic calculator. The pupils copy the numbers onto their sheets.
- In groups, the pupils fill in the other outlines to make numbers 2 to 9. If you have brought in several calculators, pupils can use these as reference. Go round the class to make sure pupils can work out how to fill in the number outlines, and help as necessary. (If pupils are unfamiliar with digital number displays, and do not have calculators to look at, you may need to demonstrate how to fill in all the outlines on your own sheet, or on the board.)
- Point to the second part of the page. Explain that the pictures show a special watch. This watch shows both ways of saying the time (i.e. analogue and digital).
- The pupils choose a time and add the hands to the face of each watch. Then they write the same time in numbers in the digital part of the watch face.
- Ask individual pupils to show their watches and say the times, like this: (pointing to the hands) *The watch says half past eight*, (pointing to the digital screen) *The watch says eight thirty.*

Fun activity

- Take an unused photocopy and colour in the first outline at the top to make the number 0. Show the pupils the number and ask *What number is that?* Teach or revise the answer *Zero.*
- Turn the sheet upside down and ask the pupils *What letter is that?* The pupils answer *O.*
- Repeat with the numbers *7 (l), 7 (l), 3 (e) and 4 (h).*
- When you have finished, turn the paper upside down and ask the pupils *What word is that?* The pupils answer *hello.*
- Show the pupils again how the numbers you have drawn become letters when you turn them upside down.
- Tell the pupils *Look at your numbers at the top of the page. What number spells 'shoe' when I turn it upside down?*
- The pupils work out the answer. (*3045*)
- On another photocopy, fill in the numbers 3045, then turn it upside down to confirm that it makes the word *shoe.*

Teaching tip

You can also show these number / word tricks on the calculator, but to make the word *hello* you will have to enter *0.7734*, with the decimal point.

- Optional activity: Let the pupils work in groups to see if they can find any other words they can write with upside-down digital numbers in this way (either in English or their own language). Let them use calculators to help if available. (Other English words could be *he* (=34), *she* (=345) and *go* (=0.6).)

Song

- Ask the pupils *Can you remember the song in this unit?*
- Write what the pupils can remember on the board. Help them to remember the bits they've forgotten, then add them on the board.
- Play the song again (Listening 1.9). The pupils check that the version on the board is correct.
- Play the song again and encourage the pupils to join in.

Lesson 12

Review and self-evaluation

CB page 10

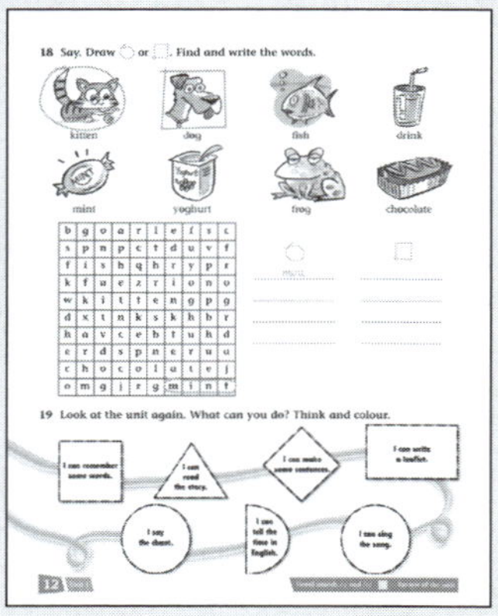

AB page 12

Objectives

- Focus on the pronunciation of vowel sounds (/ɪ/ and /ɒ/) with a chant
- Review the activities and the new language of the unit
- Complete a self-evaluation activity

Core language

Review of language used so far

Other language

drink (n), mint, frog

Materials

CD 1; Rollercoaster Game poster; Character counters and game cards; Dice (one pair per class); Picture dictionary page (PMB p2) – one photocopy per pupil (optional)

CB p10 Activity 17 Listen, find and repeat.

- Point to the pictures. The pupils say the words they know (they should know *kitten*, *dog*, *yoghurt*, and *chocolate* from Levels 1 and 2). Say the new words for them to repeat: *frog*, *drink*, *mint*.
- Play the CD. Pupils point and repeat.

1.14

drink – fish – mint – kitten [/ɪ/]
yoghurt – dog – frog – chocolate [/ɒ/]

- Say the two vowel sounds /ɪ/ and /ɒ/. The pupils find the words that share the vowel sound.
- The pupils practise saying the words chorally and individually, concentrating on the pronunciation of the vowel sounds.

CB p10 Activity 18 Listen and say the chant.

- Play the chant. The pupils point to the items as they hear them.

1.15

He's got a kitten,
She's got a dog,
He's got a fish,
And she's got a frog!

She's got a yoghurt,
He's got a drink,
She's got a chocolate,
And he's got a mint!

Focus on spelling

- Match the spelling with the vowel sounds.
- Highlight the spelling patterns:
  /ɪ/ is always spelt i
  /ɒ/ is always spelt o
- Show examples from the chant for each vowel sound.

AB p12 Activity 18 Say. Draw ● or ■. Find and write the words.

- Point to each of the pictures. The pupils say the words chorally.
- Focus on the pronunciation difference between /ɪ/ and /ɒ/, using the words *kitten* and *dog*.
- Show how *kitten* has a circle around it and *dog* has a square round it.
- Ask the pupils to identify a word with the /ɪ/ sound.
- Show the pupils how to put a circle round the word.
- Repeat with the /ɒ/ sound, putting a square around the word.
- The pupils put circles and squares around the words.
- The pupils find and circle the words in the wordsearch. They copy the words into the correct columns.
- Point to the pictures at random. The pupils say the words chorally and individually. Check the pupils' pronunciation.

Answers: circle: kitten, fish, drink, mint; square: dog, yoghurt, frog, chocolate

End-of-unit review

- Use the Rollercoaster Game poster and the Class Book to recall the main activities of the unit.
- Recall the language associated with each activity.
- Ask the pupils to let you know what they liked or didn't like, and what they found easy or difficult.

Play the Rollercoaster Game

- Tell the pupils they are going to play a game where they remember what they've done in the unit.
- Divide the class into small groups (e.g. of 3–6 pupils).
- Place the chance cards and challenge cards face down at the front of the class.
- Give each group a character counter, and let them place their characters on the *Start* square on the poster.
- Explain how to play the game. The groups take turns to throw the dice and move their counters round the rollercoaster route.
- If they land on an arrow, they stay where they are until their next turn.
- If they land on an exclamation mark, they take a 'chance' card, which will tell them to move forwards or backwards by a number of places.
- If they land on a shape (corresponding to the different sections / activity types in the unit), then they take a card which has the same shape on the front of it. They read out the card to the class and do the challenge. If they get it right, they move on two places. If they get it wrong, they stay where they are.
- There are two chants printed on the poster; encourage pupils to chant these each time a group gets a question right or wrong:
  You got it right!
  Well done to you!
  You're now allowed
  To move on two!
  If you're not sure,
  Then open your book.
  You'll find the answer
  If you look!
- The game is finished when all the characters have arrived at the *Finish* square. The character counters can then be placed together so that their separate carriages form a single train again.

AB p12 Activity 19 Look at the unit again. What can you do? Think and colour.

- Look at each of the categories with the pupils. Look back through the unit with them, and help them to remember the different activities they have done. *Do you remember? We learnt some words for personal possessions – magazine, sweets … what other words? And then we read a story – what was it called? Yes, 'Scat, cat!' And then we wrote a leaflet – what was it about? Yes, it was about a club …*, etc.
- Read the sentences for each category (*I can remember some words*, etc.) After each sentence, ask the pupils *Do you agree?* or *Can you do that?*
- The pupils who agree with the sentence colour the corresponding shape. Make sure the pupils realize that this is not a test; it's for them to be aware of their achievement and the areas that still need improvement.
- Circulate round the class as the pupils do this activity and do the following:
  1 make a note of problem areas for the group as a whole
  2 make a note of problem areas for individual pupils
  3 encourage pupils who are being over-negative about their achievement
  4 talk to pupils who are unrealistically positive about their achievement

5 congratulate pupils who are being realistic about their achievement.

Teaching tip: Picture Dictionary

Making a Picture Dictionary is optional in this level of the course. A photocopiable template is provided on page 2 of the Photocopy Masters Book, with writing lines and drawing spaces. If you wish to create Picture Dictionaries with your pupils, photocopy this page in every unit for each pupil. Pupils look back through the unit in their Class Books, and copy the words and pictures for the Lesson 1 and Lesson 9 vocabulary input onto the photocopied template.

PMB p2 Picture Dictionary (optional)

- If your pupils are making Picture Dictionaries, give out the photocopies of the template.
- Tell pupils that they are going to make an English dictionary of the new words in this level of the course, and that they will complete this page in every unit.
- Ask them to look back through their books and to copy the new words and pictures onto the page (they should look especially at the first and sixth pages of the unit in the Class Book).
- More able pupils may like to try and do this from memory first.
- Pupils can complete the Picture Dictionary at home, and can also make and decorate a cover for it.

Lesson 12a (optional)

■ = Words ◆ = Sentences

Show what you know!

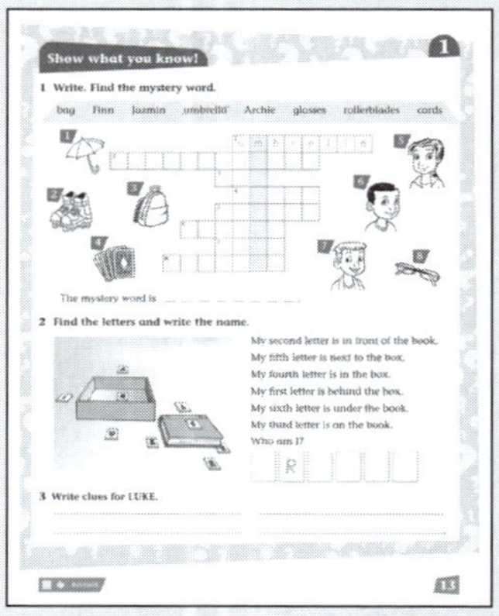

AB page 13

For suggestions on how to use *Show what you know!* see page 13.

Objectives

- Extra practice of the vocabulary of the unit
- Solve puzzles in English
- Provide extra material for homework and fast finishers

Core language

Review of language used so far

Materials

No extra materials

AB p13 Activity 1 Write. Find the mystery word.

- Read the words in the word pool to the pupils. Ask the pupils to match the words to the pictures around the crossword.
- Show the crossword to the pupils. Show the example answer for 1 across (*umbrella*) and ask the pupils to suggest a word for 2 across (*rollerblades*).
- Tell pupils that when they have completed the crossword, a mystery word will be revealed in the shaded squares.
- The pupils complete the rest of the crossword individually, using words from the word pool.

Answers: **1** umbrella **2** rollerblades **3** bag **4** cards **5** Jazmin **6** Archie **7** Finn **8** glasses
The mystery word is *magazine*.

AB p13 Activity 2 Find the letters and write the name.

- Show the picture to the pupils. Ask questions such as *What letter is behind the box? (A)* and *What letter is on the book? (C)*.
- Read the first clue to the pupils. The pupils identify the letter (*R*). Point out how this has been inserted as an example answer in the second box (because it is the second letter).
- The pupils read the other clues and write the letters in the boxes.
- The pupils read the final question (*Who am I?*). The pupils read the answer from their completed boxes.

Answer: Archie

AB p13 Activity 3 Write clues for Luke.

- Explain to the pupils that they are going to write clues for another name – Luke.
- Say *My first letter is …* The pupils complete the clue (*behind the book*).
- The pupils write this and the other three clues (they can write the clues in any order).

Answers: My first letter is behind the book. My second letter is in front of the box. My third letter is next to the book. My fourth letter is under the book.

- As a follow-up activity, ask the pupils to copy the picture of the table, box, and book in their notebooks. They should choose an English word or a character name and add the letters for it (as well as several other 'decoy' letters) to the picture, in positions that can be described with prepositions.
- The pupils use their pictures to write clues for other words or names. In pairs, they give their pictures to their partners, then read the clues for the partner to work out the word or name. (If spelling a name, the final line of their clues should be *Who am I?*, but if spelling another word it should be *What am I?*)

The pupils are now ready to sit the Unit 1 test. See pages 170–173 for both Standard and Higher levels.

2 Saturday morning

Lesson 1 = Words

Introducing vocabulary

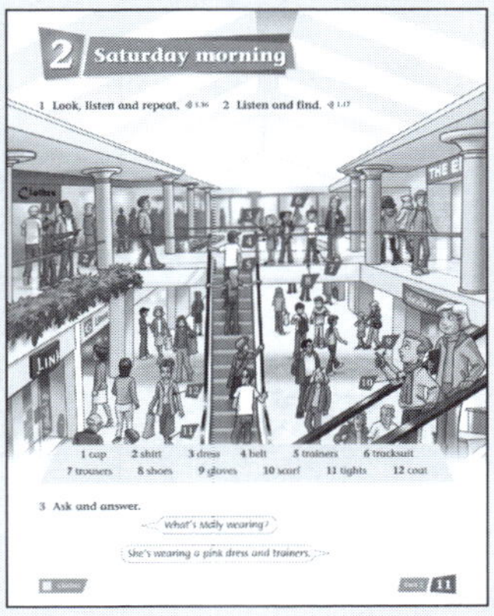

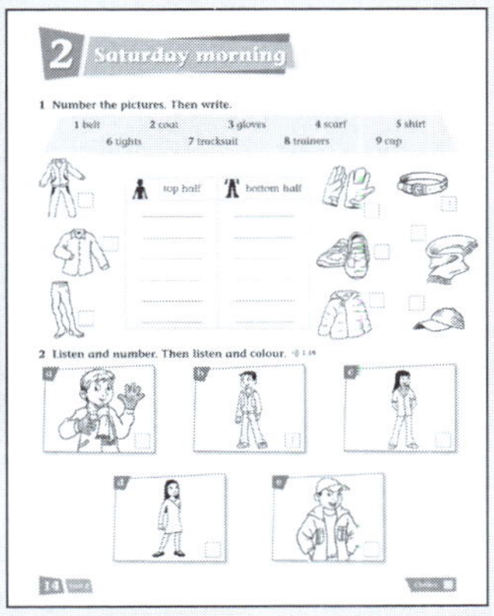

CB page 11 AB page 14

Objectives
- Understand the theme of the unit
- Become familiar with vocabulary for clothes
- Practise listening to and talking about what people are wearing
- Focus on spelling

Core language
Clothes vocabulary: *belt, coat, gloves, scarf, shirt, tights, tracksuit, trainers, cap*
Review of
- clothes vocabulary: *dress, trousers, shoes*
- language used so far

Other language
top half, bottom half

Materials
Rollercoaster Game poster; Clothes flashcards (*belt, coat, gloves, scarf, shirt, tights, tracksuit, trainers, cap, dress, trousers, shoes*); CD 1; Pupils' bookmarks (optional) (see p28)

Unit overview
- Point to the clothes you are wearing and ask the pupils to say the words in English.
- Ask the pupils to say other words in English they know for clothes.
- Ask them which words (in their own language) they would like to learn.
- Ask the pupils to look through Unit 2 in their Class Books. Talk with them about the unit and quickly write the different topics and activities on the board, relating them to the shapes on the poster:
  - ■ Words – clothes, adjectives to describe people
  - ▲ Story – *The autograph*
  - ◆ Sentences – *What colour's his jacket? / What colour are her shoes? His / her shoes are red. This is Finn's cap. / These are Molly's shoes.*
  - ■ Text work – menus
  - ● Song – *We need energy* / Chant – *Put on your skirt*
  - ◗ Other subjects – Art (portraits)
- Remind the pupils that they will use the poster again at the end of the unit.

Introduce new vocabulary *see p19*
- Use the clothes flashcards to teach the new vocabulary.
- Give each pupil a number between 1 and 12. Put all the flashcards on the board and give each one a number between 1 and 12.
- Play *That's my word!* with the pupils (see p20): take the flashcards down and jumble them up. Show them to the pupils one at a time. When they see the flashcard which had their number, they say *That's my word! Belt!*

CB p11 Activity 1 Look, listen and repeat.
- Look at the picture with the pupils. Ask questions such as *Who can you see? Where are they?* Recast pupils' answers as necessary: *Yes, the children are at a shopping centre.*
- Ask about the children's clothes: *What's Molly wearing? Yes, a pink dress.*
- The pupils listen to the recording. They repeat each word chorally and point to the correct picture.

1.16

1 cap, **2** shirt, **3** dress, **4** belt, **5** trainers, **6** tracksuit, **7** trousers, **8** shoes, **9** gloves, **10** scarf, **11** tights, **12** coat

CB p11 Activity 2 Listen and find.
- Explain that although the children are all at the shopping centre, they're not together. The children are going to describe each other's clothes to their parents.
- Play the dialogue.
- The pupils listen for the descriptions. They point to the person being described in the picture.
- Alternatively, the pupils can use their bookmarks (see p28) to focus on the pictures.

1.17

Archie: Hey, Dad! I can see Luke and Molly. And Jazmin!
Dad: Where? What's Luke wearing?
Archie: He's wearing blue trousers and brown shoes.
Dad: Er … and what's Molly wearing?
Archie: She's wearing a pink dress … and a yellow belt.
Dad: Oh yes. Jazmin's wearing a tracksuit and trainers.
Archie: Yes.

Jazmin: Look, Molly. I can see Finn and his Mum.
Molly: Where? What's Finn wearing?
Jazmin: He's wearing a green scarf … and green gloves.
Molly: Oh yes!

Finn: Mum!
Mum: Yes, Finn?
Finn: I can see Eve. Look.
Mum: Where?
Finn: There. She's wearing purple tights … and a grey coat.
Mum: Oh yes. And look – I can see Archie too.
Finn: Where? What's he wearing?
Mum: He's wearing a red shirt, and an orange cap.
Finn: Oh yes, I can see him. He's with his Dad. Let's say hello!

CB p11 **Activity 3 Ask and answer.**

- Introduce the dialogue with questions such as *What's Finn wearing?*
- The pupils answer your questions with complete sentences: *He's wearing a green scarf.*
- Practise the dialogue, asking about all the children in the picture.
- The pupils practise asking and answering the questions in pairs.
- As a variation, the pupils take turns to close their books and answer their partner's questions from memory.

Spelling

- Ask the pupils to identify:
  1 words with two vowels together (*tracksuit, trainers, coat*)
  2 words that begin with *t* (*tracksuit, tights, trainers, trousers*)
  3 words that end in *t* (*tracksuit, belt, coat, shirt*)

AB p14 **Activity 1 Number the pictures. Then write.**

- Read the words in the word pool to the pupils.
- Point to the picture of a belt and ask *What is it?* The pupils identify the item (*a belt*). Show how the example answer '1' next to the belt links the picture with the correct word in the word pool. Pupils number the remaining pictures in the same way.
- Use the pictures of the person to show the meaning of *top half* (above the waist) and *bottom half* (below the waist).
- Point to the picture of the trainers and ask *Top half or bottom half?* The pupils answer *bottom half* and write *trainers* in the correct column. Repeat with the other clothes items.
- There may be some debate over whether coat, tracksuit, and gloves are for the top half or the bottom half. You can discuss this as a class, and take a vote to decide where to write the words, or else write them in both columns.

Answers: top half – scarf, shirt, cap, (gloves), (coat), (tracksuit); bottom half – belt, tights, trainers, (gloves), (coat), (tracksuit)

Lesson 2 ■ = Words

Practising vocabulary

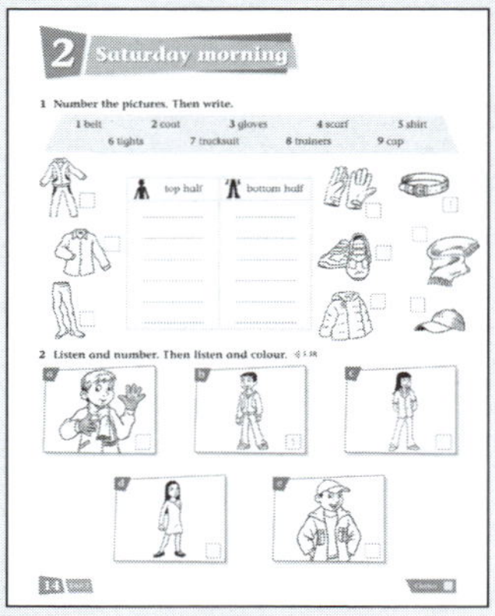

AB page 14

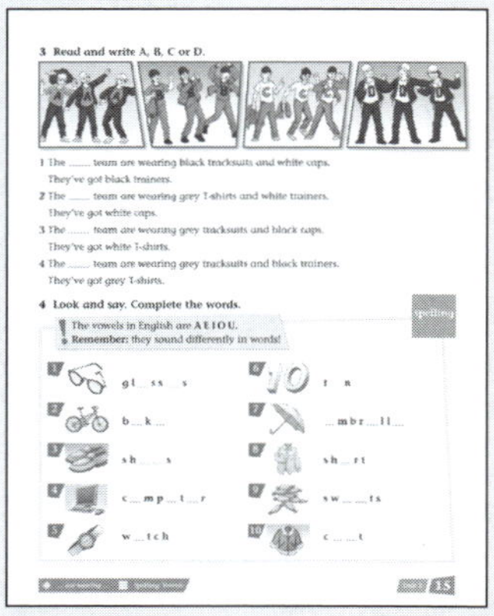

AB page 15

Objectives

- Review vocabulary for clothes
- Practise listening to and talking about what people are wearing
- Read about people's clothes
- Practise saying and writing vowel sounds

Core language

Review of

- clothes vocabulary
- language used so far

Other language

team

Materials

Clothes flashcards (x12); CD 1; Clothes picture cards (PMB p10) – one photocopied set per pupil

Review vocabulary

- Put the clothes flashcards on the board. The pupils say the words chorally and individually.
- Play *First sounds* with the pupils: say the first sound of each word and encourage the pupils to identify them.

AB p14 **Activity 2 Listen and number. Then listen and colour.**

- Point to the first boy and ask *What's he wearing?* The pupils answer *a scarf, gloves,* etc.
- Repeat with the other children in the pictures.
- Play the CD. After each conversation, pause the CD. The pupils identify the child and write the number of the conversation next to the picture.

1.18

1 Adult 1: What's he wearing?
Adult 2: He's wearing a green tracksuit and red trainers.

2 Adult 1: What's she wearing?
Adult 2: She's wearing a pink dress and black shoes.

3 Adult 1: What's she wearing?
Adult 2: She's wearing black trousers and a purple shirt.

4 Adult 1: What's he wearing?
Adult 2: He's wearing a yellow scarf and orange gloves.

5 Adult 1: What's he wearing?
Adult 2: He's wearing a grey coat and a blue cap.

Answers: a 4 b 1 c 3 d 2 e 5

- Play the first conversation again. Ask the pupils *What colour is his tracksuit? (green)* and *What colour are his trainers? (red)*. The pupils colour the picture of the first boy.
- Repeat with the other conversations.

AB p15 Activity 3 Read and write A, B, C or D.

- Point to the first team. Say *Tell me about Team A's clothes*. The pupils describe the clothes (*black tracksuits, grey T-shirts, white trainers, white caps*).
- Repeat with the other teams.
- Read the first sentence to the pupils. The pupils identify the correct team and write the letter in the description.
- Repeat with the other sentences.

Answers: 1 D 2 A 3 C 4 B

AB p15 Activity 4 Look and say. Complete the words.

- Read the text to the pupils. Ask the pupils to repeat the vowels A-E-I-O-U chorally and individually.
- Point to the first word. Ask the pupils *What word is it?* The pupils answer *glasses*.
- Spell the word letter by letter. Pause at each blank for the pupils to say the missing vowel.
- The pupils add the missing vowels to the words.

Answers: glasses, bike, shoes, computer, watch, ten, umbrella, shirt, sweets, coat

- Point out the different pronunciation of the vowel A in *glasses, watch, umbrella,* and *coat*. Show how the pronunciation is different:
  – in different words (*watch, umbrella*)
  – with another vowel next to *a* (*coat*), etc.
- Repeat with the other vowels.
- Make sure pupils understand that the vowels in English don't often 'say their sound' – they have lots of different sounds.
- Practise the vowel sounds by saying the words individually and asking pupils if they can tell you what sound the vowel makes: *What sound does 'u' make in 'umbrella'. Yes, /ʌ/. And what about in 'computer'? Yes, /u:/.*

Spelling game

- Play *Hangman* using the words for clothes which the pupils know (see p20).

PMB p11 Make the picture cards

- Give out the photocopies of the clothes picture cards. The pupils colour and cut out the picture cards.
- They can use their cards to play a game, for example *Who's got ...?* (see p21).
- If your pupils are using word cards, they can prepare them now (see p30). Pupils cut them out and match them with the picture cards.
- Remind the pupils to keep all the cards in a safe place.

Lesson 3 ▲ = Story

Story

CB page 12

CB page 13

Objectives

- Listen to a story
- Read a story
- Listen for words and phrases in a story
- Practise story language

Core language

This is Luke's CD, What colour's his jacket?

Review of
- clothes vocabulary
- language used so far

Other language

autograph, manager
Me too!; Brilliant!; Here you are.

Materials

Clothes flashcards (x12); CD 1

Review vocabulary

- Put the clothes flashcards on the board. The pupils say the words chorally and individually.
- Play *Memory numbers* with the pupils: put all the flashcards in a line on the board, with a number from 1 to 12 under each one. Say sets of three or more numbers: the pupils say the corresponding words in the same order.

Introduce the story

- Ask the pupils to imagine they are going to see someone famous at the shopping centre. The pupils talk about who they would like to see.
- Explain that in the story the children are going to get a surprise connected with a famous person.

CB pp12–13 Activity 4 First listening with the books closed

- Tell the pupils to listen to the story and decide what the surprise was.
- The pupils listen with their books closed.

1.19

[1] At the shopping centre ...

Molly:	Look, Jazmin. This is Luke's CD. It's new.
Jazmin:	Oh, The Street Boys. I like The Glitter Girls.
Molly:	Me too!

[2] Luke: Hey, look! It's Rick! From The Street Boys!
Molly: Where?
Luke: There!

[3] Jazmin: What's he wearing?
Luke: Oh … a jacket and black trousers.

[4] Molly: I can't see him. What colour's his jacket?
Luke: It's red.
Molly: Oh …

[5] Luke: Come on, let's follow him.
Jazmin: Let's get an autograph!

[6] Jazmin: Let's go this way, Molly.
Molly: OK.

[7] Five minutes later …
Molly: A red jacket … Look, he's over there!
Jazmin: Oh, yes!

[8] Jazmin: Hello! Can we have an autograph?
Man: An autograph? OK!
Luke: That's not Rick!

[9] Man: Here you are. You can have a CD too.
Molly: Thanks! Oh. It's a Glitter Girls CD!
Man: Yes, I'm their manager.

[10] Jazmin: Brilliant!
Luke: Fantastic!

- Ask the children what the surprise was (they thought the singer of a popular boy band was at the shopping centre. In fact he was the manager of a popular girl group). Encourage them to give further details of the story. Recast the pupils' answers as necessary.

CB pp12–13 Activity 4 Second listening with the books open

- Tell the pupils to open their books and look at the story.
- Ask questions about the story such as *What CD did the friends get?*
- Play the recording again while the pupils follow in their books.
- Go through any vocabulary queries with the class.

CB p13 Activity 5 Read and write *true* or *false*.

- Explain that the number of each sentence refers to the number of the picture in the story.
- Read the first sentence. Say *Look at picture 1. Is sentence number 1 true?* The pupils answer *No*, and write *false* in their notebooks.
- The pupils answer the rest of the questions in their notebooks.

Answers: 1 false **2** true **4** false **7** true **8** false **9** false **10** true

Fun expressions

- Write these 'fun expressions' from the story on the board:
  Me too!
  Brilliant!
  Here you are.
- Play the story again: the pupils put up their hands when they hear one of the phrases.
- Pause the recording. The pupils repeat the phrase chorally and individually. Encourage the pupils to copy the intonation on the CD.

Lesson 4 ◆ = Sentences

Language focus 1

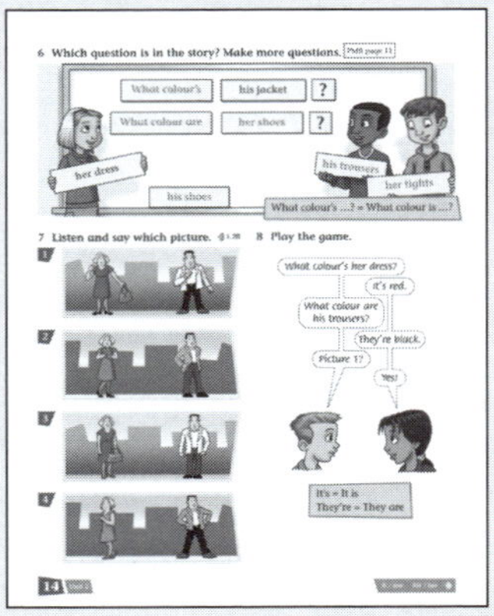

CB page 14

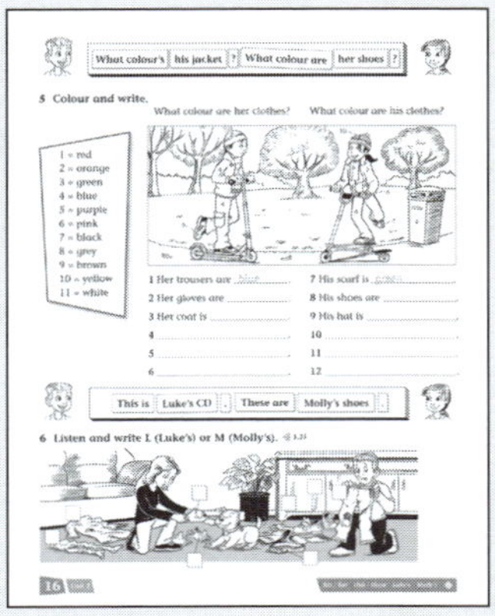

AB page 16

Objectives

- Understand the use of *his* and *her*
- Review the use of *is* and *are*
- Practise using the new language

Core language

What colour's …? / What colour are …?
his, her
Review of language used so far

Materials

Character flashcards (x7); Grammar tiles (PMB p11) – one photocopy of Set 1 per pupil (optional); CD 1

Recall the story

- Ask the pupils to remember as much as they can from the story.
- Say some sentences from the story, and ask the pupils to identify who says each one, for example:
  I like The Glitter Girls. (Jazmin)
  It's Rick! From The Street Boys! (Luke)
  Let's get an autograph! (Jazmin)
  An autograph? OK! (Man)
  You can have a CD too. (Man)

PMB p11 / CB p14 Activity 6 Which question is in the story? Make more questions.

- Ask the pupils to read the questions in the grammar tiles (*What colour's his jacket? What colour are her shoes?*).
- Ask the pupils to say which question was in the story (*What colour's his jacket?*).
- Focus on the difference between the singular and plural forms.
- Point out to pupils the reminder box: *What colour's* = *What colour is.* Remind them that *is* is often elided (run together) with the previous word to make it quicker and easier to say.
- Write *his* and *her* in big letters on the board. Point to *his* and say *We use 'his' with boys.* Point to *her* and say *We use 'her' with girls.* Show the flashcards of the characters one by one: the pupils say *his* or *her* according to the character.
- The pupils say the sentences in the grammar tiles chorally and individually.

- The pupils make more sentences using the other tiles in the picture. Alternatively, give each pupil a copy of Set 1 of the grammar tiles from the PMB: the pupils cut out the tiles and arrange them in sentences on their desks. Ask individual pupils to read out their sentences for the class.

CB p14 Activity 7 Listen and say which picture.

- Show the pupils the pictures. Ask the pupils to make sentences about the pictures, for example *She's wearing green tights.*
- Play the first conversation on the CD. The pupils match it with the correct picture.
- Repeat with the other sentences.

1.20

Jazmin:	What colour are her shoes?
Finn:	They're purple.
Jazmin:	What colour's his jacket?
Finn:	It's grey.
Presenter:	Which picture is it?
Finn:	What colour's her dress?
Jazmin:	It's red.
Finn:	What colour are his shoes?
Jazmin:	They're brown.
Presenter:	Which picture is it?
Jazmin:	What colour are her tights?
Finn:	They're pink.
Jazmin:	What colour's his jacket?
Finn:	It's white.
Presenter:	Which picture is it?
Finn:	What colour are her shoes?
Jazmin:	They're black.
Finn:	What colour are his trousers?
Jazmin:	They're blue.
Presenter:	Which picture is it?

Answers: 1 picture 4 2 picture 1 3 picture 3 4 picture 2

CB p14 Activity 8 Play the game.

- Read the conversation to the pupils.
- Say you are thinking of a picture. The pupils ask you questions about it and identify the picture.
- The pupils play the game in pairs.

AB p16 Activity 5 Colour and write.

- Read the *What colour …?* questions in the grammar tiles to the pupils. Explain that the pupils are going to colour the clothes, then write about them.
- Read the colour key to the pupils, then ask *What colour are her trousers?* The pupils answer *blue* and colour the girl's trousers blue.
- Repeat with the other items of clothing in the picture. The pupils can do most of the colouring individually as soon as they understand the idea.
- Read the first sentence to the pupils. Read the beginning of the second sentence. The pupils complete it (*… are purple*) and write the completion in their books.
- Repeat with the next sentence.
- Ask the pupils to suggest descriptions for the next three sentences, for example *Her hat is yellow.* The pupils write three more sentences about the girl's clothes.
- Repeat with the boy's clothes.

Answers: 2 Her gloves are purple. 3 Her coat is orange. 4 / 5 / 6 Her trousers are blue. / Her shoes are black. / Her scarf is pink. 8 His shoes are brown. 9 His hat is orange. 10 / 11 / 12 His trousers are grey. / His coat is blue. / His gloves are red.

Lesson 5 ◆ = Sentences

Language focus 2

AB page 16

AB page 17

Objectives

- Review vocabulary for clothes
- Understand the use of possessive *'s*
- Practise talking about people's possessions

Core language

This is Luke's CD. / These are Molly's shoes.

Review of

- clothes vocabulary
- language used so far

Materials

Grammar tiles (PMB p11) – one photocopy of Set 2 per pupil; Pupils' grammar tiles (Set 1) from Lesson 4 (optional); CD 1

Recall *this / these*

- Draw a small pencil on the board. Then draw three large pencils on the board. Point to the small pencil and say *This pencil is small.* Point to the large pencils and say *These pencils are big.*
- Say the sentences again and write the words *this* and *these* under the corresponding pictures.
- Call individual pupils up to the front to point at the pictures and say the sentences. Make sure all the pupils understand that *this* is for one object and *these* is for more than one object. Repeat with other pupils.
- Repeat with pictures of other objects (e.g. a big book and two small books).

PMB p11 / AB p16 Focus on language

- Take a pupil's pencil and say, for example, *This is Peter's pencil.* Take a pupil's books and say, for example, *These are David's books.*
- Write the sentences on the board. Point out the use of *'s* to show who the pencil and the books belong to.
- Ask the pupils to read the sentences in the second set of grammar tiles on page 16 of the Activity Book.
- Ask the pupils *Which sentence is in the story?* (*This is Luke's CD.*)

- Focus on the use of *'s* after the name to show who the object belongs to.
- The pupils say the sentences in the grammar tiles chorally and individually.
- Give each pupil a copy of Set 2 of the grammar tiles from the PMB. Ask the pupils to suggest words to put in the blank tiles (*Archie's trousers, Jazmin's belt*, etc.). Write the suggestions on the board. The pupils can choose words to copy in the blank tiles.
- The pupils cut out all the tiles and use them to make sentences on their desks. Ask pupils to read out their sentences for the class.
- Pupils can combine the Set 2 tiles with some of the Set 1 tiles to make more sentences, for example *This is his jacket. These are her tights.*

Practice

- Take several objects from the pupils and put them on your desk. Show the pupils one of the objects and say, for example, *This is Ana's bag.* The pupils repeat the sentence chorally and individually.
- Repeat with a group of objects and say, for example, *These are Sara's pencils.* The pupils repeat chorally and individually.
- Repeat with the other objects.
- Call individual pupils up to the front to pick up objects, show them to the class, and say the sentence.

AB p16 Activity 6 Listen and write L (Luke's) or M (Molly's).

- Point to the items in the picture (cap, trousers, belt, tights, scarf, gloves, dress, and shoes) and ask the pupils to say the word.
- Play the first part of the conversation (up to *This is Molly's cap.*) Pause the CD and ask the pupils *Is it Luke's cap? Is it Molly's cap?* The pupils answer *It's Molly's cap* and write *M* next to the cap in the picture.
- Play the rest of the conversation, pausing after each item is identified to give the pupils time to write *L* or *M* next to it.

1.21

Mum:	Oh, look.
Dad:	Oh no! Naughty dog! Bad dog!
Mum:	This is Molly's cap.
Dad:	Oh no! And these are Luke's trousers.
Mum:	Oh. And this is Molly's belt.
Dad:	Look at Molly's tights!
Mum:	And Luke's scarf!
Dad:	These are Luke's gloves.
Mum:	And this is Molly's dress.
Dad:	Oh dear. Look at Luke's shoes!
Mum:	Naughty dog!

Answers: cap – M, trousers – L, belt – M, tights – M, scarf – L, gloves – L, dress – M, shoes – L

AB p17 Activity 7 Write.

- Ask individual pupils to read the words in word pool 1 and word pool 2.
- Point to the picture of the car in Number 1. Ask *Is it Luke's car?* The pupils answer *No.* Say *This is Eve's car.*
- Point to the picture of the trainers in Number 2. Ask *Are they Jazmin's trainers?* The pupils answer *No.* Say *These are Archie's trainers.*
- Point to the picture of the shirt in Number 3. Help the pupils to say *This is Finn's shirt.*
- Call a pupil up to the front to write the sentence on the board. The pupils write the sentence in their books.
- Repeat with the other pictures.

Answers: **1** This is Eve's car. **2** These are Archie's trainers. **3** This is Finn's shirt. **4** These are Molly's tights. **5** This is Jazmin's belt. **6** This is Luke's football. **7** These are Eve's glasses. **8** This is Archie's cap.

AB p17 Activity 8 Look at Class Book page 3. Write the questions and answers.

- Tell the pupils to look at page 3 of their Class Books. Point to parts of the picture and say, for example, *Eve's glasses.* The pupils say *Eve's glasses are black.* You can say *Yes, they're black.*
- Read the first and second question and answer.
- Help pupils to understand that *They're* … is used to talk about plural items (instead of repeating *Eve's glasses*, or whatever) and *It's* … is used to talk about singular items.
- Point out the grammar box to pupils and make sure they understand the short forms.
- Read the third question. The pupils say the answer *They're blue.*
- Repeat with the other questions and answers.

Answers: **3** They're blue. **4** They're red and white. **5** It's orange. **7** What colour are Jazmin's trousers? **8** What colour is Eve's bag / Luke's T-shirt?

- As a follow-up activity, pupils can make up more questions about the Class Book pictures, and ask and answer in pairs.

Practice

- Ask questions about the pupil's clothes, bags, etc. For example, *What colour are Ana's trousers?* Select individual pupils to answer your questions.
- Choose individual pupils to ask more questions and other pupils to answer them.
- The pupils practise the questions and answers in pairs.

For extra grammar practice, see AB page 98.

Activity 1 Look and colour. Then write.

Answers: **2** They're brown. **3** his; It's green. **4** her; It's yellow. **5** What colour are her; They're red. **6** What colour's his; It's orange.

Activity 2 Find and write.

Answers: **2** These are Eve's glasses. **3** These are Jazmin's trainers. **4** This is Eve's umbrella. **5** these are Archie's gloves. **6** This is Jazmin's belt.

Lesson 6 ▲ = Story

Playscript

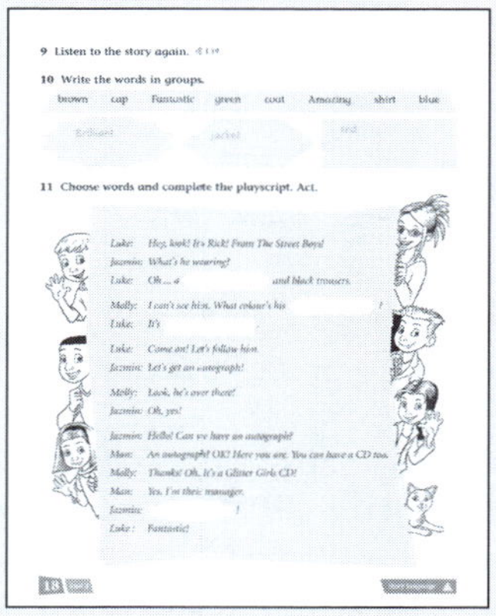

AB page 18

Objectives

- Read and complete a playscript
- Use finger puppets to act out a playscript
- Act out the play

Core language

Review of language used so far

Other language

amazing, fantastic

Materials

CD 1; Spare photocopies of the finger puppets (FMB p3)

AB p18 Activity 9 Listen to the story again.

- Tell the pupils to look at pages 12–13 in the Class Book again.
- Play the CD while the pupils listen and read.
- Alternatively, the pupils can read the story aloud in groups of four. Each pupil should read one character.

AB p18 Activity 10 Write the words in groups.

- Read the words in the word pool to the pupils.
- Point to each of the boxes and read the word in each one. Ask the pupils to suggest words from the word pool to go in each box.
- The pupils write the words from the word pool in the correct category.
- Ask pupils to talk about how they grouped the words, and to describe the categories, i.e. the first group is words to describe things, the second group is clothes, and the third group is colours.

Answers: set 1 – Brilliant, Amazing, Fantastic; set 2 – jacket, cap, shirt, coat; set 3 – red, brown, green, blue

- Ask the pupils to suggest new words for each category.

AB p18 Activity 11 Choose words and complete the playscript. Act.

- Read the playscript to the pupils. When you come to a blank, ask *Which word was in the story?* The pupils say the words from the story.
- Read the playscript again. Ask the pupils to suggest alternative words from Activity 10 to complete the blanks.
- Divide the pupils into groups of four. In their groups, the pupils decide which words to use when they read the playscript.

Finger puppets see p22

- Ask the pupils *How many characters are there in the story? (Four)*.The pupils identify the four characters (Jazmin, Molly, Luke, and the man).
- In their groups, the pupils decide who is going to take each part.
- If the pupils have got their finger puppets with them, tell them to get out the puppet for the character they are going to play.
- Give each group a photocopy of the extra finger puppet. The pupils cut out, colour, and stick the extra puppet to make the puppet for the man. If they haven't got the other puppets they need, they will have to make those too.

Practice

- Remind the pupils of the five points of successful play acting (see p34).
- Tell the pupils about the notes you made during the Unit 1 play acting. Encourage them to concentrate on the points you noticed. Say you will be watching them again this time.
- The pupils act out the play with their puppets. While they are doing this, circulate around the classroom. Make a note of the points the pupils should improve on next time.
- Ask one or two groups to come to the front to act out the play with their puppets.

Lesson 7 ▬ = Text work

Reading and writing

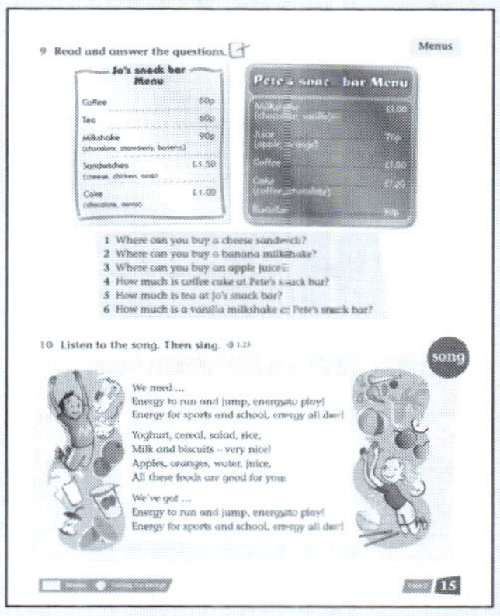

CB page 15 AB page 19

Objectives

- Review food and drink vocabulary
- Read and understand a menu with prices
- Write a menu

Core language

Review of
- clothes vocabulary
- food and drink vocabulary

Other language

menu, snack bar, coffee, tea, milkshake, strawberry, carrot, vanilla,
80 pence, one pound fifty / one pound fifty pence

Materials

Cut-outs of people in magazines with a range of different clothes; Menu template (PMB p12) – one photocopy per pupil

Review vocabulary

- Show one of the magazine cut-outs to the pupils.
- Ask the pupils to talk about the people's clothes, using *his*, *her*, or *their*. For example, *Her belt is black.*
- Hand out the magazine cut-outs to the pupils. In pairs, they talk about the clothes.
- Select individual pupils to stand up and tell the rest of the class about their picture.

CB p15 Activity 9 Read and answer the questions.

- Write these headings on the board: *milkshake, sandwich, cake, juice*. Check the meaning.
- Ask the pupils to suggest flavours and types for each heading, for example: *milkshake – chocolate, strawberry, vanilla; cake – coffee, chocolate, carrot*, etc.
- Talk with the pupils about restaurants. Ask the pupils what they do when they go to a restaurant.
- Ask pupils to look at the top of Class Book page 15. Make sure that the pupils understand they are looking at menus for two different restaurants.
- Explain how to say money in English (*80 pence, one pound fifty / one pound fifty pence*, etc.).
- Ask the pupils to read the menus.
- Read the first question to the pupils. Help them to find the answer in the menu for Jo's snack bar.
- The pupils read the rest of the questions and write the answers in their notebooks.

Answers: 1 Jo's snack bar 2 Jo's snack bar
3 Pete's snack bar 4 £1.00 5 60p 6 £1.00

AB p19 Activity 12 Listen and find the menu. Circle A or B.

- Point to the menu for Susie's snack bar. Read the items and prices to the pupils.
- Repeat with the menu for Mike's snack bar.
- Choose items from the menus, for example *apple juice* or *carrot cake*. Ask the pupils to say which menu it is, A or B.
- Play the first conversation on the CD. Ask the pupils which menu the person is looking at (*B*). Show the pupils that letter B is circled in Number 1.
- Repeat with the other conversations. The pupils circle the correct letter, A or B.

1.22

1 Child: Can I have a beef sandwich and a coffee, please?
2 Child: Can I have some chocolate cake and a strawberry milkshake, please?
3 Child: Can I have two biscuits and a chocolate milkshake, please?
4 Child: Can I have a tea and some coffee cake, please?
5 Child: Can I have a chicken sandwich and a tea, please?
6 Child: Can I have some carrot cake and a pineapple juice, please?

Answers: 1 B 2 A 3 B 4 A 5 A 6 B

AB p19 Activity 13 Look at menu A and answer the questions.

- Point out the free gifts in the menu at Susie's snack bar. Relate the amount a person spends to the free gift he / she receives.
- Read the first speech bubble. Ask the pupils *How much is that?* The pupils work out the total (£3.00).
- Read the question. The pupils identify the free gift (*stickers*).
- Repeat with the other speech bubbles.

Answers: 1 total £3.00, the gift is some stickers
2 total £2.50, the gift is a key ring
3 total £3 plus £2.50 = £5.50, the gift is a T-shirt

PMB p12 / AB p19 Activity 14 Make a menu.

- Explain to the pupils that they are going to write a menu for a snack bar.
- Remind pupils that they have to choose work for their portfolio during the course (see p198). Point out that this piece of work would be a suitable piece to include.
- Brainstorm ideas for food and drink to include in the menu.
- Choose some suggestions and write them on the board.
- Show the pupils how to write the menu, using the menus in Activity 12 as a model.
- Hand out the photocopies of the writing template. Tell the pupils to choose a name for another snack bar and write its menu.
- The pupils write a rough copy first in their notebooks for you to correct. After you have checked the rough copy, they write their final copy on the photocopied template.

Lesson 8

● = Song / chant

Learning for life

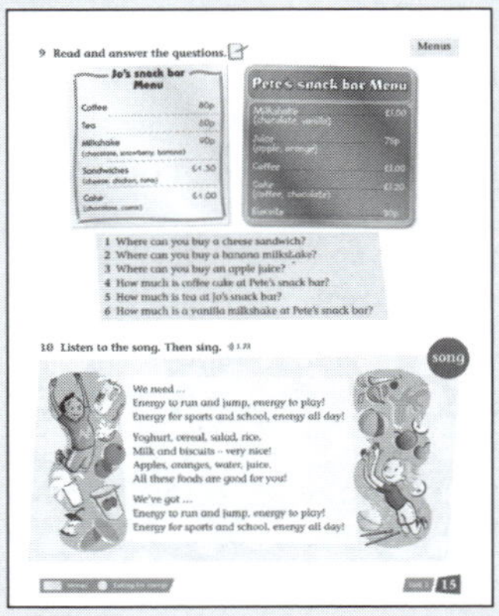

CB page 15

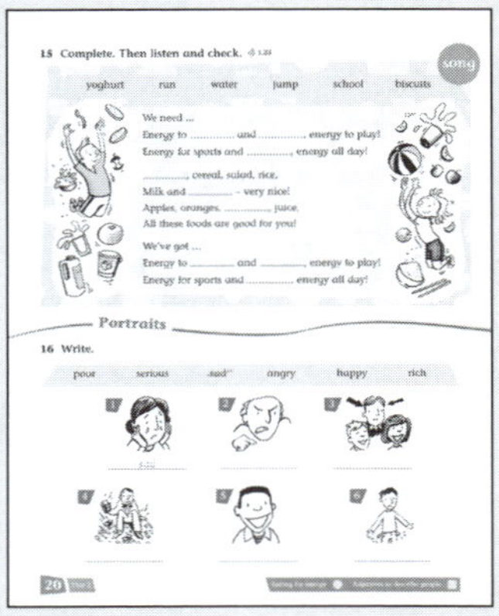

AB page 20

Objectives
- Review the unit so far
- Understand the importance of healthy eating
- Talk about what types of food are healthy
- Sing a song about healthy eating

Core language
Review of language used so far

Other language
energy

Materials
Rollercoaster Game poster; Clothes flashcards (x12); CD 1

Unit review

- Use the Rollercoaster Game poster and the Class Book to review the unit so far. Talk with the pupils about the activities they have done.
- The pupils give examples of the language they used in each activity.

Review vocabulary (categorizing)

- Ask the pupils to tell you all the new words they remember from the unit.
- Put all the flashcards on the board and ask the pupils to arrange them in these two categories: *clothes for girls only* and *clothes for boys and girls*
- Repeat with other categories, such as:
  clothes for cold weather / *clothes for all weather*
  clothes I wear / *clothes I don't wear.*

Introduce the topic

- Talk with the pupils about eating healthy food. Ask questions such as: What happens if we eat a lot of unhealthy food? What types of food are healthy? What types of food are unhealthy?
- Encourage the pupils to talk about some or all of these ideas in their answers:
  - unhealthy food isn't good for you
  - it's important to eat a balanced diet
  - vegetables, fruit, cereals, nuts, chicken, and fish are healthy foods
  - hamburgers and chips aren't healthy foods
  - it's easy to become overweight if you eat unhealthy food.
- The pupils can express their ideas in their own language. If they do, recast their answers in English.

CB p15 Activity 10 Listen to the song. Then sing.

- Read the song with the pupils. Explain any new words (e.g. *energy*).
- Play the song on the CD.

1.23

We need ...
Energy to run and jump, energy to play!
Energy for sports and school, energy all day!

Yoghurt, cereal, salad, rice,
Milk and biscuits – very nice!
Apples, oranges, water, juice,
All these foods are good for you!

We've got. ...
Energy to run and jump, energy to play!
Energy for sports and school, energy all day!

- Write a list of the food items in the song (*yoghurt, cereal, salad, rice, milk, biscuits, apples, oranges, water, juice*). Point to each one and ask the pupils to draw in the air the first letter of each one (*a* for *apples*, *o* for *oranges*, etc.).
- Read the song again to the pupils. Ask them to draw the first letters in the air as you read.
- Play the song again and encourage the pupils to join in, singing and drawing letters in the air.

AB p20 Activity 15 Complete. Then listen and check.

- Tell the pupils to close their Class Books and open their Activity Books at page 20.
- Read the first line of the song to the pupils. Ask the pupils to recall the words to go in the spaces. Write the words they suggest on the board.
- Repeat with the other lines of the song.
- Play the song again; the pupils check the words they suggested.
- Make any necessary corrections to the words on the board. The pupils copy the words in the spaces in their Activity Books.
- To finish the lesson, tell the pupils to close their books. Help them to say the whole song again, chorally, from memory.

Answers: run, jump, school; Yoghurt, biscuits, water; run, jump, school

Lesson 9 = Words = Other subjects

Learning through English

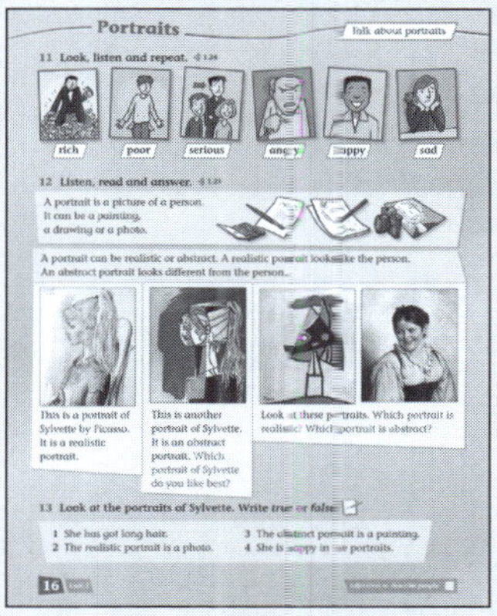

CB page 16

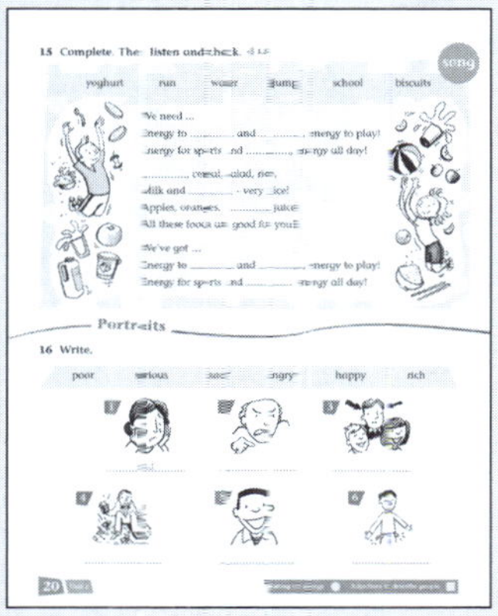

AB page 20

Objectives

- Learn some adjectives to describe people
- Learn about different types of portraits through English

Core language

Adjectives to describe people: *rich, poor, angry, serious*

Review of

- *sad, happy*
- language used so far

Other language

abstract, realistic, portrait, drawing, painting, photo

Materials

Flashcards for adjectives to describe people (*happy, rich, poor, angry, serious, sad*); CD 1; Picture cards for adjectives to describe people (PMB p10) – one photocopied set per pupil

Introduce the topic

- Show the pupils the portraits on pages 16 and 17 of the Class Book. Make sure that the pupils understand that a *portrait* is a painting of a person, not an object or a place.
- Discuss the pupils' reactions to the pictures. Encourage the pupils to say sentences such as:
  She's very pretty.
  I like this portrait.
- The pupils can express their reactions in their own language. Recast their answers as necessary.

- Tell the pupils that they are going to discuss the people in the portraits, and the way the portraits were made.

Introduce new vocabulary *see p19*

- Show the adjectives flashcards one by one to the pupils. Model the word for each flashcard clearly.
- The pupils repeat the words chorally and then individually.
- Play *What's missing?* with the pupils: take one of the flashcards from the pile, then put the other five flashcards on the board. The pupils say the word for the missing flashcard.

CB p16 Activity 11 Look, listen and repeat.

- Play the CD. The pupils repeat each word chorally and point to the correct picture.

1.24

rich – poor – serious – angry – happy – sad

CB p16 Activity 12 Listen, read and answer.

- Show the pupils the first four portraits.
- Play the CD. Pause after the first section.
- Point to each portrait and ask *What type of portrait is it?* The pupils answer *painting, drawing,* or *photo* as appropriate.
- Play the rest of the CD. Pause after each section.
- Point to each portrait and ask the pupils *Is it realistic or abstract?*

1.25

A portrait is a picture of a person. It can be a painting … a drawing … or a photo.

A portrait can be realistic or abstract. A realistic portrait looks like the person. An abstract portrait looks different from the person.

This is a portrait of Sylvette by Picasso. It is a realistic portrait.

This is another portrait of Sylvette. It is an abstract portrait. Which portrait of Sylvette do you like best?

Look at these portraits. Which portrait is realistic?

Which portrait is abstract?

CB p16 Activity 13 Look at the portraits of Sylvette. Write *true* or *false.*

- Point to the portraits of Sylvette. Make sure the pupils understand that these are both portraits of the same person.
- Read the first sentence to the pupils. The pupils answer *true.*
- The pupils read the other sentences and write *true* or *false* in their notebooks.

Answers: 1 true 2 false 3 true 4 false

AB p20 Activity 16 Write.

- Read the words in the word pool.
- Point to the first picture and ask the pupils *Which word is it?* The pupils answer *sad.*
- Repeat with the other pictures. The pupils write the words on the lines next to the pictures.

Answers: 1 sad 2 angry 3 serious 4 rich 5 happy 6 poor

PMB p10 Make the picture cards

- Give out the photocopies of the adjectives picture cards. The pupils colour and cut out the picture cards.
- They can use their cards to play a game, for example *What's missing?* (pairs version) (see p19).
- If your pupils are using word cards, they can prepare them now (see p30). Pupils cut them out and match them with the picture cards.
- Remind the pupils to keep all the cards in a safe place.

Lesson 10 = Words = Other subjects

Learning through English

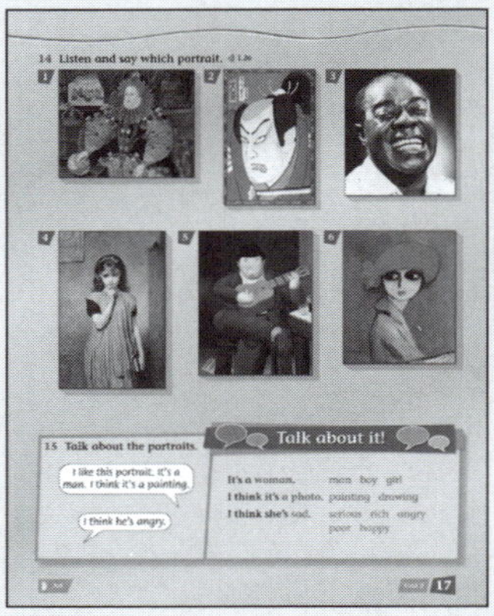

CB page 17

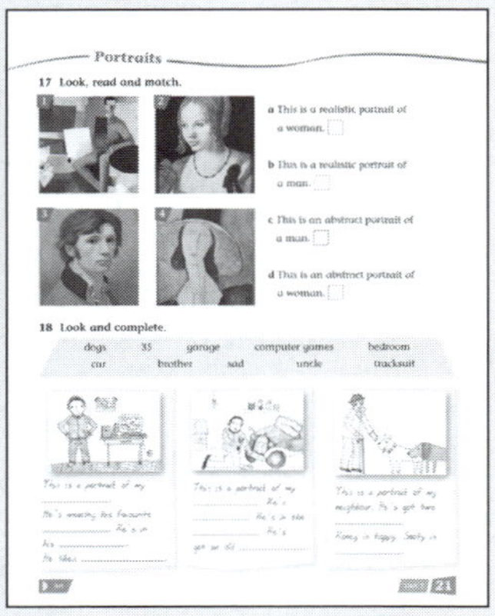

AB page 21

Objectives

- Review adjectives to describe people
- Identify portraits from descriptions
- Describe portraits

Core language

Review of language used so far

Materials

Clothes flashcards (x12); Flashcards for adjectives to describe people (x6); CD 1

Review vocabulary

- Stick half of the clothes and half of the adjectives flashcards on the board.
- Write up the words with jumbled letters.
- Ask pupils to come to the front to write the words and match them with the flashcards.
- Repeat with the other half of the flashcards.

CB p17 Activity 14 Listen and say which portrait.

- Point to the each of the portraits and ask the pupils to describe each one.
- Encourage the pupils to talk about the subjects of the portraits – their age, their feelings, what they're wearing, etc. Recast their answers if necessary.
- Tell the pupils to listen to the conversations on the CD and identify the correct portraits.
- Play the CD. Pause after each conversation and ask *Which portrait is it?*

1.26

Adult: Tell me about this portrait.
Child: Um, it's a painting. It's a woman. She's got a red hat.
Adult: Is she happy?
Child: I don't know. I think she's serious.

Adult: Tell me about this portrait.
Child: It's a photo. It's a man. He's laughing.
Adult: Is he happy?
Child: Yes, I think he's very happy!

Adult: Tell me about this portrait.
Child: It's a painting. It's a girl. She's got brown hair and a pink ribbon.
Adult: Yes …
Child: I think she's poor. I think she's sad too.

Adult: Tell me about this portrait.
Child: It's a painting. It's a woman. She's got red hair. I think she's rich.

Adult: Tell me about this portrait.
Child: It's a painting. It's a man. He's wearing a hat … and purple trousers and a purple jacket.
Adult: Yes.
Child: He's got a guitar.

Adult: Tell me about this portrait.
Child: It's a man.
Adult: Mmm… Is he happy?
Adult: No! I think he's angry.

Answers: 1 6 2 3 3 4 4 1 5 5 6 2

CB p17 Activity 15 Talk about the portraits.

- Read the speech bubbles to the pupils. The pupils identify which portrait they're talking about (2).
- Point to another portrait and say *Tell me about this portrait*. The pupils describe the portrait.
- Repeat with the other portraits. Alternatively, the pupils can practise describing the portraits in pairs.
- Remind them to look at the *Talk about it!* box to help them.

AB p21 Activity 17 Look, read and match.

- Point to each of the portraits. Ask the pupils some of these questions about each one: *Is it a man? Is it a woman? Is it realistic? Is it abstract? Is it a drawing? Is it a painting?* The pupils answer *Yes* or *No* according to each portrait.
- Read the first description to the pupils. The pupils match it with the correct portrait (2).
- Repeat with the other descriptions.

Answers: a 2 b 3 c 1 d 4

AB p21 Activity 18 Look and complete.

- Read the words in the word pool with the pupils. Then read the first sentence of the first description. The pupils choose a word from the word pool and write it in the space.
- The pupils complete the rest of the descriptions individually.

Answers: 1 brother, tracksuit, bedroom, computer games
2 uncle, 35, garage, car 3 dogs, sad

Lesson 11 = Other subjects

Learning through English (Project)

16 Make a portrait. PMB page 13
1 Draw and colour. 2 Write.
17 Listen, find and repeat. 18 Listen and say the chant.
chant
purple
yellow
Put on your skirt, your purple skirt.
Put on your shirt, your purple shirt.
Purple skirt, purple shirt.
Now you're looking good!
Put on your dress, your yellow dress.
Put on your belt, your red belt.
Yellow dress, red belt.
Now you're looking good!
18

CB page 18

Objectives

- Review adjectives to describe people
- Draw a portrait and describe it

Core language

Review of language used so far

Materials

Flashcards for adjectives to describe people (x6); 'Make a portrait' template (PMB p13) – one photocopy per pupil

Review vocabulary

- Stick the adjectives flashcards on the board
- Write up the words with jumbled letters.
- Ask pupils to come to the front to write the words and match them with the flashcards.

Present the project

- Tell the pupils they are going to draw a portrait. It can be a portrait of any person they choose.
- They are going to write some sentences describing the person in the portrait.

PMB p13 / CB p18 Activity 16 Make a portrait.

- Give out the photocopies of the 'Make a portrait' template.
- Elicit ideas for the person each pupil can draw.
- Elicit ideas for the features they can emphasize in the portrait – long hair, big eyes, a big smile, etc.
- Elicit ideas for the features they can add to the portrait – a pet, a favourite possession, etc.
- The pupils draw rough pictures first in their notebooks or on rough paper. While they are drawing, circulate around the class. Encourage the pupils to include features and make them clear.
- Look at each of the portraits and tick each one when you think it is adequate.
- The pupils draw their final portrait on the photocopy.
- Read the sentences again from Activity Book page 21, Activity 18.
- The pupils write sentences about the person in their portrait. They use the sentences in the Activity Book as a model.

Display

- Display the portraits in the classroom.
- Allow the pupils to move around the classroom, look at all the portraits, and discuss them with their friends.
- Have a feedback session in which the pupils decide on the best portrait, the friendliest person, the most interesting person, etc. Ask the pupils to give reasons for their choices. Finally, ask the pupils to decide which person they would like to meet.

Lesson 11a (optional)

Learning through English (Extension)

PMB page 14

Objectives

- Learn about facial proportions
- Use a grid to draw a facial portrait
- Learn about distorting facial proportions for different artistic effects

Core language

Review of
- adjectives to describe people
- face vocabulary (*face, eyes, nose, mouth, ears, hair*)
- language used so far

Other language

eyebrows, forehead, chin

Materials

Flashcards for adjectives to describe people (x6); Examples of faces drawn by cartoon artists; 'Drawing faces' template (PMB p14) – one photocopy per pupil; Paper – one or two pieces per pupil

Review vocabulary

- Use the flashcards to review the adjectives to describe people. Show the pupils the flashcards and ask them to say the words chorally and individually.
- Show the cartoon faces you have brought in and ask the pupils to describe them, using the adjectives, for example *I think he's sad / serious / rich.* The pupils may have different opinions, and you can discuss what features in the drawing helped them to assess the mood / status of the person (e.g. frown lines, upturned / downturned mouth, eyebrows lowered in anger, etc.).

Preparation

- Tell the pupils that in this lesson they are going to look at facial proportions, and learn how to draw faces more accurately.
- Ask them to get into pairs and study each other's faces for one minute. Tell them to look at the shape, size, and position of all the features of their partner's face. Give them some questions to think about while looking, for example: How close are the eyes to the top of the head? What shape is the nose? Where are the ears – halfway between the eyes and mouth, or higher up? Are the eyebrows straight or slanting?
- Discuss their findings, and ask if they were surprised by anything they saw. Help them to notice the following points:
  - the eyes are positioned halfway down the head (when looking at the whole head, not just the face – many people assume that the eyes sit much higher on the head than they actually do!);
  - a nose is not actually a triangular shape, although many people assume that it is;
  - the hair comes much further down (from the crown of the head onto the forehead) than many people think.
- Following on from this, talk about the importance of always drawing from observation, i.e. drawing what you actually see rather than what you *think* you see.

PMB p14 Using the Photocopy Master

- Give each pupil a photocopy of the 'Drawing faces' sheet.
- Talk with the pupils about the proportions in the template – help them to notice that the rectangle is divided into six equal squares, that the eye line is halfway down the rectangle, and that the mouth line is halfway up the bottom section.
- Look at the four stages at the top of the page with the pupils, naming the face parts in English, and commenting on the facial proportions: *Look, the eyes are halfway up the head. The nose sits on this line here.*
- Teach the new words *eyebrows, forehead,* and *chin.*
- Ask pupils, in pairs, to take turns to draw a quick sketch of their partner on the blank template. Encourage them to use the template as a guide but to really focus on what they can see.
- Optional activity: Give each pupil a blank piece of paper. Ask them to copy the blank face template onto this in pencil. They can draw a more careful portrait of their partner (using pencil, and then pen), and then rub out the template lines.

Display

- Arrange a display of the portraits in the classroom. Allow the pupils to see all the portraits and discuss them.
- Have a feedback session. Encourage the pupils to talk about the easiest features to draw and the most difficult. Have a vote on the best portraits.

Fun activity (optional)

- Give each pupil another piece of paper. Encourage them to experiment with drawing faces with deliberately distorted proportions, e.g. eyes much too high or low, and see what difference it makes.
- Talk about how artists might do this deliberately to create different effects (e.g. putting eyes lower down tends to make someone look younger).

Song

- Ask the pupils *Can you remember the song in this unit?*
- Write what the pupils can remember on the board. Help them to remember the bits they've forgotten, then add them on the board.
- Play the song again (Listening 1.23). The pupils check that the version on the board is correct.
- Play the song again and encourage the pupils to join in.

Lesson 12

Review and self-evaluation

CB page 18

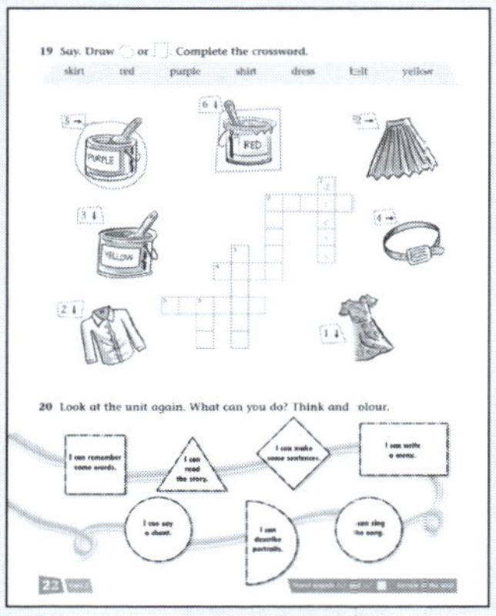

AB page 22

Objectives

- Focus on the pronunciation of vowel sounds (/ɜː/ and /e/) with a chant
- Review the activities and the new language of the unit
- Complete a self-evaluation activity

Core language

Review of language used so far

Other language

put on

Materials

CD 1; Rollercoaster Game poster; Character counters and game cards; Dice (one pair per class); Picture dictionary page (PMB p2) – one photocopy per pupil (optional)

CB p18 Activity 17 Listen, find and repeat.

- Point to the pictures. The pupils say the words.
- Play the CD. Pupils point and repeat.

1.27

purple – skirt – shirt [/ɜː/]
belt – red – dress – yellow [/e/]

- Say the two vowel sounds /ɜː/ and /e/. The pupils find the words that share the vowel sound.
- The pupils practise saying the words chorally and individually, concentrating on the pronunciation of the vowel sounds.

CB p18 Activity 18 Listen and say the chant.

- Play the chant. The pupils point to the items as they hear them.

1.28

Put on your skirt, your purple skirt.
Put on your shirt, your purple shirt.
Purple skirt, purple shirt,
Now you're looking good!

Put on your dress, your yellow dress.
Put on your belt, your red belt.
Yellow dress, red belt,
Now you're looking good!

- Teach the chant line by line. Focus on the pronunciation points. Use choral and individual repetition to check pronunciation.
- Play the chant again and encourage the pupils to join in.

Focus on spelling

- Match the spelling with the vowel sounds.
- Highlight the spelling patterns:
  /ɜː/ is usually spelt *ir* (*skirt*) or *ur* (*purple*), but the *r* is silent
  /e/ is spelt *e* (*belt*)
- Show examples from the chant for each vowel sound.
- Remind the pupils that there are lots of exceptions to spelling patterns in English.

AB p22 Activity 19 Say. Draw ● or ■. Complete the crossword.

- Point to each of the pictures. The pupils say the words chorally.
- Focus on the pronunciation difference between /ɜː/ and /e/, using the words *purple* and *red*.
- Show how *purple* has a circle around it and *red* has a square round it.
- Ask the pupils to identify a word with the /ɜː/ sound.
- Show the pupils how to put a circle round the word.
- Repeat with the /e/ sound, putting a square around the word.
- The pupils put circles and squares around the words.
- Show the pupils the word *dress* in the crossword. The pupils suggest a word for 2 across (*skirt*).
- The pupils complete the crossword individually.
- Point to the pictures at random. The pupils say the words chorally and individually. Check the pupils' pronunciation.

Answers: circle: skirt, purple, shirt; square: red, dress, belt, yellow
1 dress **2 (across)** skirt **2 (down)** shirt **3** yellow
4 belt **5** purple **6** red

End-of-unit review

- Use the Rollercoaster Game poster and the Class Book to recall the main activities of the unit.
- Recall the language associated with each activity.
- Ask the pupils to let you know what they liked or didn't like, and what they found easy or difficult.

Play the Rollercoaster Game

- Divide the class into small groups. Give each group one of the character 'counters' and let them play the game as before (see p41).
- Remind them to use the poster chants when a group gets a question right or wrong.

AB p22 Activity 19 Look at the unit again. What can you do? Think and colour.

- Let the pupils do the self-evaluation activity as before (see p41).

PMB p2 Picture Dictionary (optional)

- If your pupils are making Picture Dictionaries, give out the photocopies of the template.
- Pupils continue making the dictionaries as for Unit 1 (see p42).

Lesson 12a (optional)

■ = Words ◆ = Sentences

Show what you know!

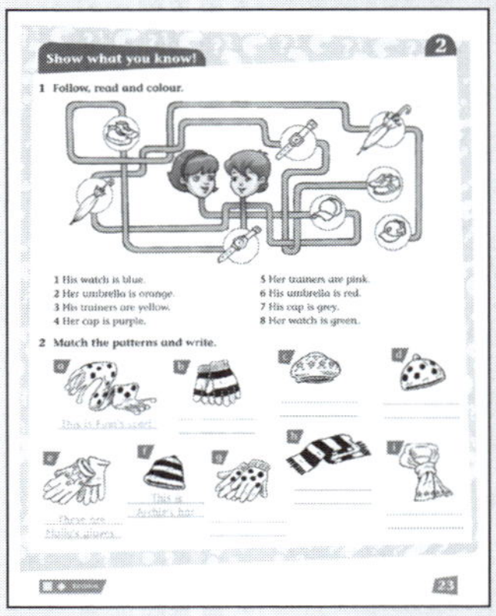

AB page 23

For suggestions on how to use *Show what you know!* see page 13.

Objectives

- Extra practice of the vocabulary of the unit
- Practise solving puzzles in English
- Provide extra material for homework and fast finishers

Core language

Review of language used so far

Materials

No extra materials

AB p23 Activity 1 Follow, read and colour.

- Show the maze to the children. Point to the objects in the maze and ask the pupils to name them.
- Read the sentences to the pupils. Then follow the line from the boy to the first object.
- Ask the pupils what colour the boy's watch is (*blue*). The pupils colour the watch blue.
- The pupils follow the rest of the line and colour the objects according to the sentences. Remind them that they need to look at the sentences beginning *His …*
- Repeat with the line from the girl. Remind pupils that this time they need to look at the sentences beginning *Her …*

AB p23 Match the patterns and write.

- Show the objects to the pupils. Ask them to find the matching sets of scarves, hats, and gloves.
- Point to Finn's scarf and read the sentence *This is Finn's scarf.*
- Repeat with Molly's gloves and Archie's hat.
- Point to the hat with the same pattern as Finn's scarf. The pupils say *This is Finn's hat* and write the sentence.
- Repeat with the gloves with the same pattern as Finn's scarf. The pupils say *These are Finn's gloves* and write the sentence.
- The pupils write the rest of the sentences individually.

Answers: **a** This is Finn's scarf. **b** These are Archie's gloves. **c** This is Molly's hat. **d** This is Finn's hat. **e** These are Molly's gloves. **f** This is Archie's hat. **g** These are Finn's gloves. **h** This is Archie's scarf. **i** This is Molly's scarf.

- As a follow-up activity, take a selection of the pupils' possessions – book, bags, pencils, etc. Call individual pupils up to the front and give them one of the objects. The pupil says, for example, *These are Ana's pencils.* Repeat with other pupils and other objects.

The pupils are now ready to sit the Unit 2 test. See pp174–177 for both Standard and Higher levels.

DVD VIDEO

Multimedia extension: you may now like to use the Art section of the optional DVD.

3 Camping

Lesson 1 ■ = Words

Introducing vocabulary

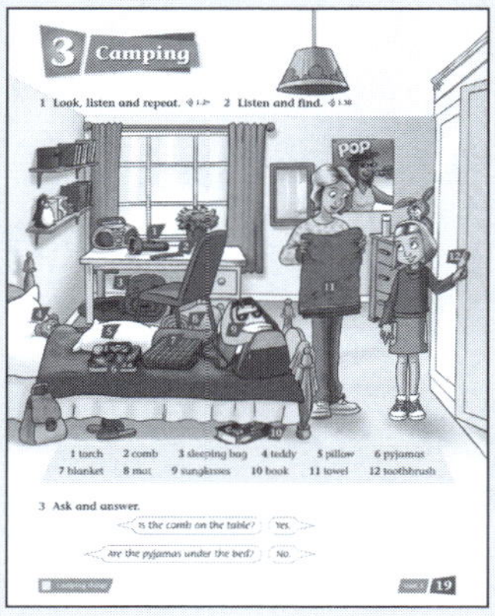

CB page 19

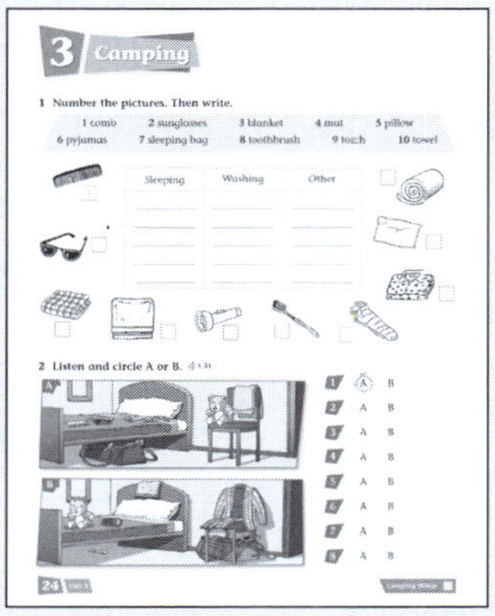

AB page 24

Objectives

- Understand the theme of the unit
- Become familiar with vocabulary for camping things
- Practise asking where things are
- Focus on spelling

Core language

Camping things: *blanket, comb, mat, pillow, pyjamas, sleeping bag, toothbrush, torch, towel, sunglasses*

Review of

- camping things vocabulary: *book, teddy*
- language used so far

Other language

What else?, spotty, Don't forget …

Materials

Rollercoaster Game poster; Camping things flashcards (*blanket, comb, mat, pillow, pyjamas, sleeping bag, toothbrush, torch, towel, sunglasses, book, teddy*); CD 1; Pupils' bookmarks (optional) (see p28)

Unit overview

- Talk to the pupils about camping. Ask them if they know any words in English connected with camping. Ask them what words they would like to know.
- Ask the pupils to look through Unit 3 in their Class Books. Talk with them about the unit and quickly write the different topics and activities on the board, relating them to the shapes on the poster:
  - ■ Words – camping things, adjectives to describe music
  - ▲ Story – *Camping at the club*
  - ◆ Sentences – *I've got a torch. I haven't got a torch. Have you got a torch?*
  - ▬ Text work – certificates
  - ● Song – *I can cook …* / Chant – *I've got a book*
  - ◗ Other subjects – Music (saying what music sounds like)
- Remind the pupils that they will use the poster again at the end of the unit.

Introduce new vocabulary *see p19*

- Use the camping things flashcards to teach the new vocabulary. The pupils repeat the words chorally and then individually.
- Place the flashcards in different parts of the classroom and play *Around the class* with the pupils. First you say the words and the pupils point to the flashcards. Then you point to the flashcards and the pupils say the words.

CB p19 Activity 1 Look, listen and repeat.

- Explain that the children in the story are going camping.
- The pupils listen to the recording. They repeat each word chorally and point to the correct picture.

1.29

1 torch, **2** comb, **3** sleeping bag, **4** teddy, **5** pillow, **6** pyjamas, **7** blanket, **8** mat, **9** sunglasses, **10** book, **11** towel, **12** toothbrush

CB p19 Activity 2 Listen and find.

- Play the dialogue.
- The pupils listen for the objects and point to each one in the picture.
- Alternatively, the pupils can use their bookmarks (see p28) to focus on the pictures.

1.30

Molly: Where's my torch, Mum? And my comb?
Mum: They're on the table.
Molly: Thanks. Here's my towel … Where's my sleeping bag?
Mum: It's under the table.
Molly: And my blanket – where's my red blanket?
Mum: It's on the bed.
Molly: Oh yes.
Where are my pyjamas?
Mum: They're here. Look, they're on the bed.
Molly: Here's my mat … and here's my pillow.
And my book? Oh, it's under the bed.
Mum: Now. What else?
Molly: Er … I can't find my sunglasses.
Mum: They're in the bag!
Molly: Oh. Where's my teddy? My pink spotty teddy?
Mum: I don't know.
Molly: Oh, he's here. He's in the bed. Phew!
I think I've got everything!

CB p19 Activity 3 Ask and answer.

- Introduce the dialogue with questions about Molly's possessions: *Are the sunglasses on the table?*, etc.
- The pupils answer your questions with *Yes* or *No*, and point to the object in the picture.
- Practise the dialogue with more of Molly's possessions.
- The pupils practise asking and answering questions in pairs.
- As a variation, the pupils take turns to close their books and answer their partner's question from memory.

Spelling

- Ask the pupils to identify:
  1 words that are similar in their language (highlight the differences in spelling)
  2 words with three or more consonants together (*sunglasses*, *toothbrush*, etc.)
  3 words with double letters (*sunglasses*, *pillow*, etc.).

AB p24 Activity 1 Number the pictures. Then write.

- Read the words in the word pool to the pupils. Ask the pupils to match the words to the pictures.
- Read the categories (*Sleeping*, *Washing*, *Other*) to the pupils. Ask *Which words go with sleeping?* The pupils choose suitable words.
- Repeat with the other categories.

Answers: sleeping - sleeping bag, pillow, mat, blanket, pyjamas; washing – toothbrush, comb, towel; other – torch, sunglasses

Lesson 2 ■ = Words

Practising vocabulary

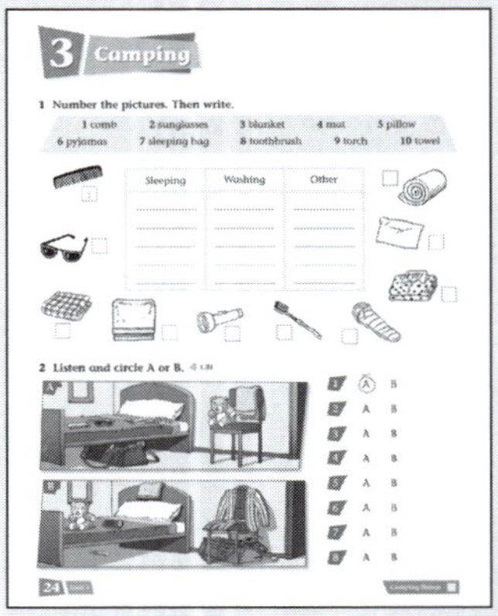

AB page 24

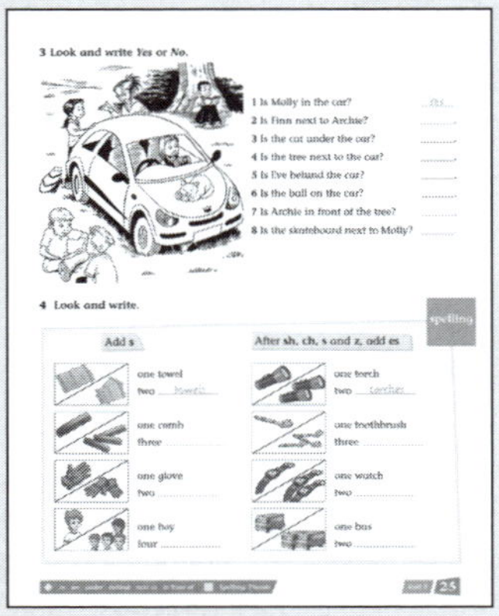

AB page 25

Objectives

- Review camping things vocabulary
- Practise listening and talking about where things are
- Practise irregular plural forms
- Arrange vocabulary in pronunciation / spelling categories

Core language

Review of
- camping things vocabulary
- language used so far

Materials

Camping things flashcards (x12); A CD of music with a strong beat (for *Musical flashcards*); CD 1; Camping things picture cards (PMB p15) – one photocopied set per pupil

Review vocabulary

- Put the camping things flashcards on the board. The pupils say the words chorally and individually.
- Play *Musical flashcards* with the pupils (see p21): they say the word for the flashcard your hand is on when the music stops.

AB p24 Activity 2 Listen and circle A or B.

- Point to the two pictures. Say *The comb is on the bed. Which picture is it?* The pupils answer *A*.
- Say *The comb is under the bed. Which picture is it?* The pupils answer *B*.
- Ask the pupils to find more differences between Picture A and Picture B.
- Play the first conversation on the CD. The pupils identify the correct picture (*A*). Show the pupils how A is circled in Number 1.
- Play the rest of the conversations. After each conversation, the pupils circle A or B.

1.31

1 Adult: Where's the comb?
Child: It's on the bed.

2 Adult: Where's the teddy?
Child: It's on the chair.

3 Adult: Where's the bag?
Child: It's under the chair.

4 Adult: Where are the sunglasses?
Child: They're in the bag.

5 Adult: Where are the pyjamas?
Child: They're under the pillow.

6 Adult: Where's the toothbrush?
Child: It's behind the bag.

7 Adult: Where's the torch?
Child: It's next to the teddy.

8 Adult: Where's the towel?
Child: It's on the chair.

Answers: 1 A 2 A 3 B 4 B 5 A 6 B 7 B 8 A

- Play a guessing game: tell the pupils you are thinking of one of the pictures. The pupils ask questions such as *Where's the comb?* and guess the picture from your answers. The pupils can play this game in pairs.

AB p25 Activity 3 Look and write *Yes* or *No*.

- Show the picture to the pupils. Ask *Where …?* questions about it, such as *Where's the cat? (It's on the car).*
- Read the first question to the pupils. The pupils answer *Yes*. Show the pupils how the answer *Yes* is written on the line.
- Read the other questions to the pupils. They write *Yes* or *No* after each question.
- More confident groups can do this activity in pairs.

Answers: 1 Yes 2 No 3 No 4 Yes 5 Yes 6 No 7 Yes 8 No

AB p25 Activity 4 Look and write.

- Point to the first set of plurals on the left of the page. Point out the plural 's' (*one towel, two towels*).
- The pupils complete the plural forms in the rest of the first set.
- Read the nouns in the second set (*torch, toothbrush, watch, bus*). Explain that words which end in *ch, sh, s,* and *z* make the plural with *-es*. Show the example with *torch* (*one torch, two torches*).
- Point to the pictures of the toothbrushes. Read *one toothbrush*, then ask the pupils to say the plural form (*three toothbrushes*). The pupils write the plural form on the line.
- Repeat with the other pictures in the second set.

Answers: three combs, two gloves, four boys, three toothbrushes, two watches, two buses

Spelling game

- The pupils make a crossword using plural forms which the pupils know.

PMB p15 Make the picture cards

- Give out the photocopies of the camping things picture cards. The pupils colour and cut out the picture cards.
- They can use their cards to play a game, for example *That's my word!* (picture cards version) (see p20).
- If your pupils are using word cards, they can prepare them now (see p30). Pupils cut them out and match them with the picture cards.
- Remind the pupils to keep all the cards in a safe place.

Lesson 3

▲ = Story

Story

CB page 20

CB page 21

Objectives

- Listen to a story
- Read a story
- Listen for words and phrases in a story
- Practise story language

Core language

Have you got a torch?; I haven't got my teddy.

Review of

- camping things vocabulary
- language used so far

Other language

clubhouse, ready, scared (of), the dark, scaredy cat, owl, bear, everything
What's that?; Help!; Look, it's a …

Materials

Camping things flashcards (x12); CD 1

Review vocabulary

- Stick the camping things flashcards on the board. The pupils say the words chorally and individually.
- Play *Memory words* with the pupils. Say sequences of three words (for example, *blanket, toothbrush, pyjamas*); the pupils repeat the words in the same sequence and point to the flashcards on the board.

Introduce the story

- Ask the pupils to imagine that they are going to camp overnight in a garden. Ask if they would enjoy it, and what things they would be frightened of.
- Explain that in the story the children are going to camp in the garden of the clubhouse.
- Ask the pupils what animals they think the children will hear. Ask which animals they think the children will be scared of.

CB pp20–21 Activity 4 First listening with the books closed

- Tell the pupils to listen and answer this question: *What were the children frightened of?*
- The pupils listen with their books closed.

1.32

[1]	In the clubhouse garden …	
	Eve:	Is everyone ready?
	All:	YES!
	Luke:	Have you got a torch?
	Archie:	Yes! And I've got a sleeping bag, and a pillow, and my guitar …
[2]	Molly:	Oh no. I haven't got my teddy. My pink spotty teddy.
	Luke:	Oh. Molly!
	Eve:	It's in the clubhouse. Wait a minute.
[3]	Molly:	I'm scared.
	Jazmin:	I don't like the dark.
	Finn:	Scaredy cats!
[4]	Eve:	Molly, here's your teddy.
	Molly:	Thanks.
		(sound of an owl)
	Archie:	What's that noise?
[5]	Luke:	It's just an owl.
	Finn:	Archie's scared of an owl! Scaredy cat!
[6]	Luke:	What's that?
	Finn:	It's just the cat. You're all scared of everything!
[7]	Molly:	I've got my toothbrush, and my towel … and here's my teddy. My pink spotty teddy.
[8]	Luke:	Look at that!
	Finn:	Help!
[9]	Jazmin:	What's the matter?
	Finn:	Look, it's a bear! I'm scared!
[10]	Molly:	Finn is scared of my pink spotty teddy!
	Finn:	Everyone's a scaredy cat!

- Ask the pupils what the children were frightened of (an owl, a cat, and a bear / teddy bear). Encourage them to give further details of the story. Recast the pupils' answers as necessary.

CB pp20–21 Activity 4 Second listening with the books open

- Tell the pupils to open their books and look at the story.
- Ask questions about the story such as *Were there any animals in the camp?*
- Play the recording again while the pupils follow in their books.
- Go through any vocabulary queries with the class.

CB p21 Activity 5 Read and write *true* or *false*.

- Explain that the number of each sentence refers to the number of the picture in the story.

- Ask the pupils to read the first sentence, then look at picture 2. Ask *Is that true or false?* The pupils answer *False*.
- The pupils read the sentences and write *true* or *false* in their notebooks.

Answers: **2** false **3** false **5** false **7** true **8** true **9** false **10** true

Fun expressions

- Write these 'fun expressions' from the story on the board:
  What's that?
  Help!
  Look, it's a bear! I'm scared.
- Play the story again: the pupils put up their hands when they hear one of the phrases.
- Pause the recording. The pupils repeat the phrase chorally and individually. Encourage the pupils to copy the intonation on the CD.

Lesson 4 ◆ = Sentences

Language focus 1

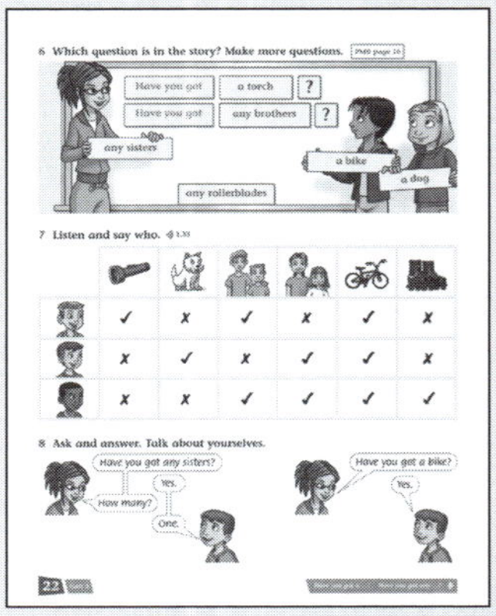

CB page 22

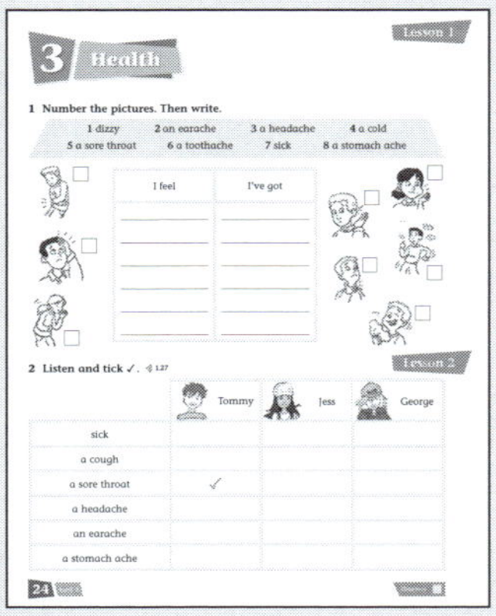

AB page 26

Objectives

- Understand the use of *Have you got a / any …?*
- Review the use of *I've got …*
- Practise using the new language

Core language

Have you got a / any …?
Review of language used so far

Materials

Grammar tiles (PMB p16) – one photocopy of Set 1 per pupil (optional); CD 1

Recall the story

- Ask the pupils to remember as much as they can from the story.
- Say the following sentences from the story, and ask the pupils to identify who says each one:
  I haven't got my teddy. (Molly)
  Molly, here's your teddy. (Eve)
  It's just an owl. (Luke)
  Archie's scared of an owl! (Finn)
  Everyone's a scaredy cat! (Finn)

PMB p16 / CB p22 Activity 6 Which question is in the story? Make more questions.

- Ask the pupils to read the questions in the grammar tiles.
- Ask the pupils to say which question is in the story (*Have you got a torch?*).
- Write *I've got a torch* and *Have you got a torch?* on the board. Use a mime gesture to show how the order of *have* and *I / You* changes to make a question.
- Also point out the use of *any* for asking about more than one thing: *Have you got a torch? Have you got any brothers?*
- The pupils say the questions in the grammar tiles chorally and individually.
- The pupils use the remaining tiles in the picture to make questions with *Have you got …?* Choose other pupils to answer with *yes* or *no*. Alternatively, give each pupil a copy of Set 1 of the grammar tiles from the PMB: the pupils cut out the tiles and arrange them in questions on their desks. Ask individual pupils to read out their questions for the class.

CB p22 Activity 7 Listen and say who.

- Show the pictures to the pupils.
- Play the first dialogue to the pupils. The pupils identify who is answering the questions.
- Repeat with the second dialogue.

1.33

Eve:	Have you got a torch?
Luke:	No.
Eve:	Have you got a dog?
Luke:	Yes!
Eve:	Have you got any brothers?
Luke:	No.
Eve:	Have you got any sisters?
Luke:	Yes.
Eve:	How many?
Luke:	One.
Presenter:	Who is it?
Eve:	Have you got a bike?
Finn:	Yes.
Eve:	Have you got any rollerblades?
Finn:	No.
Eve:	Have you got any brothers?
Finn:	Yes, I've got two brothers.
Eve:	Have you got any sisters?
Finn:	No.
Presenter:	Who is it?

Answers: **1** Luke **2** Finn

CB p22 Activity 8 Ask and answer. Talk about yourselves.

- Read the conversations to the pupils.
- Say you are pretending to be one of the characters in the table. The pupils ask you questions using *Have you got … ?* and identify the character.
- Select individual pupils and ask them about their possessions and family: *Ana, have you got a bike?*, etc.
- The pupils practise asking about each other's possessions and family in pairs.

AB p26 **Activity 5 Look and complete.**

- Read the words in the word pool to the pupils.
- Point to the first picture. Point out Eve's thought bubble with sunglasses. Read the question and answer. Make sure the pupils understand that Molly hasn't got any sunglasses.
- Point to the second picture. Read the beginning of the question and point to the comb in Archie's thought bubble. The pupils ask the complete question (*Have you got a comb?*). The pupils complete the question in their books.
- Repeat with the other questions and answers. The pupils write the questions and answers in their books.

Answers: 1 Have you got any sunglasses? No. **2** Have you got a comb? No. **3** Have you got any pyjamas? Yes. **4** Have you got a sleeping bag? Yes. **5** Have you got a pillow? No.

Lesson 5 ◆ = Sentences

Language focus 2

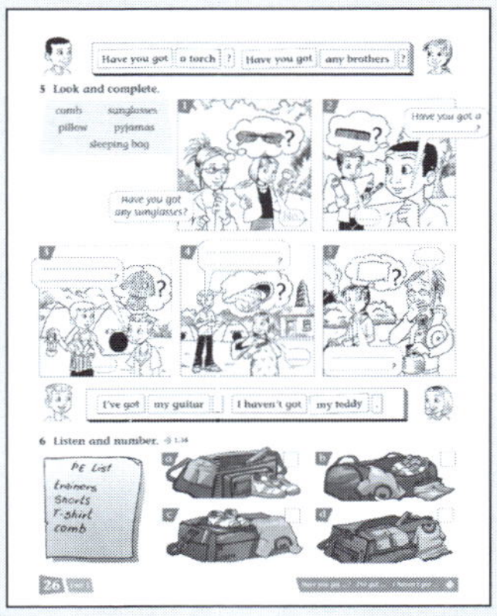

AB page 26

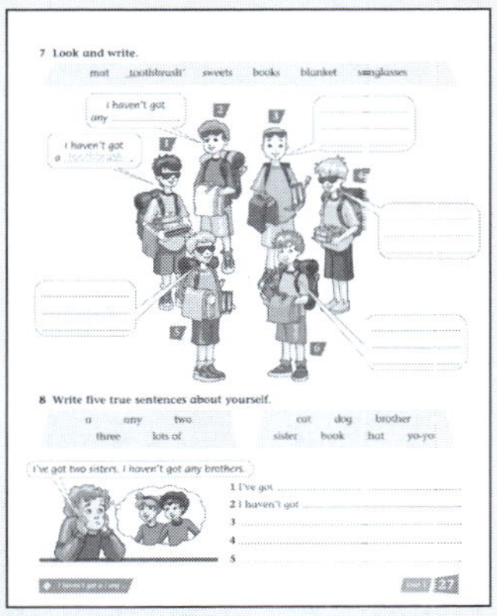

AB page 27

Objectives

- Review *I've got …* and *Have you got …?*
- Understand the use of *I haven't got a / any …*
- Practise talking about your possessions

Core language

I haven't got my teddy. / I haven't got any sunglasses.

Review of language used so far

Materials

Grammar tiles (PMB p16) – one photocopy of Set 2 per pupil; Pupils' grammar tiles (Set 1) from Lesson 4 (optional); Personal possessions flashcards (x10); CD 1

PMB p16 **AB p26** **Focus on language**

- Read the sentences in the second set of grammar tiles on Activity Book page 26 to the pupils. Ask the pupils *Which sentence is in the story?* (*I haven't got my teddy.*)
- Point out the difference between the affirmative form (*I've got* …) and the negative form (*I haven't got* …).
- On the board, write the contractions and the long forms: *I've got* = *I have got* and *I haven't got* = *I have not got*. Use mime gestures to show how the long forms 'contract' to the short forms.
- The pupils say the sentences in the grammar tiles chorally and individually.
- Give each pupil a copy of Set 2 of the grammar tiles from the PMB. Ask the pupils to suggest words to put in the blank tiles (*my cat, my torch, my magazine,* etc.). Write the suggestions on the board. The pupils can choose words to copy in the blank tiles.
- The pupils cut out all the tiles and use them to make sentences on their desks. Ask pupils to read out their sentences for the class.
- Pupils can combine the Set 2 tiles with some of the Set 1 tiles to make more sentences, for example *I've got a torch, I haven't got any brothers,* etc.

Practice

- Show the pupils one of the personal possessions flashcards. Select a pupil and say *Make a sentence with 'I've got' or 'I haven't got'.*
- The pupil says, for example, *I haven't got a watch.* Ask several pupils to make a sentence about the same flashcard.
- Repeat with the other flashcards.

Teaching tip

To keep this activity simple, you can encourage pupils to follow the model of the grammar tiles and just use *my* with the sentences, e.g. *I've got my sweets, I haven't got my rollerblades,* etc. (This avoids the use of *some* and *any*). With more confident groups, however, you might like to encourage them to say *I've got some sweets, I haven't got any rollerblades,* etc. (Pupils will do further work on *I haven't got any …* later in this lesson.)

AB p26 **Activity 6 Listen and number.**

- Point to each of the pictures. Ask the pupils *What's in the bag?* The pupils say a list of the items in (or next to) each bag, for example: *a comb, shorts, trainers.*
- Play the first conversation on the CD. Ask the pupils *Which bag is it?* The pupils answer *b*, and write *1* next to bag *b*.
- Repeat with the other conversations. The pupils number the bags in the order they hear about them.

1.34

1 Adult: Remember, you've got PE today.
Child: Yes. Look, here's my sports bag.
Adult: Let's check it.
Child: Look. I've got my trainers, my shorts and my T-shirt … Oh, I haven't got my comb!

2 Adult: Have you got your sports bag?
Child: Yes.
Adult: Let's check it.
Child: OK. I've got my shorts and my T-shirt. I've got my comb … Oh, I haven't got my trainers!

3 Adult: Remember, you've got PE today.
Child: Yes. Look, here's my sports bag.
Adult: Let's check it.
Child: Look. I've got my comb. I've got my shorts and my trainers … Oh, I haven't got my T-shirt!

4 Adult: Have you got your sports bag?
Child: Yes.
Adult: Let's check it.
Child: OK. I've got my trainers and my T-shirt. I've got my comb … Oh, I haven't got my shorts!

Answers: a 3 b 1 c 4 d 2

- As a follow-up activity, ask pupils to say which item is missing from each bag (*a – T-shirt, b – comb, c – shorts, d – trainers*).

AB p27 Activity 7 Look and write.

- Read the words in the word pool to the pupils.
- Point to each of the children in the picture. The pupils say a list of what each child has got, for example: Number 1 – *he's got some books, a mat, a pair of sunglasses, a blanket and some sweets.*
- Read the first speech bubble to the pupils: *I haven't got a toothbrush.* Point out how child number 1 doesn't have a toothbrush.
- Read the beginning of second speech bubble to the pupils. They complete the sentence about child number 2 (*… books*), and write the completion in their books.
- Repeat with the other sentences about the other children.

Answers: 1 toothbrush 2 books 3 I haven't got a mat. 4 I haven't got a blanket. 5 I haven't got any sweets. 6 I haven't got any sunglasses.

Teaching tip

Make sure that pupils understand the use of *any* to talk about plural things which they haven't got, for example *I haven't got any (sweets).* Drill this as necessary with the class. Draw pictures of plural and singular camping things on the board with a large cross at the top. Point to each picture and encourage pupils to say *I haven't got any blankets, I haven't got a mat, I haven't got any toothbrushes,* etc. Do this chorally and then individually.

AB p27 Activity 8 Write five true sentences about yourself.

- Read the words in the first and second word pool to the pupils.
- Say sentences about yourself using these words, for example *I've got a brother. I haven't got three dogs.*
- Ask the pupils to say similar sentences about themselves. Encourage them to use *I've got …* and *I haven't got …*
- The pupils write five sentences about themselves.

For extra grammar practice, see AB page 99.

Activity 1 Find the words. Then write questions and answers.

Answers: 1 pillow 2 Have you got any pyjamas? Yes. 3 Have you got a towel? Yes. 4 Have you got any sunglasses? No.

Activity 2 Look and write.

Answers: 1 mat 2 got my sleeping bag 3 I haven't got my comb. 4 I've got my torch. 5 I haven't got my blanket. 6 I've got my toothbrush.

Lesson 6 ▲ = Story

Playscript

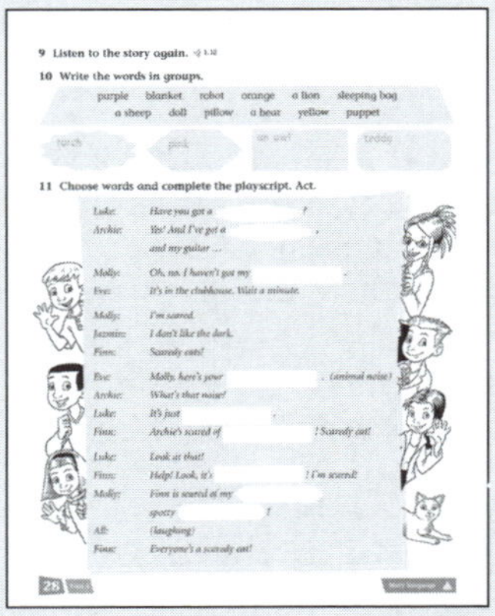
9 Listen to the story again.

10 Write the words in groups.

purple blanket robot orange a lion sleeping bag a sheep doll pillow a bear yellow puppet

torch pink an owl teddy

11 Choose words and complete the playscript. Act.

Luke: Have you got a ______?
Archie: Yes! And I've got a ______, and my guitar …
Molly: Oh, no. I haven't got my ______.
Eve: It's in the clubhouse. Wait a minute.
Molly: I'm scared.
Jazmin: I don't like the dark.
Finn: Scaredy cats!
Eve: Molly, here's your ______. (animal noise)
Archie: What's that noise?
Luke: It's just ______.
Finn: Archie's scared of ______! Scaredy cat!
Luke: Look at that!
Finn: Help! Look, it's ______! I'm scared!
Molly: Finn is scared of my spotty ______!
All: (laughing)
Finn: Everyone's a scaredy cat!

AB page 28

Objectives

- Read and complete a playscript
- Use finger puppets to act out a playscript
- Act out the play

Core language

Review of language used so far

Materials

CD 1; Spare photocopies of the finger puppets (PMB p3)

AB p28 Activity 9 Listen to the story again.

- Tell the pupils to look at pages 20–21 in their Class Books again.
- Play the CD while the pupils listen and read.
- Alternatively, the pupils can read the story aloud in groups of six. Each pupil should read one character.

AB p28 Activity 10 Write the words in groups.

- Read the words in the word pool to the pupils.
- Point to each of the boxes and read the word in each one. Ask the pupils to suggest words from the word pool to go in each box.
- The pupils write the words from the word pool in the correct category.

Answers: set 1 – torch, blanket, pillow, sleeping bag; set 2 – pink, yellow, orange, purple; set 3 – an owl, a bear, a sheep, a lion; set 4 – teddy, doll, robot, puppet

- Ask the pupils to suggest new words for each category.

AB p28 Activity 11 Choose words and complete the playscript. Act.

- Read the playscript to the pupils. When you come to a blank, ask *Which word was in the story?* The pupils say the words from the story.
- Read the playscript again. Ask the pupils to suggest alternative words from Activity 10 to complete the blanks.
- Divide the pupils into groups of six. In their groups, the pupils decide which words to use when they read the playscript.

Finger puppets *see p22*

- Ask the pupils *How many characters are there in the story? (six)*. The pupils identify the six characters. (Eve, Molly, Finn, Archie, Jazmin, and Luke).
- In their groups, the pupils decide who is going to take each part.
- If the pupils have got their finger puppets with them, tell them to get out the puppet for the character they are going to play.
- If the pupils haven't got their finger puppets, they will have to make them now. Give each pupil a photocopy of the finger puppets. The pupils cut out, colour, and stick the photocopy of the character they are going to play.

Practice

- Remind the pupils of the five points of successful play acting:
  1 Listen to the other actors.
  2 Wait for your turn.
  3 Speak clearly.
  4 When the puppets are speaking to each other, they should face each other.
  5 Don't move your puppets unnecessarily.
- Tell the pupils about the notes you made during the Unit 2 play acting. Encourage them to concentrate on the points you noticed. Say you will be watching them again this time.
- The pupils act out the play with their puppets. While they are doing this, circulate around the classroom. Make a note of the points the pupils should improve on next time.
- Ask one or two groups to come to the front to act out the play with their puppets.

Lesson 7

= Text work

Reading and writing

CB page 23

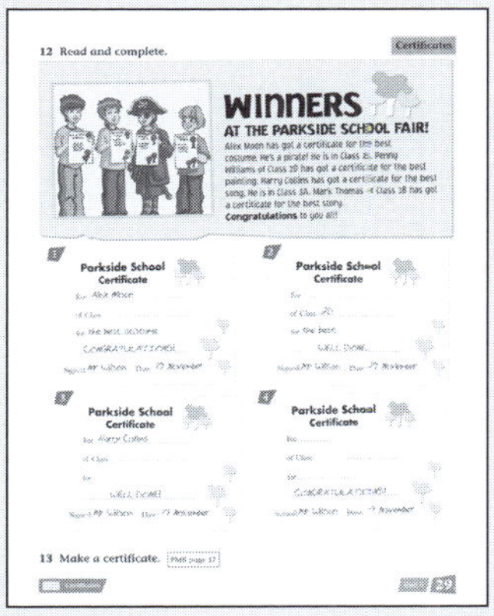

AB page 29

Objectives

- Review camping things vocabulary
- Read and understand certificates
- Write a certificate

Core language

Review of language used so far

Other language

certificate, tidy, congratulations, pirate, costume

Materials

Camping things flashcards (x12); Certificate template (PMB p17) – one photocopy per pupil

Review vocabulary

- Write the camping things vocabulary words on the board like this: *b_____t, p_____s, t_____sh*, etc.
- Call pupils to the front to complete the words.
- Call other pupils to the front to put the flashcards next to each word.

CB p23 Activity 9 Read and find the pictures. Then answer the questions about a, b and c.

- Read certificate a to the pupils. Ask the pupils to match the certificate with the picture.
- Repeat with the other two certificates.

Answers: a 2 b 1 c 4

- Read the first question and point to certificate a. The pupils answer *The Incredible Club*. Repeat with the other questions about certificate a.

Answers: Certificate a: **1** The Incredible Club **2** Archie Taylor **3** a very tidy tent

- The pupils answer the same questions about certificate b and certificate c. They write the answers in their notebooks.

Answers: Certificate b: **1** The Park Road Club **2** Simon Price **3** a fantastic hat Certificate c: **1** The Riverside Club **2** Clare Jones **3** learning to swim

AB p29 Activity 12 Read and complete.

- Read the article from the school newsletter to the pupils. Explain any new vobabulary, e.g. *costume* and *pirate*.
- Point to the first certificate. Read it to the pupils and pause after *Class*. Ask the pupils *Which class is Alex Moon in?* The pupils answer *2C* and write it on the certificate.
- Read the rest of the certificate to the pupils.
- Repeat with the other certificates. The pupils say and write the missing information.

Answers: **2** Penny Williams, the best painting **3** Class 3A, the best song **4** Mark Thomas, Class 3B, the best story

PMB p17 / AB p29 Activity 13 Make a certificate.

- Explain to the pupils that they are going to write a certificate.
- Remind pupils that they have to choose work for their portfolio during the course (see p193). Point out that this piece of work would be a suitable piece to include.
- Brainstorm ideas for school / organization names, classes, and awards for the certificate.
- Choose some suggestions and write them on the board.
- Show the pupils how to write the certificates, using the certificates in Activity 12 as a model.
- Hand out the photocopies of the writing template. Tell the pupils to choose another school / organization and write about it.
- The pupils write a rough copy in their notebooks for you to correct. After you have checked the rough copy, they write their final copy on the photocopied template.

Lesson 8 ● = Song / chant

Learning for life

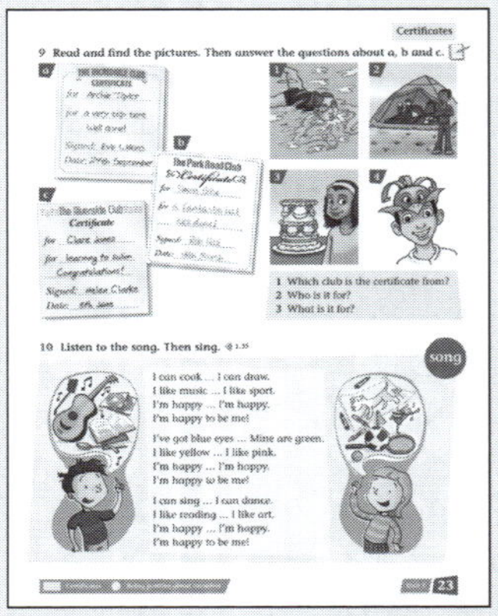

CB page 23

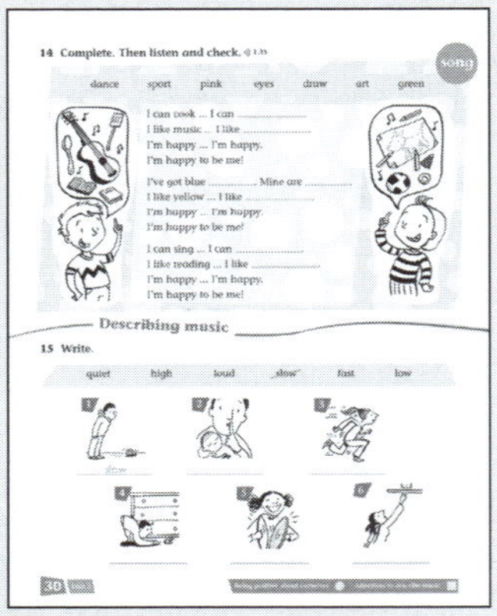

AB page 30

Objectives
- Review the unit so far
- Understand how different people have different abilities and skills
- Talk about positive attitudes
- Sing a song about abilities and skills

Core language
Review of language used so far

Materials
Rollercoaster Game poster; Camping things flashcards (x12); CD 1

Unit review
- Use the Rollercoaster Game poster and the Class Book to review the unit so far. Talk with the pupils about the activities they have done.
- The pupils give examples of the language they used in each activity.

Review vocabulary (categorizing)
- Ask the pupils to tell you all the new words they remember from the unit.
- Put the camping things flashcards on the board. Write *For sleeping in / on* on the board. Ask the pupils to choose words for this category (*blanket, mat, pyjamas, sleeping bag*).
- Repeat with other categories, such as:
  for keeping clean and tidy
  for keeping warm

Introduce the topic
- Write *I like …* on the board. Ask the pupils *What do you like?* Write some of their answers on the board.
- Write *I can …* on the board. Ask the pupils *What can you do?* Write some of their answers on the board.
- Talk with the pupils about how they feel when they do things they like, and when they learn to do things.
- Encourage the pupils to talk about some or all of these ideas in their answers:
  – learning new things is good
  – I feel good / clever / happy when I learn new things
  – I want to learn to …
- The pupils can express their ideas in their own language. If they do, recast their answers in English as necessary.

CB p23 Activity 10 Listen to the song. Then sing.
- Read the song with the pupils. Explain any new words.
- Play the song on the CD.
- Work out simple mime gestures for the verbs (*cook, draw, sing, dance*) in the song. Work out another mime gesture for *I'm happy to be me!*
- Read through the song again and ask the pupils to use the mime gestures as you read.
- Play the song again and encourage the pupils to join in, singing and miming.

1.35

I can cook … I can draw.
I like music … I like sport.
I'm happy, I'm happy,
I'm happy to be me!

I've got blue eyes … Mine are green.
I like yellow … I like pink.
I'm happy, I'm happy,
I'm happy to be me!

I can sing … I can dance.
I like reading … I like art.
I'm happy, I'm happy,
I'm happy to be me!

AB p30 Activity 14 Complete. Then listen and check.
- Tell the pupils to close their Class Books and open their Activity Books at page 30.
- Read the first line of the song to the pupils. Ask the pupils to recall the words to go in the spaces. Write the words they suggest on the board.
- Repeat with the other lines of the song.
- Play the song again; the pupils check the words they suggested.
- Make any necessary corrections to the words on the board. The pupils copy the words in the spaces in their Activity Books.
- To finish the lesson, tell the pupils to close their books. Help them to say the whole song again, chorally, from memory.

Answers: draw, sport, swim, pink, dance, art

Lesson 9 ■ = Words ◗ = Other subjects

Learning through English

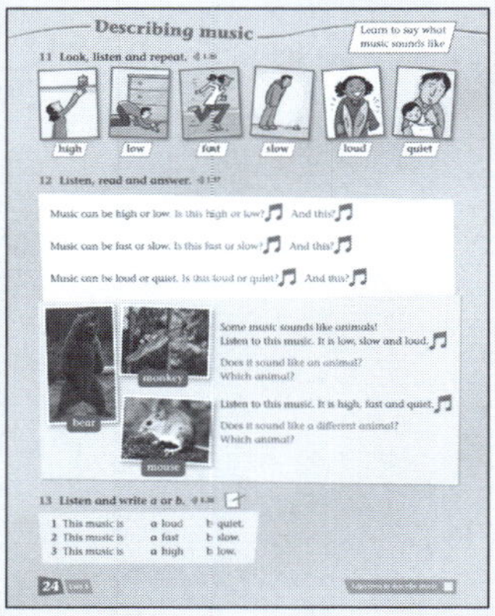

CB page 24

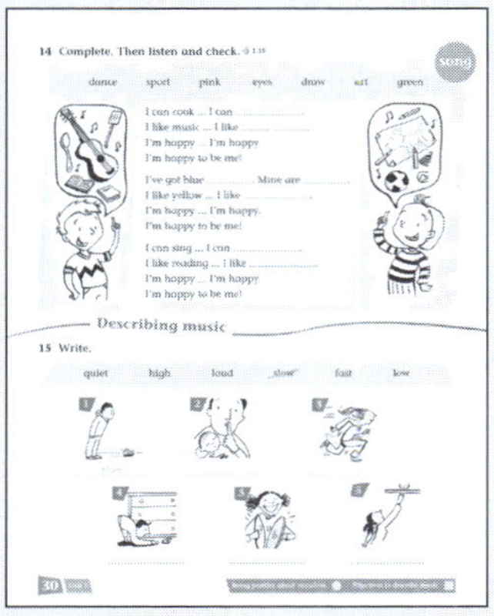

AB page 30

Objectives

- Learn some adjectives to describe music
- Listen to music and describe it

Core language

Adjectives to describe music: *high, low, fast, slow, loud, quiet*

Review of language used so far

Other language

sound like

Materials

CD 1; Flashcards for adjectives to describe music (*high, low, fast, slow, loud, quiet*); Picture cards for adjectives to describe music (PMB p15) – one photocopied set per pupil

Introduce the topic

- Talk with the pupils about music. Ask questions such as *What type of music do you like? When do you listen to music?*
- Ask the pupils to say words that describe music.
- Tell the pupils that they are going to learn some more words for describing music.

Introduce new vocabulary

- Use the flashcards to teach the new vocabulary (adjectives to describe music). The pupils repeat the words chorally and then individually.
- Stick the flashcards on the board in three rows of two, like this:
  [*high*] [*low*]
  [*fast*] [*slow*]
  [*loud*] [*quiet*]
- Point to the flashcards: the pupils say the words chorally and individually.
- Play *Where is it?* with the pupils (see p20): turn the flashcards face down on the board, then ask where each flashcard is.

CB p24 Activity 11 Look, listen and repeat.

- Put the flashcards on the board. Point to each one in turn. Emphasize the meaning of the picture with mime gestures (stretching up for *high*, etc.).
- Play the CD. The pupils repeat each word chorally and point to the correct picture.

1.36

high – low – fast – slow – loud – quiet

CB p24 Activity 12 Listen, read and answer.

- Explain to the pupils they are going to listen to very short pieces of music. They are going answer a question about each piece of music.
- Play the CD while the pupils listen and read.
- Pause the CD after each question for the pupils to answer.

1.37

Music can be high … *(high note)*
or low. *(low note)*
Is this high or low? *(low note)*
And this? *(high note)*

Music can be fast … *(fast beat)*
or slow. *(slow beat)*
Is this fast or slow? *(fast beat)*
And this? *(slow beat)*

Music can be loud … *(loud notes)*
or quiet. *(quiet notes)*
Is this loud or quiet? *(quiet note)*
And this? *(loud note)*

Some music sounds like animals! Listen to this music. It is low, slow and loud.
(excerpt of low, slow, loud music)
Does it sound like an animal? Which animal?

Listen to this music. It is high, fast and quiet.
(excerpt of high, fast and quiet music)
Does it sound like a different animal? Which animal?

Answers: low, high, fast, slow, quiet, loud (the remaining answers depend on the pupils' opinions, but suggested answers are bear and mouse)

CB p24 Activity 13 Listen and write *a* or *b*.

- Read the sentence opener and answer options to the pupils.
- Play the first piece of music. The pupils say which answer option describes it (*a*). They write the number of the piece of music and the letter of the description in their notebooks.
- Play the other pieces of music. The pupils write the numbers of each piece and the letters of the descriptions.
- Let pupils listen again to check their answers.

1.38

1 *(loud music)*
2 *(fast music)*
3 *(low music)*

Answers: 1 a 2 a 3 a

AB p30 Activity 15 Write.

- Read the words in the word pool to the pupils.
- Point to the first picture and say the answer *slow*.
- Point to the second picture. The pupils say the answer (*quiet*) and write it on the line.
- Repeat with the other pictures.

Answers: 1 slow 2 quiet 3 fast 4 low 5 loud 6 high

PMB p15 Make the picture cards

- Give out the photocopies of the picture cards for music adjectives. The pupils colour and cut out the picture cards.
- If your pupils are using word cards, they can prepare them now (see p30). Pupils cut them out and match them with the picture cards.
- They can use their cards to play a game, for example *Memory (pairs)* (see p20).
- Remind the pupils to keep all the cards in a safe place.

Lesson 10 ■ = Words ◗ = Other subjects

Learning through English

CB page 25

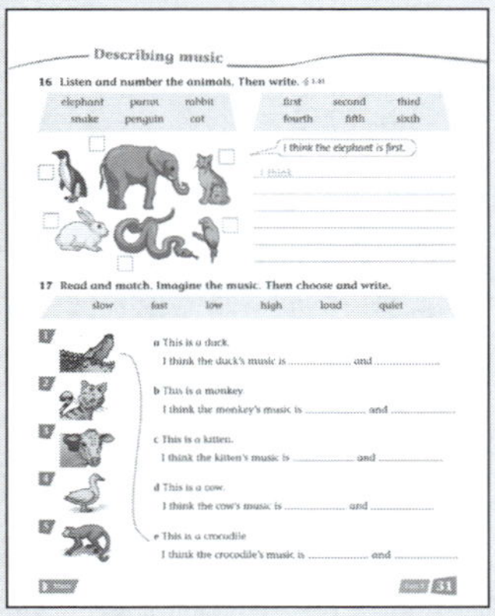

AB page 31

Objectives

- Review adjectives to describe music
- Talk about your impressions of music
- Describe pieces of music

Core language

Review of language used so far

Other language

elephant, I think it sounds like …

Materials

Flashcards for adjectives to describe music (x6)

Review vocabulary

- Stick the flashcards for music adjectives on the board.
- Ask the pupils to write the corresponding adjective next to each one.
- Say *fast* and ask the pupils to say the opposite.
- Repeat with the other adjectives.

CB p25 Vocabulary for animals

- Point to each of the animals in Activity 14. The pupils say the name of the animal.
- Point to the elephant and ask the pupils to describe it. The pupils use adjectives such as *grey, big, slow,* etc.
- Repeat with the other animals.
- Point to the elephant again. Say *Imagine music about an elephant. Is it fast or slow?*
- The pupils give you their opinion. Repeat with *Is it low or high?* and *Is it quiet or loud?*

CB p25 Activity 14 Listen and find the animals.

- Play the first piece of music and the conversation. The pupils identify the animal.
- Repeat with the other pieces of music.

1.39

(music)
Child 1: It's low and quiet.
Child 2: I think it sounds like a snake.
Child 1: Me too.
(music)
Child 1: It's slow, quiet and low.
Child 2: I think it sounds like a lion.
(music)
Child 1: It's low and slow.
Child 2: I think it sounds like an elephant.
(music)
Child 1: It's loud and high.
Child 2: I think it sounds like a parrot.
(music)
Child 1: It's fast and high.
Child 2: I think it sounds like a horse.
Child 1: Me too.
(music)
Child 1: It's fast and high.
Child 2: I think it sounds like a hen.

Answers: 1 snake 2 lion 3 elephant 4 parrot 5 horse 6 hen

CB p25 Activity 15 Listen. Talk about the music.

- Play the first piece of music. Read the comments about it.
- Play the other pieces of music. The pupils comment on the music, using the music vocabulary and choosing an animal. They can either do this in pairs, or as a whole-class activity.
- Point out how the *Talk about it!* box gives them all the language they need.

1.40

(six 'animal' musical excerpts)

Answers: (the answers depend on the pupils' opinions)

AB p31 Activity 16 Listen and number the animals. Then write.

- Read the animal words in word pool 1 to the pupils. Ask them to identify the animals in the pictures.
- Read the ordinal numbers in word pool 2 to the pupils, and check they remember the meaning.
- Tell the pupils that they are going to hear six pieces of 'animal' music, and that they should number the animals in the order which they think matches the music. Explain that there are no right or wrong answers – it is just their opinion.
- Play the first piece of music on the CD. Ask the pupils *What animal do you think that is?* Recast the pupils' suggestions like this: *An elephant – You think the elephant is first. So, you write number 1 next to the elephant.*
- Play the remaining pieces of music for pupils to listen and number.
- Play the music again for pupils to check and revise their answers.
- Show pupils how to write their opinions on the answer lines, for example *I think the elephant is first.*
- Make sure the pupils use the correct ordinal number – *first, second, third fourth, fifth, sixth* – in their sentences.

1.41

1 *(music for elephants – low and slow)*
2 *(music for parrots – loud and high)*
3 *(music for rabbits – high and fast)*
4 *(music for snakes – low and quiet)*
5 *(music for penguins – fast and low)*
6 *(music for cats – high and quiet)*

Answers: (these are suggested answers only) **1** I think the elephant is first. **2** I think the parrot is second. **3** I think the rabbit is third. **4** I think the snake is fourth. **5** I think the penguin is fifth. **6** I think the cat is sixth.

AB p31 Activity 17 Read and match. Imagine the music. Then choose and write.

- Read the words in the word pool to the pupils.
- The pupils match the animals with the sentences.

Answers: **1** e **2** c **3** d **4** a **5** b

- Tell pupils to imagine the kind of music which would represent each animal.
- Say to the pupils *Choose words from the word pool to describe the music.* The pupils suggest adjectives for each animal.
- Write the name of the animal and the adjectives the pupils suggest for each animal's music on the board.
- The pupils choose the adjectives they want for each animal and write them in the descriptions.

Answers: (these are suggested answers only) **1** slow, quiet **2** high, fast **3** slow, low **4** slow, loud **5** fast, loud

Lesson 11 = Other subjects

Learning through English (Project)

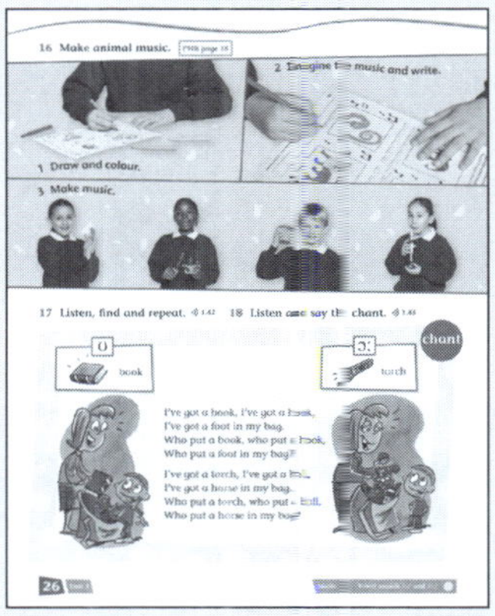

CB page 26

Objectives
- Review words to describe music
- Make music about animals and write about it

Core language
Review of language used so far

Materials
Flashcards for adjectives to describe music (x6); 'Make animal music' (PMB p18) – one photocopy per pupil

Review vocabulary

- Use the flashcards to review the adjectives to describe music. The pupils say the words chorally and individually.
- Ask the pupils to remember the music for the animals. The pupils describe the music using the vocabulary. For example *The elephant music was slow and low.*

Present the project

- Tell the pupils they are going to make music to describe animals.
- They are going to choose four animals, then decide what the music for each animal is like.
- They are going to write a sentence about the music for each animal.

PMB p18 / CB p26 Activity 16 Make animal music.

- Give each pupil a copy of the 'Make animal music' sheet.
- Elicit ideas for animals to write about. The pupils draw pictures of four animals on the photocopy.
- Ask the pupils for ideas about the music for each animal. The pupils say, for example, *The music for the elephant is low and slow. It's loud.*
- The pupils write their sentences about each animal in their notebooks or on rough paper. They can use the sentences from Activity Book page 31, activity 17, as a model. While they are writing, circulate around the class. Encourage the pupils to think about what the music will sound like. Look at the sentences and tick each one when you think it is adequate.
- The pupils write their sentences on their photocopies.
- Ask the pupils to choose one of their animals and think about how they can make music for it in the classroom. Encourage the pupils to think about all

the resources they have to make sounds (apart from any musical instruments in the classroom, they can use rulers, paper, elastic bands, plus using their own voices or whistling).

- Give the pupils five minutes to practise their music. Then select individual pupils to play their music to the class. For most pupils, it's probably best to name the animal before they perform the music. However, if your pupils have some very good examples, you can arrange a guessing game; the other pupils guess the animal after they hear the music.

Display

- Display the mini-projects around the classroom.
- Allow the pupils to move around the classroom, look at all the projects and discuss them with their friends.
- Have a feedback session in which the pupils decide on the most attractive drawings and the best descriptions. Ask pupils to give reasons for their choices.

Lesson 11a (optional)

Learning through English (Extension)

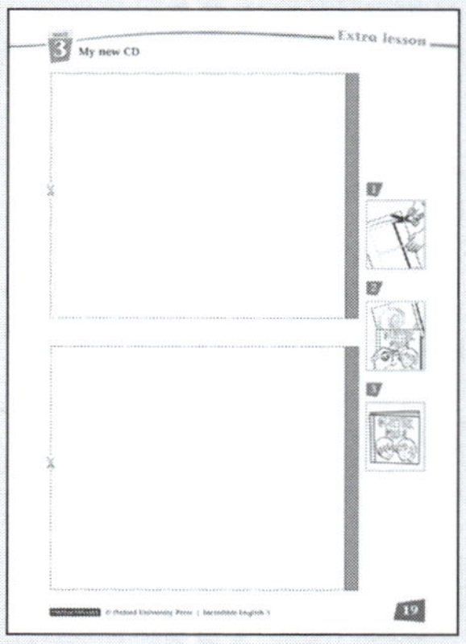

PMB page 19

Objectives

- Review adjectives to describe music
- Discuss how information and pictures are combined on CD covers
- Discuss CDs and music
- Design a cover for a CD

Core language

Review of

- adjectives to describe music
- language used so far

Other language

Words for parts of a CD cover: *cover, back, front, spine, tracks*

Materials

Some CDs; Flashcards for adjectives to describe music (x6); 'My new CD' (PMB p19) – one photocopy per pupil; A cut-out and stuck template from PMB p19; Glue; Scissors; Empty CD cases (optional)

Review vocabulary

- Use the flashcards to review the music vocabulary with the pupils; show the pupils the flashcards and ask them to say the words chorally and individually.

Preparation

- Show the pupils the CDs you have brought in. Ask them to name the musicians and the music.
- Ask the pupils (use L1 as necessary) *What information is on the front?* and point to the front of the CD. The pupils answer *The name of the CD. / The name of the group. / The name of the orchestra*, etc. Recast the pupils' answers as necessary.
- Ask the pupils *What information is on the back?* and point to the back of the CD. The pupils answer *A list of the songs / tracks*, etc. Recast the pupils' answers as necessary.
- Ask the pupils *What information is on the spine?* and point to the spine of the CD. The pupils answer *The name of the CD. / The name of the group. / The name of the orchestra*, etc. Recast the pupils' answers as necessary.
- Ask the to pupils to find CD covers which are:
  – easy to read
  – difficult to read
  – interesting / attractive
  – boring / unattractive.

PMB p19 Using the Photocopy Master

- Give each pupil a photocopy of the 'My new CD' sheet, a pair of scissors, and glue.
- Say *You are going to make a cover for a CD.* Show the pupils the template for the CD cover on the photocopy.
- Show the pupils a template you have cut out, stuck, and folded, so that they can see how it forms the front, spine, and back. Slot it into an empty CD case so that they can see how the template works.
- Tell the pupils they are going to make a cover for a CD of animal music. Ask the pupils to recall the animals they talked about in the previous lesson. Tell them that they can choose six animals for their CD.
- The pupils decide which animals they are going to have on the CD. Then they decide on a name for the CD. They cut out and make the CD cover by sticking the shaded areas together, and folding the edges to create a spine.
- The pupils design a cover for their new CD. The cover should include:
  – the name of the CD on the front (for example, *Animal Magic*)
  – the name of the class as the musicians (for example, *Form 3C Orchestra*)
  – a picture on the front
  – the name of the CD on the spine
  – the list of tracks on the back (the tracks can be just the names of the animals, e.g. *1 Penguins, 2 Cows*, etc.).

Display

- Arrange a display of the CD covers in the classroom. For a more effective display, pupils should insert their covers into blank CD cases.
- Allow the pupils to see all the CD covers and comment on them. Arrange a feedback session with the pupils, and vote on the best artwork, the best lettering, and the best overall cover.

Play a game

- The pupils draw a grid in their notebooks ten squares wide and ten squares high.

- They add the adjectives to describe music to the wordsquare. Encourage them to write some words vertically and some words horizontally.
- The pupils complete the empty squares in the wordsquare with random letters.
- They show their wordsquares to their partners and try to find the words in each other's wordsquares.

Song

- Ask the pupils *Can you remember the song in this unit?*
- Write what the pupils can remember on the board. Help them to remember the bits they've forgotten, then add them on the board.
- Play the song again (Listening 1.35). The pupils check that the version on the board is correct.
- Play the song again and encourage the pupils to join in.

Lesson 12

Review and self-evaluation

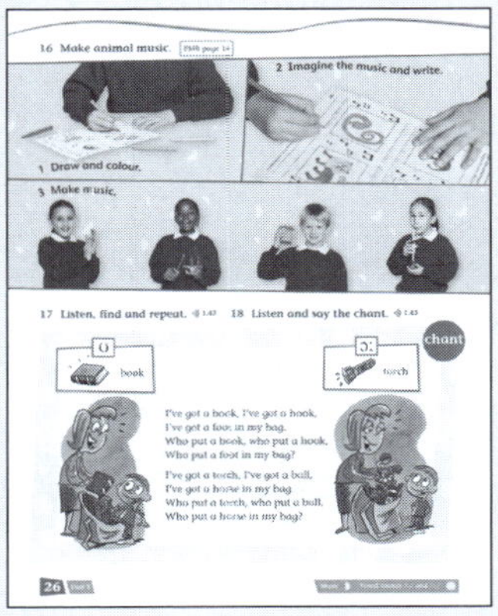

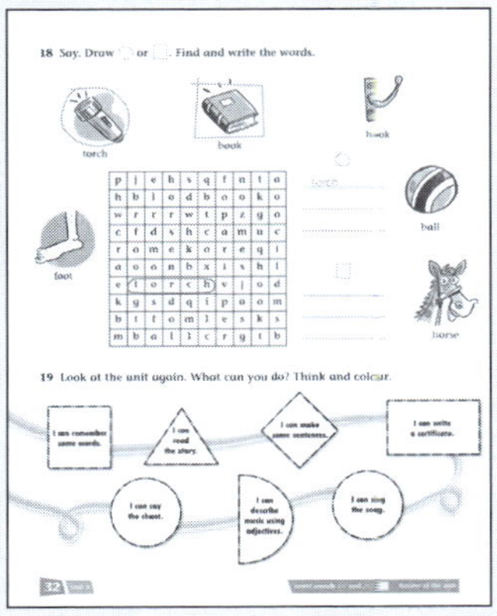

CB page 26 AB page 32

Objectives

- Focus on the pronunciation of vowel sounds (/ʊ/ and /ɔ:/) with a chant
- Review the activities and the new language of the unit
- Complete a self-evaluation activity

Core language

Review of language used so far

Other language

hook

Materials

CD 1; Rollercoaster Game poster; Character counters and game cards; Dice (one pair per class); Picture dictionary page (PMB p2) – one photocopy per pupil (optional)

CB p26 Activity 17 Listen, find and repeat.

- Point to the pictures. The pupils say the words. Teach the new word *hook*.
- Play the CD. Pupils point and repeat.

1.42

foot – book – hook [/ʊ/]
horse – ball – torch [/ɔ:/]

- Say the two vowel sounds /ʊ/ and /ɔ:/. The pupils find the words that share the vowel sound.
- The pupils practise saying the words chorally and individually, concentrating on the pronunciation of the vowel sounds.

CB p26 Activity 18 Listen and say the chant.

- Play the chant. The pupils point to the items as they hear them.

1.43

I've got a book, I've got a hook,
I've got a foot in my bag.
Who put a book, who put a hook,
Who put a foot in my bag?

I've got a torch, I've got a ball,
I've got a horse in my bag.
Who put a torch, who put a ball,
Who put a horse in my bag?

- Teach the chant line by line. Focus on the pronunciation points. Use choral and individual repetition to check pronunciation.
- Play the chant again and encourage the pupils to join in.

Focus on spelling

- Match the spelling with the vowel sounds.
- Focus on the spelling patterns:
  /ʊ/ is often spelt *oo* (*foot*)
  /ɔ:/ is often spelt *or* (*torch*) but the *r* is silent
- Show examples from the chant for each vowel sound.
- Remind the pupils that there are lots of exceptions to spelling patterns in English.

AB p32 Activity 13. Say. Draw ● or ■. Find and write the words.

- Point to each of the pictures. The pupils say the words chorally.
- Focus on the pronunciation difference between /ʊ/ and /ɔ:/, using the words *book* and *torch*.
- Show how *book* has a square around it and *torch* has a circle round it.
- Ask the pupils to identify a word with the /ʊ/ sound.
- Show the pupils how to put a square round the word.
- Repeat with the /ɔ:/ sound, putting a circle around the word.
- The pupils put circles and squares around the words.
- The pupils find and circle the words in the wordsearch. They copy the words into the correct columns.
- Point to the pictures at random. The pupils say the words chorally and invidually. Check the pupils' pronunciation.

Answers: circle: torch, ball, horse; square book, hook, foot

p	j	e	h	s	q	f	n	t	a
h	b	l	o	d	b	o	o	k	o
w	r	r	r	w	t	p	z	g	o
c	f	d	s	h	c	a	m	u	c
r	o	m	e	k	o	r	e	q	i
a	o	o	n	b	x	i	s	h	l
e	t	o	r	c	h	v	j	o	d
k	g	s	d	q	i	p	a	o	m
b	t	f	o	m	l	e	s	k	s
m	b	a	l	l	c	r	g	t	b

End-of-unit review

- Use the Rollercoaster Game poster and the Class Book to recall the main activities of the unit.
- Recall the language associated with each activity.
- Ask the pupils to let you know what they liked or didn't like, and what they found easy or difficult.

Play the Rollercoaster Game

- Divide the class into small groups. Give each group one of the character 'counters' and let them play the game as before (see p41).
- Remind them to use the poster chants when a group gets a question right or wrong.

AB p32 Activity 19 Look at the unit again. What can you do? Think and colour.

- Let the pupils do the self-evaluation activity as before (see p41).

PMB p2 Picture Dictionary (optional)

- If your pupils are making Picture Dictionaries, give out the photocopies of the template.
- Pupils continue making the dictionaries as for Unit 1 (see p42).

Lesson 12a (optional)

■ = Words ◆ = Sentences

Show what you know!

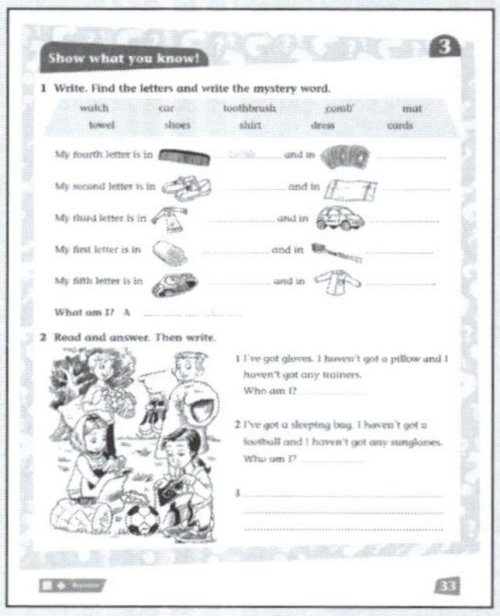
Show what you know!
3
1 Write. Find the letters and write the mystery word.
watch car toothbrush comb mat
towel shoes shirt dress cards
My fourth letter is in .... and in ....
My second letter is in .... and in ....
My third letter is in .... and in ....
My first letter is in .... and in ....
My fifth letter is in .... and in ....
What am I? A ....
2 Read and answer. Then write.
1 I've got gloves. I haven't got a pillow and I haven't got any trainers. Who am I? ....
2 I've got a sleeping bag. I haven't got a football and I haven't got any sunglasses. Who am I? ....
3 ....
33

AB page 33

For suggestions on how to use *Show what you know!* see page 13.

Objectives

- Extra practice of the vocabulary of the unit
- Solve puzzles in English
- Provide extra material for homework and fast finishers

Core language

Review of language used so far

Materials

No extra materials

AB p33 Activity 1 Write. Find the letters and write the mystery word.

- First, quickly revise ordinal numbers with the class. For example, get ten pupils to stand in a row at the front of the class. Call out the ordinal numbers in random order and ask the class to say the correct pupil's name, e.g. *first – Maria, seventh – Tomàs …*
- Then read the words in the word pool to the pupils.
- Write five lines on the board (_ _ _ _ _). Say *We are going to guess the word.*
- Read the beginning of the first sentence to the pupils (*My fourth letter is in …*). Ask the pupils to identify the picture (*comb*) and write the word on the board.
- Continue with the rest of the sentence (*and in …*). Ask the pupils to identify the next picture (*cards*) and write the word on the board.
- Ask the pupils *What letter is in comb and in cards?* The pupils answer *c*. Ask the pupils *Where does the letter c go in the word?* The pupils answer *It's the fourth letter* (recast their answers if necessary). Write the letter *c* in the fourth space.
- Repeat with the other sentences. The pupils copy the words on the lines in their books, and add the letters to the mystery word as they find them. The second and fifth letters have two possibilities (*shoes* and *towel* contain both *e* and *o*, of which the correct letter is *o*, and *watch* and *shirt* contain both *t* and *h*, of which the correct letter is *h*), so pupils will have to work out which letters can be used to make a word once they have worked out all the other letters.

Answer: My fourth letter is in comb and in cards.
My second letter is in shoes and in towel.
My third letter is in dress and in car.
My first letter is in mat and in toothbrush.
My fifth letter is in watch and in shirt.
The mystery word is *torch*.

AB p33 Activity 2 Read and answer. Then write.

- Point to the picture of the children. Say to the pupils *Tell me about Jazmin. She's got ….*
- The pupils make sentences about the things that Jazmin has got (e.g. *She's got sunglasses*) and the things she hasn't got (e.g. *She hasn't got gloves*).
- Read the first description to the pupils. They identify the person (*Molly*).
- Repeat with the second description.
- Pupils complete a third description about one of the other characters.
- In pairs, the pupils read their sentences to each other and try to guess the person.

Answers: 1 Molly **2** Finn **3** (possible answers) I've got gloves. I haven't got a sleeping bag and I haven't got any trainers. (Luke) I've got a football. I haven't got a pillow and I haven't got a sleeping bag. (Jazmin)

- As a follow-up activity, the pupils can make sentences about themselves, using other objects. For example: *I've got a radio. I haven't got a bicycle and I haven't got a computer.*

The pupils are now ready to sit the Unit 3 test. See pp178–181 for both Standard and Higher levels. They are also ready to sit the Term 1 test on pp206–207 and p212.

The pupils are now ready to do the culture lessons on 'My country' (see p160).

4 Looking at animals

Lesson 1 ■ = Words

Introducing vocabulary

CB page 27

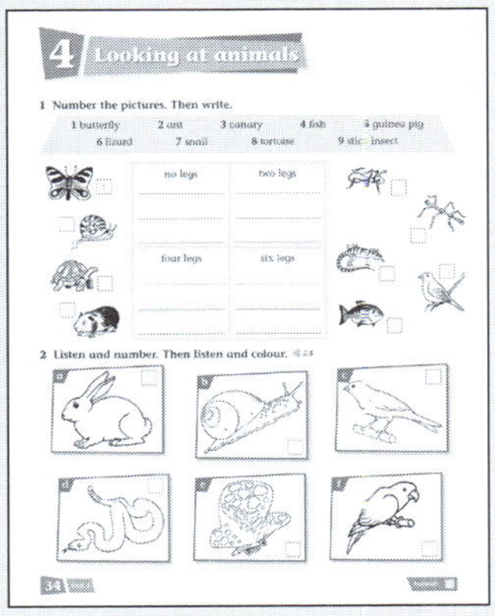

AB page 34

Objectives

- Understand the theme of the unit
- Become familiar with vocabulary for animals
- Practise talking about animals
- Focus on spelling

Core language

Animal vocabulary: *ant, guinea pig, lizard, stick insect, tortoise, butterfly, canary, snail*

Review of

- animal vocabulary: *rabbit, parrot, snake, fish*
- language used so far

Other language

beautiful

Materials

Rollercoaster Game poster; Animals flashcards (*ant, guinea pig, lizard, stick insect, tortoise, butterfly, canary, snail, rabbit, parrot, snake, fish*); CD 2; Pupils' bookmarks (optional) (see p28)

Unit overview

- Talk to the pupils about animals. Ask them what words for animals they know in English.
- Ask them which words (in their own language) they would like to learn.
- Ask the pupils to look through Unit 4 in their Class Books. Talk with them about the unit and quickly write the different topics and activities on the board, relating them to the shapes on the poster:
  - ■ Words – animals, insects
  - ▲ Story – *Reptile rescue*
  - ◆ Sentences – *He's got a … / He hasn't got a … / Has he got a …?*
  - ▬ Text work – postcards
  - ● Song – *Parrots fly in the jungle.* / Chant – *Clap, clap, clap!*
  - ◗ Other subjects – Science (learn about insects)
- Remind the pupils that they will use the poster again at the end of the unit.

Introduce new vocabulary *see p19*

- Use the animals flashcards to teach the new vocabulary. The pupils repeat the words chorally and then individually.
- Play *Just a little bit* with the pupils: cover each flashcard with a sheet of paper and slowly pull down the paper, showing more and more of the flashcard. The pupils try to guess what it is.

CB p27 **Activity 1 Look, listen and repeat.**

- Explain that the children are looking at a book about animals.
- The pupils listen to the recording. They repeat each word chorally and point to the correct picture.

2.1

1 ant, **2** tortoise, **3** snake, **4** butterfly, **5** canary, **6** parrot, **7** lizard, **8** stick insect, **9** snail, **10** fish, **11** guinea pig, **12** rabbit

CB p27 **Activity 2 Listen and find.**

- Play the dialogue.
- The pupils listen for the animals and point to each one in the picture.
- Alternatively, the pupils can use their bookmarks (see p28) to focus on the pictures.

2.2

Molly:	Oh look, an ant. It's very small.
Luke:	And look – a snake.
Molly:	It's beautiful!
Luke:	I like this tortoise.
Molly:	Oh, look at this butterfly!
Luke:	Wow!
Finn:	Look – a guinea pig. I like guinea pigs.
Eve:	I've got a guinea pig. Have you got any pets, Finn?
Finn:	Yes, I've got a rabbit!
Archie:	Do you like lizards, Jazmin?
Jazmin:	Lizards? Yes. And I like stick insects! I've got three stick insects. Have you got any pets, Archie?
Archie:	Yes. I've got a canary, and a parrot, and a fish … and a snail.
Jazmin:	Oh!

CB p27 **Activity 3 Ask and answer.**

- Read the dialogue to the pupils.
- Ask individual pupils questions such as *Do you like stick insects?*, etc. The pupils answer the questions with *Yes* or *No*.
- The pupils practise asking and answering the questions in pairs.

Spelling

- Ask the pupils to identify:
  1. words that are similar in their language (highlight the differences in spelling)
  2. words with combinations of two vowels (for example, *guin<u>ea</u> pig, tort<u>oi</u>se*, etc.)
  3. words with double letters (for example, *bu<u>tt</u>erfly*).

AB p34 Activity 1 Number the pictures. Then write.

- Read the words in the word pool to the pupils. Ask the pupils to match the words to the pictures.
- Read the categories (*no legs, two legs, four legs, six legs*) to the pupils. Ask *Which animals go in the 'no legs' category?* The pupils choose suitable animals.
- Repeat with the other categories.

Answers: no legs: snail, fish; two legs: canary; four legs: guinea pig, lizard, tortoise; six legs: ant, butterfly, stick insect

Lesson 2 ■ = Words

Practising vocabulary

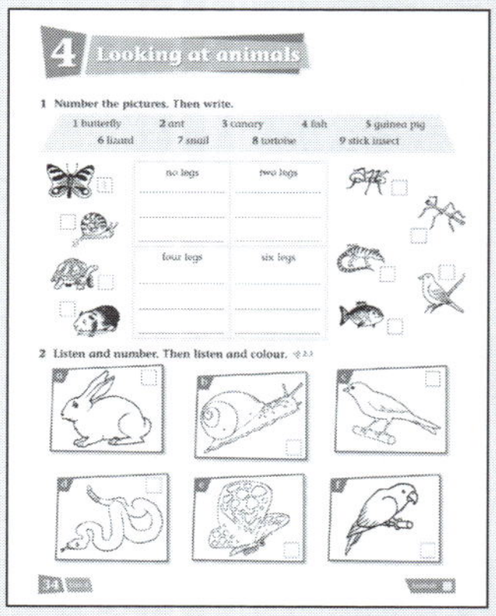
4 Looking at animals
1 Number the pictures. Then write.
1 butterfly 2 ant 3 canary 4 fish 5 guinea pig 6 lizard 7 snail 8 tortoise 9 stick insect
no legs two legs four legs six legs
2 Listen and number. Then listen and colour.

AB page 34

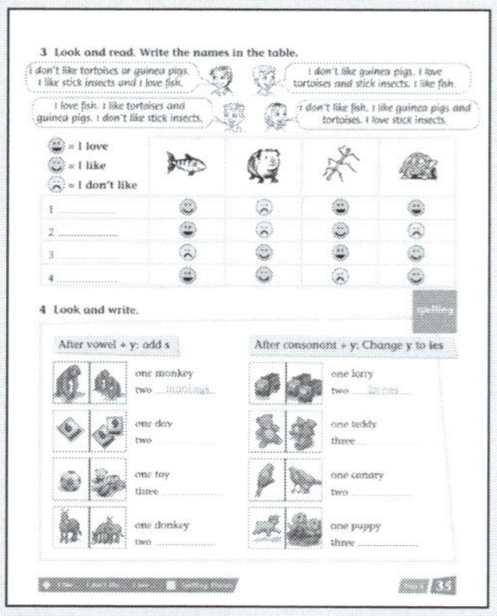
3 Look and read. Write the names in the table.
4 Look and write.

AB page 35

Objectives

- Review the vocabulary for animals
- Practise listening and talking about people and animals
- Read about people and animals
- Arrange vocabulary in pronunciation / spelling categories

Core language

Review of

- animal vocabulary
- language used so far

Other language

lorry

Materials

Animals flashcards (x12); Animals picture cards (PMB p20) – one photocopied set per pupil

Review vocabulary

- Put the animals flashcards on the board. The pupils say the words chorally and individually.
- Say each animal and ask the pupils *What colour is it?* Decide on one colour for each animal.
- Allocate one animal to each pupil and play *Colours* with the pupils: when they hear their colour, they say the word for their animal.

AB p34 Activity 2 Listen and number. Then listen and colour.

- Point to each animal and ask *What is it?* The pupils say the name of each animal.
- Play the first conversation on the CD. Ask *What animal is it?* The pupils answer *butterfly* and write *1* in the box next to the butterfly.
- Repeat with the other conversations. The pupils number each animal with the number of the conversation.

2.3

1 Adult: Have you got a pet?
Girl 1: Yes. I've got a butterfly.
Adult: Oh. What colour is it?
Girl 1: It's red and purple.

2 Adult: Have you got a pet?
Girl 2: Yes. I've got a snail.
Adult: Oh. What colour is it?
Girl 2: It's black and brown.

3 Adult: Have you got a pet?
Girl 3: Yes. I've got a parrot.
Adult: Oh. What colour is it?
Girl 3: It's pink and blue.

4 Adult: Have you got a pet?
Girl 4: Yes. I've got a snake.
Adult: A snake? What colour is it?
Girl 4: It's green and orange.

5 Adult: Have you got a pet?
Girl 5: Yes. I've got a rabbit.
Adult: Oh. What colour is it?
Girl 5: It's brown and white.

6 Adult: Have you got a pet?
Girl 5: Yes. I've got a canary.
Adult: Oh. What colour is it?
Girl 5: It's yellow and grey.

Answers: **a** 5 **b** 2 **c** 6 **d** 4 **e** 1 **f** 3

- Say *Now listen for the colours of the animals.* Play the conversations again. After each conversation, the pupils colour the animals.

Answers: **a** brown and white **b** black and brown **c** yellow and grey **d** green and orange **e** red and purple **f** pink and blue

AB p35 Activity 3 Look and read. Write the names in the table.

- Read the key to the pupils. Make sure they understand the difference between *I like …* and *I love …*
- Point to each animal in the table and ask *What is it?* The pupils say the name of each animal.
- Point to the first speech bubble and the picture of Jazmin. Read out the speech bubble text. Point out how Jazmin uses the plural form of the nouns.
- Ask pupils to find the line in the table which matches what Jazmin says (you can ask them first to find the picture which represents *I don't like tortoises*, then *I like stick insects*, etc.).
- Ask *Which number is Jazmin? Yes, line number 2.*
- Repeat with one of the other characters' speech bubbles.
- The pupils read the last two sentences individually, and write the names in the table. Check the answers orally.

Answers: **1** Luke **2** Jazmin **3** Molly **4** Finn

- For extra practice, ask pupils to cover the speech bubbles, and make sentences using the table: *Look at row 1 – Luke. What does Luke say about tortoises? Yes, 'I love tortoises'.*

AB p35 Activity 4 Look and write.

- Point to the first set of plurals on the left of the page. Point out the plural *s* (*one monkey, two monkeys*).

- The pupils complete the plural forms in the rest of the first set.
- Read the nouns in the second set (*lorry, teddy, canary, puppy*). Explain that these words are different to the words in the first set. In the first set, the words end in a vowel + y. In the second set, the words end in a consonant + y. Words that end in a consonant + y make the plural with *-ies*. Show the example with *lorry* (*one lorry, two lorr<u>ies</u>*).
- Point to the pictures of the teddies. Read *one teddy*, then ask the pupils to say the plural form (*three teddies*). The pupils write the plural form on the line.
- Repeat with the other pictures in the second set.

Answers: two days, three toys, two donkeys; three teddies, two canaries, three puppies

PMB p20 Make the picture cards

- Give out the photocopies of the animals picture cards. The pupils colour and cut out the picture cards.
- They can use their cards to play a game, for example *Bingo* (picture cards version) (see p21).
- If your pupils are using word cards, they can prepare them now (see p30). Pupils cut them out and match them with the picture cards.
- Remind the pupils to keep all the cards in a safe place.

Lesson 3 ▲ = Story

Story

CB page 28

CB page 29

Objectives

- Listen to a story
- Read a story
- Listen for words and phrases in a story
- Practise story language

Core language

Has she got a python?; She hasn't got a tiger.

Review of

- animal vocabulary
- language used so far

Other language

reptile, owner, python, chameleon, Shame!, Too bad!, find, Wow!, That's big, Hurry up, hold, She's just like a ..., stripy

Materials

Animals flashcards (x12); CD 2

Review vocabulary

- Put the animals flashcards on the board. The pupils say the words chorally and individually.
- Place the flashcards in different parts of the classroom and play *Around the class* with the pupils. First you say the words and the pupils point to the flashcards. Then you point to the flashcards and the pupils say the words.

Introduce the story

- Ask the pupils to imagine they are going to visit a zoo. Ask them to say what animals they would like to see.
- Explain that in the story the children are going to visit a reptile zoo. Ask the pupils to give examples of reptiles, such as lizard, snake, crocodile, and tortoise. (Note: a frog is an amphibian, not a reptile.)

CB pp28–29 Activity 4 First listening with the books closed

- Tell the pupils to listen and answer this question: *What animal is lost in the zoo?*
- The pupils listen with their books closed

2.4

[1]	Eve:	Here's the reptile centre.
	Archie:	Who's Mrs Ripley?
	Eve:	She's the owner. She loves reptiles!
[2]	Archie:	Has she got a python?
	Luke:	Has she got a crocodile?
	Eve:	Yes! And she's got a giant tortoise!
	Archie:	She's got LOTS of reptiles.
[3]	Molly:	Has she got a tiger?
	Luke:	No. She hasn't got a tiger. A tiger isn't a reptile!
[4]	Molly:	Oh, yes. Shame. I like tigers!
	Luke:	Too bad!
[5]	Eve:	Hello Mrs Ripley! What's the matter?
	Mrs Ripley:	I can't find Camilla, my chameleon.
[6]	Eve:	Oh dear!
	Archie:	Come on. Let's look at the snakes.
	Luke:	Hurry up, Molly!
	Molly:	But look ...
[7]	Archie:	The python is five metres long.
	Luke:	Wow That's big.
	Molly:	Look! Look!
[8]	Molly:	Look at the table. It's Camilla the chameleon. She's here!
[9]	Mrs Ripley:	Well done, Molly!
	Molly:	Can I hold her?
	Mrs Ripley:	Yes, of course.
[10]	Luke:	Oh look – now she's stripy!
	Molly:	Fantastic. She's just like a tiger!

- Check the pupils' answers to your question (*a chameleon*).
- Ask the pupils if they know why it was difficult to find the chameleon (Because it changes colour to match the environment). Recast the pupils' answers as necessary.

CB pp28–29 Activity 4 Second listening with the books open

- Tell the pupils to open their books and look at the story.
- Ask questions about the story such as *Which animal does Molly want to see?* and *Is there a snake in the zoo?*

- Play the recording again while the pupils follow in their books.
- Go through any vocabulary queries with the class.

CB p29 Activity 5 Read and find the picture.

- Explain that each sentence refers to a particular picture in the story.
- Ask the pupils to identify the frame for the first sentence (frame 8).
- The pupils read each sentence and match it with a picture. This can be done as a whole-class activity or individually.
- The pupils write the answers in their notebooks.

Answers: a 8 b 10 c 6 d 1 e 9 f 2 g 7

Fun expressions

- Write these 'fun expressions' from the story on the board:
  Too bad!
  Hurry up!
  Wow! That's big.
- Play the story again: the pupils put up their hands when they hear one of the phrases.
- Pause the recording. The pupils repeat the phrase chorally and individually. Encourage the pupils to copy the intonation on the CD.

Lesson 4 ◆ = Sentences

Language focus 1

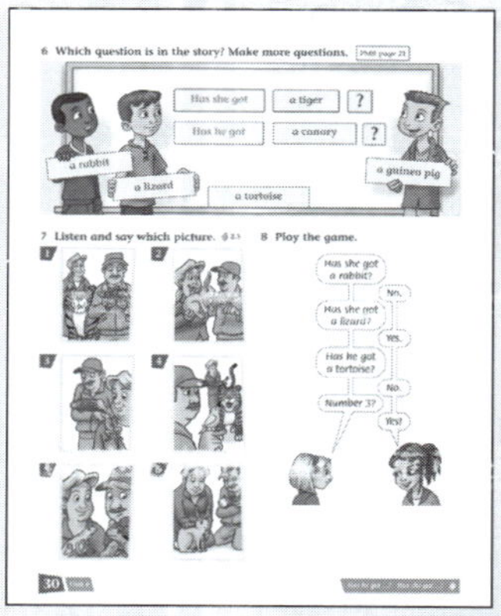

CB page 30

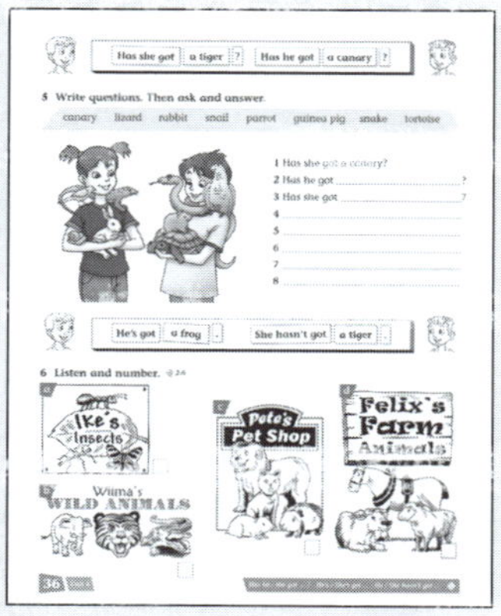

AB page 36

Objectives

- Understand the use of *Has he / she got a …?*
- Review the use of *She's got a …*
- Practise using the new language

Core language

Has he got …? / Has she got …?
Review of language used so far

Materials

CD 2; Grammar tiles (PMB p21) – one photocopy of Set 1 per pupil (optional)

Recall the story

- Ask the pupils to remember as much as they can from the story.
- Describe people and animals from the story, like this:
  She's the owner of the Reptile Centre. (Mrs Ripley)
  She's got a stripy T-shirt. (Molly)
  Mrs Ripley can't find this animal. (Camilla the chameleon)
  He wants to see the snakes. (Archie)
  It's a very long animal. (the python)
- After each description, ask *Who is it?* or *What is it?* The pupils identify the people and animals.

PMB p21 / CB p30 Activity 6 Which question is in the story? Make more questions.

- Ask the pupils to read the questions in the grammar tiles.
- Ask the pupils to say which question is in the story (*Has she got a tiger?*).
- Focus on the use of *he* for men and boys, and *she* for women and girls.
- Write *She has got a tiger* on the board. Under this, write *Has she got a tiger?* Use a mime gesture to show how the order of *she* and *has* changes to make the question.
- The pupils say the questions in the grammar tiles chorally and individually.
- The pupils use the remaining tiles in the picture to make questions with *Has he / she got …?* Choose other pupils to answer with *yes* or *no*. Alternatively, give each pupil a copy of Set 1 of the grammar tiles from the PMB: the pupils cut out the tiles and arrange them in sentences on their desks. Ask individual pupils to read out their sentences for the class.

CB p30 Activity 7 Listen and say which picture.

- Show the pupils the pictures. Ask the pupils to say sentences about each one, for example *She's got a tiger in picture 1.*
- Play the first sentence on the CD. The pupils match it with the correct picture.
- Repeat with the other sentences.

2.5

Eve:	Has she got a lizard?
Molly:	Yes.
Eve:	Has he got a guinea pig?
Molly:	No.
Presenter:	Which picture is it?
Molly:	Has she got a rabbit?
Eve:	No.
Molly:	Has she got a tiger?
Eve:	Yes.
Molly:	Has he got a canary?
Eve:	Yes.
Presenter:	Which picture is it?
Eve:	Has she got a tiger?
Molly:	No.
Eve:	Has she got a rabbit?
Molly:	Yes.
Eve:	Has he got a canary?
Molly:	No.
Presenter:	Which picture is it?
Molly:	Has she got a lizard?
Eve:	Yes.
Molly:	Has he got a tortoise?
Eve:	No.
Presenter:	Which picture is it?

Answers: 5, 4, 6, 3

CB p30 **Activity 8 Play the game.**

- Read the conversation to the pupils.
- Say you are thinking of a picture. The pupils ask you questions about it, with *Has she got a ...?* and *Has he got a ...?*
- The pupils identify the picture you are thinking of.
- The pupils play the game in pairs.

AB p36 **Activity 5 Write questions. Then ask and answer.**

- Read the words in the word pool to the pupils.
- Point to the picture. Ask *What animals has the boy got?* The pupils name the boy's animals.
- Repeat with the girl's animals.
- Read the first question, then read the beginning of the second question. The pupils suggest a suitable ending, for example *a parrot.*
- Repeat with the third question.
- The pupils write five more questions with *Has he got ...?* and *Has she got ...?*
- Ask individual pupils to read a question each. Choose other pupils to answer the questions.
- The pupils ask and answer their questions in pairs. As a variation, this can be played as a memory game: one pupil in each pair closes his / her book and tries to answer the questions from memory.

Lesson 5 ◆ = Sentences

Language focus 2

AB page 36

AB page 37

Objectives

- Review vocabulary for animals
- Understand the use of *He / She hasn't got a / any ...*
- Review *He's / She's got ...* and *Has he / she got ...?*
- Practise talking about what people have and haven't got

Core language

He / She hasn't got a tiger.

Review of language used so far

Other language

He / she hasn't got any rollerblades.

Materials

Grammar tiles (PMB p21) – one photocopy of Set 2 per pupil; Pupils' grammar tiles (Set 1) from Lesson 4 (optional); CD 2; Camping things flashcards (singular items only, i.e. *comb, blanket, mat, pillow, sleeping bag, toothbrush, torch, towel, book, teddy*)

PMB p21 **AB p36** **Focus on language**

- Read the sentences in the second set of grammar tiles on Activity Book 36 to the pupils. Ask the pupils *Which sentence is in the story? (She hasn't got a tiger.)*
- Point out the difference between the affirmative form (*He's got ...*) and the negative form (*He hasn't got ...*). Write the contractions and the long forms on board: *He's got = He has got*, and *He hasn't got = He has not got.* Use mime gestures to show how the long forms 'contract' to the short forms.
- The pupils say the sentences in the grammar tiles chorally and individually.
- Give each pupil a copy of Set 2 of the grammar tiles from the PMB. Ask the pupils to suggest words to put in the blank tiles (*an ant, a butterfly*, etc.). Write the suggestions on the board. The pupils can choose words to copy in the blank tiles.
- The pupils cut out all the tiles and use them to make sentences on their desks. Ask pupils to read out their sentences for the class.
- Pupils can combine the Set 2 tiles with some of the Set 1 tiles to make more sentences, for example *She's got a tortoise, He hasn't got a guinea pig*, etc.

Practice

- Call a pupil to the front and give him / her three of the camping things flashcards to hold up, e.g. *teddy, comb*, and *towel*. Stick the other flashcards on the board.
- Select a pupil and say *Make a sentence with 'He's got' or 'He hasn't got'.* The pupil says, for example, *He hasn't got a toothbrush.* Ask other pupils to make sentences.
- Repeat with other pupils at the front, with other flashcards. Use girls and boys so that the pupils have to use *he* and *she*.

AB p36 **Activity 6 Listen and number.**

- Point to each of the places. Ask the pupils *What animals can you see?* The pupils say the animals in each place.
- Play the first conversation. Ask the pupils *Which place is it?* The pupils answer *Pete's Pet Shop* and write 1 next to the picture.
- Repeat with the other conversations.

2.6

1 Adult: Here we are.
Child 1: Ooh, look. He's got hamsters and guinea pigs!
Child 2: I want to see a horse!
Child 1: He hasn't got any horses.
Child 2: Oh.
Adult: Never mind. Come on.

2 Adult: Here we are.
Child 1: Ooh, look. She's got tigers and elephants.
Child 2: I want to see a snake!
Child 1: She hasn't got any snakes.
Child 2: Oh.
Adult: Never mind. Come on.

3 Adult: Here we are.
Child 1: Ooh, look. He's got horses and sheep.
Child 2: I want to see a crocodile.
Child 1: He hasn't got a crocodile.
Child 2: Oh.
Adult: Never mind. Come on.

4 Adult: Here we are.
Child 1: Ooh, look. He's got ants and butterflies.
Child 2: I want to see some grasshoppers.
Child 1: He hasn't got any grasshoppers.
Child 2: Oh.
Adult: Never mind. Come on.

Answers: a 4 b 2 c 1 d 3

AB p37 Activity 7 Circle the differences. Complete.

- Read the words in the word pool to the pupils.
- Point to the two pictures and say *Find a difference.* The pupils find differences in the picture, for example *In Picture A the woman is wearing a hat. In Picture B she isn't wearing a hat / she's wearing a cap.*
- Recast the answers with *has got / hasn't got,* for example: *In Picture A she's got a hat. In Picture B she hasn't got a hat.*
- Point to sentence 1. Match the picture at the side with the person in pictures A and B. Point out the example answer to the pupils.
- Point to sentence 2. Match the person with the pictures again. Read the first part of the sentence to the pupils (*In picture ...*). The pupils say *A* and write the letter in the sentence. Ask what they could write for the second sentence. Ask them to look at what the man is holding in picture B, and guide them towards the answer *He hasn't got a magazine.*
- For numbers 3 to 6, the pupils write their own sentences (or they can work in pairs).

Answers: 1 B 2 A magazine 3 (example answer) In picture A she's got a fish. She hasn't got a lizard. 4 (example answer) In picture B he's got a dog. He hasn't got a cat. 5 (example answer) In picture A, she's got a snake. She hasn't got a guinea pig. 6 (example answer) In picture B, he's got a bag. He hasn't got an umbrella.

AB p37 Activity 8 Look and write the names. Write about picture B.

- Read the words in the word pools to the pupils.
- Point to the children in Picture A. Read sentence 1. The pupils suggest names for sentences 2 and 3.

Answers: 2 Luke 3 Archie

- Point to the children in Picture B. Say to the pupils *Make sentences with 'hasn't got'.* The pupils suggest a sentence about each child, for example *Finn hasn't got a lizard.* They write the sentences in their books.

Answers: (in any order) 4 Finn hasn't got a lizard. 5 Jazmin hasn't got a guinea pig. 6 Eve hasn't got any ants.

- Ask the pupils to say similar sentences about people in their family and their friends. Encourage them to use *He / She hasn't got ...*

For extra grammar practice, see AB page 100.

Activity 1 Look and write.

Answers: 1 got a 2 Has she got a; No. 3 Has she got a; Yes. 4 got a; No. 5 Has he got a; Yes. 6 Has he got a; Yes.

Activity 2 Find and write.

Answers: 1 She's got a 2 He's got a 4 She hasn't got a 5 He's got a

Teaching tip: *any*

Use of *hasn't got <u>any</u> ...* with plurals isn't overtly focused on as target language at this stage. However, pupils have met this structure already in Unit 3. For sentence 6, encourage pupils to produce the answer *Eve hasn't got any ants* by copying the model of *Archie hasn't got any rollerblades* in sentence 2, but also accept answers such as *Eve hasn't got an ant* or *Eve hasn't got ants* as correct.

Lesson 6 ▲ = Story

Playscript

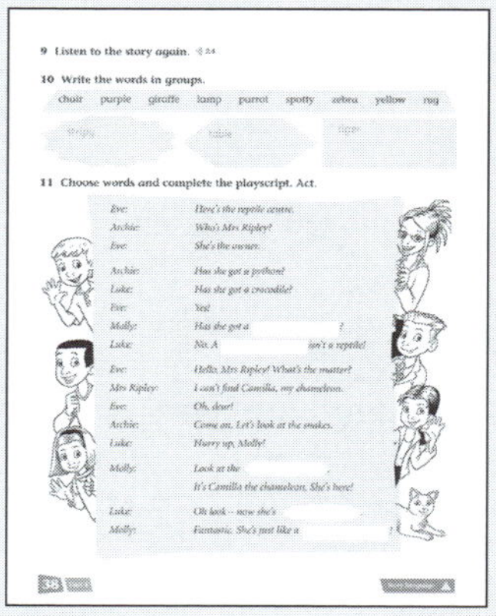

AB page 38

Objectives
- Read and complete a playscript
- Use finger puppets to act out a playscript
- Act out the play

Core language
Review of language used so far

Other language
stripy, spotty, lamp, zebra, giraffe

Materials
CD 2; Spare photocopies of the finger puppets (PMB p3)

AB p38 Activity 9 Listen to the story again.

- Tell the pupils to look at pages 28–29 in their Class Books again.
- Play the CD while the pupils listen and read.
- Alternatively, the pupils can read the story aloud in groups of five. Each pupil should read one character.

AB p38 Activity 10 Write the words in groups.

- Read the words in the word pool to the pupils.
- Point to each of the boxes and read the word in each one. Ask the pupils to suggest words from the word pool to go in each box.
- The pupils write the words from the word pool in the correct category.

Answers: set 1 – stripy, spotty, purple, yellow; set 2 – table, chair, lamp, rug; set 3 – tiger, zebra, giraffe, parrot

- Ask the pupils to suggest new words for each category.

AB p38 **Activity 11 Choose words and complete the playscript. Act.**

- Read the playscript to the pupils. When you come to a blank, ask *Which word was in the story?* The pupils say the words from the story.
- Read the playscript again. Ask the pupils to suggest alternative words from Activity 10 to complete the blanks.
- Divide the pupils into groups of four. In their groups, the pupils decide which words to use when they read the playscript.

Finger puppets *see p22*

- Ask the pupils *How many characters are there in the story? (five)*. The pupils identify the five characters. (Eve, Archie, Molly, Luke, and Mrs Ripley.)
- Say *We have four pupils for five characters. It isn't a problem. Look!* Write this table on the board:
  Pupil 1 – Eve
  Pupil 2 – Molly and Mrs Ripley
  Pupil 3 – Archie
  Pupil 4 – Luke
- In their groups, the pupils decide who is going to take each part. They should also choose an object to be Camilla the chameleon, or draw a picture and cut it out.
- If the pupils have got their finger puppets with them, tell them to get out the puppet for the character they are going to play.
- Give each group a photocopy of the extra finger puppet. The pupils cut out, colour, and stick the extra puppet to make the Mrs Ripley puppet. If they haven't got the other puppets they need, they will have to make those too.

Practice

- Remind the pupils of the five points of successful play acting:
  1 Listen to the other actors.
  2 Wait for your turn.
  3 Speak clearly.
  4 When the puppets are speaking to each other, they should face each other.
  5 Don't move your puppets unnecessarily.
- Tell the pupils about the notes you made during the Unit 3 play acting. Encourage them to concentrate on the points you noticed. Say you will be watching them again this time.
- The pupils act out the play with their puppets. While they are doing this, circulate around the classroom. Make a note of the points the pupils should improve on next time.
- Ask one or two groups to come to the front to act out the play with their puppets.

Lesson 7 = Text work

Reading and writing

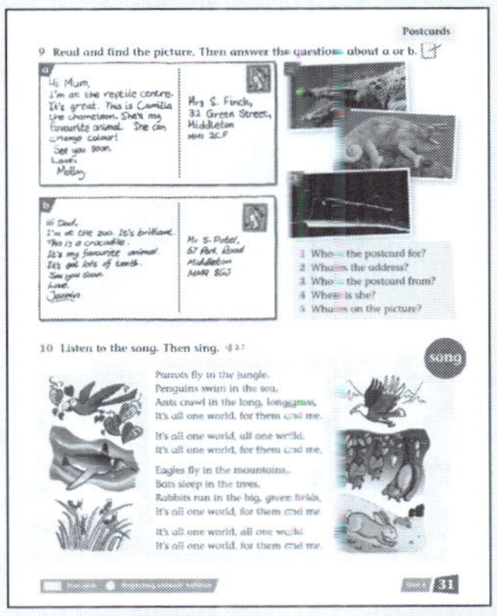

CB page 31

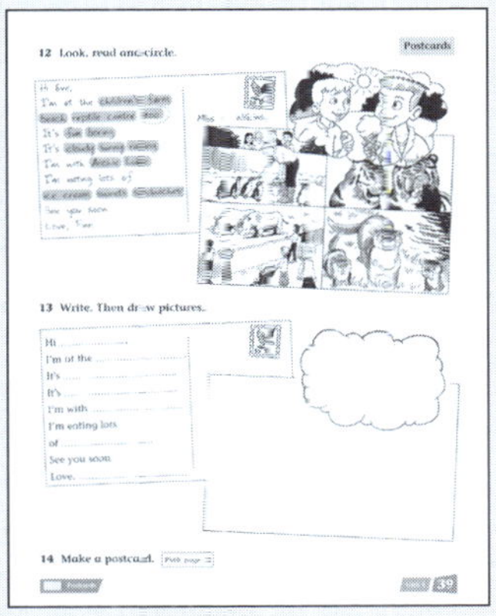

AB page 39

Objectives
- Review animal vocabulary
- Read and understand postcards
- Write a postcard

Core language
Review of language used so far

Other language
postcard, address, change colour, teeth, fun, boring

Materials
Animals flashcards (x12); Postcard template (PMB p22) – one photocopy per pupil; Glue

Review vocabulary

- Write the animal words on the board with the letters in a jumbled order.
- Call pupils to the front to write the letters in the correct order to form the words.
- Call other pupils to the front to put the flashcards next to the correct spellings.

CB p31 **Activity 9 Read and find the picture. Then answer the questions about a or b.**

- Talk to the pupils about postcards. Ask questions such as *Where can you buy postcards? When do you send postcards? Do you write a lot on a postcard?* (Use L1 as necessary.)
- Ask the pupils about the postcards in the Class Book. Point to each one and ask *Who wrote it?* and *Who did he / she send it to?*
- Ask the pupils what they can tell you about the design and layout of postcards (the address goes on the right, the message goes on the left, and there is usually a vertical line to divide these two sections).
- Tell the pupils to read the postcards. The pupils match the back of each postcard with the pictures on the front of the postcards.

Answers: a 2 b 1

- Ask the pupils to answer the questions about postcard a or postcard b. They write the answers in their notebooks.

Answers: postcard a: **1** Mrs S. Finch **2** 32 Green Street, Middleton, MM1 2CF **3** Molly **4** at the reptile centre **5** a chameleon / Camilla
postcard b: **1** Mr S. Patel **2** 67 Park Road, Middleton, MM9 8GJ **3** Jazmin **4** at the zoo **5** a crocodile

AB p39 Activity 12 Look, read and circle.

- Show the picture of Luke and Finn to the pupils. Explain that they are on holiday.
- Show the picture on the postcard to the pupils. Ask the pupils where Luke and Finn are (*the zoo*).
- Explain that Finn is writing a postcard to Eve. Point to the text of the postcard and say *Choose words for the postcard.* The pupils choose suitable words and circle them. Ask the pupils to tell you the words they chose, and write a complete version of the text on the board. Check that pupils have understood the meaning of *fun* and *boring*.

Answers: zoo, fun, sunny, Luke, ice cream

AB p39 Activity 13 Write. Then draw pictures.

- Point to the empty bubble and say *Draw yourselves here on holiday.* The pupils draw a picture of themselves in the bubble.
- Point to the front of the postcard and say *Draw a picture of the place where you are on holiday.* The pupils draw a suitable picture.
- Point to the text of the postcard. Say *Write the postcard.* The pupils complete the postcard using words and phrases from Activity 12.

PMB p22 / AB p39 Activity 14 Make a postcard.

- Explain to the pupils that they are going to draw and write a postcard. Show them the PMB template.
- Remind pupils that they have to choose work for their portfolio (see p198) during the course. Point out that this piece of work would be a suitable piece to include.
- Brainstorm ideas for the front and back of the postcard: pictures for the front and text for the back.
- Choose some suggestions and write them on the board.
- Remind pupils that they are drawing a picture of a place, not a picture of themselves. Show them how they could divide the front of the postcard up and draw four different pictures if they want to. Write some example greetings on the board to go on the front of the postcard, for example *Greetings from … (name of place).*
- Show the pupils how to write the postcards, using the postcard in Activity 12 as a model. Show them how to write an address at the side.
- Hand out the photocopies of the writing template. Tell the pupils to draw a picture in the frame at the bottom of the page and then write their postcard, with the address, in the top part of the page.
- The pupils write a rough copy of the text and address in their notebooks for you to correct. After you have checked the rough copy, they write their final copy on the photocopied template.
- When they have finished writing and drawing, pupils can cut out the two parts of the template and stick them together to make a realistic postcard.

Lesson 8 ● = Song / chant

Learning for life

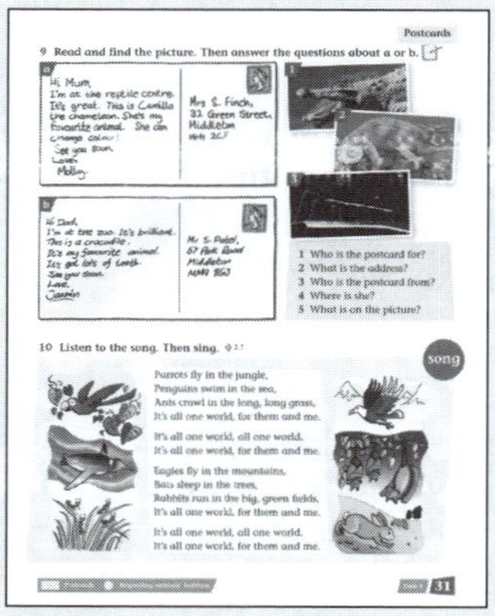

CB page 31

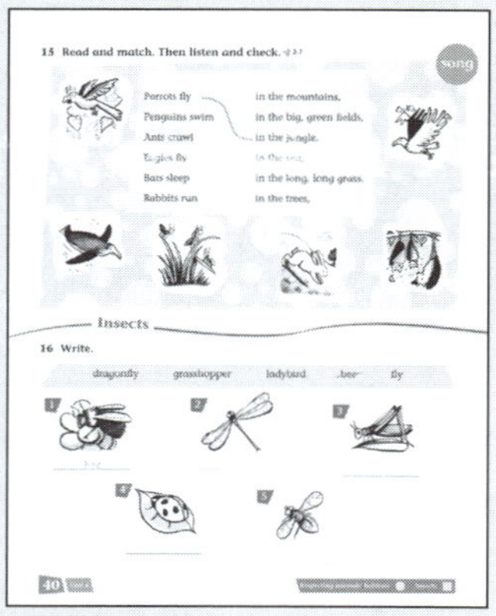

AB page 40

Objectives

- Review the unit so far
- Understand the importance of looking after the environment
- Talk about solutions for environmental problems
- Sing a song about animals

Core language

Review of language used so far

Other language

penguin, eagle, jungle, sea, field, grass, mountain, world, them, fly (v), crawl

Materials

Rollercoaster Game poster; Animals flashcards; CD 2

Unit review

- Use the Rollercoaster Game poster and the Class Book to review the unit so far. Talk with the pupils about the activities they have done.
- The pupils give examples of the language they used in each activity.

Review vocabulary (categorizing)

- Ask the pupils to tell you all the new words they remember from the unit.
- Put all the flashcards on the board and ask the pupils to arrange them in these two categories: *They can fly* and *They can't fly.*
- Repeat with other categories, such as:
  They're good pets / They aren't good pets
  I like … / I don't like …
  Insects / Birds / Others

Introduce the topic

- Talk about the problems facing wild animals. Encourage the pupils to talk about some or all of these ideas:
  – some animals are in danger of extinction
  – we are destroying their habitat
  – we are hunting them
  – pollution is killing them
  – we should respect the needs of animals
  – we should protect animals and their habitats
- The pupils can express their ideas in their own language. If they do, recast their answers in English.

CB p31 **Activity 10 Listen to the song. Then sing.**

- Read the song with the pupils. Explain any new words.
- Play the song on the CD.

2.7

Parrots fly in the jungle,
Penguins swim in the sea,
Ants crawl in the long, long grass,
It's all one world, for them and me.

It's all one world, all one world,
It's all one world, for them and me.

Eagles fly in the mountains,
Bats sleep in the trees,
Rabbits run in the big, green fields,
It's all one world, for them and me.

It's all one world, all one world,
It's all one world, for them and me.

- Work out simple mime gestures for the verbs (*fly, swim, crawl, sleep, run*) in the song. Work out another mime gesture for *It's all one world.*
- Read through the song again and ask the pupils to use the mime gestures as you read.
- Play the song again and encourage the pupils to join in, singing and miming.

AB p40 **Activity 15 Read and match. Then listen and check.**

- Tell the pupils to close their Class Books and open their Activity Books at page 40.
- Read the first sentence opener *Parrots fly …* to the pupils. Ask the pupils to recall the correct place. Write their suggestions on the board.
- Repeat with the other animals in the song.
- Play the song again; the pupils check the places they suggested.
- Make any necessary corrections to the words on the board. The pupils then link the lines in their Activity Books.
- To finish the lesson, tell the pupils to close their books. Help them to say the whole song again, chorally, from memory.

Answers: Parrots fly in the jungle. Penguins swim in the sea. Ants craw in the long, long grass. Eagles fly in the mountains. Bats sleep in the trees. Rabbits run in the big, green fields.

Lesson 9 ■ = Words ◗ = Other subjects

Learning through English

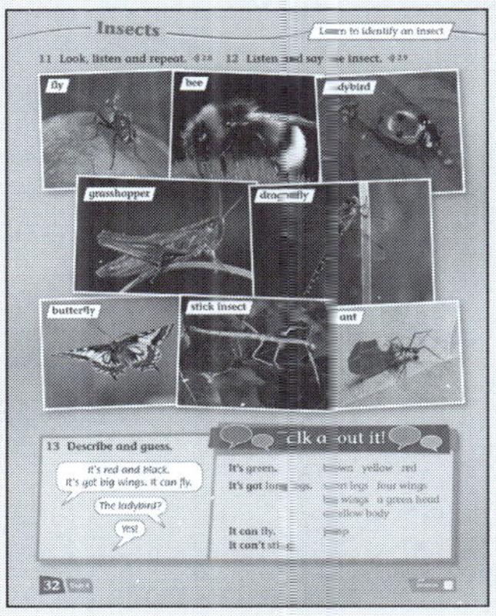

CB page 32

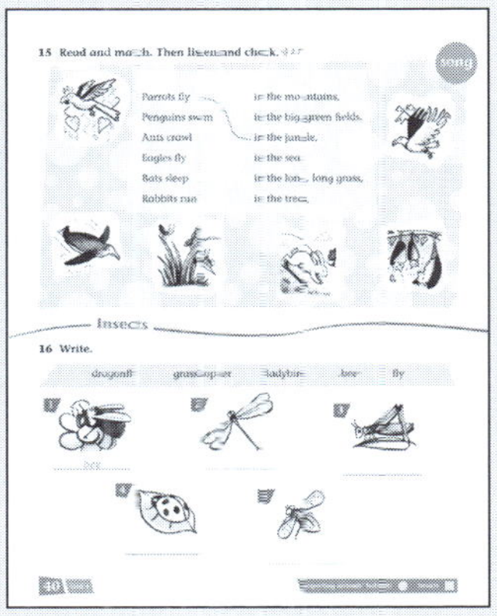

AB page 40

Objectives

- Learn some words for insects
- Learn how to identify insects
- Identify some insects

Core language

Insect vocabulary: *fly, bee, ladybird, grasshopper, dragonfly*

Review of

- insect vocabulary: *butterfly, ant, stick insect*
- language used so far

Other language

sting (v)

Materials

CD 2; Insects flashcards (new words: *fly, bee, ladybird, grasshopper, dragonfly;* revised words: *butterfly, ant, stick insect* from the animals flashcard set); Insects picture cards (PMB p20) – one photocopied set per pupil

Introduce the topic

- Show the pupils the flashcards of all the insects. Ask the pupils to name as many as they can, using their own language if necessary.
- Explain that in this lesson they are going to talk about how to identify insects.

Introduce new vocabulary *see p19*

- Use the flashcards to teach the new insect vocabulary. The pupils repeat the words chorally and then individually.
- Give each pupil a number between 1 and 5. Put the flashcards for the new insect vocabulary on the board and give each one a number between 1 and 5.
- Play *That's my word!* with the pupils (see p20).

CB p32 **Activity 11 Look, listen and repeat.**

- Put all the insects flashcards on the board and say the words again.
- Play the CD and drill the words chorally.

2.8

fly – bee – ladybird – grasshopper – dragonfly – butterfly – stick insect – ant

CB p32 **Activity 12 Listen and say the insect.**

- Play the first description to the pupils.
- The pupils identify the insect.
- Repeat with the other descriptions.

2.9

Child 1: It's got a long, brown body.
It's got long legs.
It can't fly.

Child 2: It's green.
It's got four short legs and two long legs.
It's got wings.
It can jump.

Child 1: It's yellow and black.
It's got big wings.
It can fly.

Child 2: It's orange and black.
It's got four wings.
It can sting.

Answers: 1 stick insect **2** grasshopper **3** butterfly **4** bee

CB p32 **Activity 13 Describe and guess.**

- Read the model conversation to the pupils.
- Describe one of the insects. The pupils guess which insect it is.
- Choose individual pupils to describe insects. The rest of the class guess which insect it is.
- The pupils practise describing and guessing insects in pairs. Remind them to look at the *Talk about it!* box to help them.

AB p40 **Activity 16 Write.**

- Read the words in the word pool to the pupils.
- The pupils write labels for the picures using the words in the word pool.

Answers: 1 bee **2** dragonfly **3** grasshopper **4** ladybird **5** fly

PMB p20 **Make the picture cards**

- Give out the photocopies of the insects picture cards. The pupils colour and cut out the picture cards.
- They can use their cards to play a game, for example *What's missing?* (picture card version) (see p19).
- If your pupils are using word cards, they can prepare them now (see p30). Pupils cut them out and match them with the picture cards.
- Remind the pupils to keep all the cards in a safe place.

Lesson 10

■ = Words ◗ = Other subjects

Learning through English

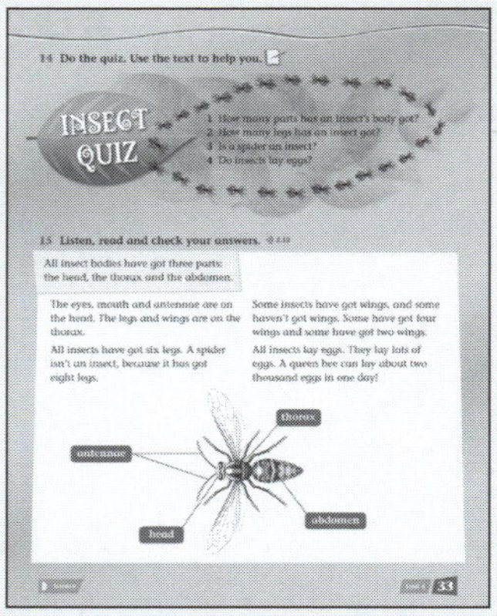

CB page 33

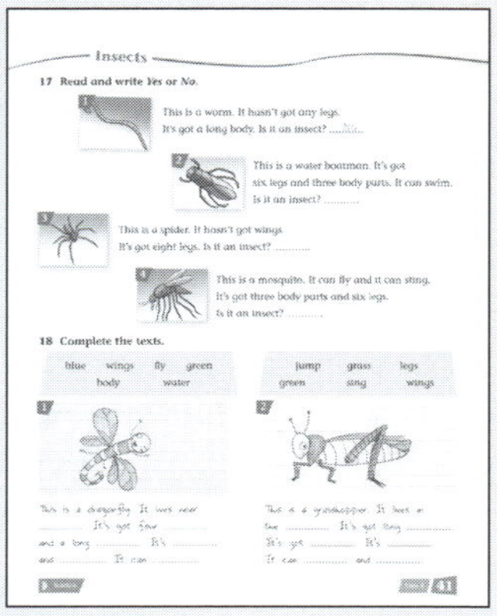

AB page 41

Objectives

- Review words for insects
- Learn about the characteristics of insects
- Identify animals that are insects and that aren't insects

Core language

Review of language used so far

Other language

head, thorax, abdomen, antennae, spider, lay eggs, queen

Materials

Insects flashcards (x5); Animals flashcards (x12)

Review vocabulary

- Stick the insects and animals flashcards on the board, in three rows of five or six flashcards each.
- Ask questions such as *Where's the stick insect?*
- Ask individual pupils to answer with *next to*. For example, *It's next to the ant.*
- Repeat with other pupils asking and answering questions.

CB p33 **Activity 14 Do the quiz. Use the text to help you.**

- Read the questions to the pupils. Explain any new words.
- The pupils take turns to read one sentence of the text each.
- Read the first question again. The pupils answer *three.*
- The pupils answer the rest of the questions individually and write the answers in their notebooks.
- Don't check the answers: go straight on to the next activity.

Answers: 1 three **2** six **3** no **4** yes

CB p33 **Activity 15 Listen, read and check your answers.**

- Explain that the pupils are going to read and listen to the text again. They can use the information to check the answers.
- Show the pupils the picture of the insect. Focus on the words in the labels (*head, thorax, abdomen, antennae*) and make sure the pupils understand them.
- Play the CD to the pupils. They check their answers and correct any that are wrong.

2.10

All insect bodies have got three parts: the head, the thorax and the abdomen.

The eyes, mouth and antennae are on the head. The legs and wings are on the thorax.

All insects have got six legs. A spider isn't an insect, because it has got eight legs.

Some insects have got wings, and some haven't got wings. Some have got four wings and some have got two wings.

All insects lay eggs. They lay lots of eggs. A queen bee can lay about two thousand eggs in one day!

AB p41 Activity 17 Read and write *Yes* or *No*.

- Read the first description to the pupils. Point out the example answer *No*. Ask pupils what information in the description tells them that a worm isn't an insect (*It hasn't got any legs*).
- Read the second description. Ask *Is it an insect?* The pupils answer *Yes* and write the answer on the line.
- Repeat with the other descriptions.

Answers: **2** Yes **3** No (It has got eight legs.) **4** Yes

AB p41 Activity 18 Complete the texts.

- Read the words in the first word pool to the pupils.
- Read the first description to the pupils. Pause at the lines: the pupils suggest words from the word pool to complete the sentence. They complete the description by writing the correct words.
- Read the words in the second word pool to the pupils. They complete the description individually.

Answers: text 1: water, wings, body, blue, green, fly; text 2: grass, legs, wings, green, jump, sing

Lesson 11 = Other subjects

Learning through English (Project)

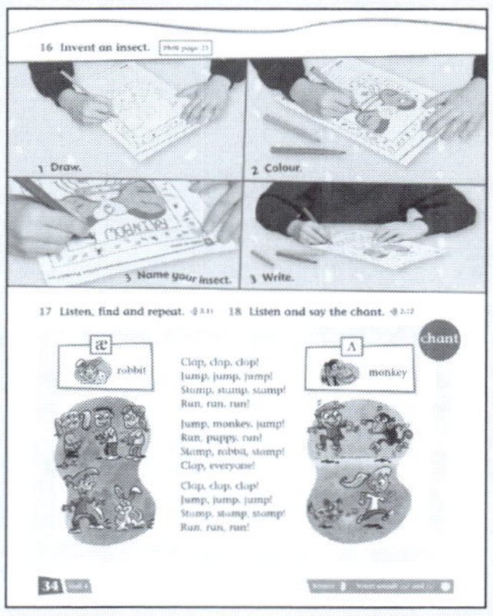

CB page 34

Objectives

- Review insect vocabulary
- Invent an insect
- Draw the insect and write a description of it

Core language

Review of language used so far

Materials

Insects flashcards (x8); 'Invent an insect' template (PMB p23) – one photocopy per pupil

Review vocabulary

- Put all the insects flashcards on the board. The pupils say the words chorally and individually.
- Play *Memory numbers* with the pupils: put all the flashcards in a line on the board, then turn them face down with a number from 1 to 8 under each one. Say sets of three or more numbers: the pupils say the corresponding words in the same order.
- Leave the flashcards on the board to give the pupils ideas for the next activity.

Present the project

- Tell the pupils they are going to invent an insect. They can use the insects on the board for ideas.
- They are going to invent a name for the insect, draw it, and write sentences about it.
- Review the characteristics of insects – all have bodies in three parts (head, thorax, abdomen), antennae, and six legs. Some have wings.

PMB p23 / CB p34 Activity 16 Invent an insect.

- Give out the photocopies of the 'Invent an insect' template.
- Elicit ideas for insects.
- The pupils draw rough pictures of the insects first in their notebooks or on rough paper. While they are drawing, circulate around the class. Encourage the pupils to use their imagination for the colours of the insect and its name.
- Look at each of the rough drawings and tick each one when you think it is adequate.
- The pupils draw their final insects on the photocopy.
- Read the sentences from Activity Book page 41, Activity 18 again with the pupils.
- The pupils write sentences about their insect. They use the sentences on Activity Book page 41 as a model.

Display

- Display the insect projects in the classroom.
- Allow the pupils to move around the classroom, look at all the insects, and discuss them with their friends.
- Have a feedback session in which the pupils decide on the most beautiful insect, the most frightening insect, the funniest insect, etc. Ask the pupils to give reasons for their choices.
- Finally, ask the pupils to decide on the best project.

Lesson 11a (optional)

Learning through English (Extension)

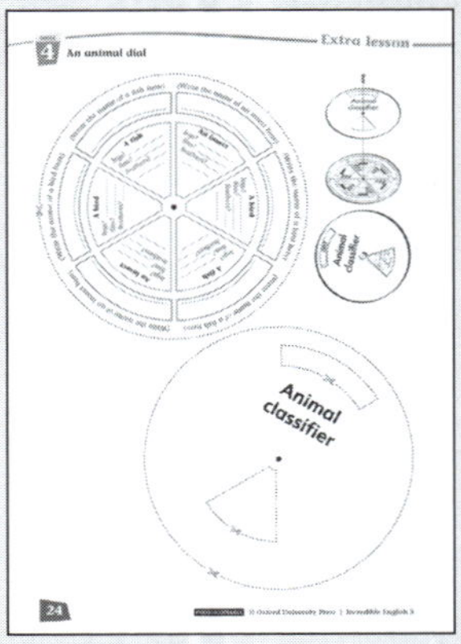

PMB page 24

Objectives

- Review insect vocabulary
- Review the characteristics of insects
- Learn about other types of animals (*fish, birds*)
- Learn the characteristics of these types

Core language

Review of
- insect vocabulary
- animal vocabulary
- language used so far

Other language

parts of an animal: *feathers, fins*

names of animals: *goldfish, salmon, cod*

Materials

Insects flashcards (x8); Scissors; Split pins – one per pupil; 'An animal dial' (PMB p24) – one photocopy per pupil (if possible, photocopy the template onto A3 rather than A4 paper)

Review vocabulary

- Use the flashcards to review the insect vocabulary: show the flashcards to the pupils and ask them to say the words chorally and individually.
- Ask pupils what they can remember about the characteristics of insects. Say *Insects have got …* and encourage the pupils to complete the sentence in as many different ways as possible, e.g. *… three body parts / six legs / a thorax / an abdomen / antennae.*

Preparation

- Talk with the pupils about different types of animals. Ask them to name as many different types of animal category as they can (e.g. insects, reptiles, mammals, fish, birds, crustaceans, etc.) and to tell you anything they know about the characteristics of the different categories.
- Tell them they are going to look at a few of the categories in more detail today: insects, fish, and birds.
- Write *fish* on the board, and ask the pupils for examples of fish in their own language. Give them at least two English words (for example, *goldfish / cod / salmon*).
- Write *birds* on the board, and ask the pupils for examples of birds in their own language. Give them at least two English words (for example, *parrot / canary / owl*).

PMB p24 Using the Photocopy Master

- Give each pupil a photocopy of the animal dial template, and a pair of scissors.
- The pupils cut out the bottom dial (with the text on it) and the top dial (with the title *Animal classifier* on it).
- Point to the outside edge of the bottom dial. Say *We are going to write the names of animals here.* Ask the pupils to suggest some insects, fish, and birds. Write their suggestions on the board and recast into English as necessary.
- The pupils choose two animals from each category and write them in the relevant places on the dial.
- Point to the inner section of the bottom dial. Read the three headings: *An insect, A fish, A bird.*
- Point to the first description word (*legs*). Ask *Have insects got legs?* The pupils answer *Yes.* Ask *How many?* The pupils answer *six*, and write *6* in the space for their insect boxes.
- Repeat with the other animal groups:
  birds (2)
  fish (0).
- Point to the second description word (*fins*). Make sure the pupils understand the meaning. Ask *Have insects got fins?* The pupils answer *No* and write the answer in the space.
- Repeat with the other animal groups:
  fish (yes)
  birds (no).
- Point to the third description word (*feathers*). Make sure the pupils understand the meaning. Ask *Have insects got feathers?* The pupils answer *No* and write the answer in the space.
- Repeat with the other animal groups:
  fish (no)
  birds (yes).
- Pupils cut out the top dial, including the 'windows', and draw some animals to illustrate the classifier.
- Give each pupil a split pin. They use it to make a small hole in the centre of each dial. Then they push the split pin through it to hold the two dials together.
- Show the pupils how to move the top dial round so that it shows the name of each animal, and the relevant information.
- Pupils use their dials to help them say sentences, for example *A grasshopper is an insect. It's got six legs. It hasn't got (any) fins and it hasn't got (any) feathers.*
- They can do this in pairs or you can select individual pupils to say sentences for the class.

Play a game

- Write *bird, insect, fish* on the board.
- Divide the class into two teams. Choose one pupil from each team and ask them to come to the front of the class with their dials.
- Say one of these descriptions, and ask them to tell you which of the animal categories on their dials it is:
  It's got two legs. It's got feathers. (a bird)
  It's got six legs. It hasn't got feathers. (an insect)
  It hasn't got legs. It's got fins. (a fish)
  It hasn't got fins. It hasn't got feathers. (an insect)
  It hasn't got legs. It hasn't got feathers. (a fish)
  It hasn't got fins. It's got feathers. (a bird)

- The pupils say *It's a (bird / insect / fish)* and put their hand on the correct word on the board. The first pupil to do this correctly gets a point for his / her team.
- The pupils can refer to their dials for help.
- Repeat with other descriptions and other pupils until all the pupils have had a turn.
- Add the scores to see which team won.

Song

- Ask the pupils *Can you remember the song in this unit?*
- Write what the pupils can remember on the board. Help them to remember the bits they've forgotten, then add them on the board.
- Play the song again (Listening 2.7). The pupils check that the version on the board is correct.
- Play the song again and encourage the pupils to join in.

Lesson 12

Review and self-evaluation

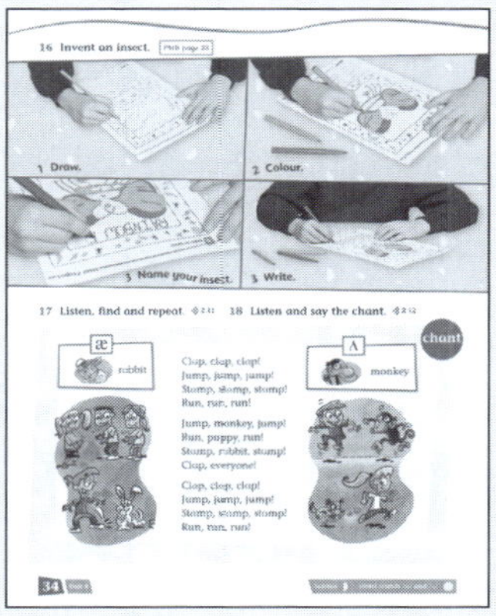

CB page 34

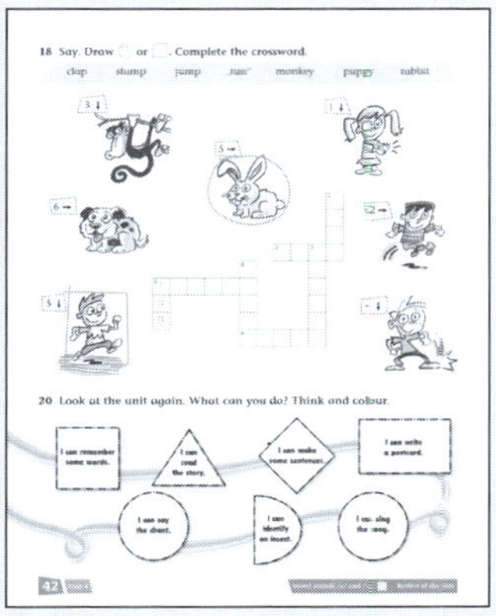

AB page 42

Objectives

- Focus on the pronunciation of vowel sounds (/æ/ and /ʌ/) with a chant
- Review the activities and the new language of the unit
- Complete a self-evaluation activity

Core language

Review of language used so far

Other language

clap, stamp

Materials

CD 2; Rollercoaster Game poster; Character counters and game cards; Dice (one pair per class); Picture dictionary page (PMB p2) – one photocopy per pupil (optional)

CB p34 Activity 17 Listen, find and repeat.

- Point to the pictures. The pupils say the words.
- Play the CD. Pupils point and repeat.

2.11

rabbit – clap – stamp [/æ/]
run – monkey – jump – puppy [/ʌ/]

- Say the two vowel sounds /æ/ and /ʌ/. The pupils find the words that share the vowel sound.
- The pupils practise saying the words chorally and individually, concentrating on the pronunciation of the vowel sounds.

CB p34 Activity 18 Listen and say the chant.

- Play the chant. The pupils point to the items as they hear them.

2.12

Clap, clap, clap!
Jump, jump, jump!
Stamp, stamp, stamp!
Run, run, run!

Jump, monkey, jump!
Run, puppy, run!
Stamp, rabbit, stamp!
Clap, everyone!

Clap, clap, clap!
Jump, jump, jump!
Stamp, stamp, stamp!
Run, run, run!

- Teach the chant line by line. Focus on the pronunciation points. Use choral and individual repetition to check pronunciation.
- Play the chant again and encourage the pupils to join in. This chant is ideal for using with mime actions; if you choose to do this, work out mime actions for each of the verbs (*clap, jump, stamp,* and *run*) after the pupils have said the chant chorally for the first time.

Focus on spelling

- Match the spelling with the vowel sounds.
- Highlight the spelling patterns:
  /ʌ/ is often spelt *u* (*run*) or *o* (*monkey*)
  /æ/ is often spelt *a* (*rabbit*)
- Show examples from the chant for each vowel sound.
- Remind the pupils that there are lots of exceptions to spelling patterns in English.

AB p42 Activity 19 Say. Draw ● or ■. Complete the crossword.

- Point to each of the pictures. The pupils say the words chorally.
- Focus on the pronunciation difference between /ʌ/ and /æ/, using the words *run* and *rabbit*.
- Show how *rabbit* has a circle around it and *run* has a square round it.
- Ask the pupils to identify a word with the /ʌ/ sound.
- Show the pupils how to put a square round the word.
- Repeat with the /æ/ sound, putting a circle around the word.
- The pupils put circles and squares around the words.
- Show the pupils the word *run* in the crossword. The pupils suggest a word for 5 across (*rabbit*).
- The pupils complete the crossword individually.
- Point to the pictures at random. The pupils say the words chorally and invidually. Check the pupils' pronunciation.

Answers: circle: clap, stamp, rabbit; square: jump, run, monkey, puppy
1 clap 2 jump 3 monkey 4 stamp 5 (across) rabbit
5 (down) run 6 puppy

End-of-unit review

- Use the Rollercoaster Game poster and the Class Book to recall the main activities of the unit.
- Recall the language associated with each activity.
- Ask the pupils to let you know what they liked or didn't like, and what they found easy or difficult.

Play the Rollercoaster Game

- Divide the class into small groups. Give each group one of the character 'counters' and let them play the game as before (see p41).
- Remind them to use the poster chants when a group gets a question right or wrong.

AB p42 Activity 19 Look at the unit again. What can you do? Think and colour.

- Let the pupils do the self-evaluation activity as before (see p41).

PMB p2 Picture Dictionary (optional)

- If your pupils are making Picture Dictionaries, give out the photocopies of the template.
- Pupils continue making the dictionaries as for Unit 1 (see p42).

Lesson 12a (optional)

■ = Words ◆ = Sentences

Show what you know!

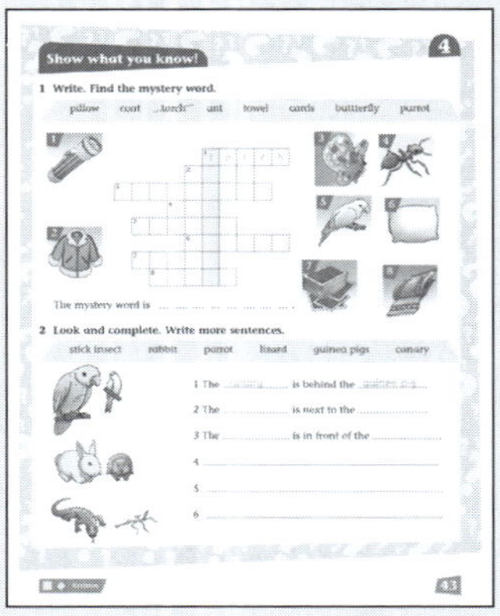

AB page 43

For suggestions on how to use *Show what you know!* see page 13.

Objectives

- Extra practice of the vocabulary of the unit
- Solve puzzles in English
- Provide extra material for homework and fast finishers

Core language

Review of language used so far

Materials

No extra materials

AB p43 Activity 1 Write. Find the mystery word.

- Read the words in the word pool to the pupils.
- Show the pupils how *torch* has been added to the crossword. Ask the pupils *What word goes in Number 2?* The pupils make suggestions and write in the answer (*coat*).
- The pupils complete the rest of the crossword individually, using words from the word pool.
- Show the pupils how there is a word going down, starting at the *t* of *torch*. Ask the pupils *What word is it?* The pupils say *tortoise* and write the word in the space.

Answer: **1** torch **2** coat **3** butterfly **4** ant **5** parrot **6** pillow **7** cards **8** towel
The mystery word is *tortoise*.

AB p43 Activity 2 Look and complete. Write more sentences.

- Read the words in the word pool to the pupils. The pupils identify the animals in the picture.
- Look at the first sentence and the example answers with the class.
- Ask the pupils to suggest words to go in the second sentence.
- Pupils complete the third sentence by themselves, and then write full sentences for numbers 4 to 6.

Answers: **1** The canary is behind the guinea pig.
2 (possible answer) The lizard is next to the stick insect.
3 (possible answer) The rabbit is in front of the parrot.
4–6 (possible answers) The stick insect is in front of the guinea pig. (etc.)

The pupils are now ready to sit the Unit 4 test. See pp182–185 for both Standard and Higher levels.

5 At the supermarket

Lesson 1 = Words

Introducing vocabulary

CB page 35

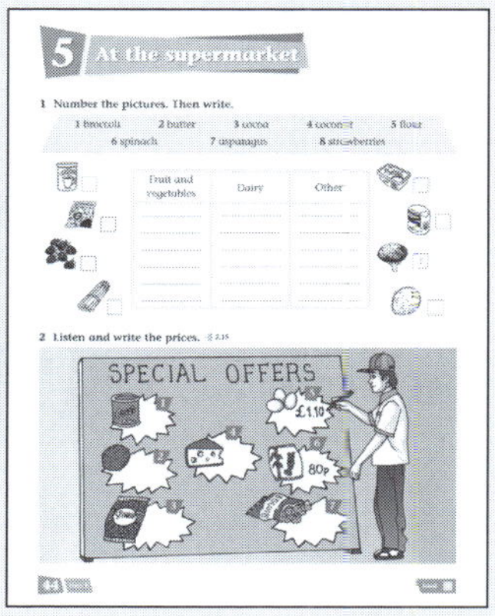

AB page 44

Objectives
- Understand the theme of the unit
- Become familiar with vocabulary for food
- Practise asking about the price of food
- Focus on spelling

Core language

Food vocabulary: *broccoli, butter, cocoa, coconut, flour, spinach, asparagus, strawberries*

Review of
- food vocabulary: *biscuits, sugar, cheese, eggs*
- language used so far

Other language

need, buy

Materials

Rollercoaster Game poster; Food flashcards (*broccoli, butter, cocoa, coconut, flour, spinach, asparagus, strawberries, biscuits, sugar, cheese, eggs*); CD 2; Pupils' bookmarks (optional) (see p28)

Unit overview
- Talk to the children about food. Ask them to say the words they know in English for food. Ask them what words they would like to learn.
- Ask the pupils to look through Unit 5 in their Class Books. Talk with them about the unit and quickly write the different topics and activities on the board, relating them to the shapes on the poster:
  - Words – food, parts of plants
  - Story – *A surprise for Finn*
  - Sentences – *He likes mice. He doesn't broccoli. Does he / she like …?*
  - Text work – recipes
  - Song – *I'm cooking in the kitchen* / Chant – *Pasta for my sister*
  - Other subjects – Science (identifying parts of plants)
- Remind the pupils that they will use the poster again at the end of the unit.

Introduce new vocabulary *see p19*
- Use the food flashcards to teach the new vocabulary. The pupils repeat the words chorally and then individually.
- Say each word and ask the pupils *What colour is it?* Decide on one colour for each food item (for example, the strawberry is red).
- Allocate one food item to each pupil and play *Colours* with the pupils: when they hear their colour, they say the word for their food.

CB p35 Activity 1 Look, listen and repeat.
- Play the CD. The pupils repeat each word chorally and point to the correct picture.

2.13

1 flour, 2 eggs, 3 cheese, 4 butter, 5 biscuits, 6 broccoli, 7 spinach, 8 strawberries, 9 sugar, 10 cocoa, 11 asparagus, 12 coconuts

CB p35 Activity 2 Listen and find.
- Explain that the children are buying food in a supermarket.
- The pupils listen for food words and point to the items they hear.
- Alternatively, the pupils can use their bookmarks to focus on the pictures.

2.14

Luke: I've got butter and sugar and eggs.
Jazmin: We need flour. Where's the flour?
Luke: Here. No, that's cocoa. Oh look, here's the flour
Jazmin: How much is flour?
Luke: Ninety p.

Jazmin: We need strawberries too.
Luke: Oh yes. How much are strawberries?
Jazmin: One pound fifty.
Luke: OK.

Eve: OK. I've got cheese … and a coconut … and broccoli.
Archie: What's this, Eve?
Eve: It's spinach.
Archie: Oh. I like spinach. And look – here's some asparagus.
Eve: Yum! How much is asparagus?
Archie: It's two pounds.

Jazmin: Let's buy some chocolate biscuits.
Luke: Yum! I like chocolate biscuits.

CB p35 Activity 3 Ask and answer.
- Explain to the pupils how to say prices in English:
  90p is *ninety pence* or *ninety p*
  £1.50 is *one pound fifty* or *one pound fifty pence* (or *p*)
  £2.00 is *two pounds*.
- Introduce the dialogue with *How much …?* questions. Make sure the pupils understand that we ask about uncountable nouns (for example, *flour*) with *How much is …?* and about plural countable nouns (for example, *strawberries*) with *How much are …?*

Teaching tip

If you wish to practise identifying countable / uncountable nouns before practising the dialogue, put all the food flashcards on the board, and ask pupils to help you group them into the two categories.

- Practise the dialogue with different food items.
- The pupils practise asking and answering questions about prices in pairs.

Spelling

- Ask the pupils to identify:
  1 words that are similar in their language (highlight the differences in spelling)
  2 words with double letters (for example, *bro<u>cc</u>oli*)
  3 words that end with vowels (*broccol<u>i</u>, coc<u>oa</u>*)
  4 words that end in *-s* but aren't plural (*asparagu<u>s</u>*)

AB p44 Activity 1 Number the pictures. Then write.

- Read the words in the word pool to the pupils. Ask the pupils to match the words to the pictures.
- Read the categories (*Fruit and vegetables, Dairy, Other*) to the pupils. Ask *Which words go in the 'Fruit and vegetables' list?* The pupils choose suitable words.
- Repeat with the other categories.

Answers: Fruit and vegetables: spinach, strawberries, asparagus, broccoli, coconut; Dairy: butter; Other: cocoa, flour

Lesson 2 ■ = Words

Practising vocabulary

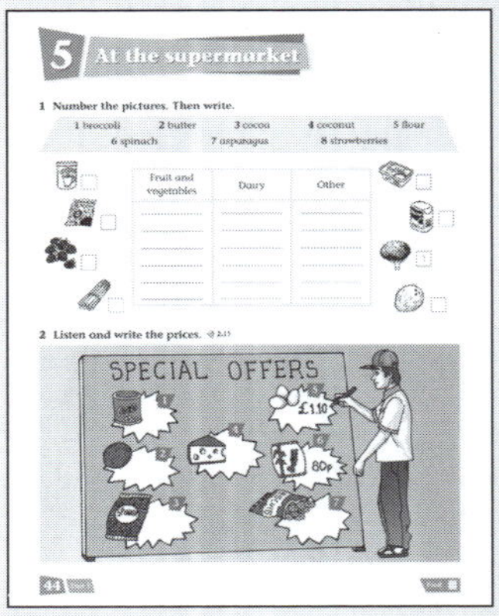

AB page 44

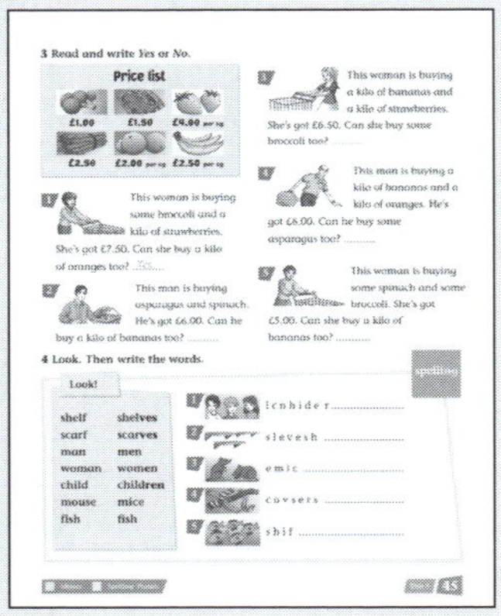
AB page 45

Objectives

- Review vocabulary for food
- Practise listening and talking about how much things cost
- Arrange vocabulary in pronunciation / spelling categories

Core language

Review of
- food vocabulary
- language used so far

Materials

Food flashcards (x12); CD 2; Food picture cards (PMB p25) – one photocopied set per pupil

Review vocabulary

- Put the food flashcards on the board. The pupils say the words chorally and individually.
- Place the flashcards in different parts of the classroom and play *Around the class* with the pupils. First you say the words and the pupils point to the flashcards. Then you point to the flashcards and the pupils say the words.

AB p44 Activity 2 Listen and write the prices.

- Point to each of the food items on the special offers board and ask *What is it?* The pupils say the name of the food.
- Point to the sugar and ask *How much is sugar?* The pupils answer *80 p / pence.*
- Play the first conversation. Show the pupils the price marked next to the sugar.
- Play the second conversation. After the conversation, ask *What are they talking about?* The pupils answer *eggs.* Ask *How much are eggs?* The pupils answer *one pound ten (pence).*
- Play the other conversations. Pupils write the prices.

2.15

Shop assistant:	How much is sugar?
Manager:	Eighty p.
Shop assistant:	Eighty p *(speaking slowly, as he writes).*
Shop assistant:	How much are eggs?
Manager:	One pound ten.
Shop assistant:	One pound ten …
Shop assistant:	How much are biscuits?
Manager:	Sixty-five p.
Shop assistant:	Sixty-five p …
Shop assistant:	How much is cheese?
Manager:	Two pounds.
Shop assistant:	Two pounds …
Shop assistant:	How much is cocoa?
Manager:	One pound thirty.
Shop assistant:	One pound thirty …
Shop assistant:	How much is spinach?
Manager:	One pound fifty.
Shop assistant:	One pound fifty …
Shop assistant:	How much is a coconut?
Manager:	One pound ninety.
Shop assistant:	One pount ninety … (*speaking slowly, as he writes*). Now I've finished. Thanks!

Answers: cocoa £1.30, cheese £2.00 (or £2), coconut £1.90, sugar 80p, biscuits 65p, spinach £1.50, eggs £1.10

AB p45 Activity 3 Read and write *Yes* or *No*.

- Point to the price list and ask questions such as *How much is broccoli?* Make sure the pupils express the money amounts correctly in their replies.
- Read the first question to the pupils. Go through the price of each item the woman is spending, like this:
  How much is broccoli? (£1.00)
  How much is a kilo of strawberries? (£4.00)
  What is the total? (£5.00)
  How much money does she have after she buys them? (£2.50)
  How much is a kilo of oranges? (£2.00)
  Can she buy a kilo of oranges? (Yes)
- The pupils answer the rest of the questions in pairs. When they have finished, go through each of the calculations with the whole class, as above, to check the answers.

Answers: 1 Yes (total £7.00) 2 No (total £4.00) 3 No (total £6.50) 4 No (total £4.50) 5 Yes (total £5.00)

AB p45 **Activity 4 Look. Then write the words.**

- Read each of the singular and plural forms to the pupils. Point out that:
  - words ending in *f* make the plural with *-ves* (*shelf – shelves*)
  - some words have irregular plurals (*man – men*)
- Point to the first picture. Ask the pupils *What are they?* The pupils say *children*. Ask them to look at the jumbled letters, and write the word on the line.
- Repeat with the other pictures.

Answers: 1 shelves 2 children 3 mice 4 scarves 5 fish

Spelling game

- Play a game using food vocabulary and plural forms which the pupils know. Say *this words begins with* (say the sound or the letter(s)). Pupils guess the word.

PMB p25 **Make the picture cards**

- Give out the photocopies of the food picture cards. The pupils colour and cut out the picture cards.
- They can use their cards to play a game, for example *Show me!* (see p21).
- If your pupils are using word cards, they can prepare them now (see p30). Pupils cut them out and match them with the picture cards.
- Remind the pupils to keep all the cards in a safe place.

Lesson 3 ▲ = Story

Story

CB page 36

CB page 37

Objectives

- Listen to a story
- Read a story
- Listen for words and phrases in a story
- Practise story language

Core language

Does he like marbles?; He likes mice.

Review of

- food vocabulary
- language used so far

Other language

mouse / mice, birthday, Happy Birthday!, present, delicious
Off you go; Ready, steady, go!; Look out!

Materials

Food flashcards (x12); CD 2

Review vocabulary

- Use the flashcards to review the food vocabulary. The pupils repeat the words chorally and then individually.
- Play *Memory words* with the pupils. Say sequences of three food words (for example, *broccoli, biscuits, flour*); the pupils repeat the words in the same sequence and point to the flashcards on the board.

Introduce the story

- Ask the pupils to imagine they are planning a birthday party for a friend. The pupils talk about what they need to do. Recast their answers if necessary.
- Explain that in the story the children are planning a birthday party.

CB pp36–37 **Activity 4 First listening with the books closed**

- Tell the pupils to listen and answer these questions: *What is Finn's present? What problem does it cause?*

2.16

[1] At the clubhouse …
Molly: What are you doing?
Luke: It's Finn's birthday today! We're making a cake.
Jazmin: Come and help!
Molly: OK!

[2] Molly: Butter and flour …
Jazmin: … and eggs and sugar.
Luke: And strawberries, and cream … Oh. We haven't got any cream!

[3] In the supermarket …
Molly: Where's the cream?
Jazmin: It's here.
Luke: Let's buy a present for Finn.
Jazmin: Good idea, Luke.

[4] In the toy shop . .
Molly: Does he like marbles?
Jazmin: No, he doesn't.
Luke: He likes mice. Let's buy this mouse. It's funny!

[5] Jazmin: Here's Coco! Hello, Coco.
Luke: Look! Coco likes mice too!
Molly: No, Coco! That's not for you! It's for Finn!

[6] Later, back at the clubhouse …
All: Happy birthday, Finn!
Luke: We've got a present for you

[7] Finn: A mouse! Thanks, everyone.
Luke: Off you go, mouse. Ready, steady, GO!

[8] Finn: Coco, be careful!

[9] Jazmin: Look out!
Finn: Oh NO!

[10] Jazmin: Oh dear! What a mess!
Finn: Yum. This cake is delicious!
All: *(laughing)*

- Check the answer to your questions (*His present is a mouse. The cat tries to catch it*). Recast the pupils' answers if necessary.

CB pp36–37 **Activity 4 Second listening with the books open**

- Tell the pupils to open their books and look at the story.
- Ask questions about the story such as *What do they put in the cake?*
- Play the recording again while the pupils follow in their books.
- Go through any vocabulary queries with the class.

CB p37 Activity 5 Read and write *true* or *false*.

- Explain that the number of each sentence refers to the number of the picture in the story.
- Ask the pupils to read the first sentence, then look at picture 1. Ask *Is that true or false?* The pupils answer *False*.
- The pupils read the sentences and write the answers (*true* or *false*) in their notebooks.

Answers: **1** false **2** true **3** true **4** true **5** true **8** false **9** false

Fun expressions

- Write these 'fun expressions' from the story on the board:
  Ready, steady, go!
  Look out!
  This cake is delicious!
- Play the story again: the pupils put up their hands when they hear one of the phrases.
- Pause the recording. The pupils repeat the phrase chorally and individually. Encourage the pupils to copy the intonation on the CD.

Lesson 4 ◆ = Sentences

Language focus 1

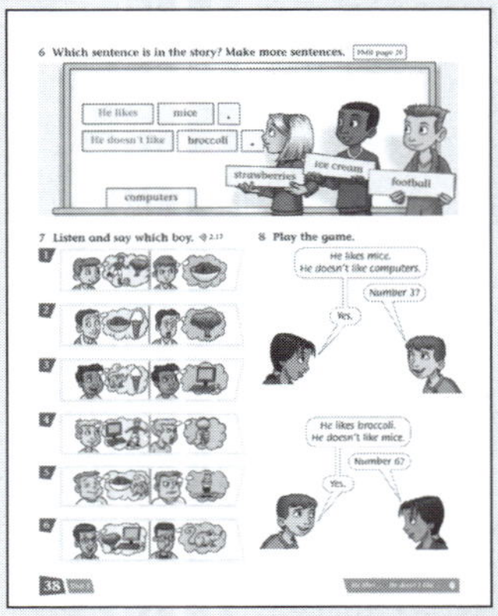
CB page 38

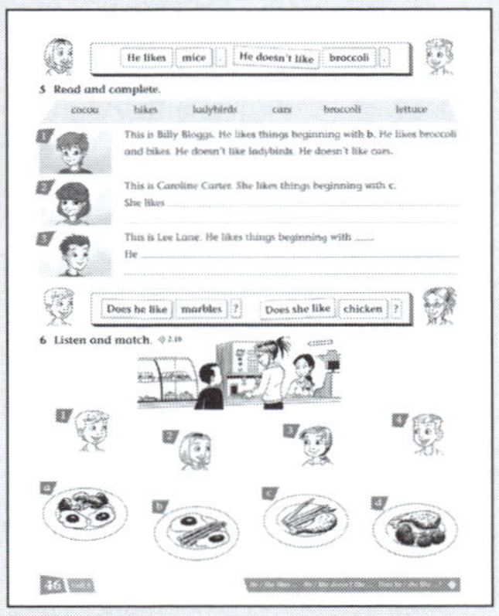
AB page 46

Objectives

- Understand the use of *He likes … / He doesn't like …*
- Practise using the new language

Core language

He / She
He likes … / He doesn't like …
Review of language used so far

Materials

Grammar tiles (PMB 26) – one photocopy of Set 1 per pupil (optional); CD 2

Recall the story

- Ask the pupils to remember as much as they can from the story.
- Say the following sentences from the story, and ask the pupils to identify who says each one:
  Let's buy a present for Finn. (Luke)
  Look! Coco likes mice too! (Luke)
  Ready, steady, go! (Luke)
  What a mess! (Jazmin)
  This cake is delicious! (Finn)

PMB p26 / CB p38 Activity 6 Which sentence is in the story? Make more sentences.

- Ask the pupils to read the sentences in the grammar tiles.
- Ask the pupils to say which sentence is in the story (*He likes mice*).
- Focus on the difference between the affirmative form (*He likes …*) and the negative form (*He doesn't like …*). Write the contraction and the short form on the board: *He doesn't like … = He does not like …* Use mime gestures to show how the long form 'contracts' to the short form.
- Make sure the pupils understand that the sentences could begin with *She*.
- The pupils say the sentences in the grammar tiles chorally and individually.
- The pupils make more sentences using the other tiles in the picture. Alternatively, give each pupil a copy of Set 1 of the grammar tiles from the PMB: the pupils cut out the tiles and arrange them in sentences on their desks. Ask individual pupils to read out their sentences for the class.

CB p38 Activity 7 Listen and say which boy.

- Show the pupils the pictures. Ask the pupils to talk about the first boy (*He likes broccoli. He doesn't like strawberries,* etc.).
- Play the first set of sentences on the CD. The pupils say which boy it is.
- Repeat with the other sentences.

2.17

Jazmin: He likes computers. He doesn't like ice cream.
Presenter: Which boy is it?

Luke: He likes mice. He doesn't like football.
Presenter: Which boy is it?

Jazmin: He likes broccoli. He doesn't like strawberries.
Presenter: Which boy is it?

Luke: He likes ice cream. He doesn't like broccoli.
Presenter: Which boy is it?

Answers: **1** picture 4 **2** picture 5 **3** picture 1 **4** picture 2

CB p38 Activity 8 Play the game.

- Read the conversation to the pupils.
- Say you are thinking of a picture. Say two sentences about it.
- The pupils identify the picture you are thinking of.
- The pupils play the game in pairs.

AB p46 Activity 5 Read and complete.

- Read the words in the word pool to the pupils.
- Read the first text. Point out the *b*s in *Billy Bloggs, broccoli,* and *bikes*. Make sure pupils understand why Billy doesn't like *ladybirds* or *cars* (they don't begin with *b*).
- Read out the first part of the text about Caroline Carter. Ask pupils to suggest which things from the list she likes (*cocoa* and *cars*). Ask the pupils to suggest what she doesn't like. The pupils answer with anything that doesn't begin with *c*, for example *bikes, broccoli, ladybirds,* or *lettuce*. The pupils complete the text in their books.

- The pupils complete the third text in pairs. Call individual pupils up to the front to write a sentence each on the board.

Answers: Caroline – She likes cocoa and cars. She doesn't like bikes / broccoli / ladybirds / lettuce. Lee – He likes things beginning with l. He likes ladybirds and lettuce. He doesn't like cocoa / bikes / cars / broccoli.

- Encourage the pupils to invent new characters, for example: *This is Sam Stone. He likes things beginning with S. He likes strawberries and sweets. He doesn't like fish. He doesn't like oranges.*
- The pupils can also make up texts about themselves, using their first names, for example: *My name is Ana. I like things beginning with A*, etc.

Lesson 5 ◆ = Sentences

Language focus 2

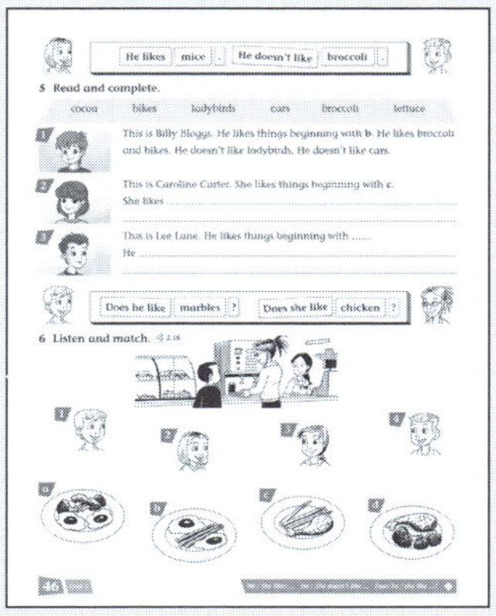
AB page 46

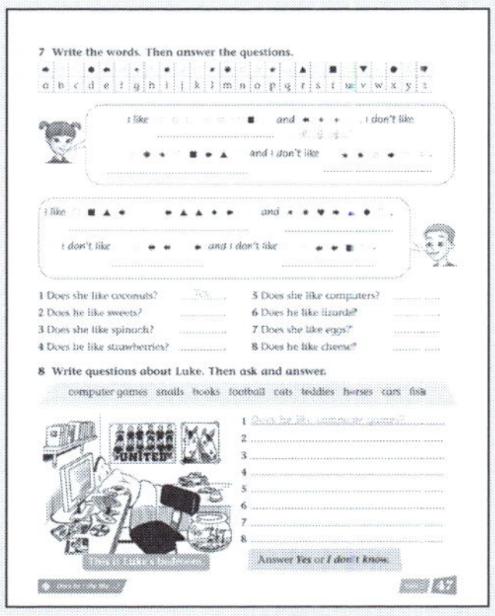
AB page 47

Objectives

- Review vocabulary for food
- Review *He likes … / He doesn't like …*
- Understand the question form *Does he like …?*
- Practise the question form

Core language

Does he like …?

Review of

- food vocabulary
- language used so far

Other language

plate, tray

Materials

Grammar tiles (PMB p26) – one photocopy of Set 2 per pupil; Pupils' grammar tiles (Set 1) from Lesson 4 (optional); CD 2

PMB p26 AB p46 Focus on language

- Read the questions in the second set of grammar tiles on Activity Book page 46 to the pupils. Ask the pupils *Which question is in the story?* (*Does he like marbles?*)
- Write *He likes marbles* on the board. Under this, write *Does he like marbles?* Show how we add *does* to make the question. Also show that the verb doesn't have *-s* in the question.
- The pupils say the questions in the grammar tiles chorally and individually.
- Give each pupil a copy of Set 2 of the grammar tiles from the PMB. Ask the pupils to suggest words to put in the blank tiles (*coconut, asparagus*, etc.). Write the suggestions on the board. The pupils can choose words to copy in the blank tiles.
- The pupils cut out all the tiles and use them to make sentences on their desks. Ask pupils to read out their sentences for the class.
- Pupils can combine the Set 2 tiles with some of the Set 1 tiles to make more questions, for example *Does he like broccoli?, Does she like football?*, etc.

Practice

- Call a pupil to the front. On one side of him, draw a happy face on the board and stick two of the food flashcards under it. On the other side, draw an unhappy face on the board and stick two of the food flashcards under it.
- Select a pupil and say *Make a question with 'Does he like …?'* The pupil says, for example, *Does he like broccoli?* Select another pupil to answer the sentence with *Yes* or *No*. Ask other pupils to make questions.
- Repeat with other pupils at the front, with other flashcards. Use girls and boys so that the pupils have to use *he* and *she*.

AB p46 Activity 5 Listen and match.

- Point to the picture of Eve and Archie. Ask the pupils *Who are they?* and *Where are they?*
- Point to the pictures of the other children. Ask the pupils *Who are they?*
- Explain that Eve and Archie are choosing meals for the rest of the club members. Play the first conversation. Ask the pupils *Which tray is it?* and *Who is it for?* The pupils answer *Tray D* and *For Luke*. They draw a line from Luke to tray D
- Repeat with the other conversations.

2.18

1 Eve: Come on, Archie. Let's get a plate for Luke.
Archie: OK. Which one?
Eve: Well, does he like chicken?
Archie: Yes.
Eve: Does he like asparagus?
Archie: No.
Eve: Oh … does he like broccoli?
Archie: Yes.
Eve: OK. Luke can have this plate.

2 Eve: Let's get a plate for Molly.
Archie: OK. Which one?
Eve: Well, does she like eggs?
Archie: Yes.
Eve: Does she like broccoli?
Archie: No.
Eve: Oh … does she like asparagus?
Archie: Yes.
Eve: OK. Molly can have this plate.

3 Eve: Let's get a plate for Jazmin.
Archie: OK. Which one?
Eve: Well, does she like broccoli?
Archie: Yes.
Eve: Does she like chicken?
Archie: No.
Eve: Oh … does she like eggs?
Archie: Yes.
Eve: OK. Jazmin can have this plate.

4 Eve: Let's get a plate for Finn.
Archie: OK. Which one?

Eve: Well, does he like asparagus?
Archie: Yes.
Eve: Does he like eggs?
Archie: No.
Eve: Oh … does he like chicken?
Archie: Yes.
Eve: OK. Finn can have this plate.

Answers: **1** d **2** b **3** a **4** c

AB p47 Activity 7 Write the words. Then answer the questions.

- Explain the code to the pupils. Show how each letter has a special symbol in the code. Draw some of the symbols on the board and ask *What letter is it?*
- Point to the first word in code. Ask the pupils *What word is this?* The pupils decode it and say the answer (*coconuts*).
- Repeat with the other words in code.

Answers: Girl – coconuts, eggs, computers, spinach; Boy – strawberries, lizards, cheese, sweets

- Read the first question and answer to the pupils.
- Read the second question. The pupils answer *No* and write the answer on the writing line.
- Repeat with the other questions.

Answers: **1** Yes **2** No **3** No **4** Yes **5** No **6** Yes **7** Yes **8** No

AB p47 Activity 8 Write questions about Luke. Then ask and answer.

- Read the words in the word pool to the pupils.
- Point to the computer games in the picture of Luke's room. Say *He has computer games in his room. Does he like computer games?* The pupils answer *Yes.*
- Say *There aren't any teddies in his room. Does he like teddies?* The pupils answer *I don't know.* (You will probably need to recast their answers. Discourage the pupils from saying *No*; make it clear that perhaps he likes them, perhaps he doesn't.)
- Say *Make a question about books.* The pupils answer *Does he like books?* Repeat with other items from the word pool.
- Write seven of the pupils' questions on the board. The pupils copy them in their Activity Books.
- Alternatively, the pupils can write the questions individually or in groups. Circulate around the class while they do this to check.
- Select one pupil to ask a question about Luke and another to answer it. Repeat with other pupils and other questions.
- The pupils practise the questions and answers in pairs.

Answers: (examples) Does he like football? Yes, he does. Does he like teddies? I don't know.

For extra grammar practice, see AB page 101.

Activity 1 Look and write.

Answers: **1** eggs **2** He likes cocoa. He doesn't like asparagus. **3** She likes strawberries. She doesn't like coconut. **4** He likes spinach. He doesn't like butter.

Activity 2 Write questions and answers.

1 ice cream? **2** Does she like cheese? No. **3** Does he like eggs? Yes. **4** Does she like oranges? Yes. **5** Does he like bananas? No. **6** Does he like biscuits? Yes.

Lesson 6 ▲ = Story

Playscript

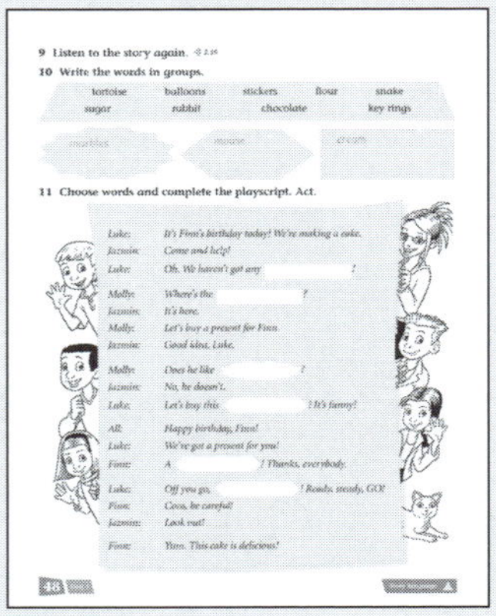

AB page 48

Objectives
- Read and complete a playscript
- Use finger puppets to act out a playscript
- Act out the play

Core language
Review of language used so far

Materials
CD 2; Spare photocopies of the finger puppets (PMB p3)

AB p48 Activity 9 Listen to the story again.

- Tell the pupils to look at pages 36–37 in the Class Book again.
- Play the CD while the pupils listen and read.
- Alternatively, the pupils can read the story aloud in groups of four. Each pupil should read one character.

AB p48 Activity 10 Write the words in groups.

- Read the words in the word pool to the pupils.
- Point to each of the boxes and read the word in each one. Ask the pupils to suggest words from the word pool to go in each box.
- The pupils write the words from the word pool in the correct category.

Answers: set 1 – marbles, stickers, balloons, key rings; set 2 – mouse, rabbit, snake, tortoise; set 3 – cream, chocolate, flour, sugar

- Ask the pupils to suggest new words for each category.

AB p48 **Activity 11 Choose words and complete the playscript. Act.**

- Read the playscript to the pupils. When you come to a blank, ask *Which word was in the story?* The pupils say the words from the story.
- Read the playscript again. Ask the pupils to suggest alternative words from Activity 10 to complete the blanks.
- Divide the pupils into groups of four. In their groups, the pupils decide which words to use when they read the playscript.

Finger puppets *see p22*

- Ask the pupils *How many characters are there in the story? (four, plus the cat).* The pupils identify the four characters (Molly, Luke, Jazmin, and Finn).
- In their groups, the pupils decide who is going to take each part. One pupil can also take the part of Coco the cat.
- If the pupils have got their finger puppets with them, tell them to get out the puppet for the character they are going to play.
- If the pupils haven't got their finger puppets, they will have to make them now. Give each pupil a photocopy of the finger puppets. The pupils cut out, colour, and stick the photocopy of the character they are going to play.

Practice

- Remind the pupils of the five points of successful play acting:
  1 Listen to the other actors.
  2 Wait for your turn.
  3 Speak clearly.
  4 When the puppets are speaking to each other, they should face each other.
  5 Don't move your puppets unnecessarily.
- Tell the pupils about the notes you made during the Unit 4 play acting. Encourage them to concentrate on the points you noticed. Say you will be watching them again this time.
- The pupils act out the play with their puppets. While they are doing this, circulate around the classroom. Make a note of the points the pupils should improve on next time.
- Ask one or two groups to come to the front to act out the play with their puppets.

Lesson 7 = Text work

Reading and writing

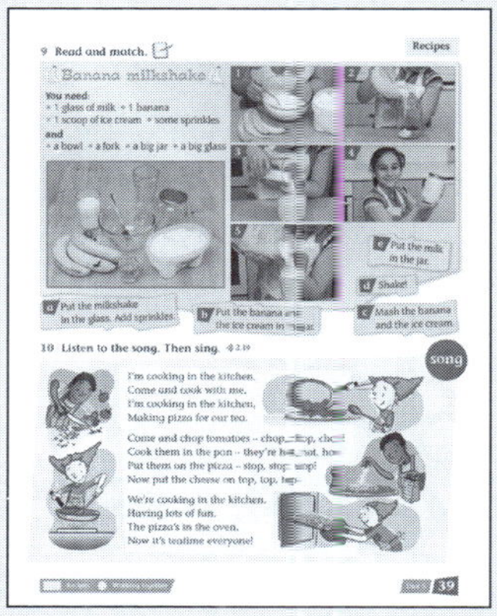

CB page 39

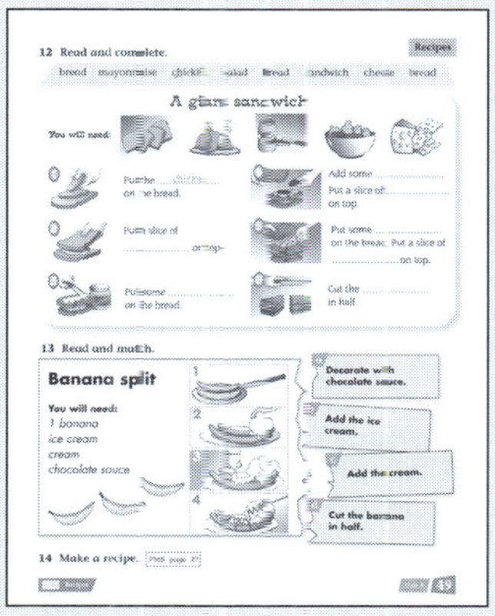

AB page 49

Objectives

- Review food vocabulary
- Read and understand a recipe
- Write a recipe

Core language

Review of language used so far

Other language

recipe, glass, scoop, sprinkles, bowl, fork, jar, mash, shake, salad, mayonnaise

Materials

Food flashcards (x12); Recipe template (PMB p27) – one photocopy per pupil

Review vocabulary

- Write the food vocabulary on the board like this: *b_____i, b_____r, c_____a*, etc.
- Call pupils to the front to complete the words.
- Call other pupils to the front to put the flashcards next to each word.

CB p39 **Activity 9 Read and match.**

- Talk with the pupils about recipes. Ask questions such as: Where can you find recipes? What recipes do people use in your house? Have you got a favourite recipe? Recast the pupils' answers as necessary.
- Point to the recipe in the Class Book. Explain that recipes usually have two parts: the ingredients and the instructions.
- Read the ingredients with the pupils. Explain any unfamiliar words.
- Read the first instruction (a). The pupils match the instruction with the picture (5).
- The pupils read the instructions and write the letter of the picture for each one in their notebooks.

Answers: 1 c 2 b 3 e 4 d 5 a

AB p49 **Activity 12 Read and complete.**

- Read the words in the word pool to the pupils.
- Read the list of ingredients for the sandwich, then read the first instruction. Start reading the second instruction (*Put a slice of …*). The pupils say *bread* and write it in the space. Repeat with the other instructions.

Answers: 1 chicken 2 bread 3 mayonnaise 4 salad, bread 5 cheese, bread 6 sandwich

AB p49 Activity 13 Read and match.

- Ask questions about the recipe such as *What is it for?* and *What are the ingredients?*
- Read the first instruction. The pupils match it with the picture (*4*) and draw a line from the instruction to picture 4.
- Repeat with the other instructions.

Answers: 1 d 2 b 3 c 4 a

PMB p27 / AB p49 Activity 14 Make a recipe.

- Explain to the pupils that they are going to write a recipe.
- Remind pupils that they have to choose work for their portfolio during the course (see p198). Point out that this piece of work would be a suitable piece to include.
- Brainstorm ideas for dishes, names, and ingredients for the recipe.
- Choose some suggestions and write them on the board.
- Show the pupils how to write the recipe, using the recipe in Activity 12 as a model.
- Hand out the photocopies of the writing template. Tell the pupils to choose another recipe and write and illustrate it (they should draw a picture at the top to illustrate the ingredients and then pictures for the different stages).
- The pupils write a rough copy in their notebooks for you to correct. After you have checked the rough copy, they write their final copy on the photocopied template.

Lesson 8 ● = Song / chant

Learning for life

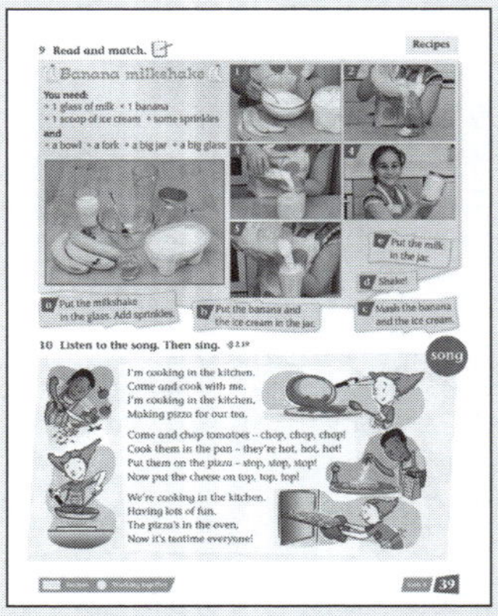

CB page 39

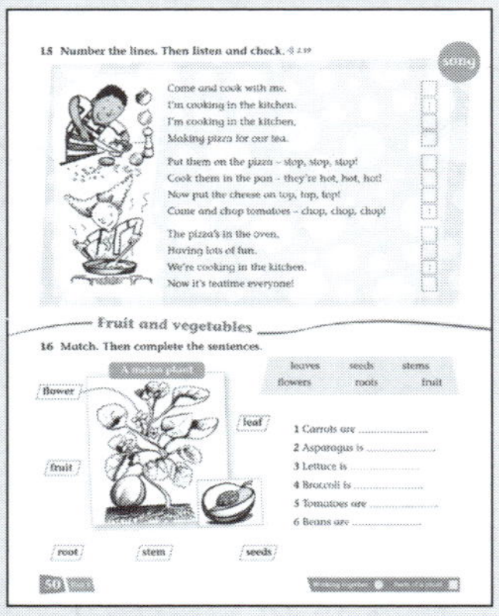

AB page 50

Objectives

- Review the unit so far
- Understand why working together is important
- Talk about ways of working together
- Sing a song about working together

Core language

Review of language used so far

Other language

chop, stop, top, teatime

Materials

Rollercoaster Game poster; Food flashcards (x12); CD 2

Unit review

- Use the Rollercoaster Game poster and the Class Book to review the unit so far. Talk with the pupils about the activities they have done.
- The pupils give examples of the language they used in each activity.

Review vocabulary (categorizing)

- Ask the pupil to tell you all the new words they remember from the unit.
- Put the food flashcards on the board and ask the pupils to arrange them in these two categories: *food I like* and *food I don't like.*
- Repeat with other categories, such as:
  I often eat … / I don't often eat …
  countable nouns / uncountable nouns.

Introduce the topic

- Talk with the pupils about working together. Ask questions such as: When do you work together? Why is it good to work together? Do you enjoy working together?
- Encourage the pupils to talk about some or all of these ideas in their answers:
  - we can help each other
  - we can do the work more quickly
  - we can divide the work
  - we can have more fun.
- The pupils can express their ideas in their own language. If they do, recast their answers in English.

CB p39 Activity 10 Listen to the song. Then sing.

- Read the song with the pupils. Explain any new words.
- Play the song on the CD.

2.19

Boy:	I'm cooking in the kitchen, Come and cook with me. I'm cooking in the kitchen, Making pizza for our tea.
Boy:	Come and chop tomatoes.
Boy and girl:	Chop, chop, chop!
Boy:	Cook them in the pan.
Boy and girl:	They're hot, hot, hot!
Boy:	Put them on the pizza.
Boy and girl:	Stop, stop, stop!
Boy:	Now put the cheese on …
Boy and girl:	Top, top, top!
Boy and girl:	We're cooking in the kitchen, Having lots of fun. The pizza's in the oven, Now it's teatime, everyone!

- Work out simple mime gestures for these words: *chop, hot, stop, top* in the song.
- Read through the song again and ask the pupils to use the mime gestures as you read.
- Play the song again and encourage the pupils to join in, singing and miming.

AB p50 Activity 15 Number the lines. Then listen and check.

- Tell the pupils to close their Class Books and open their Activity Books at page 50.
- Show them the lines of the song. Ask the pupils to find the first line of the song (*I'm cooking in the kitchen*).
- Ask them to find the next line (*Come and cook with me*) and to write *2* in the box next to it.

- Repeat until they have numbered all the lines of the song.
- Play the song again; the pupils check the order they suggested.
- To finish the lesson, divide the pupils into four groups. Give each group a number from one to four. The pupils say the whole song again, chorally, with each group doing the corresponding line of each verse (for example, group 1 says the first line of each verse, group 2 says the second line of each verse, etc.).

Answers: verse 1: 2 1 3 4 verse 2: 3 2 4 1 verse 3: 3 2 1 4

Lesson 9 = Words = Other subjects

Learning through English

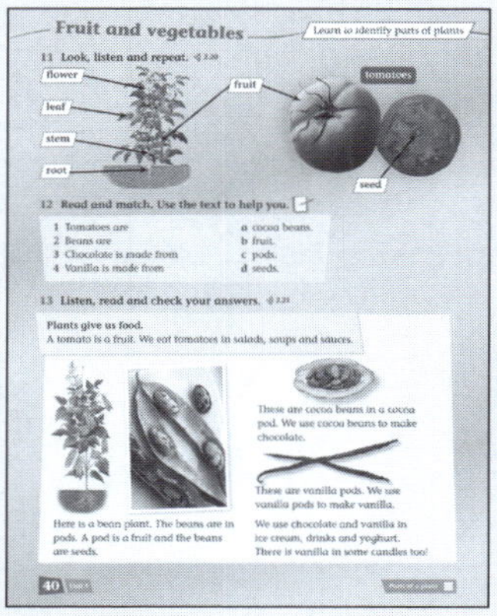

CB page 40

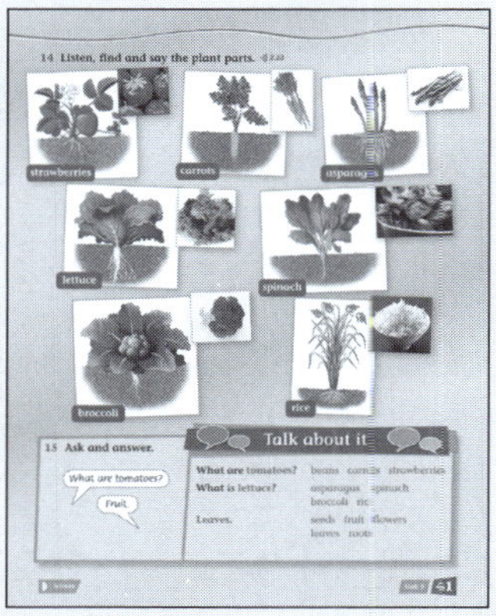

CB page 41

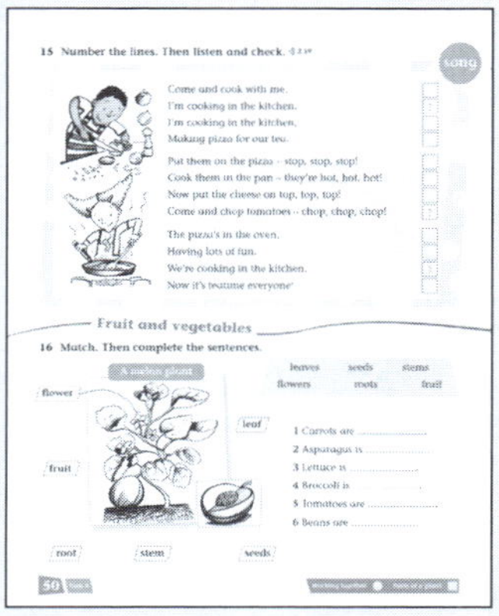

AB page 50

Objectives

- Learn some words for parts of plants
- Get to know, through English, about parts of plants that we eat
- Identify food plants as fruits, roots, stems, seeds, or leaves

Core language

Parts of a plant vocabulary: *flower, stem, root, fruit, leaf, seed*

Review of language used so far

Other language

bean, vanilla, pod, soup, sauce, candle, melon

Materials

Some fruit and vegetables: Parts of a plant flashcards (*flower, stem, root, fruit, leaf, seed*); CD 2; Parts of a plant picture cards (PMB p25) – one photocopied set per pupil

Introduce the topic

- Show the pupils the fruit and vegetables you have brought in. The pupils name them.
- Talk with the pupils about where the plants grow. Explain, for example, that a carrot grows under the ground, and a lettuce above the ground.
- Tell the pupils they are going to learn about the parts of plants.

Introduce new vocabulary *see p19*

- Show the flashcards for parts of a plant one by one to the pupils. Model the word for each flashcard clearly.
- The pupils repeat the words chorally and then individually.
- Play *What's missing?* with the pupils: take one of the flashcards from the pile, then put the other five flashcards on the board. The pupils say the word for the missing flashcard.

CB p40 Activity 11 Look, listen and repeat.

- Talk about the picture with the pupils. Explain that it's a tomato plant.
- Ask the pupils to show you the part you eat.
- The pupils listen to the recording. They repeat each word chorally and point to the correct part of the picture.

2.20

flower – leaf – stem – root – fruit – tomatoes – seed

CB p40 Activity 12 Read and match. Use the text to help you.

- Look at the split sentences with the pupils. Explain any new words.
- Ask the pupils to guess the answers (or they can quickly skim read the text in Activity 13 to help them). Write their answers on the board.

CB p40 Activity 13 Listen, read and check your answers.

- Explain to the pupils that they are going to read and listen to information about plants. They can use the information to check the answers on the board.
- Play the CD to the pupils. Go through the answers on the board and correct any that are wrong.

Answers: 1 b 2 d 3 a 4 c

2.21

Plants give us food.

A tomato is a fruit. We eat tomatoes in salads, soups and sauces.

Here is a bean plant. The beans are in pods. A pod is a fruit and the beans are seeds.

These are cocoa beans in a cocoa pod. We use cocoa beans to make chocolate.

These are vanilla pods. We use vanilla pods to make vanilla.

We use chocolate and vanilla in ice cream, drinks and yoghurt. There is vanilla in some candles too!

CB p41 Activity 14 Listen, find and say the plant parts.

- Show the pupils the pictures of the plants and the photos of the food that comes from them.
- Play the CD while the pupils listen, read, and point to the correct photo.

- The pupils repeat each answer chorally.

2.22

Child 1: What is rice?
Child 2: Seeds.

Child 1: What is asparagus?
Child 2: Stems.

Child 1: What are strawberries?
Child 2: Fruit.

Child 1: What is spinach?
Child 2: Leaves.

Child 1: What is broccoli?
Child 2: Flowers.

Child 1: What are carrots?
Child 2: Roots.

Child 1: What is lettuce?
Child 2: Leaves.

AB p50 Activity 16 Match. Then complete the sentences.

- Ask pupils if they recognize the plant (a melon plant). Read the words around the picture (*flower, stem, leaf,* etc.) to the pupils. The pupils draw lines from the words to the correct part of the plant.

Answers:

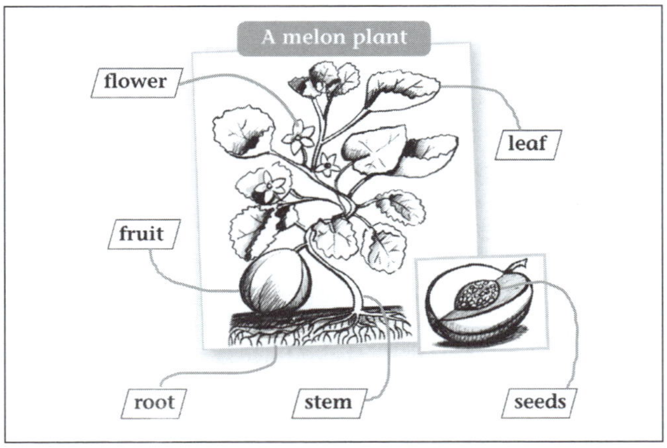

- Read the beginning of sentence 1. The pupils complete it with a word from the word pool (*roots*) and write the word on the line.
- Repeat with the other sentences.

Answers: **1** roots **2** stems **3** leaves **4** flowers **5** fruit **6** seeds

PMB p25 Make the picture cards

- Give out the photocopies of the picture cards for the parts of a plant. The pupils colour and cut out the picture cards.
- They can use their cards to play a game, for example *That's my word!* (word card version) (see p20).
- If your pupils are using word cards, they can prepare them now (see p30). Pupils cut them out and match them with the picture cards.
- Remind the pupils to keep all the cards in a safe place.

Lesson 10

= Words = Other subjects

Learning through English

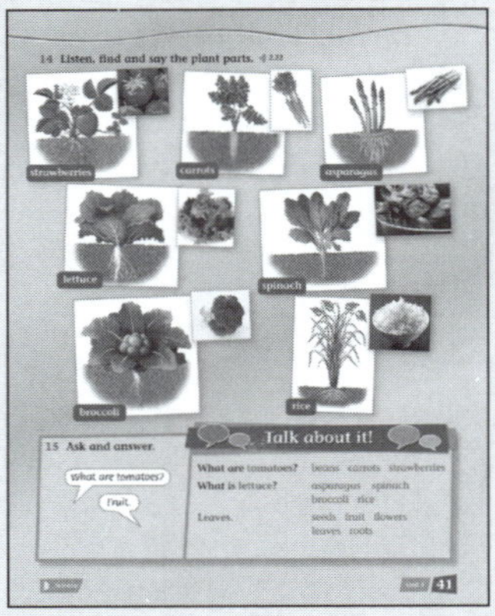

CB p41

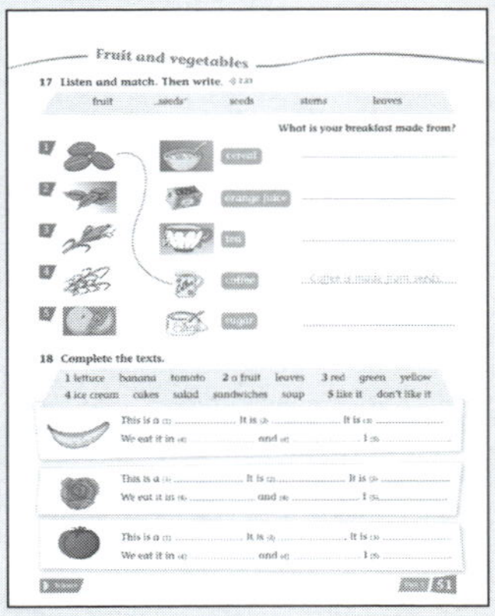

AB p51

Objectives

- Review food vocabulary
- Learn about how some types of food are made
- Describe food

Core language

Review of language used so far

Other language

maize, sugar cane, tea leaves, breakfast

Materials

Food flashcards (x12); Parts of a plant flashcards (x6)

Review vocabulary

- Stick half of the food flashcards and half of the parts of a plant flashcards on the board.
- Write up the words with jumbled letters.
- Ask pupils to come to the front to write the words and match them with the cards.
- Repeat with the other half of the flashcards.

CB p41 Activity 15 Ask and answer.

- Read the model conversation to the pupils.
- Ask a pair of pupils to have a similar conversation about carrots.
- Point out how the *Talk about it!* box gives them all the language they need.
- The pupils practise talking about fruit and vegetables in pairs.

AB p51 Activity 17 Listen and match. Then write.

- Read the words in the word pool to the pupils.
- Play the first conversation to the pupils. Ask *What do the seeds go with?* The pupils answer *coffee*. Point out how there is a line from the seeds to the coffee.
- Repeat with the other conversations. Pupils draw lines to link the items.

2.23

1 Child: What are these? Are they seeds?
Adult: Yes, they are seeds. They're coffee beans. We use coffee beans to make coffee.

2 Child: What are these?
Adult: They're leaves – tea leaves. We use tea leaves to make tea.

3 Child: What are these?
Adult: They're seeds – maize seeds.
We use maize seeds to make cereal for breakfast.

4 Child: What are these?
Adult: They're stems. It's sugar cane.
We use sugar cane to make sugar.

5 Child: Oh, an orange!
Adult: Yes, it's a fruit. We use oranges to make orange juice.

- Point to the coffee beans and the mug of coffee. Say *Coffee is made from seeds.* Write the sentence on the board. Point out the phrase *is made from*, and translate it into the pupils' own language if necessary.
- Say *Tell me about tea.* The pupils reply *Tea is made from leaves.* Recast their answers if necessary.
- Repeat with the other breakfast foods in the table. The pupils write the sentences on the writing lines.

Answers: 1 Coffee is made from seeds. 2 Tea is made from leaves. 3 Cereal is made from maize. 4 Sugar is made from stems. 5 Orange juice is made from fruit.

AB p51 Activity 18 Complete the texts.

- Read the words in the word pool to the pupils.
- Read the texts to the pupils. At each blank, ask the pupils to suggest a word from the appropriate group in the word pool (1–4). The pupils write the correct words in the blanks.

Answers: text 1: 1 banana 2 a fruit 3 yellow 4 ice cream, cakes 5 like it / don't like it. text 2: 1 lettuce 2 leaves 3 green 4 salad, sandwiches 5 like it / don't like it. text 3: 1 tomato 2 a fruit 3 red 4 salad, soup (pupils can also write 'sandwiches' here) 5 like it / don't like it.

Lesson 11 = Other subjects

Learning through English (Project)

CB page 42

Objectives

- Review vocabulary for food and parts of a plant
- Make a mini-book about fruit and vegetables
- Write about the fruit and vegetables

Core language

Review of language used so far

Materials

Food flashcards (x12); Parts of a plant flashcards (x6): Fruit and vegetable book template (PMB p28) – one photocopy per pupil

Review vocabulary

- Put the food flashcards and parts of a plant flashcards on the board. The pupils say the words chorally and individually.
- Play *Bingo* with the pupils: they choose six of the words and write them in the notebooks to use as their Bingo cards.

Present the project

- Tell the pupils they are going to make a mini-book about fruits and vegetables. They can choose the fruits and vegetables they write about.
- They are going to draw a picture of each one.
- They are going to write some sentences about each one.
- They are going to design and make a cover for their mini-book

PMB p28 / CB p42 Activity 16 Make a fruit and vegetable book

- Give out the photocopies of the mini-book template.
- Elicit ideas for fruit and vegetables to include in the mini-book.
- The pupils decide which fruit and vegetables they want to include. They draw rough pictures of them in their notebooks or on rough paper. While they are drawing, circulate around the class. Encourage the pupils to think about what part of the plant each one is, what colour it is, etc.
- Look at each of the rough pictures and tick each one you think is adequate.
- Show the pupils how to cut, fold, and stick the photocopy to make a mini-book.
- The pupils draw their final pictures in the mini-book.
- Read the sentences from Activity Book page 51, Activity 18 again with the pupils.
- The pupils write sentences about their fruit and vegetables. They use the sentences in Activity 18 as a model.
- The pupils write and draw a cover for their mini-book. They can add a title, for example *My book of fruit and vegetables.*

Display

- Display the mini-books in the classroom.
- Allow the pupils to move around the classroom, look at all the mini-books, and discuss them with their friends.
- Have a feedback session in which the pupils decide on the most attractive cover, the best pictures, and the best descriptions. Ask the pupils to give reasons for their choices. Finally, ask the pupils to decide on the best mini-book.

Lesson 11a (optional)

Learning through English (Extension)

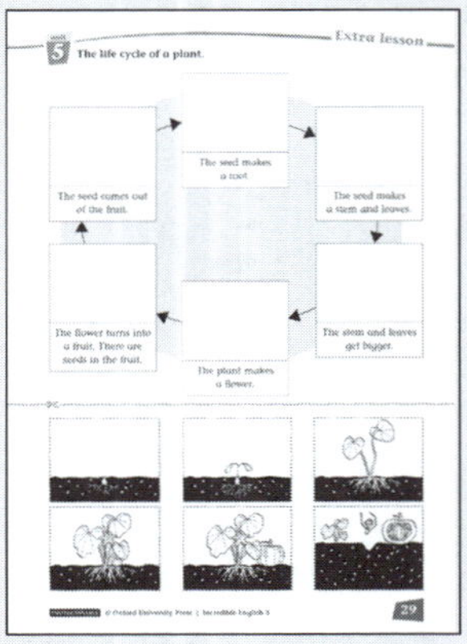

PMB page 29

Objectives

- Practise parts of a plant vocabulary
- Learn about the life cycle of a plant

Core language

Review of

- parts of a plant vocabulary
- language used so far

Other language

come out of, get bigger, turn into

Materials

Parts of a plant flashcards (x6); Some examples of seeds (for example, apple pips, orange pips, seeds from a garden flower); Scissors; Glue; 'The life cycle of a plant' (PMB p29) – one photocopy per pupil

Review vocabulary

- Review the parts of a plant vocabulary; show the flashcards to the pupils and ask them to say the words chorally and individually.

Preparation

- Show the pupils the seeds and write *seed* on the board. Ask questions such as *Where do we find seeds?* (In fruit) and *What are seeds for?* (They make new plants). Recast the pupils' answers as necessary.

PMB p29 Using the Photocopy Master

- Give each pupil a photocopy of the life cycle sheet and a pair of scissors.
- Read the sentences to the pupils. Use their own language to explain any sentences that aren't clear.
- The pupils cut out the pictures. Ask the pupils to match the pictures with the sentences.
- Hand out the glue. The pupils stick the pictures in the correct places to complete the life cycle.
- The pupils colour the pictures.
- The pupils take turns to read aloud one stage each of the life cycle.
- Ask the pupils to turn over their photocopies so they can't read them. Write the sentences from the Photocopy Master on the board with blanks, like this:

  1 The seed makes a ______.
  2 The seed makes a ______ and leaves.
  3 The stem and ______ get bigger.
  4 The plant makes a ______.
  5 The flower turns into a ______. There are ______ in the fruit.
  6 The ______ comes out of the fruit.

- Ask individual pupils to come to the front to complete the sentences.

Fun activity

- Copy the blank squares for this crossword on the board. Write the first letter of each word in the box.

						L	
				S	E	E	D
F	R	U	I	T		A	
L				E		F	
O				M			
W							
E							
R	O	O	T				

- Stick up the parts of a plant flashcards or write the words on the board as a reference
- Call pupils to the front of the class to complete the words.

Play a game

- Write the words *leaf*, *root*, and *fruit* on the board. Divide the class into two teams.
- Call one pupil from each team up to the front. Say a vegetable or fruit, such as *carrot*; the first pupil to say what it is (in this case, *root*) and put his / her hand on the word gets a point for his / her team.
- Continue with other fruits and vegetables until all the pupils have had a turn. Add up the points to find out which team won.

Song

- Ask the pupils *Can you remember the song in this unit?*
- Write what the pupils can remember on the board. Help them to remember the bits they've forgotten, then add them on the board.
- Play the song again (Listening 2.19). The pupils check that the version on the board is correct.
- Play the song again and encourage the pupils to join in.

Lesson 12

Review and self-evaluation

CB page 42

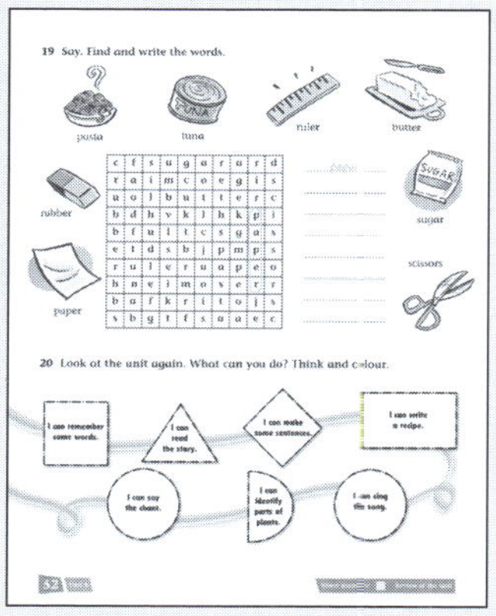

AB page 52

Objectives

- Focus on the pronunciation of a vowel sound (/ə/) with a chant
- Review the activities and the new language of the unit
- Complete a self-evaluation activity

Core language

Review of language used so far

Other language

paper, ruler, pasta, scissors, rubber

Materials

CD 2; Rollercoaster Game poster; Character counters and game cards; Dice (one pair per class); Picture dictionary page (PMB p2) – one photocopy per pupil (optional)

CB p42 Activity 17 Listen, find and repeat.

- Point to the pictures. The pupils say the words.
- Play the CD. Pupils point and repeat.

2.24

paper – rulers – pasta – sugar – scissors – rubbers – butter – tuna

- Say the vowel sound /ə/. The pupils practise saying the words chorally and individually, concentrating on the pronunciation of the vowel sound.

CB p42 Activity 18 Listen and say the chant.

- Play the chant. The pupils point to the items as they hear them.

2.25

Pasta for my sister,
Tuna for my brother,
Butter for my father,
Sugar for my mother!

Paper for my sister,
Scissors for my brother,
Rulers for my father,
Rubbers for my mother!

- Teach the chant line by line. Focus on the pronunciation point. Use choral and individual repetition to check pronunciation.
- Play the chant again and encourage the pupils to join in.

Focus on spelling

- Match the spelling with the vowel sound.
- Show the pupils that vowels *a*, *e*, and *o* can make this sound (*tun<u>a</u>*, *butt<u>e</u>r*, *sciss<u>o</u>rs*, etc.).
- Show the pupils that sometimes combinations of the vowels + *r* make this sound too.
- Remind the pupils that these vowels can make other sounds (*cat*, *pet*, *bath*, etc.).

AB p52 Activity 19 Say. Find and write the words.

- Point to each of the pictures. The pupils say the words chorally.
- Focus on the pronunciation of the schwa sound (/ə/) in the last syllable of all these words.
- The pupils repeat the word chorally and individually, concentrating on the schwa sound.
- The pupils find and circle the words in the wordsearch. They copy the words into the column.
- Point to the pictures at random. The pupils say the words chorally and individually. Check the pupils' pronunciation.

Answers:

c	f	s	u	g	a	r	a	r	d
r	a	i	m	c	o	e	g	i	s
u	o	l	b	u	t	t	e	r	c
b	d	h	v	k	l	h	k	p	i
b	f	u	l	t	c	s	g	a	s
e	t	d	s	b	j	p	m	p	s
r	u	l	e	r	u	a	p	e	o
h	n	e	i	m	o	s	e	r	r
b	a	f	k	r	i	t	o	j	s
s	b	g	t	f	s	a	a	e	c

End-of-unit review

- Use the Rollercoaster Game poster and the Class Book to recall the main activities of the unit.
- Recall the language associated with each activity.
- Ask the pupils to let you know what they liked or didn't like, and what they found easy or difficult.

Play the Rollercoaster Game

- Divide the class into small groups. Give each group one of the character 'counters' and let them play the game as before (see p41).
- Remind them to use the poster chants when a group gets a question right or wrong.

AB p52 Activity 20 Look at the unit again. What can you do? Think and colour.

- Let the pupils do the self-evaluation activity as before (see p41).

PMB p2 Picture Dictionary (optional)

- If your pupils are making Picture Dictionaries, give out the photocopies of the template
- Pupils continue making the dictionaries as for Unit 1 (see p42).

Lesson 12a (optional)

■ = Words ◆ = Sentences

Show what you know!

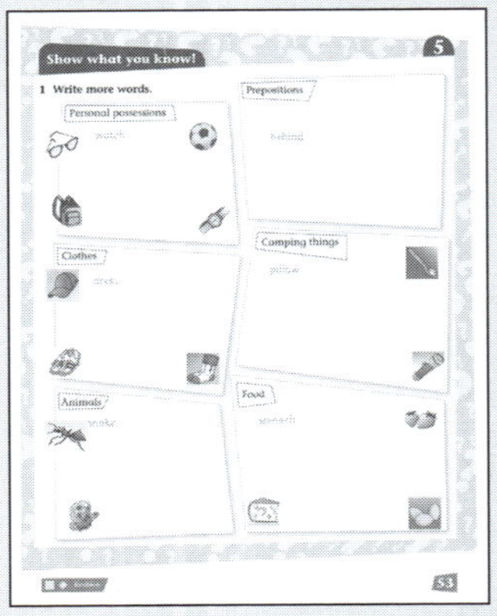

AB page 53

For suggestions on how to use *Show what you know!* see page 13.

Objectives
- Extra practice of the vocabulary of the unit
- Solve puzzles in English
- Provide extra material for homework and fast finishers

Core language

Review of language used so far

Materials

No extra materials

AB p53 Activity 1 Write more words.

- Look at the boxes for different vocabulary categories with the pupils.
- Point to the first box (*Personal possessions*). Read the word in the box (*watch*) and ask the pupils *Can you think of some more words for this box?* Write suitable suggestions on the board.
- The pupils copy the words from the board into the boxes.
- Repeat with the other boxes. Alternatively, the pupils can work in pairs or groups to complete the boxes.

Teaching tip

Pupils should be encouraged to classify the words in ways that make sense to them, rather than sticking rigidly to the categories in the book – e.g. *cat* (from Unit 1) would fit better in the 'Animals' category than the 'Personal possessions' category.

Answers: (these are suggested answers only – pupils may suggest more words from this level or previous levels, and they may choose to group them differently) Personal possessions: watch, sweets, glasses, skates, magazine, yo-yo, football, bike, car, bag; Prepositions: behind, in front of, next to, in, on, under; Clothes: belt, coat, gloves, scarf, shirt, tights, tracksuit, trainers, cap, dress, trousers, shoes; Camping things: pillow, blanket, comb, mat, pyjamas, sleeping bag, toothbrush, torch, towel, sunglasses, book, teddy; Animals: ant, fish, guinea pig, lizard, stick insect, tortoise, butterfly, canary, snail, rabbit, parrot, snake, fly, bee, ladybird, grasshopper, dragonfly; Food: spinach, broccoli, butter, coca, coconut, flour, asparagus, strawberries, biscuits, sugar, cheese, eggs

The pupils are now ready to sit the Unit 5 test. See pp186–189 for both Standard and Higher levels.

DVD VIDEO

Multimedia extension: you may now like to use the Science 1 section of the optional DVD.

6 Our town

Lesson 1 ▪ = Words

Introducing vocabulary

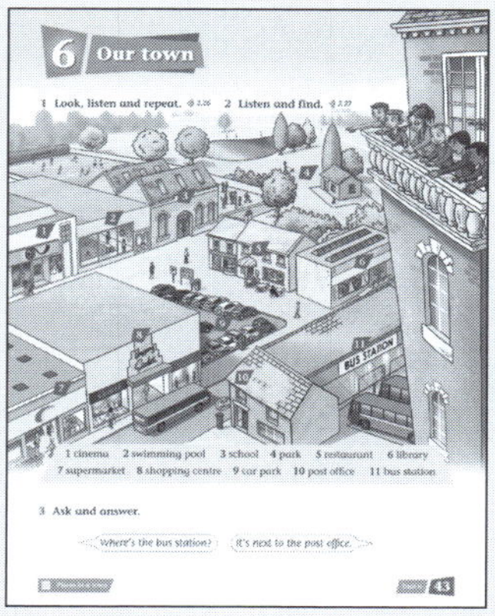

CB page 43

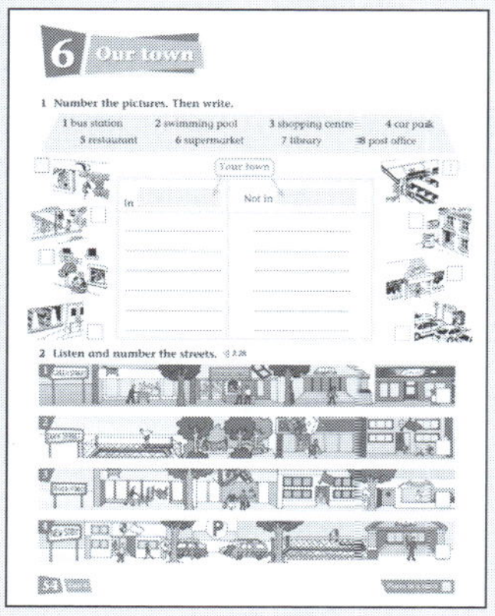

AB page 54

Objectives

- Understand the theme of the unit
- Become familiar with vocabulary for places in a town
- Practise listening to and asking where places are
- Focus on spelling

Core language

Places in a town vocabulary: *supermarket, swimming pool, restaurant, library, bus station, shopping centre, car park, post office*

Review of

- places in a town vocabulary: *school, park, cinema*
- prepositions: *next to*
- language used so far

Other language

our

Materials

Rollercoaster Game poster; Places in a town flashcards (*supermarket, swimming pool, restaurant, library, bus station, shopping centre, car park, post office, school, park, cinema*); CD 2; Pupils' bookmarks (optional) (see p28)

Unit overview

- Tell the pupils that they are going to talk about places in a town in this unit.
- Ask them to say the words they already know for places in a town.
- Ask them to say (in their own language) the words they would like to know.
- Ask the pupils to look through Unit 6 in their Class Books. Talk with them about the unit and quickly write the different topics and activities on the board, relating them to the shapes on the poster:
  - ▪ Words – places in a town, places in the countryside
  - ▲ Story – *The visitors*
  - ◆ Sentences – *There's a slide. There are eight swings. Is there a slide? Are there any swings?*
  - ▬ Text work – Web pages
  - ● Song – *Don't drop rubbish* / Chant – *I like scooters*
  - ◗ Other subjects – Geography (learn to find places on a map)
- Remind the pupils that they will use the poster again at the end of the unit.

Introduce new vocabulary *see p19*

- Use the flashcards to teach the new vocabulary for places in a town. The pupils repeat the words chorally, then individually.
- Work out a gesture for each place (for example, pushing a shopping trolley for the supermarket, swimming for the swimming pool).
- Play *Get moving!* with the pupils. First do the gestures and ask the pupils to say the place. Then ask individual pupils to do the gestures for the other pupils to guess.

CB p43 Activity 1 Look, listen and repeat.

- The pupils listen to the recording. They repeat each word chorally and point to the correct picture.

2.26

1 cinema, **2** swimming pool, **3** school, **4** park, **5** restaurant, **6** library, **7** supermarket, **8** shopping centre, **9** car park, **10** post office, **11** bus station

CB p43 Activity 2 Listen and find.

- Play the dialogue.
- The pupils listen for the places and point to each one in the picture.
- Alternatively, the pupils can use their bookmarks (see p28) to focus on the pictures.

2.27

Luke: Where's the swimming pool?
Finn: Over there. It's next to the cinema.
Luke: Oh yes!

Eve: I can see the library.
Molly: Where is it?
Eve: There. It's next to the park.

Finn: Where's the post office?
Luke: Er … it's next to the bus station.
Finn: Oh yes. Look at the buses – they're very small!

Jazmin: Where's our school?
Archie: Oh! … There! It's next to the swimming pool.

Eve: Where's the shopping centre?
Molly: It's next to the car park. Look.
Eve: Oh yes. And I can see the supermarket, too.

Archie: Oh, I can see my favourite restaurant!
Jazmin: Where?
Archie: There. It's next to the park.
Jazmin: Oh yes. I can see it. It's my favourite restaurant too!

Luke: Hey, I can see the clubhouse. Look.
Finn: Oh yes. And I can see Coco! She's next to the clubhouse.
Luke: Oh yes!
Finn: *(shouting)* Hello, Coco!
All: *(laughing)*

CB p43 Activity 3 Ask and answer.

- Review *next to* using the picture: point to places for the pupils to say *It's next to the …*
- Introduce the dialogue with questions such as *Where's the …?*
- The pupils answer your questions with complete sentences: *It's next to the …*

- Practise the dialogue with all the places.
- The pupils practise asking and answering the questions in pairs.
- As a variation, the pupils take turns to close their books and answer their partner's question from memory.

Spelling

- Ask the pupils to identify:
  1 words that are similar in their language (highlight the differences in spelling)
  2 places that are compound nouns (for example, *car park*)
  3 words with double letters (for example, *shopping*).

AB p54 Activity 1 Number the pictures. Then write.

- Read the words in the word pool to the pupils. Ask the pupils to match the words to the pictures.
- Read the categories (*In, Not in*) to the pupils. Ask *Which places have we got in our town / area?* The pupils choose suitable words.
- Ask *Which places haven't we got in our town / area?* The pupils choose suitable words.

Answers: (answers will depend on where the pupils live)

Lesson 2 ■ = Words

Practising vocabulary

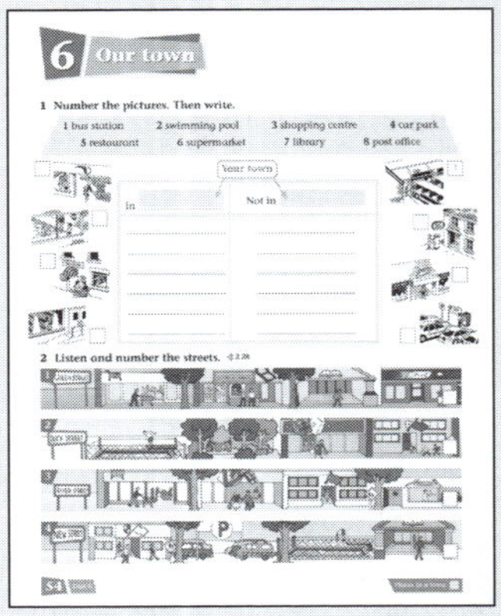

AB page 54

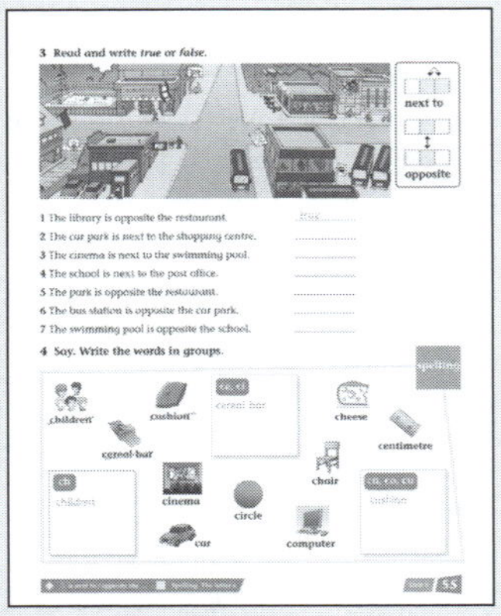

AB page 55

Objectives

- Review vocabulary for places in a town
- Practise listening and talking about the places in a street
- Read about the places in a street
- Arrange vocabulary in pronunciation / spelling categories

Core language

Prepositions: *opposite*

Review of

- places in a town vocabulary
- prepositions: *next to*
- language used so far

Other language

Excuse me?

Materials

Places in a town flashcards (x11); CD 2; Places in a town picture cards (PMB p30) – one photocopied set per pupil

Review vocabulary

- Stick the flashcards for places in a town on the board. The pupils repeat the words chorally and then individually.
- Give each pupil a number between 1 and 11. Put all the flashcards on the board and give each one a number between 1 and 11.
- Play a variation of *That's my word!* with the pupils: when they hear you say their number, they point to the flashcard on the board and say the word.

AB p54 Activity 2 Listen and number the streets.

- Point to each of the streets: the pupils say the name.
- Ask *What can you see in Green Street?* Repeat with the other streets.
- Play the CD. After each conversation, the pupils identify the street that the people are talking about. They number the streets in the order they hear about them.

2.28

1 Girl: Excuse me?
Adult: Yes?
Girl: Where's the shopping centre?
Adult: Look, over there. It's next to the park.
Girl: Oh, thank you.

2 Boy: Excuse me?
Adult: Yes?
Boy: Where's the library?
Adult: Look, over there. It's next to the swimming pool.
Boy: Thank you.

3 Girl: Excuse me?
Adult: Yes?
Girl: Where's the supermarket?
Adult: Look, over there. It's next to the cinema.
Girl: Oh yes, thank you.

4 Girl: Excuse me?
Adult: Yes?
Girl: Where's the school?
Adult: Look, over there. It's next to the restaurant.
Girl: Oh yes, thank you.

Answers: Duck Street – 1, New Street – 2, Green Street – 3, River Street – 4

- Play a guessing game: one pair of pupils choose a street and ask each other questions about the places in it, such as *Where's the supermarket?* The other pupils listen and guess the name of the street.

AB p55 Activity 3 Read and write *true* or *false*.

- Teach the pupils the meaning of *opposite*: point to the cinema and the post office in the map and say *The cinema is opposite the post office.* Repeat with other pairs of opposite buildings.
- Read the first sentence and ask the pupils if it is true or false. Show the pupils the answer (*true*) in the answer space.
- Repeat with the other sentences. The pupils write *true* or *false* after each one.
- With more confident groups, this activity can be done in pairs.

Answers: 1 true **2** false **3** true **4** true **5** false **6** false **7** true

AB p55 Activity 4 Say. Write the words in groups.

- Look at the three example answers with the pupils, and write them on the board. Point out the underlined key sounds in each one:
  cereal bar (/s/)
  cushion (/k/)
  children (/tʃ/)
- Select a pupil to read the next word from the word bank: *cinema*.
- Ask *Which group is it in?* The pupils identify the group. Ask *Why?*
- Recast the pupils' answers in this form: *That's right, the first sound is /s/ and the first letter is c.*
- Repeat with the other words.
- Call individual pupils to the front to write one word each in the correct category.

Answers: Box 1: cereal bar, cinema, circle, centimetre; Box 2: children, chair, cheese; Box 3: cushion, car, computer

Spelling game

- Play *Guess the word* using the words for places which the pupils know (see p20).

PMB p30 Make the picture cards

- Give out the photocopies of the picture cards for places in a town. The pupils colour and cut out the picture cards.
- If your pupils are using word cards, they can prepare them now (see p30). Pupils cut them out and match them with the picture cards.
- Remind the pupils to keep all the cards in a safe place.

Lesson 3 ▲ = Story

Story

CB page 44

CB page 45

Objectives

- Listen to a story
- Read a story
- Listen for words and phrases in a story
- Practise story language

Core language

There's a ... / There are ...; Is there a ....?

Review of

- places in a town vocabulary
- language used so far

Other language

visitor, late, enormous, slide, swings, good friends, train station

There aren't any ...; No, there isn't; No, it's mine! Me first!

Materials

Places in a town flashcards (x11); CD 2

Review vocabulary

- Stick the flashcards for places in a town on the board. The pupils repeat the words chorally and then individually.
- Take the flashcards down again and play *Just a little bit* with the pupils: cover each card with a sheet of paper and gradually lower the paper, showing more and more of the flashcard. The pupils try to guess what it is.

Introduce the story

- Ask the pupils to imagine some visitors are coming to their town or their school. The pupils suggest places for the visitors to see.
- Explain that in the story some visitors are coming to the town.

CB pp44–45 Activity 4 First listening with the books closed

- Tell the pupils to listen and answer this question: *Do the visitors like Middleton?*
- The pupils listen with their books closed.

2.29

[1]	At the bus station …	
	Eve:	Where are the visitors? They're late.
	Luke:	They're over there – on that bus.
[2]	Eve:	Welcome to Middleton.
	Jazmin:	Hi!
	Visitors:	Hello!
	Jazmin:	Come and see our town. It's great!
[3]	Luke:	Look! There's the toy shop!
	Visitor girl:	There's a VERY big toy shop in OUR town.
[4]	Jazmin:	This is the park. Look. There's a slide.
	Visitor boy 1:	Oh. There aren't any swings!
[5]	Visitor girl:	In our park, there are eight swings … and an enormous slide!
[6]	Eve:	Here's the train station. It's big!
	Visitor boy 2:	Is there an airport?
	Eve *(a bit crossly)*:	No, there isn't!
[7]	Back at the clubhouse …	
	Luke:	This is Coco the cat.
	Visitor boy 1:	There are TWO cats in our club. And a horse!
	Visitor girl:	The horse is mine.
	Visitor boy 2:	No, it's mine!
[8]	Visitor girl:	Oh, a computer! Let's play on the computer.
	Visitor boy 2:	OK. Me first!
	Visitor boy 1:	No! Me first!
[9]	Visitor girl:	At our club we've got SIX computers.
	Visitor boy 1:	… and a TV.
	Visitor boy 2:	What have you got?
[10]	Eve:	We've got …
	Children:	… very good friends!

- Check the answer to your question (*No, they don't*), and ask pupils to give reasons for their replies (e.g. the visitors have got more computers in their club, there isn't an airport, etc.). Recast the pupils' answers as necessary.

CB pp44–45 Activity 4 Second listening with the books open

- Tell the pupils to open their books and look at the story.
- Ask questions about the story such as *Are the visitors good friends?*
- Play the recording again while the pupils follow in their books.
- Go through any vocabulary queries with the class.

CB p45 Activity 5 Read and find the picture.

- Explain that each sentence refers to a particular frame in the story.
- Ask the pupils to identify the frame for the first sentence (frame 3).
- The pupils read each sentence and match it with a frame. This can be done as a whole-class activity or working in pairs.
- The pupils write the answers in their notebooks.

Answers: a 3 b 8 c 7 d 4 e 6 or 9 f 2 g 6

Fun expressions

- Write these 'fun expressions' from the story on the board:
  Come and see our town. It's great!
  OK. Me first!
  No, it's mine!
- Play the story again: the pupils put up their hands when they hear one of the phrases.
- Pause the recording. The pupils repeat the phrase chorally and individually. Encourage the pupils to copy the intonation on the CD.

Lesson 4 ◆ = Sentences

Language focus 1

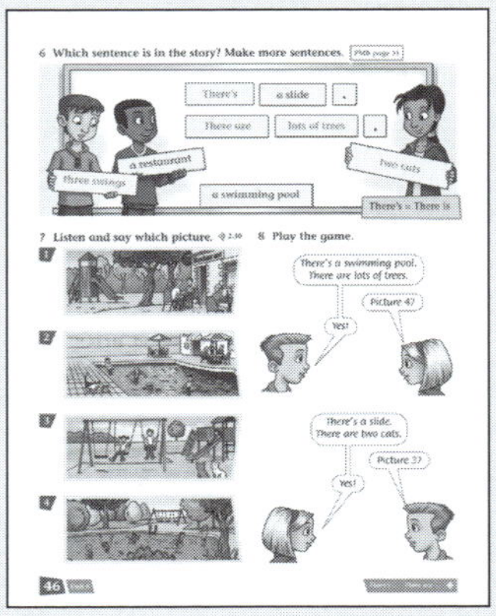

CB page 46

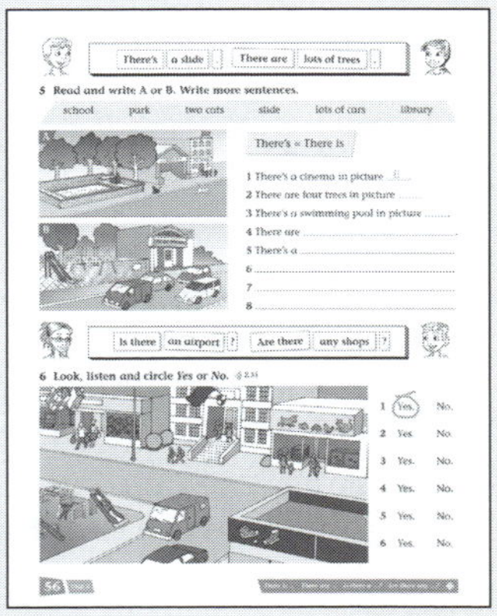

AB page 56

Objectives

- Understand the use of *There is* … and *There are* …
- Practise using the new language

Core language

There's … / There are …

Review of language used so far

Materials

Grammar tiles (PMB 31) – one photocopy of Set 1 per pupil (optional); CD 2

Recall the story

- Ask the pupils to remember as much as they can from the story.
- Say sentences with key structures such as:
  Come and see our town! (Jazmin)
  There's a very big toy shop in our town. (Visitor girl)
  There aren't any swings! (Visitor boy (1))
  In our park, there are eight swings. (Visitor girl)
  Is there an airport? (Visitor boy (2))
- The pupils identify who says each sentence (the pupils can identify the visitors as *one of the visitors*).

PMB p31 / CB p46 Activity 6 Which sentence is in the story? Make more sentences.

- Ask the pupils to read the sentences in the grammar tiles.
- Ask the pupils to say which sentence is in the story (*There's a slide*).
- Write the contraction and the long forms on the board: *There's = There is*. Use a mime gesture to show how the long form 'contracts' to the short form.

- Focus on the differences between the singular and plural forms. Establish the connection between *there is* with singular nouns and *there are* with plural nouns. Ask the pupils to suggest words that can be used with *there is* and *there are*.
- The pupils say the sentences in the grammar tiles chorally and individually.
- The pupils make more sentences using the other tiles in the picture. Alternatively, give each pupil a copy of Set 1 of the grammar tiles from the PMB: the pupils cut out the tiles and arrange them in sentences on their desks. Ask individual pupils to read out their sentences for the class.

CB p46 Activity 7 Listen and say which picture.

- Show the pupils the pictures.
- Play the first sentence on the CD. The pupils match it with the correct picture.
- Repeat with the other sentences.

2.30

Molly: There's a restaurant. There are two cats.
Presenter: Which picture is it?

Finn: There's a slide. There are three swings.
Presenter: Which picture is it?

Molly: There's a slide. There are two cats.
Presenter: Which picture is it?

Finn: There's a slide. There's a restaurant.
Presenter: Which picture is it?

Molly: There's a swimming pool. There are lots of trees.
Presenter: Which picture is it?

Answers: **1** picture 2 **2** picture 3 **3** picture 3 **4** picture 1 **5** picture 4

CB p46 Activity 8 Play the game.

- Read the conversation to the pupils.
- Say you are thinking of a picture. Say two sentences about it.
- The pupils identify the picture you are thinking of.
- The pupils play the game in pairs.

AB p56 Activity 5 Read and write A or B. Write more sentences.

- Read the first sentence (with the example answer) to the pupils. Show them that there is a cinema in picture B, but no cinema in picture A.
- Read the second sentence to the pupils. They identify the picture, A or B, and write the letter in the space.
- Repeat with the third sentence.
- The pupils write their own sentences about the pictures.

Answers: **1** B **2** A **3** A **4** (example) There are two cats in picture A. **5** (example) There's a park in picture B. **6–8** (examples) There's a school in picture A. There's a slide in picture B. There's a library in picture A. There are lots of cars in picture B. There are two swings in picture B.

Lesson 5 ◆ = Sentences

Language focus 2

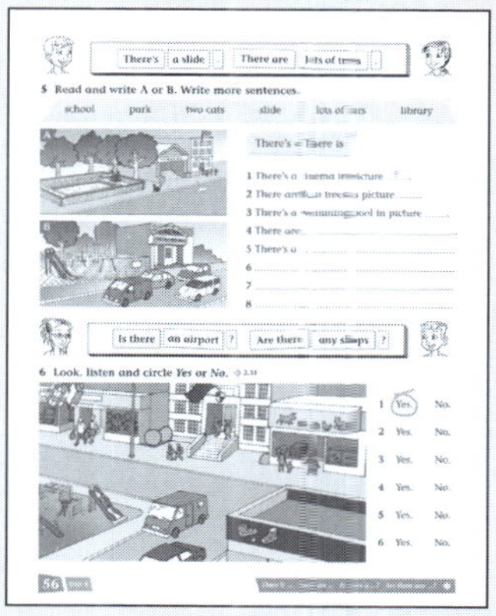

AB page 56

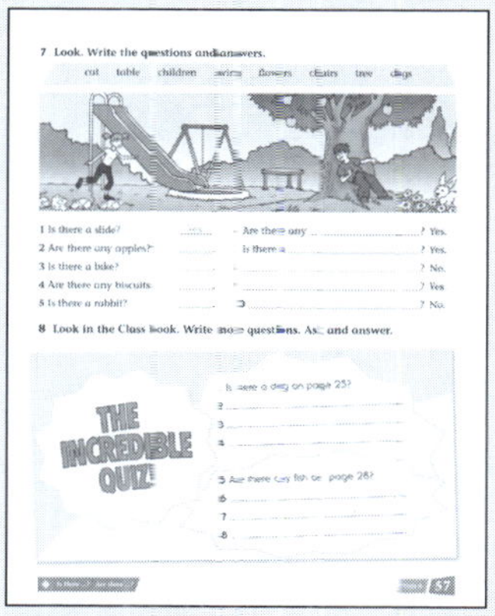

AB page 57

Objectives

- Understand the question forms *Is there a …?* and *Are there any …?*
- Review *There is …* and *There are …*
- Practise the question forms
- Practise asking and answering questions about a street

Core language

Is there an airport?; Are there any shops?

Review of

- places in a town
- language used so far

Materials

Grammar tiles (PMB p31) – one photocopy of Set 2 per pupil; Pupils' grammar tiles (Set 1) from Lesson 4 (optional); PMB town picture cards; CD 2

Recall *There is / are …*

- Say true or false sentences about the classroom, such as:
  There are twenty chairs.
  There's a slide.
- The pupils stand up if the sentence is true. If the sentence is false, they move their hand from side to side in front of their face to indicate *No*.

PMB p31 / AB p56 Focus on language

- Read the questions in the second set of grammar tiles to the pupils.
- Point out the question marks and explain that these sentences are questions.
- Ask the pupils to identify the question which is in the story (*Is there an airport?*).
- Write *There is a slide* and *Is there a slide?* on the board. Use a mime gesture to show how the order of *there* and *is* changes to make a question.
- Repeat with *There are twenty chairs* and *Are there any chairs?* Point out the use of *any* in plural questions.
- The pupils say the questions in the grammar tiles chorally and individually. Encourage them to use your mime gesture as they say each question.
- Give each pupil a copy of Set 2 of the grammar tiles from the PMB. Ask the pupils to suggest words to put in the blank tiles (*a car park, any cinemas, any libraries,*

etc.). Write the suggestions on the board. The pupils can choose words to copy in the blank tiles.

- The pupils cut out all the tiles and use them to make questions on their desks. Ask pupils to read out their questions for the class.
- Pupils can combine the Set 2 tiles with some of the Set 1 tiles to make more questions, for example *Is there a slide?*, *Are there lots of trees?*, *Are there three swings?*, etc.

Teaching tip

You can point out that although *any* is normally used in plural questions (*Are there any swings?*), it can be substituted by a number (*Are there three swings?*) or a phrase which describes quantity (*Are there lots of swings? / Are there many swings?*).

Practice

- Ask the pupils to help you make a list of things in the classroom (*pens*, *a table*, etc.). Write the list on the board.
- Write these two categories on the board: *singular nouns*, *plural nouns*. Call individual pupils to the front to write words from the list in the correct category. For example:

Singular nouns	*Plural nouns*
board	*pens*
teacher	*pencils*
bin	*books*

- Ask the pupils to suggest objects that are not in the classroom. They can make humorous suggestions such as *a crocodile*, *pyjamas*, etc.
- Point to items in the list and make a question, for example;
  board – Is there a board?
  pens – Are there any pens?
- The pupils answer *Yes* or *No*.
  Note: Some pupils may want to give complete answers (*Yes, there is / are. / No, there isn't / aren't.*) Accept both types of answer.
- Cue questions like this: *Make a question about chairs.* The pupils reply with *Are there any chairs?*
- Practise the questions and answers chorally, then select pairs of pupils to ask and answer questions.
- The pupils practise the questions in pairs.

AB p56 Activity 6 Look, listen and circle *Yes* or *No*.

- Point to the picture and say *Tell me about the picture.* The pupils make sentences with *There's* … and *There are* … (*There's a school. There are some shops*, etc.).
- Play the first conversation. The pupils answer *Yes* and circle *Yes* in their Activity Books.
- Repeat with the other conversations.

2.31

1 Adult: Look at the picture. Is there a park?
2 Adult: Are there any trees?
3 Adult: Is there a bus station?
4 Adult: Are there any shops?
5 Adult: Is there a school?
6 Adult: Is there an airport?

Answers: 1 Yes **2** No **3** No **4** Yes **5** Yes **6** No

AB p57 Activity 7 Look. Write the questions and answers.

- Read the words in the word pool to the pupils.
- Read the first question. The pupils answer *Yes* and write the answer on the line.
- Repeat with questions 2 to 5
- For questions 6 and 7, ask the pupils for suggestions to complete the question. Write suitable suggestions on the board. The pupils choose one suggestion for each question and write them on the lines.
- For questions 8, 9, and 10, ask the pupils to suggest questions. Write suitable questions on the board. The pupils copy a question onto each of the lines.

Answers: 1 Yes **2** Yes **3** No **4** No **5** Yes **6** Are there any flowers / children? **7** (example) Is there a swing / tree / table? **8** Are there any dogs / chairs? **9** (as for questions 6 and 7) **10** (example) Is there a cat?

AB p57 Activity 8 Look in the Class Book. Write more questions. Ask and answer.

- Read the first question to the pupils. Say *Look at page 25 in your Class Books. What's the answer?*
- The pupils answer *No.*
- Choose another page in the Class Book, for example, page 19. Ask the pupils to suggest questions with *Is there …*, for example *Is there a comb on page 19?* (*Yes.*) Select other pupils to answer the questions.
- The pupils write three more questions beginning *Is there …* on the lines.
- Read question 5 to the pupils. Say *Look at page 28 in your Class Books. What's the answer?*
- The pupils answer *No.*
- Choose another page in the Class Book, for example, page 32. Ask the pupils to suggest questions with *Are there any …?*, for example *Are there any insects?* (*Yes.*). Select other pupils to answer the questions.
- The pupils write three more questions beginning *Are there any …?* on the lines.
- Select individual pupils to read their questions and other pupils to answer them.
- The pupils ask and answer their questions in pairs.

Make a street

- Tell the pupils to get out their picture cards of places in a town.
- Make a 'street' with five of the cards, but don't let the pupils see it.
- The pupils ask questions about your street, in two stages:
- First they ask questions with *Is there …?* (*Is there a car park? Yes.*)
- Then they ask questions about positions with *Where …?* (*Where is the car park? It's next to the library.*)
- The pupils select and lay out the picture cards in the correct positions according to your answers.
- Draw your street on the board for pupils to check against.
- The pupils play the game in pairs.

For extra grammar practice, see AB page 102.

Activity 1 Look and write.

2 There are lots of girls. 3 There's a lizard. 4 There are lots of trees. 5 There are lots of apples 6 There's a swing.

Activity 2 Write questions and answers about your town.

Answers: 1 swimming pool? 2 there any car parks? 3 Is there a post office? 4 Are there any restaurants? 5 Are there any supermarkets? 6 Is there a library?

Pupils' own answers to the questions.

Lesson 6 ▲ = Story

Playscript

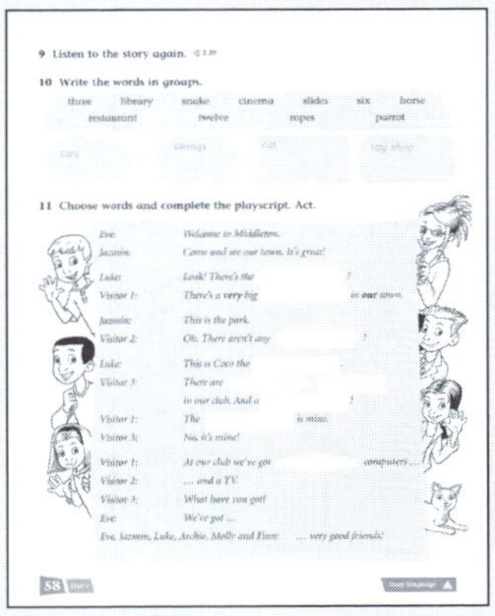

AB page 58

Objectives

- Read and complete a playscript
- Use finger puppets to act out a playscript
- Act out the play

Core language

Review of language used so far

Materials

CD 2; Spare photocopies of the finger puppets (PMB p3)

AB p58 Activity 9 Listen to the story again.

- Tell the pupils to look at pages 44–45 in the Class Book again.
- Play the CD while the pupils listen and read.
- Alternatively, the pupils can read the story aloud in groups of six. Each pupil should read one character.

AB p58 Activity 10 Write the words in groups.

- Read the words in the word pool to the pupils.
- Point to each of the boxes and read the word in each one.
- The pupils write the words from the word pool in the correct category.

Answers: set 1 – two, six, three, twelve; set 2 – swings, slides, ropes; set 3 – cat, horse, snake, parrot; set 4 – toy shop, library, cinema, restaurant

- Ask the pupils to suggest new words for each category.

AB p58 Activity 11 Choose words and complete the playscript. Act.

- Read the playscript to the pupils. When you come to a blank, ask *Which word was in the story?* The pupils say the words from the story.
- Read the playscript again. Ask the pupils to suggest alternative words from Activity 10 to complete the blanks.
- Divide the pupils into groups of four.
- In their groups, the pupils decide which words to use when they read the playscript.

Finger puppets *see p22*

- Ask the pupils *How many characters are there in the story? (six).* The pupils identify the six characters. (Eve, Jazmin, Luke, Visitor 1, Visitor 2, Visitor 3). Say *We have four pupils for six characters. It isn't a problem. Look!* Write this table on the board:
  Pupil 1 – Eve
  Pupil 2 – Jazmin and Visitor 1
  Pupil 3 – Visitor 3
  Pupil 4 – Luke and Visitor 2
- In their groups, the pupils decide who is going to take each part.
- If the pupils have got their finger puppets with them, tell them to get out the puppet for the character they are going to play.
- Give each group three photocopies of the extra finger puppet. The pupils cut out, colour, and stick the extra puppets to make the Visitor 1, Visitor 2, and Visitor 3 puppets. If they haven't got the other puppets they need, they will have to make those too.

Teaching tip

You may prefer to divide the class into groups of six for this playscript, to avoid Pupil 4 having to talk to him / herself in role as different characters.

Practice

- Remind the pupils of the five points of successful play acting:
  1 Listen to the other actors.
  2 Wait for your turn.
  3 Speak clearly.
  4 When the puppets are speaking to each other, they should face each other.
  5 Don't move your puppets unnecessarily.
- Tell the pupils about the notes you made during the Unit 5 play acting. Encourage them to concentrate on the points you noticed. Say you will be watching them again this time.
- The pupils act out the play with their puppets. While they are doing this, circulate around the classroom. Make a note of the points the pupils should improve on next time.
- Ask one or two groups to come to the front to act out the play with their puppets.

Lesson 7 = Text work

Reading and writing

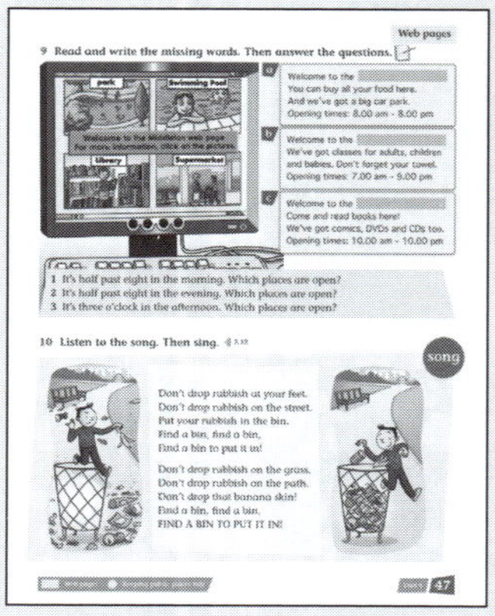

CB page 47

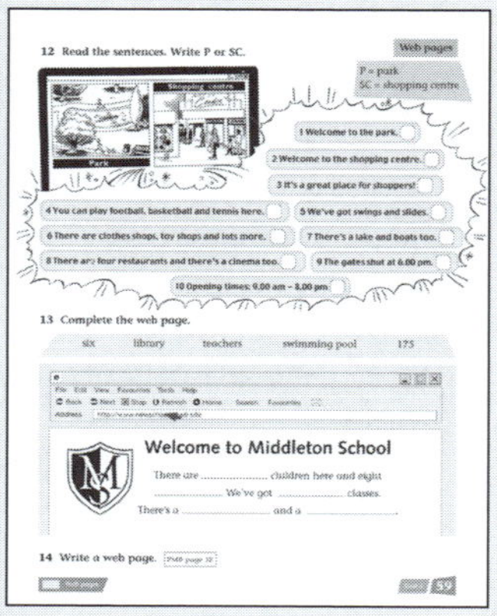

AB page 59

Objectives
- Review vocabulary for places in a town
- Read and understand a web page about a town
- Write a web page about a place

Core language
Review of language used so far

Other language
opening times, adults, babies

Materials
Places in a town flashcards (x11); Web page template (PMB p32) – one photocopy per pupil

Review vocabulary
- Stick the flashcards for places in a town on the board. Point to each one; the pupils say the words chorally.
- Write these words on the board: *buses, cars, tickets, books, trees, letters, ice cream, teachers, shops, biscuits, towels.* Teach the pupils the meaning of *tickets.*
- Call individual pupils up to the front and say one of the words in the list, for example *towels.* The pupil selects one or more flashcards to go with the word (in this case, *swimming pool*) and puts it next to the word.
- Repeat with other pupils and other words.

Answers: (examples) buses – bus station; cars – car park; tickets – bus station, cinema, library; books – school, library; trees – park; letters – post office; ice cream – park, restaurant, supermarket, cinema; teachers – school; shops – shopping centre; biscuits – supermarket; towels – swimming pool

CB p47 Activity 9 Read and write the missing words. Then answer the questions.
- Talk to the pupils about their favourite websites and other websites they visit.
- Explain the difference between a *website* (a set of connected web pages) and a *web page* (a single page that is part of a website).
- Ask the pupils about the web page on the screen. The pupils identify that it's about a town and name the places.
- Tell the pupils to read texts a–c and match them with the places on the web page. The pupils write the answers in their notebooks.

Answers: **a** supermarket **b** swimming pool **c** library

- Tell the pupils to read sentences 1–3 and say which places are open at these times.

Answers: **1** The supermarket and the swimming pool.
2 The swimming pool and the library.
3 The supermarket, the swimming pool and the library.

AB p59 Activity 12 Read the sentences. Write P or SC.
- Point to each picture and ask *What place is it?* The pupils identify the places as a park and a shopping centre.
- Read the first sentence with the pupils. They decide if it describes the park or the shopping centre, and write *P* or *SC* next to it.
- Repeat with the other sentences. More confident groups can do this work individually.

Answers: **1** P **2** SC **3** SC **4** P **5** P **6** SC **7** P **8** SC **9** P **10** SC

- Ask a pupil to read the sentences about the park, in the order they appear on the page. Point out how this makes a good description of the park.
- Repeat for the sentences about the shopping centre.

AB p59 Activity 13 Complete the web page.
- Read the words in the word pool to the pupils.
- Read the first part of the web page to the pupils (from *Welcome …* to the first blank). Ask *What number goes here? (175).* The pupils write the number in the text, then complete the rest of the text individually.
- Point out how the text is a good short description of a school.

Answers: There are 175 children here and eight teachers. We've got six classes. There's a library and a swimming pool.

PMB p32 AB p59 Activity 14 Write a web page.
- Explain to the pupils that they are going to write a web page about a place in their town.
- Remind pupils that they have to choose work for their portfolio during the course (see p198). Point out that this piece of work would be a suitable piece to include.
- Brainstorm ideas for places to write about, and for information to include for each place.
- Choose one and write the pupils' suggestions about it on the board.
- Show the pupils how to make complete sentences, using the texts in Activity 12 as a model.
- Hand out the photocopies of the writing template. Tell the pupils to choose another place and write about it.
- The pupils write a rough copy first in their notebooks for you to correct. After you have checked the rough copy, they write their final copy on the photocopied template.

Lesson 8 ● = Song / chant

Learning for life

CB page 47

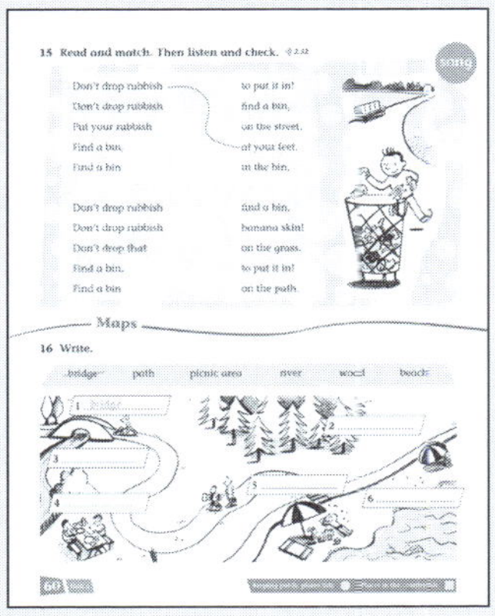

AB page 60

Objectives

- Review the unit so far
- Understand why litter in the street is a problem
- Talk about solutions for the problem
- Sing a song about keeping public places tidy

Core language

Review of language used so far

Other language

drop, rubbish, banana skin, street, path, Find a bin to put it in

Materials

Rollercoaster Game poster; Places in a town flashcards (x11); CD 2

Unit review

- Use the Rollercoaster Game poster and the Class Book to review the unit so far. Talk with the pupils about the activities they have done.
- The pupils give examples of the language they used in each activity.

Review vocabulary (categorizing)

- Ask the pupils to tell you all the new words they remember from the unit.
- Put the town flashcards on the board and ask the pupils to arrange them in these two categories: *near our school* and *not near our school.*
- Repeat with other categories, such as: commercial places and non-commercial places inside places and outside places

Introduce the topic

- Talk with the pupils about the problem of street litter in their town. Ask questions such as: Are the streets clean or dirty? What sort of rubbish is there? Do you prefer a clean or a dirty street? Why?
- Encourage the pupils to talk about some or all of these ideas in their answers:
  – too much packaging on the products we buy
  – irresponsible behaviour
  – selfish behaviour
  – litter ruins the appearance of our streets
  – litter encourages rats and other pests
  – enough / not enough litter bins on our streets
  – fines for people who drop litter.
- The pupils can express their ideas in their own language. If they do, recast their answers in English.

CB p47 Activity 10 Listen to the song. Then sing.

- Read the song with the pupils. Explain any new words (e.g. *drop, rubbish, street, banana skin*).
- Play the song on the CD.

2.32

Don't drop rubbish at your feet,
Don't drop rubbish on the street.
Put your rubbish in the bin –
Find a bin, find a bin,
Find a bin to put it in!

Don't drop rubbish on the grass,
Don't drop rubbish on the path.
Don't drop that banana skin!
Find a bin, find a bin,
FIND A BIN TO PUT IT IN!

- Work out simple mime gestures for the actions in the song, for example *drop rubbish* (mime throwing something down) *put your rubbish in the bin* (mime putting something in a bin), *find a bin* (mime looking around), *don't drop that banana skin* (mime slipping over).
- Read through the song again and ask the pupils to use the mime gestures as you read.
- Play the song again and encourage the pupils to join in, singing and miming.
- Have a follow-up discussion with the pupils. Encourage them to talk about these ideas:
  – why litter can be dangerous (people can slip on a banana skin or other rubbish)
  – if the pupils always use a litter bin.
  – what you can do if there isn't a litter bin (take the rubbish home)
  – if the pupils keep their school and classroom tidy.
- Recast their language as necessary.

AB p60 Activity 15 Read and match. Then listen and check.

- Tell the pupils to close their Class Books and open their Activity Books at page 60.
- Read the first sentence opener *Don't drop rubbish* to the pupils. Ask the pupils to recall the second part of the line. Write their suggestions on the board.
- Repeat with the other lines of the song.
- Play the song again; the pupils check their suggestions.
- Make any necessary corrections to the words on the board. The pupils then link the lines in their Activity Books.
- To finish the lesson, tell the pupils to close their books. Help them to say the whole song again, chorally, from memory.

Answers: (see song lyrics above)

Lesson 9 ▪ = Words ◗ = Other subjects

Learning through English

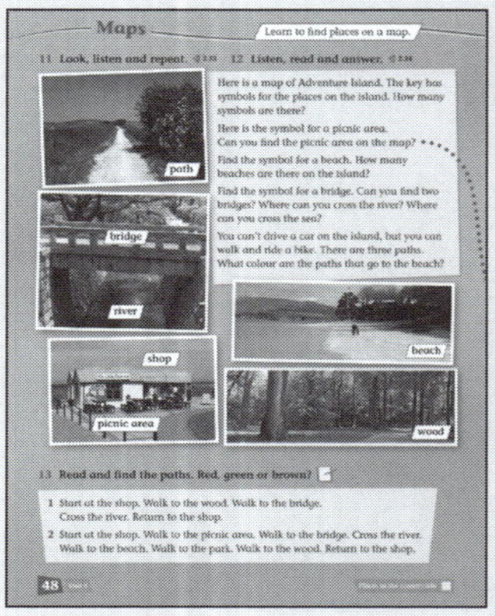

CB page 48

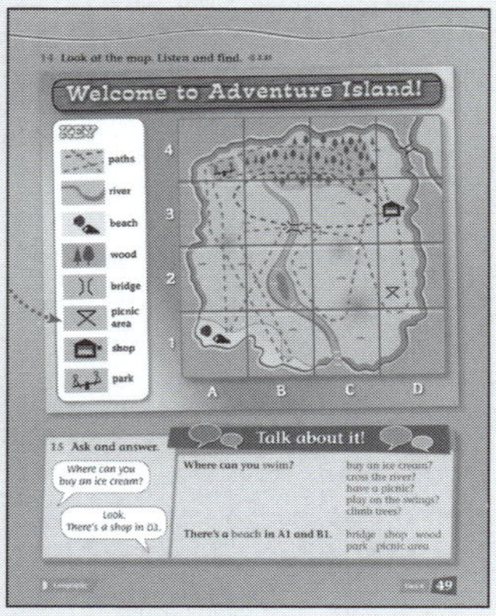

CB page 49

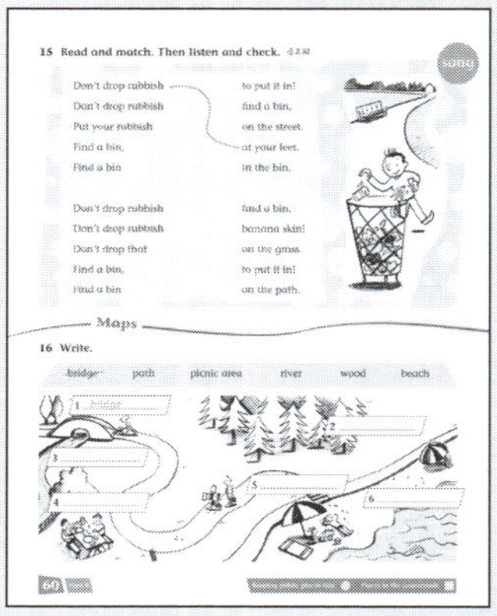

AB page 60

Objectives

- Learn some words for places in the countryside
- Identify symbols on a map using a key
- Use a key to find places on a map

Core language

Countryside vocabulary: *path, bridge, river, picnic area, beach, wood, shop*

Review of language used so far

Other language

map, adventure, island, key, symbol, cross (verb), drive, sea, return

Materials

CD 2; A map (or several maps, if possible, e.g. a world map, a country map, and a local map); Countryside flashcards (*path, bridge, river, picnic area, beach, wood, shop*); Countryside picture cards (PMB p30) – one photocopied set per pupil

Introduce the topic

- Show the pupils a map. Ask what it is used for.
- Discuss the information you can get from a map. Encourage the pupils to say these ideas:
  - You can see how to get to a place.
  - You can see what there is in a place.
  - You can see what kind of roads there are.
  - You can see hills and mountains.
  - You can discover the distances between places.
- If possible, show the pupils a variety of maps: a country map, a world map, a local map, etc.
- Tell the pupils they are going to use the sort of map that people use when they plan a walk. They're going to learn words for places in the countryside.

Introduce new vocabulary *see p19*

- Use the countryside flashcards to teach the new vocabulary. The pupils repeat the words chorally and then individually.
- Play *Just a little bit* with the pupils: cover each flashcard with a sheet of paper and gradually lower the paper, showing more and more of the flashcard. The pupils try to guess what it is.

CB p48 Activity 11 Look, listen and repeat.

- Play the CD. The pupils repeat each word chorally and point to the correct picture.

2.33

path – bridge – river – shop – picnic area – beach – wood

CB pp48–49 Activity 12 Listen, read and answer.

- Show the pupils the text on page 48, and the map on page 49.
- Play the CD while the pupils listen and read.
- Pause the CD after each question for the pupils to answer.

2.34

Here is a map of Adventure Island. The key has symbols for the places on the island. How many symbols are there?

Here is the symbol for a picnic area.
Can you find the picnic area on the map?

Find the symbol for a beach.
How many beaches are there on the island?

Find the symbol for a bridge. Can you find two bridges? Where can you cross the river? Where can you cross the sea?

You can't drive a car on the island, but you can walk and ride a bike. There are three paths.
What colour are the paths that go to the beach?

Answers: There are eight symbols. The picnic area is in D2. There is one beach on the island. You can cross the river in B3. You can cross the sea in D4. The paths that go to the beach are red and brown.

CB pp48–49 Activity 13 Read and find the paths. Red, green or brown?

- Show the pupils the different colours of the paths.
- The pupils read the route instructions and identify the paths by their colour.

Answers: 1 green **2** brown

AB p60 Activity 16 Write.

- Read the words in the word pool to the pupils.
- The pupils write labels for the pictures using the words in the word pool.

Answers: 1 bridge **2** wood **3** river **4** picnic area **5** path **6** beach

PMB p30 Make the picture cards

- Give out the photocopies of the countryside picture cards. The pupils colour and cut out the picture cards.

- If your pupils are using word cards, they can prepare them now (see p30). Pupils cut them out and match them with the picture cards.
- They can use their cards to play a game, for example, *Memory (pairs)* (see p20).
- Remind the pupils to keep all the cards in a safe place.

Lesson 10

■ = Words ◗ = Other subjects

Learning through English

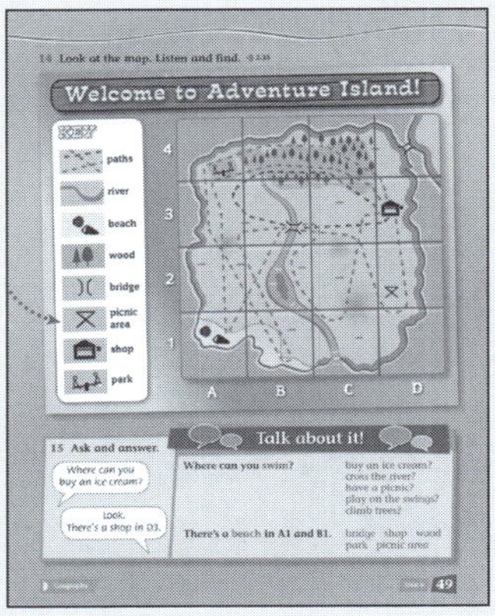

CB page 49

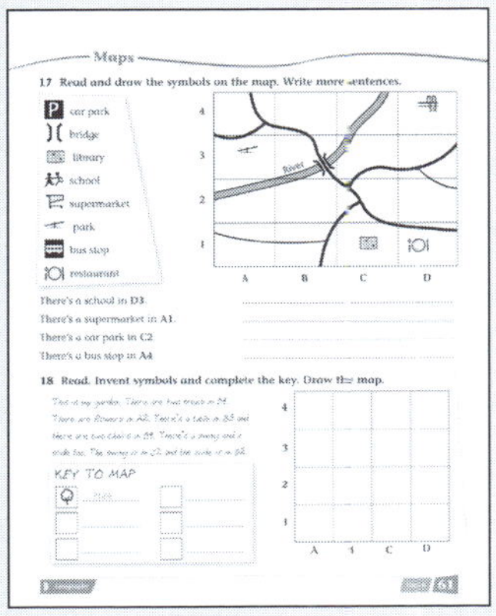

AB page 61

Objectives

- Use grid references to locate things on a map
- Complete a map using symbols and grid references

Core language

Review of language used so far

Materials

Places in a town flashcards (x11); Countryside flashcards (x7)

Review vocabulary

- Ask pupils to look at the map on Class Book page 49 again.
- Stick half of the town and countryside flashcards on the board.
- Write up the words with jumbled letters.
- Ask pupils to come to the front to write the words and match them with the flashcards.
- Repeat with the other half of the flashcards.

CB p49 Presentation of grid references

- Ask the pupils to look at the map on Class Book page 49 again.
- Explain that you can identify any square on the map with a letter and a number.
- If relevant, remind pupils of work they did on this in previous levels (Unit 9 in Levels 1 and 2).
- Explain that we say first the letter and then the number, and that this is a *grid reference*. (Note: this is a complex phrase for the pupils. To help them understand when you use it, write *grid reference* on the board, and point to it each time you say it in a sentence.)
- Give some grid references and check that the pupils can identify the symbol in that square on the map.
- Say some places on the map and ask the pupils to tell you the grid references.

CB p49 Activity 14 Look at the map. Listen and find.

- Tell the pupils to listen to the CD and point to the places.

2.35

Child 1: Where can you have a picnic?
Child 2: Look. There's a picnic area in D2.
Child 1: Oh yes.

Child 2: Where can you play on the swings?
Child 1: Er … there's a park in A4.

Child 1: Where can you swim?
Child 2: At the beach. There's a beach in A1 and B1.

Child 2: Where can you cross the river?
Child 1: Look. There's a bridge in B3.

Child 1: Where can you climb trees?
Child 2: In the wood. There's a wood in B4 and C4.

Child 2: Where can you buy an ice cream?
Child 1: Er … there's a shop in D3.

- Focus on the language, and how to use the grid references, in the dialogues (*Where can you …? / Look. There's a … in …*).

CB p49 Activity 15 Ask and answer.

- Read the model conversation to the pupils.
- Read *Where can you …?* and point to the first cue in the list (*buy an ice cream*). Elicit the dialogue from two pupils.
- Point out how the *Talk about it!* box gives them all the language they need.
- The pupils practise asking and answering about places on the map in pairs.

AB p61 Activity 17 Read and draw the symbols in the map. Write more sentences.

- Read the text with the pupils. The pupils add the missing symbols to the map.
- Guide the pupils to finding other places on the map which don't have a sentence about them.
- The pupils write more sentences about these other places.

Answers: four of the following sentences: There's a library in C1. There's a restaurant in D1. There's a swimming pool in D4. There's a park in A3. There's a bridge in B3.

AB p61 Activity 18 Read. Invent symbols and complete the key. Draw the map.

- Read the text with the pupils. The pupils identify the things in the garden (*trees, flowers, table, chair, swing, slide*).
- Help them to invent symbols for the objects in the text. Draw the new symbols on the board.
- The pupils copy the symbols onto the map, according to the text.

Lesson 11 = Other subjects

Learning through English (Project)

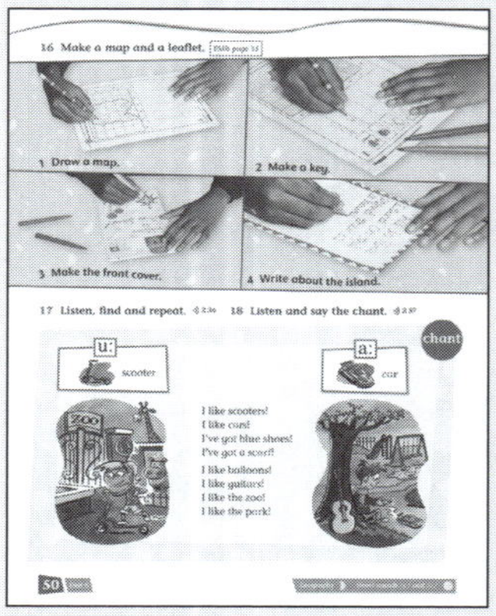

CB page 50

Objectives

- Review vocabulary associated with maps
- Invent symbols for a map
- Invent an island
- Draw a map of the island and write about it

Core language

Review of language used so far

Materials

Countryside flashcards (x7); 'Make a map and a leaflet' template (PMB p33) – one photocopy per pupil

Review vocabulary

- Use the countryside flashcards to review the vocabulary. The pupils repeat the words chorally and then individually.
- Ask the pupils what other things can be marked on a map (for example houses, parks, airports, railways, and hotels). Write the suggestions on the board.
- Call pupils to the front to draw new map symbols next to the new suggestions.

Present the project

- Tell the pupils they are going to invent an island. They can put anything they like on it.
- They are going to draw a map of the island and include symbols for the features, as well as a key.
- They are going to write some sentences about it for visitors.

PMB p33 / CB p50 Activity 16 Make a map and a leaflet.

- Give out the photocopies of the map grid.
- Elicit ideas for things to put on the map.
- The pupils draw rough maps first in their notebooks or on rough paper. While they are drawing, circulate around the class. Encourage the pupils to use their imagination in the shape of the island, its features, and the symbols they use for places on the map. Also encourage them to think about how you get to the island – by boat, bridge, aeroplane, etc.
- Look at each of the rough maps and tick each one when you think it is adequate.
- The pupils draw their final maps on the photocopy. They then complete and colour the key.
- Pupils cut out the template and fold it in half to form a leaflet (so the map and the key are on the inside).
- They illustrate the front of the leaflet, and write a title, e.g. *Welcome to Pirate Island.*
- Read the sentences from Activity Book page 61, Activity 18 again with the pupils.
- The pupils write sentences about their island on the back cover of the leaflet. They use the sentences in the Activity Book as a model.

Display

- Display the maps in the classroom.
- Allow the pupils to move around the classroom, look at all the maps and discuss them with their friends.
- Have a feedback session in which the pupils decide on the most attractive map and the most interesting island. Ask the pupils to give reasons for their choices. Finally, ask the pupils to decide on the best island for a holiday.

Lesson 11a (optional)

Learning through English (Extension)

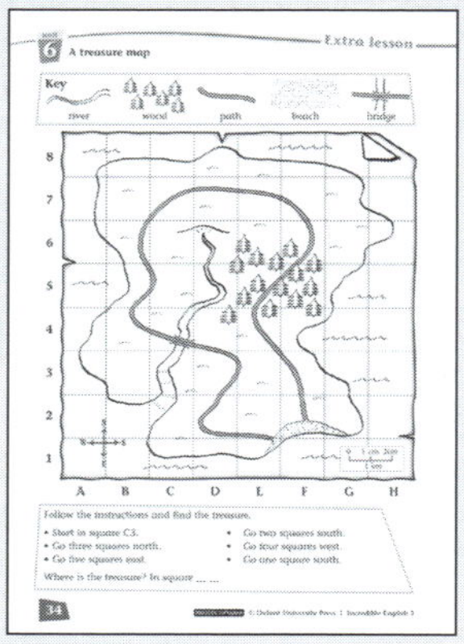

PMB page 34

Objectives

- Review vocabulary for places in the countryside
- Practise using grid references
- Learn the points of the compass – *north, south, east* and *west*
- Describe a route on a map using *north, south, east* and *west*

Core language

Review of

- places in the countryside vocabulary
- language used so far

Other language

Points of the compass (*north, south, east ,west*)

Materials

Countryside flashcards (x7); A compass (optional); A treasure map (PMB p34) – one photocopy per pupil; Paper (one piece per pupil) (optional)

Review vocabulary

- Review the countryside vocabulary with the pupils; show the flashcards to the pupils and ask them to say the words chorally and individually.

Preparation

- Draw and write the four compass directions (*north, south, east, west*) on the board.
- Use a compass to find the directions of north, south, east, and west in the classroom. Mark these with a cross on the floor, or labels on the walls.
- Say the words and ask the pupils to point in the correct direction.
- Play a quick TPR game with the pupils. Say *One step south, two steps east*, etc. Pupils move according to your instructions.
- Ask pupils if they know where *north* is normally situated on a map (at the top).

PMB p34 Using the Photocopy Master

- Give each pupil a photocopy of the treasure map.
- Say grid references from the map and ask what is in them. For example, *What is in square D3?* (*a path*).
- Point out to pupils that the key at the top of the map helps them identify the features in the map.
- Ask individual pupils to ask similar questions and other pupils to answer them.
- The pupils colour the features in the key and the map.
- Tell the pupils that you have hidden some treasure somewhere on the map.
- Tell the pupils to listen and follow your route.
- Read the instructions from the photocopy (*Start in square C3. Go three squares north*, etc.).
- Give the pupils time to follow your instructions on the map.
- When you have finished, ask the pupils where the treasure is. (*D3*)
- Say *Now you are going to hide some treasure. First decide where you are going to hide it.* The pupils decide where to hide their treasure (they should write the grid reference on a piece of paper or in their notebooks and hide it from their partner).
- Say *Now choose where to start.* The pupils choose a square in the map. They write the grid reference at the top of a piece of paper, or a page in their notebooks, as follows: *Start in (A5).*
- Say *Now write a set of instructions to find the treasure.* Underneath the grid reference, they write a set of instructions from the starting square to get to the treasure.
- The pupils read their instructions to their partners. They follow each other's instructions and find the treasure.

Fun activity

- Tell the pupils that you have a treasure chest. You are going to tell them some of the objects in the chest. They must guess some other ones.
- Say *In my treasure chest there's a book and a ball.*
- The pupils must guess what else is in your treasure chest. They ask e.g. *Is there a dog?* If the object they ask about begins with *b*, say *Yes*, otherwise say *No*.
- The pupils listen to your answers and try to work out what the rule is.
- Repeat with other rules for the pupils to guess. For example, words beginning with *t* or words of four letters.
- The pupils can play the game in small groups. They will probably need time to prepare some lists of items first, by referring to their books, Picture Dictionaries, etc.

Song

- Ask the pupils *Can you remember the song in this unit?*
- Write what the pupils can remember on the board. Help them to remember the bits they've forgotten, then add them on the board.
- Play the song again (Listening 2.32). The pupils check that the version on the board is correct.
- Play the song again and encourage the pupils to join in.

Lesson 12

Review and self-evaluation

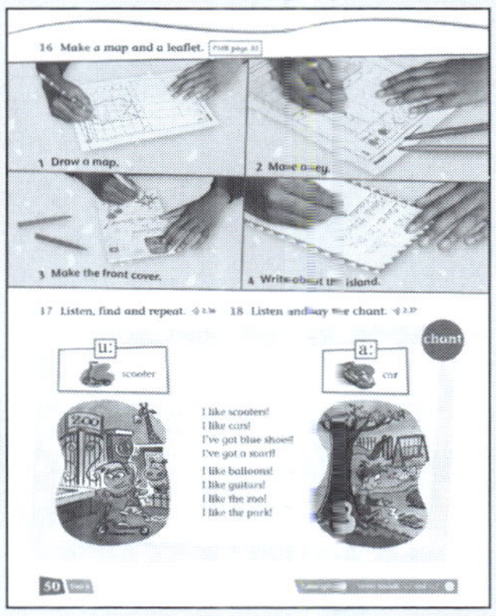

CB page 50

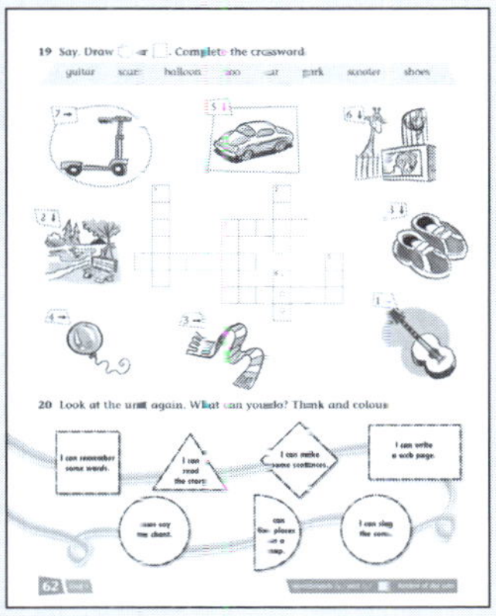

AB page 62

Objectives

- Focus on the pronunciation of vowel sounds (/a:/ and /u:/) with a chant
- Review the activities and the new language of the unit
- Complete a self-evaluation activity

Core language

Review of language used so far

Materials

CD 2; Rollercoaster Game poster; Character counters and game cards; Dice (one pair per class); Picture dictionary page (PMB p2) – one photocopy per pupil (optional)

CB p50 Activity 17 Listen, find and repeat.

- Point to the pictures. The pupils say the words.
- Play the CD. Pupils point and repeat.

2.36

zoo – scooter – shoes – balloon [/u:/]
park – car – scarf – guitar [/a:/]

- Say the two vowel sounds /u:/ and /a:/. The pupils find the words that share the vowel sound.
- The pupils practise saying the words chorally and individually, concentrating on the pronunciation of the vowel sounds.

CB p50 Activity 18 Listen and say the chant.

- Play the chant. The pupils point to the items as they hear them.

2.37

Girl: I like scooters
Boy: I like cars!
Girl: I've got blue shoes!
Boy: I've got a scarf!

Girl: I like balloons!
Boy: I like guitars!
Girl: I like the zoo!
Boy: I like the park!

- Teach the chant line by line. Focus on the pronunciation points. Use choral and individual repetition to check pronunciation.
- Play the chant again and encourage the pupils to join in.

Focus on spelling

- Match the spelling with the vowel sounds.
- Focus on the spelling patterns:
  /a:/ is often spelt *ar* (*guitar*), but the *r* is silent
  /u:/ is often *oo* (*balloon*)
- Show examples from the chant for each vowel sound.
- Remind the pupils that there are lots of exceptions to spelling patterns in English.

AB p62 Activity 19 Say. Draw ● or ■. Complete the crossword.

- Point to each of the pictures. The pupils say the words chorally.
- Focus on the pronunciation difference between /u:/ and /a:/, using the words *scooter* and *car*.
- Show how *scooter* has a circle around it and *car* has a square round it.
- Ask the pupils to identify a word with the /u:/ sound.
- Show the pupils how to put a circle round the word.
- Repeat with the /a:/ sound, putting a square around the word.
- The pupils put circles and squares around the words.
- Show the pupils the word *zoo* in the crossword. The pupils suggest a word for 7 across (*scooter*).
- The pupils complete the crossword individually.
- Point to the pictures at random. The pupils say the words chorally and individually. Check the pupils' pronunciation.

Answers: circle: scooter, zoo, shoes, balloon; square: guitar, scarf, car, park
1 guitar **2** park **3 (across)** scarf **3 (down)** shoes
4 balloon **5** car **6** zoo **7** scooter

End-of-unit review

- Use the Rollercoaster Game poster and the Class Book to recall the main activities of the unit.
- Recall the language associated with each activity.

Play the Rollercoaster Game

- Divide the class into small groups. Give each group one of the character 'counters' and let them play the game as before (see p41).
- Remind them to use the poster chants when a group gets a question right or wrong.

AB p62 Activity 20 Look at the unit again. What can you do? Think and colour.

- Let the pupils do the self-evaluation activity as before (see p41).

PMB p2 Picture Dictionary (optional)

- If your pupils are making Picture Dictionaries, give out the photocopies of the template.
- Pupils continue making the dictionaries as for Unit 1 (see p42).

Lesson 12a (optional)

■ = Words ◆ = Sentences

Show what you know!

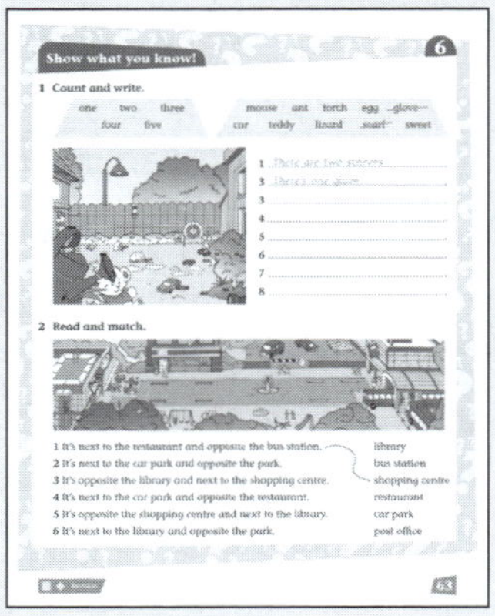

AB page 63

For ideas on how to use *Show what you know!* see page 13.

Objectives

- Extra practice of the vocabulary of the unit
- Solve puzzles in English
- Provide extra material for homework and fast finishers

Core language

Review of language used so far

AB p63 Activity 1 Count and write.

- Read the words in the word pools to the pupils.
- Point to the scarves in the picture and ask *How many scarves are there?* The pupils answer *Two.* Repeat with other objects.
- Point to the example answer for Number 1 and read it.
- Repeat with *gloves* for Number 2.
- Point to other objects in the picture. The pupils make sentences with *There's …* or *There are …* Write two or three of the sentences on the board.
- The pupils write six more sentences about the picture individually or in pairs.

AB p63 Activity 2 Read and match.

- Point to the picture and ask *Where is …?* questions about it, for example *Where is the library?* Encourage the pupils to use prepositions (*next to, opposite*) in their answers.
- Read the first sentence to the pupils. They identify the building. Show the pupils the line from sentence number 1 to the world *shopping centre.*
- The pupils match the other sentences to the words individually or in pairs.

The pupils are now ready to sit the Unit 6 test. See pp190–193 for both Standard and Higher levels. They are also ready to sit the Term 2 test on pp208–209 and p213.

The pupils are now ready to do the culture lessons on 'My town' (see p162).

DVD VIDEO
Multimedia extension: you may now like to use the Geography 1 section of the optional DVD.

7 At the sports centre

Lesson 1 ■ = Words

Introducing vocabulary

CB page 51

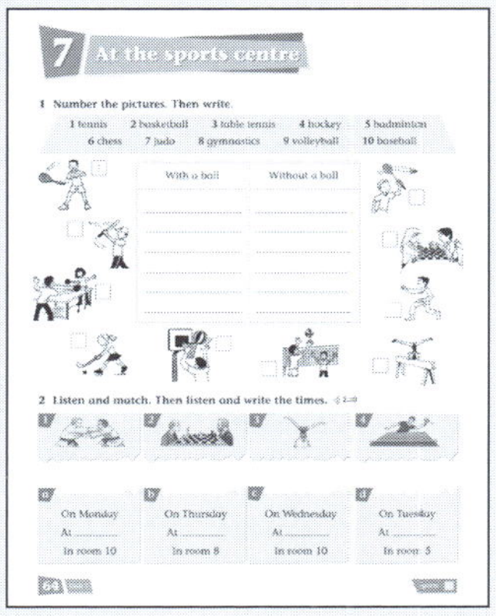

AB page 64

Objectives

- Understand the theme of the unit
- Become familiar with vocabulary for sports
- Practise listening and talking about when things happen
- Focus on spelling

Core language

Sports vocabulary: *badminton, baseball, basketball, chess, gymnastics, hockey, judo, table tennis, tennis, volleyball*

Review of

- sports vocabulary: *football*
- language used so far

Other language

timetable, class, with, without

Materials

Rollercoaster Game poster; Sports flashcards (*badminton, baseball, basketball, chess, gymnastics, hockey, judo, table tennis, tennis, volleyball, football*); CD 2; Pupils' bookmarks (optional) (see p28)

Unit overview

- Talk with the pupils about sports. Ask them questions such as *What sports do you play? Do you watch sports on television? What's your favourite sport?*
- Ask them what words they know in English for sports. Ask them what words (in their own language) they would like to learn.
- Ask the pupils to look through Unit 7 in their Class Books. Talk with them about the unit and quickly write the different topics and activities on the board, relating them to the shapes on the poster:
  - ■ Words – sports / football things
  - ▲ Story – *On the other side*
  - ◆ Sentences – *I play tennis. I don't do judo. Do you play chess?*
  - ▬ Text work – Signs and notices
  - ● Song – *Signs everywhere!* / Chant – *I can see a green tree*
  - ◗ Other subjects – Maths (learn about fractions)
- Remind the pupils that they will use the poster again at the end of the unit.

Introduce new vocabulary *see p19*

- Use the sports flashcards to teach the new vocabulary. The pupils repeat the words chorally, then individually.
- Work out a mime gesture for each sport (for example, bouncing a ball for basketball, stretching out your hands for gymnastics).
- Play *Get moving!* with the pupils. First do the gestures and ask the pupils to say the sport or activity. Then ask individual pupils to do the gestures for the other pupils to guess.

CB p51 Activity 1 Look, listen and repeat.

- The pupils listen to the recording. They repeat each word chorally and point to the correct picture.

2.38

1 baseball, **2** badminton, **3** gymnastics, **4** hockey, **5** basketball, **6** football, **7** tennis, **8** judo, **9** chess, **10** table tennis, **11** volleyball

CB p51 Activity 2 Listen and find.

- Explain that the children are looking at a sports timetable. They want to find classes for their favourite sports.
- The pupils listen to the conversations and point to the sports pictures on the timetable.
- Alternatively, the pupils can use their bookmarks (see p28) to focus on the pictures.

2.39

Finn: Let's look at the sports timetable.
Jazmin: Is there a tennis class?
Finn: Yes, look. It's on Thursday.
Jazmin: Great. And I want to do judo.
Finn: Judo?
Jazmin: Yes. Oh, there's a judo class on Monday.
Finn: Is there a football class?
Jazmin: Yes. There's a football class on Wednesday, at five o'clock.
Finn: And I like chess. Is there a chess class?
Jazmin: Yes. It's on Tuesday.
Finn: Oh good.
Molly: I like gymnastics. Is there a gymnastics class?
Luke: Yes! On Thursday.
Molly: And is there a baseball class? I like baseball.
Luke: Yes, there is a baseball class. It's on Monday at four thirty.
Molly: Great!
Luke: Hmmm, I like hockey, and I like table tennis. And I love basketball. Is there a basketball class?
Molly: Yes, it's on Tuesday!
Luke: What about you, Archie?
Archie: Well, I like badminton … and I like volleyball. Is there a volleyball class?
Luke: Yes. It's on Friday.

CB p51 Activity 3 Ask and answer.

- Read the conversation to the pupils.
- Ask *Is there a football class on Wednesday?* The pupils answer *Yes.*

- Choose pupils to ask the questions and other pupils to answer them.
- The pupil practise asking and answering the questions in pairs.

Spelling
- Ask the pupils to identify:
  1 words that are similar in their language (highlight the differences in spelling)
  2 words that end with *-ball* (*football*, *baseball*, etc.)
  3 word with double letters (*baseball*, *chess*, etc.).

AB p64 Activity 1 Number the pictures. Then write.
- Read the words in the word pool to the pupils. Ask the pupils to match the words to the pictures.
- Read the categories (*With a ball / Without a ball*) to the pupils. Ask *Which sports go in the 'With a ball' group?* The pupils choose suitable sports.
- Ask *Which sports go in the 'Without a ball' group?* The pupils choose suitable sports.

Answers: With a ball: tennis, basketball, table tennis, hockey, volleyball, baseball
Without a ball: badminton, chess, judo, gymnastics

Lesson 2 ■ = Words
Practising vocabulary

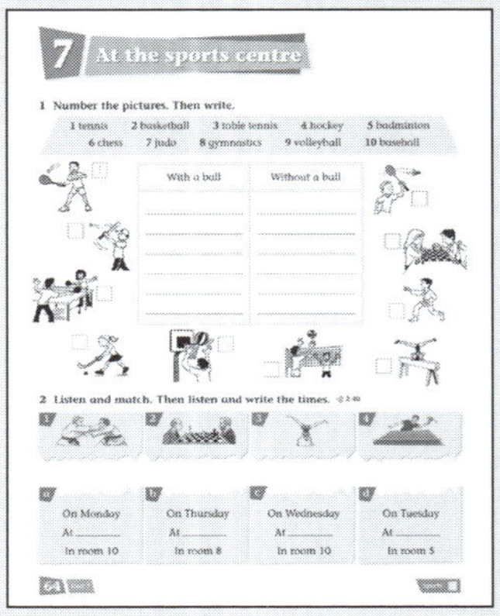
AB page 64

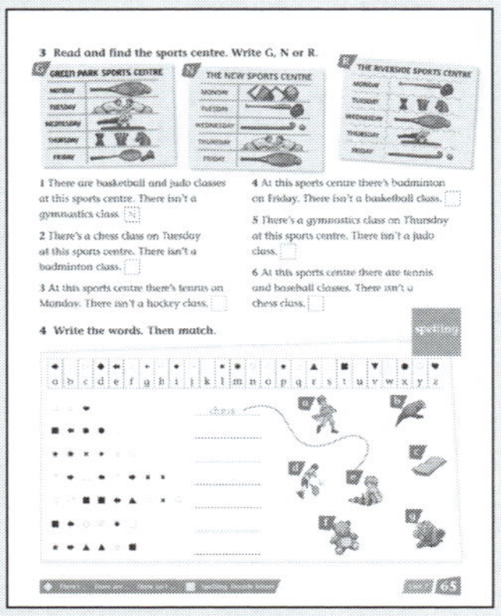
AB page 65

Objectives
- Review vocabulary for sports
- Practise listening and talking about when things happen
- Read about events at a sports centre
- Use a code to spell words

Core language
Review of
- sports vocabulary
- language used so far

Other language
Can I help you?; Let me see.

Materials
Sports flashcards (x11); Sports picture cards (PMB p35) – one photocopied set per pupil

Review vocabulary
- Show the sports flashcards one by one to the pupils. The pupils repeat the words chorally and then individually.
- Play *What's missing?* with the pupils: take one of the flashcards from the pile, then put the other ten flashcards on the board. The pupils say the word for the missing flashcard.

AB p64 Activity 2 Listen and match. Then listen and write the times.
- Point to the pictures of the sports. The pupils name each sport.
- Explain that the pupils have to match the sport with the bottom half of the poster, and add the times.
- Play the first conversation. Ask *What sport is it?* The pupils answer *Judo.* Ask *What day is judo?* The pupils answer *On Wednesday.* Ask *What time is judo?* The pupils answer *At half past six.*
- The pupils draw a line from the judo picture to the Wednesday text, and add the time (*half past six*).
- Repeat with the other conversations on the CD.

2.40
Child: Excuse me, is there a judo class today?
Adult: No, there isn't. Judo is on Wednesday.
Child: What time?
Adult: At half past six.
Child: OK, half past six on Wednesday. Thank you.

Child: Excuse me.
Adult: Yes, can I help you?
Child: Is there a chess class today?
Adult: Yes there is. Chess is on Tuesday.
Child: What time?
Adult: At half past five.
Child: OK, thanks.

Child: Excuse me, is there a gymnastics class today?
Adult: No, there isn't.
Child: Oh, when is it?
Adult: Gymnastics is on Monday.
Child: What time?
Adult: At eight o'clock.
Child: Thanks, Monday at eight o'clock.

Child: Excuse me.
Adult: Yes, can I help you?
Child: Is there a table tennis class today?
Adult: Let me see. Yes, table tennis is on Thursday at half past four.
Child: Thursday at half past four. Thank you.

Answers: 1 c (half past six) **2** d (half past five)
3 a (eight o'clock) **4** b (half past four)

AB p65 Activity 3 Read and find the sports centre. Write G, N or R.
- Point to the Green Park Sports Centre timetable. Say *It's Monday. What can I do? (tennis).* Ask other questions like this about all three sports centres.
- Read the first sentence to the pupils. Ask *Which sports centre is it?* The pupils answer *The New Sports Centre.* Show the pupils how the answer is written as *N*, and explain the answer code: *G* = Green Park, *N* = New, *R* = Riverside.
- Read the next sentence. The pupils identify the sports centre (Riverside) and write *R* in the box.
- Repeat with the other sentences.

Answers: 1 N **2** R **3** G **4** G **5** R **6** N

AB p65 Activity 4 Write the words. Then match.

- Tell the pupils to look at the code on page 65 of their Activity Books. Point to the first word written in code and look at the example answer (*chess*). Point to the second word and ask the pupils to decode it (*teddy*). The pupils write the word, then match it with the picture.
- Repeat with the other code words. The pupils can do this activity individually or in pairs.

Answers: chess (e), teddy (f), pillow (c), baseball (a), butterfly (g), tennis (d), parrot (b)

Spelling game

- The pupils make a wordsearch with four sports words (see p21).

PMB p35 Make the picture cards

- Give out the photocopies of the sports picture cards. The pupils colour and cut out the picture cards.
- They can use their cards to play a game, for example *Show me!* (see p21).
- If your pupils are using word cards, they can prepare them now (see p30). Pupils cut them out and match them with the picture cards.
- Remind the pupils to keep all the cards in a safe place.

Lesson 3 ▲ = Story

Story

CB page 52

CB page 53

Objectives

- Listen to a story
- Read a story
- Listen for words and phrases in a story
- Practise story language

Core language

I don't play basketball; Do you play chess?

Review of

- sports vocabulary
- language used so far

Other language

pass, ladder, over, hedge, hole

Come on!; No thanks; On the other side

Materials

Sports flashcards (x11); CD 2

Review vocabulary

- Put the sports flashcards on the board. The pupils say the words chorally and individually.
- Place the flashcards in different parts of the classroom and play *Around the class* with the pupils. First you say the words and the pupils point to the flashcards. Then you point to the flashcards and the pupils say the words.

Introduce the story

- Ask the pupils to talk about the games they like to play.
- Explain that in the story the children are playing games.

CB pp52–53 Activity 4 First listening with the books closed

- Tell the pupils to listen and answer this question: *What's the problem with the basketball?*
- The pupils listen with their books closed.

2.41

[1] At a country park …
Eve: Five children and one adult, please.
Assistant: Twenty pounds, please.
Jazmin: Wow, there's a lake!

[2] Archie: Look. We can play tennis.
Luke: And basketball!
Archie: Come on, let's go!

[3] Jazmin: Eve! Come and play basketball!
Eve: No, thanks. I don't play basketball.
Luke: What about you, Archie?
Archie: No, thanks. I prefer tennis.

[4] Molly: What about me? Can I play?'
Jazmin: You're too small.
Molly: Oh, please!
Luke: OK

[5] Molly: Pass it to me! Pass it to me!
(sounds of ball being passed)
Oh, JAZMIN!

[6] Jazmin: Can you climb over the hedge?
Luke: No. It's too high.
Jazmin: We need a ladder.
Luke: Oh no. Now what?

[7] Jazmin: Look – there's a hole in the hedge.

[8] Luke: You're small, Molly. You go through the hedge!
Molly: Oh … OK.

[9] On the other side of the hedge …
Woman: Hello! Who are you?
Molly: I'm Molly.

[10] Woman: Do you play chess?
Molly: Yes, I do. I love chess.
Luke: Molly! The ball! Please!

- Check the answer to your question (*They lose it*). Recast the pupils' answers as necessary.

CB pp52–53 Activity 4 Second listening with the books open

- Tell the pupils to open their books and look at the story.
- Ask questions about the story such as *Is Jazmin good at basketball?*
- Play the recording again while the pupils follow in their books.
- Go through any vocabulary queries with the class.

CB p53 Activity 5 Read and find the picture.

- Explain that each sentence refers to a particular frame in the story.
- Ask the pupils to identify the frame for the first sentence (frame 6).
- The pupils read each sentence and match it with a frame. This can be done as a whole-class activity or working in pairs.
- The pupils write the answers in their notebooks.

Answers: a 6 **b** 9 **c** 1 **d** 8 **e** 10 **f** 7 **g** 5 (2nd part of frame)

Fun expressions

- Write these 'fun expressions' from the story on the board:
  Wow! There's a lake!
  Come on, let's go!
  Oh, please!
- Play the story again: the pupils put up their hands when they hear one of the phrases.
- Pause the recording. The pupils repeat the phrase chorally and individually. Encourage the pupils to copy the intonation on the CD.

Lesson 4 ◆ = Sentences

Language focus 1

CB page 54

AB page 66

Objectives

- Understand the use of *Do you play / do ...?*
- Practise using the new language.

Core language

Do you play ...? / Do you do ...?
Review of language used so far

Materials

Grammar tiles (PMB p36) – one photocopy of Set 1 per pupil (optional); CD 2

Recall the story

- Ask the pupils how much they can remember from the story.
- Say the following sentences from the story, and ask the pupils to identify who says each one:
  Five children and one adult, please. (Eve)
  Come and play basketball! (Jazmin)
  You're too small. (Jazmin)
  You're small, Molly. You go through the hedge! (Luke)
  I love chess. (Molly)

PMB p36 / CB p54 Activity 6 Which question is in the story? Make more questions.

- Ask the pupils to read the questions in the grammar tiles.
- Ask the pupils to say which question is in the story (*Do you play chess?*).
- Write *I play chess* on the board. Under this, write *Do you play chess?* Show how we add *do* to make the question.
- The pupils say the questions in the grammar tiles chorally and individually.
- Point out that to talk about some activities we use *play*, and for others we use *do*, i.e. *play football*, but *do judo*.
- The pupils use the remaining tiles in the picture to make questions with *Do you ...?* Choose other pupils to answer with *yes* or *no*. Alternatively, give each pupil a copy of Set 1 of the grammar tiles from the PMB: the pupils cut out the tiles and arrange them in questions on their desks. Ask individual pupils to read out their questions for the class.

CB p54 Activity 7 Listen and say who.

- Point to the pictures of sports equipment. Ask the pupils to say the sport for each piece.
- Show the pupils the table. Ask the pupils to say the sports for each character.
- Play the first conversation on the CD. The pupils listen and identify the person.
- Repeat with the other conversations.

2.42

Luke:	Do you do judo?
Jazmin:	No.
Luke:	Do you do gymnastics?
Jazmin:	Yes.
Luke:	Do you play basketball?
Jazmin:	Yes.
Presenter:	Who is it?
Luke:	Do you play volleyball?
Molly:	No.
Luke:	Do you play basketball?
Molly:	No.
Luke:	Do you play football?
Molly:	Yes!
Presenter:	Who is it?

Answers: 1 Jazmin **2** Molly

CB p54 Activity 8 Ask and answer. Talk about yourselves.

- Read the two conversations to the pupils.
- Say you are pretending to be one of the characters in the table. The pupils ask you questions using *Do you do / play ...?* and identify the character.
- Ask a pupil *Do you play basketball?* Point to the pupil as you ask, to make sure that he / she answers the question about himself / herself.
- The pupils ask and answer questions about sports in pairs.

AB p66 Activity 5 Complete.

- Read the words in the word pool to the pupils.
- Point to the picture of the girl with the sports equipment in the first picture. Ask *What sports does she play?* The pupils answer *hockey and badminton.*

- Read the first question and ask the pupils what the answer is (*Yes*). The pupils write the answer in the speech bubble.
- Repeat with the other questions and answers.

Answers: Yes, No, Yes

- Point to the picture of the boy with the sports equipment in the second picture. Ask *What sports does he play?* The pupils answer *judo and tennis.*
- Read the answer to the first question. Ask the pupils to say suitable questions, for example *Do you play hockey?* or *Do you play football?* Choose one of the questions and write it on the board. The pupils write the question in their Activity Books.
- Repeat with the other questions and answers.

Answers: Do you play hockey / football / chess? / Do you do gymnastics? (No.) Do you do judo? (Yes.) Do you play tennis? (Yes.)

- Point to the picture of the girl with the sports equipment in the third picture. Ask *What sports does she play?* The pupils answer *gymnastics and football.*
- Ask pupils to complete the dialogue for this picture.

Answers: (the order may vary) Do you play hockey / chess / tennis? / Do you do gymnastics? (No.) Do you play football? (Yes.) Do you do gymnastics? (Yes.)

Lesson 5 ◆ = Sentences

Language focus 2

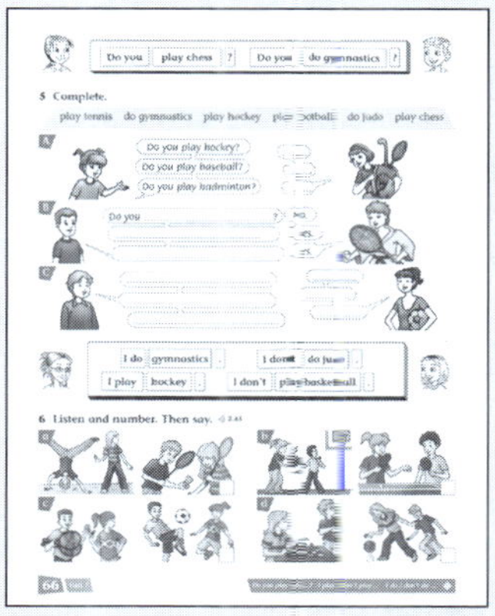

AB page 66

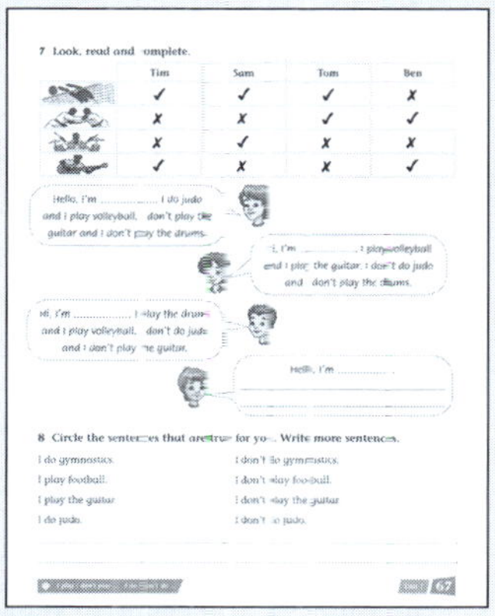

AB page 67

Objectives

- Review vocabulary for sports
- Understand the use of *I don't play …*
- Review *I play …* and *Do you play …?*
- Practise talking and writing about the sports you do

Core language

I don't play …

Review of

- sports vocabulary
- language used so far

Materials

Grammar tiles (PMB p36) – one photocopy of Set 2 per pupil; Pupils' grammar tiles (Set 1) from Lesson 4 (optional); Sports flashcards (x11); CD 2

PMB p36 / AB p66 Focus on language

- Read the sentences in the second set of grammar tiles to the pupils. Ask the pupils *Which sentence is in the story? (I don't play basketball.)*
- Focus on the difference between the affirmative form (*I play …*) and the negative form (*I don't play …*).
- Write the contraction and the long forms on board: *I don't play = I do not play.* Use a mime gesture to show how the long form 'contracts' to the short form.
- The pupils say the sentences in the grammar tiles chorally and individually.
- Give each pupil a photocopy of Set 2 of the grammar tiles from the PMB. Ask the pupils to suggest words to put in the blank tiles (*play table tennis, play hockey, play the violin,* etc. – remind pupils that *play* can be used with the musical instrument vocabulary from Level 2, as well as with sports). Write the suggestions on the board. The pupils copy the words in the blank tiles.
- The pupils cut out all the tiles and use them to make sentences on their desks. Ask pupils to read out their sentences for the class.
- Pupils can combine the Set 2 tiles with some of the Set 1 tiles to make more sentences, for example *I don't play volleyball. Do you play hockey?*

Practice

- Show the pupils one of the sports flashcards. Select a pupil and say *Make a sentence with 'I play' or 'I don't play'.*

- The pupil says, for example *I don't play tennis.* Ask several pupils to make a sentence about the same flashcard.
- Repeat with the other flashcards. Remember that with some flashcards (judo and gymnastics) the pupils will have to say *I do* or *I don't do.*

AB p66 Activity 6 Listen and number. Then say.

- Point to each of the pictures in the cartoons. Ask *What sport is it? (gymnastics, badminton,* etc.)
- Play the first conversation. Ask the pupils *Which cartoon is it?* The pupils find the cartoon (*c*).
- Repeat with the other conversations.

2.43

1 Girl: Come and play basketball.
Boy: No, thanks. I don't play basketball.
Girl: Well, come and play table tennis!
Boy: OK.

2 Boy: Let's do gymnastics.
Girl: No, thanks. I don't do gymnastics.
Boy: Well, let's play badminton.
Girl: OK!

3 Girl: Let's play chess.
Boy: No, thanks. I don't play chess.
Girl: Well, come and play basketball.
Boy: OK!

4 Boy: Let's play tennis.
Girl: No, thanks. I don't play tennis.
Boy: Well, come and play football.
Girl: OK!

Answers: a 2 b 1 c 4 d 3

- Point to each cartoon. Say *Make a sentence with 'I play / don't play ...' or 'I do / don't do ...'.* The pupils make sentences about each cartoon.

Answers: **a** I don't do gymnastics. I play badminton. **b** I don't play basketball. I play table tennis. **c** I don't play tennis. I play football. **d** I don't play chess. I play basketball.

AB p67 Activity 7 Look, read and complete.

- Point to the pictures in the table. The pupils name the activities (*play volleyball, do judo, play the drums, play the guitar*).
- Read the first text to the pupils. Ask *Who is it?* The pupils answer *Tom* and write the name in the text.
- Repeat with the second and third texts.
- Say *Who is the fourth text about? (Ben).* The pupils complete the text about Ben.

Answers: 1 Tom 2 Tim 3 Sam 4 Hello, I'm Ben. I play the guitar and I do judo. I don't play the drums and I don't play volleyball.

AB p67 Activity 8 Circle the sentences that are true for you. Write more sentences.

- Write the first pair of sentences (*I do gymnastics. I don't do gymnastics*) on the board.
- Circle the answer that is true for you. Use mime gestures (pointing at yourself) to make it clear you are talking about yourself.
- Point to the pupils and say *Circle the correct sentence for you.* The pupils circle the sentences in their Activity Books.
- Repeat with the other sentence pairs.
- Write more sentences on the board about yourself with *play* and *do*, for example: *I play table tennis. I don't play the drums.*
- Ask the pupils to write four similar sentences about themselves in their Activity Books.
- Ask individual pupils to read their sentences to the class.

For extra grammar practice, see AB page 103.

Activity 1 Look and write questions.

Answers: **2** Do you play hockey? **3** Do you play basketball? **4** Do you play badminton? **5** Do you play chess? **6** Do you play volleyball?

Activity 2 Find and write.

Answers: **1** do gymnastics. **2** I play tennis. **3** I play table tennis. **4** I don't play chess. **5** I don't play baseball.

Lesson 6 ▲ = Story

Playscript

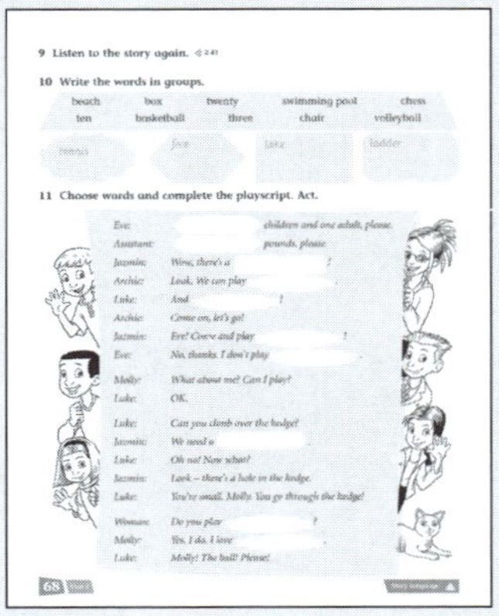
9 Listen to the story again.

10 Write the words in groups.

beach box twenty swimming pool chess
ten basketball three chair volleyball

11 Choose words and complete the playscript. Act.

AB page 68

Objectives

- Read and complete a playscript
- Use finger puppets to act out a playscript
- Act out the play

Core language

Review of language used so far

Materials

CD 2; Spare photocopies of the finger puppets (PMB p3)

AB p68 Activity 9 Listen to the story again.

- Tell the pupils to look at pages 52–53 in the Class Book again.
- Play the CD while the pupils listen and read.
- Alternatively, the pupils can read the story aloud in groups of seven. Each pupil should read one character.

AB p68 Activity 10 Write the words in groups.

- Read the words in the word pool to the pupils.
- Point to each of the boxes and read the word in each one. Ask the pupils to suggest words from the word pool to go in each box.

- The pupils write the words from the word pool in the correct category.

Answers: set 1 – tennis, basketball, chess, volleyball; set 2 – five, three, twenty, ten; set 3 – lake, swimming pool, beach; ladder, box, chair

- Ask the pupils to suggest new words for each category.

AB p68 Activity 11 Choose words and complete the playscript. Act.

- Read the playscript to the pupils. When you come to a blank, ask *Which word was in the story?* The pupils say the words from the story.
- Read the playscript again. Ask the pupils to suggest alternative words from Activity 10 to complete the blanks.
- Divide the pupils into groups of four. In their groups, the pupils decide which words to use when they read the playscript.

Finger puppets *see p22*

- Ask the pupils *How many characters are there in the story? (seven).* The pupils identify the seven characters. (Eve, Jazmin, Luke, Archie, Molly, Woman, Shop assistant).
  Say *We have four pupils for seven characters. It isn't a problem. Look!* Write this table on the board:
  Pupil 1 – Eve and Molly
  Pupil 2 – Jazmin and Woman
  Pupil 3 – Luke
  Pupil 4 – Archie and Shop assistant.
- In their groups, the pupils decide who is going to take each part.
- If the pupils have got their finger puppets with them, tell them to get out the puppet for the character they are going to play.
- Give each group two photocopies of the extra finger puppet. The pupils cut out, colour and stick the extra puppets to make the Woman and Assistant puppet. If they haven't got the other puppets they need, they will have to make those too.

Practice

- Remind the pupils of the five points of successful play acting:
  1 Listen to the other actors.
  2 Wait for your turn.
  3 Speak clearly.
  4 When the puppets are speaking to each other, they should face each other.
  5 Don't move your puppets unnecessarily.
- Tell the pupils about the notes you made during the Unit 6 play acting. Encourage them to concentrate on the points you noticed. Say you will be watching them again this time.
- The pupils act out the play with their puppets. While they are doing this, circulate around the classroom. Make a note of the points the pupils should improve on next time.
- Ask one or two groups to come to the front to act out the play with their puppets.

Lesson 7 = Text work

Reading and writing

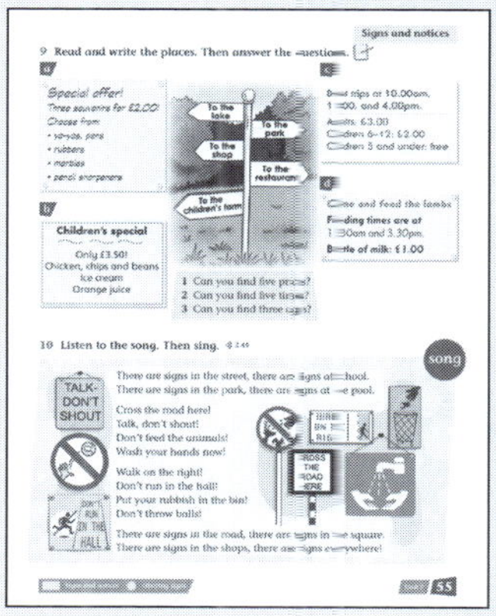

CB page 55

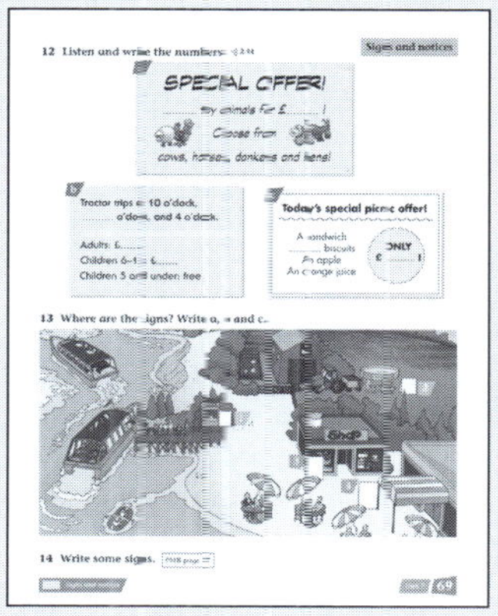

AB page 69

Objectives

- Review sports vocabulary
- Read and understand signs and notices
- Write some signs and notices

Core language

Review of language used so far

Other language

special offer, souvenir, pencil sharpener, farm, free, feed, tractor

Materials

Sports flashcards (x11); Sign template (PMB p37) – one photocopy per pupil

Review vocabulary

- Write the sports words on the board with the letters in a jumbled order.
- Call pupils to the front to write the letters in the correct order.
- Call other pupils to the front to put the flashcards next to the correct spellings.

CB p55 Activity 9 Read and write the places. Then answer the questions.

- Read the directions on the signpost to the pupils. Explain any new words (e.g. *farm*).
- Read the notices to the pupils. Explain any new words.
- Point to one of the signs on the signpost, for example *To the shop*. Ask the pupils to identify the notice that goes with this place (*a*).
- Repeat with the other places and notices. The pupils write the letter and the place in their notebooks.

Answers: a shop **b** restaurant **c** lake **d** farm

- Read the first question to the pupils. The pupils say the five prices.
- Repeat with the questions about times and ages. The pupils write the answers in their notebooks.

Answers: 1 £2.00, £3.00, £2.00, £3.50, £1.00 **2** 10.00 am, 12.00, 4.00 pm, 11.30 am, 3.30 pm **3** 6, 12, 5 (and under)

AB p69 Activity 12 Listen and write the numbers.

- Point to each of the signs and ask *What can you do at this place? (buy toy animals, ride on a tractor, have a meal).* Tell the pupils they are going to listen and complete the numbers in the signs.
- Play the first advertisement. The pupils write the numbers in the sign.
- Repeat with the second and third advertisements.

2.44

Come and visit the Country Park!
Come and buy some toy animals at the shop. We've got cows, horses, donkeys, ducks and hens.
You can buy three toy animals for only two pounds!

Come and ride on a tractor!
The trips are at ten o'clock, twelve o'clock and four o'clock.
Adults – five pounds.
Children aged six to twelve – two pounds.
And children under five are free!
It's fun! Come and have a tractor ride today!

Eat at Rosie's Restaurant.
Buy your picnic for only four pounds.
A sandwich, two biscuits, an apple and an orange juice.
Only four pounds!

Answers: a 3, 2 **b** 12, 5, 2 **c** 2, 4

AB p69 Activity 13 Where are the signs? Write a, b and c.

- Point to the picture. Say *Find a place for sign a.* The pupils choose the shop and write *a* in the box.
- Repeat with the other signs.

Answers: 2 b **3** a **4** c (the boat kiosk (no. 1) doesn't have a sign – it is a 'red herring'

PMB p37 / AB p69 Write some signs.

- Explain to the pupils that they are going to write signs for two of the following: a shop, a restaurant, a tourist attraction.
- Remind pupils that they have to choose work for their portfolio during the course (see p198). Point out that this piece of work would be a suitable piece to include.
- Brainstorm ideas for the signs.
- Choose some suggestions and write them on the board.
- Show the pupils how to write the signs, using the signs in Activity 12 as a model.
- Hand out the photocopies of the writing template. Ask the pupils to choose which two places to write signs for. Tell the pupils to write the signs for each one.
- The pupils write a rough copy in their notebooks for you to correct. After you have checked the rough copy, they write their final copy on the photocopied template.

Lesson 8 ● = Song / chant

Learning for life

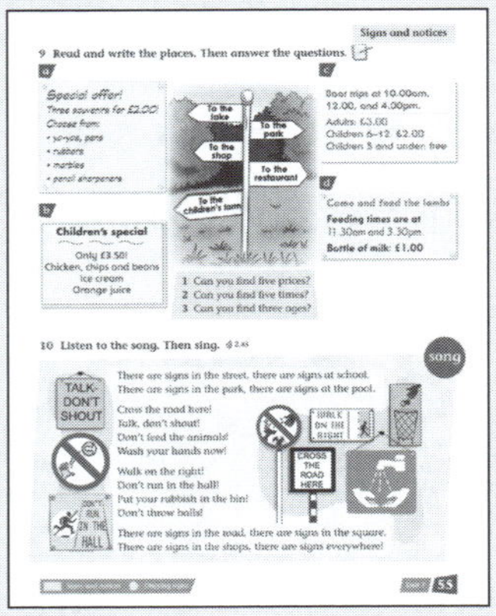
CB page 55

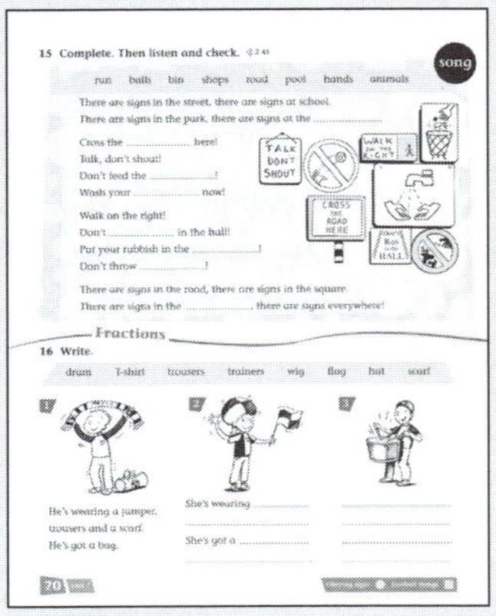
AB page 70

Objectives

- Review the unit so far
- Understand the importance of following instructions
- Talk about different types of instructions
- Sing a song about instructions

Core language

Review of language used so far

Other language

shout, right, hall

Materials

Rollercoaster Game poster; Sports flashcards (x11); CD 2

Unit review

- Use the Rollercoaster Game poster and the Class Book to review the unit so far. Talk with the pupils about the activities they have done.
- The pupils give examples of the language they used in each activity.

Review vocabulary (categorizing)

- Ask the pupils to tell you all the new words they remember from the unit.
- Put the sports flashcards on the board and ask the pupils to arrange them in these two groups: *sports we do at school* and *sports we don't do at school.*
- Repeat with other categories such as:
  Sports I can do / Sports I can't do
  Easy sports / Difficult sports
  Indoor sports / Outdoor sports

Introduce the topic

- Talk with the pupils about signs and instructions. Ask questions such as: Where do you see signs and instructions? What signs and instructions do you see in the street? What are they for?
- Encourage the pupils to talk about some or all of these ideas in their answers:
  - they tell us where places are and how to get there
  - they tell us what to do and what not to do
  - they give us information about places such as opening and closing times
  - they help us
  - they warn us about dangerous things
  - they warn us about doing damage to ourselves, other people, and other things.

- The pupils can express their ideas in their own language. If they do, recast their answers in English.

CB p55 **Listen to the song. Then sing.**

- Read the song with the pupils. Explain any new words.
- Play the song on the CD.

2.45

There are signs in the street, there are signs at school.
There are signs in the park, there are signs at the pool.

Cross the road here!
Talk, don't shout!
Don't feed the animals!
Wash your hands now!

Walk on the right!
Don't run in the hall!
Put your rubbish in the bin!
Don't throw balls!

There are signs in the road, there are signs in the square.
There are signs in the shops, there are signs everywhere!

- Work out simple mime gestures for these places: *street, school, park, pool.*
- Read through the song again and ask the pupils to use the mime gestures as you read.
- Play the song again and encourage the pupils to join in, singing and miming.

AB p70 **Activity 15 Complete. Then listen and check.**

- Tell the pupils to close their Class Books and open their Activity Books at page 70.
- Read the words in the word pool to the pupils.
- Read the first line of the song to the pupils. Ask the pupils to use the words in the word pool to complete the song. Write the words they suggest on the board.
- Repeat with the other lines of the song.
- Play the song again; the pupils check the words they suggested.
- Make any necessary corrections to the words on the board. The pupils copy the words in the spaces in their Activity Books.
- To finish the lesson, tell the pupils to close their books. Help them to say the whole song again, chorally, from memory.

Answers: pool, road, animals, hands, run, bin, balls, shops

Lesson 9 = Words = Other subjects

Learning through English

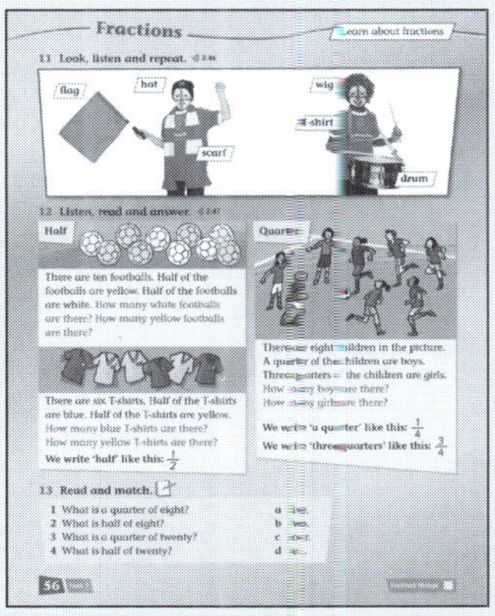

CB page 56

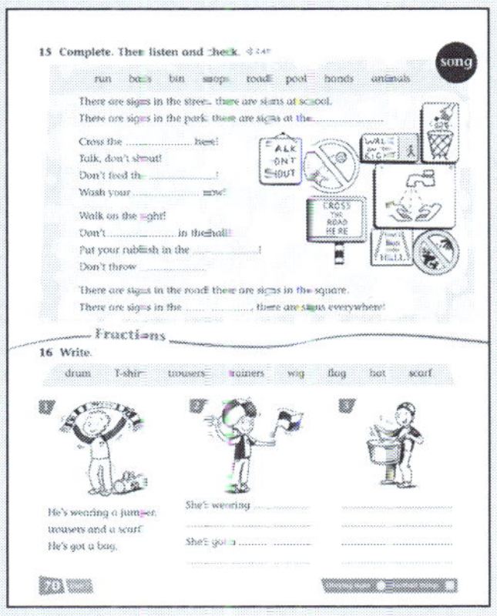

AB page 70

Objectives

- Learn words for football things
- Learn about fractions

Core language

Football things: *drum, flag, wig, hat, scarf, T-shirt*
Fractions: *half, a quarter, three quarters*
Review of language used so far

Materials

Some football fan gear (scarves, etc.), or a picture of football fans wearing fan gear; Football things flashcards (*drum, flag, wig, hat, T-shirt* and *scarf* – re-use from Unit 2); CD 2; Football things picture cards (PMB p35) – one photocopied set per pupil

Introduce the topic

- Show the pupils the pictures of the football fan gear. Ask *What is it for?* Recast the pupils' answers as necessary
- Talk with the pupils about why supporters wear fan gear. Encourage the pupils to say these ideas:
  – You can show your support for the team
  – You can know what team other people support
  – It's fun.
- Recast the pupils' answers as necessary.
- Tell the pupils that they are going use fractions with fan gear.

Introduce new vocabulary *see p19*

- Use the football things flashcards to teach the new vocabulary (pupils may remember *hat, scarf,* and *T-shirt* from previous units / levels). The pupils repeat the words chorally, then individually.
- Stick the flashcards face down on the board. Above each flashcard, write the first letter of the word. Play *Cards and letters* with the pupils: the pupils say the words for the flashcards you point to.

CB p56 **Activity 11 Look, listen and repeat.**

- Talk about the picture with the pupils. Explain that the children are football supporters.
- Play the CD. The pupils repeat each word chorally and point to the correct picture.

2.46

flag – hat – scarf – wig – T-shirt – drum

CB p56 **Activity 12 Listen, read and answer.**

- Show the pupils the pictures of the footballs, T-shirts, and children.
- Play the CD while the pupils listen and read.
- Pause the CD after each question for the pupils to answer.
- Make sure that the pupils understand the idea of half, quarter, and three quarters.

2.47

Half
There are ten footballs. Half of the footballs are yellow. Half of the footballs are white.
How many white footballs are there?

How many yellow footballs are there?

There are six T-shirts. Half of the T-shirts are blue. Half of the T-shirts are yellow.
How many blue T-shirts are there?

How many yellow T-shirts are there?

We write 'half' like this …

Quarters
There are eight children in the picture.
A quarter of the children are boys. Three quarters of the children are girls.
How many boys are there?

How many girls are there?

We write 'a quarter' like this …
We write 'three quarters' like this …

Answers: (white footballs) five, (yellow footballs) five, (blue T-shirts) three, (yellow T-shirts) three, (boys) two, (girls) six

CB p56 **Activity 13 Read and match.**

- Read the first sentence to the pupils. The pupils say the answer or write it in their notebooks.
- Repeat with the other sentences.

Answers: 1 b **2** c **3** a **4** d

AB p70 **Activity 16 Write.**

- Read the words in the word pool to the pupils.
- Point to the first picture and read the text about the boy.
- Point to the second picture. The pupils complete the text about the girl with words from the word pool.
- Point to the third picture. The pupils write a text about the boy.

Answers: 2 She's wearing a T-shirt, trousers / trainers and a wig. She's got a flag. **3** He's wearing a T-shirt, trousers / trainers and a hat. He's got a drum.

PMB p35 **Make the picture cards**

- Give out the photocopies of the football things picture cards. The pupils colour and cut out the picture cards.
- They can use their cards to play a game, for example, *Who's got …?* (see p21).
- If your pupils are using word cards, they can prepare them now (see p30). Pupils cut them out and match them with the picture cards.
- Remind the pupils to keep all the cards in a safe place.

Lesson 10

■ = Words ◗ = Other subjects

Learning through English

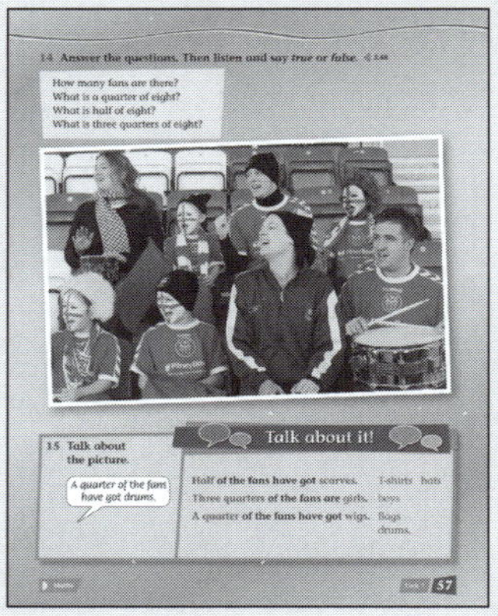

CB page 57

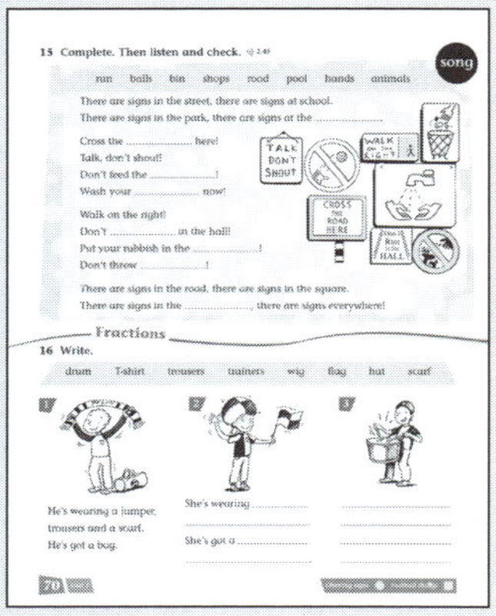

AB page 70

Objectives

- Review words for football things and fractions
- Work out and talk about fractions

Core language

Review of language used so far

Materials

Sports flashcards (x11); Football things flashcards (x6); CD 2

Review vocabulary

- Stick half of the sports flashcards and half of the football things flashcards on the board.
- Write up the words with jumbled letters.
- Ask the pupils to come to the front to write the words and match them with the flashcards.
- Repeat with the other half of the flashcards.

CB p57 **Activity 14 Answer the questions. Then listen and say *true* or *false*.**

- Read the first question to the pupils. They count and answer.
- Repeat with the other questions.

Answers: eight, two, four, six

- Show the picture to the pupils. Ask them to count how many fans are wearing wigs, scarves, hats, and T-shirts, and how many are holding flags and drums.
- Play the CD to the pupils. Pause after the first sentence. The pupils say *true*. They write the answers in their notebooks.
- Repeat with the other sentences.

2.48

Half of the fans have got drums.
Half of the fans are wearing wigs.
A quarter of the fans are wearing hats.
Half of the fans are wearing scarves.
A quarter of the fans are wearing T-shirts.
A quarter of the fans have got flags.

Answers: 1 false **2** false **3** false **4** true **5** false **6** true

CB p57 Activity 15 Talk about the picture.

- Read the example to the pupils. Read the sentences and other words in the *Talk about it!* box.
- Ask a pupil to make a sentence with *a quarter*, for example *A quarter of the fans are wearing wigs.*
- Repeat with other cues from the *Talk about it!* box.
- The pupils talk about the picture in pairs.

AB p71 Activity 17 Answer, circle and complete.

- Read the words in the word pool to the pupils.
- Point to the first picture. Read the text. Show how half of six is three.
- Point to the second picture. Say *Count the boys.* (*Ten.*) The pupils circle half the boys (five), then complete the sentence.
- Repeat with the third and fourth pictures.

Answers: 2 ten, ten, five 3 sixteen, sixteen, four 4 eight, eight, six

AB p71 Activity 18 Read and write.

- Read the words in the word pool to the pupils.
- Point to the picture and ask *How many children are there?* (*Eight.*)
- Ask more questions about the picture, such as *How many girls are there? (Six.) How many children are wearing trainers? (Six.) How many children are wearing trousers? (Four.)*
- Look at the example sentence with the pupils. Ask them what they could write for sentence 2.
- Repeat with the other sentences.

Answers: 2 are wearing trousers 3 / 4 are wearing jackets / are boys 5 are girls 6 have got bags

Lesson 11 = Other subjects

Learning through English (Project)

CB page 58

Objectives

- Review vocabulary for football things
- Draw a picture of some football fans
- Write about the fans

Core language

Review of language used so far

Materials

Football things flashcards (x6); Football fans template (PMB p38) – one photocopy per pupil

Review vocabulary

- Put the football things flashcards on the board. The pupils repeat the words chorally and then individually.
- Play *Memory words* with the pupils. Say sequences of three football words (for example *drum, scarf, wig*); the pupils repeat the words in the same sequence and point to the flashcards on the board.

Present the project

- Tell the pupils they are going to draw a group of football fans.
- They are going to draw the fans with fan gear.
- They are going to write some sentences about the fans.

PMB p38 / CB p58 Activity 16 Make a picture of football fans.

- Give out the photocopies of the football fans.
- Go through the questions: *What is half of sixteen?* (*Eight.*) *What is a quarter of sixteen?* (*Four.*) *What is three quarters of sixteen?* (*Twelve.*)
- Elicit ideas for things to draw on the football fans.
- Read the sentences from Activity Book page 71, Activity 18 again with the pupils.
- The pupils write sentences about their football fans. They use the sentences in Activity 18 as a model.
- The pupils draw the fan gear on the football fans, to match their sentences. While they are drawing, circulate round the class. Encourage the pupils to use their imagination.

Display

- Display the pictures in the classroom.

- Allow the pupils to move around the classroom, look at all the football fan pictures and discuss them with their friends.
- Have a feedback session in which the pupils decide on the best pictures. Ask the pupils to give reasons for their choices.

Lesson 11a (optional)

Learning through English (Extension)

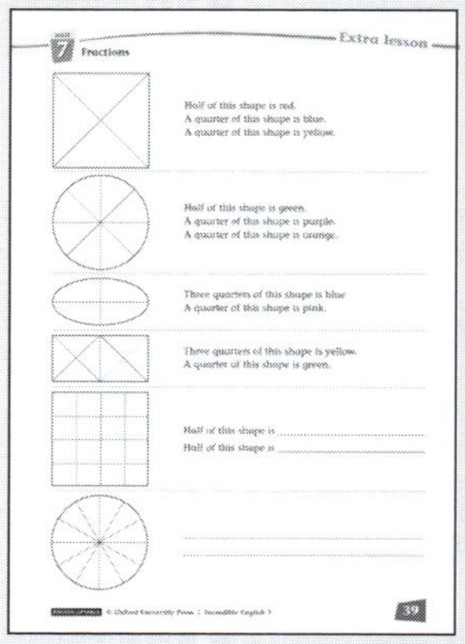
7 Fractions
Extra lesson
Half of this shape is red.
A quarter of this shape is blue.
A quarter of this shape is yellow.
Half of this shape is green.
A quarter of this shape is purple.
A quarter of this shape is orange.
Three quarters of this shape is blue
A quarter of this shape is pink.
Three quarters of this shape is yellow.
A quarter of this shape is green.
Half of this shape is ....
Half of this shape is ....
39

PMB page 39

Objectives

- Practise using fractions
- Divide shapes into segments
- Write about fractions of shapes
- Make patterns using a grid

Core language

fractions (*quarter, half, three quarters*)

Review of

- shapes vocabulary: *square, triangle, circle*
- numbers up to 100

Materials

'Fractions' worksheet (PMB p39) – one photocopy per pupil; Paper – one or two pieces per pupil (optional)

Review vocabulary

- Review the vocabulary for fractions: write ½, ¼, and ¾ on the board and ask the pupils to say the words chorally and individually.
- Practise the fractions: draw squares and circles on the board and divide them into half, quarter, and three quarters. Point to the sections and ask the pupils to say the correct fraction.

Preparation

- Draw a shape on the board, with an even number of squares. Ask the pupils to count the squares. Then ask a pupil to come to the front and colour half of the squares. Talk about different ways of doing this, for example:

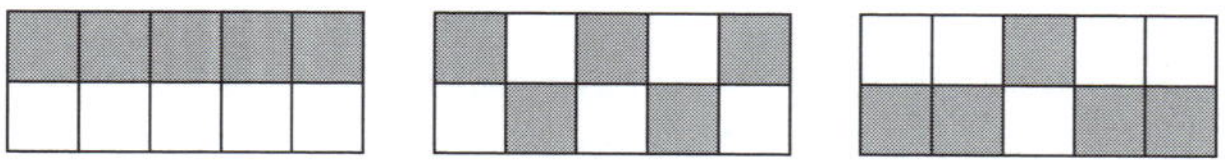

- Tell the pupils that in this lesson they are going to colour and write about fractions of shapes.

Using the Photocopy Master

- Give each pupil a photocopy of the 'Fractions' worksheet.
- Ask the pupils how many different shapes they can see on the page. Remind them of the vocabulary *square, circle*, and *triangle* (from Level 1).
- Look at the first shape with the pupils, and read the description. Ask what shape the quarters of the square are (*triangles*). Ask what other shape they could be (*squares*). (Draw a picture to illustrate, if necessary).
- The pupils colour the square according to the description. Make sure that they understand what to do, and then ask them to read and colour the next three shapes.
- For the last two shapes, pupils choose the colours themselves, and complete or write the description.

Display

- Arrange a display of the worksheets in the classroom. Allow the pupils to see all the shapes and discuss them, for example how they have coloured the first few shapes in different ways, although the fractions remain the same.
- Have a feedback session. Encourage the pupils to talk about each other's final shape on the worksheet. They can read the description, or you can cover the description and get pupils to describe the shape without the written prompt.

Fun activity (optional)

- Give each pupil a piece of paper. Ask them to draw a grid of squares, e.g. 6 by 6, or 10 by 10. Help them to work out what half / quarter of these numbers is. Explain that to find the total number of squares in each grid, you multiply the number along each side, e.g. 6x6 (=36) or 10x10 (=100).
- Ask the pupils to work out what half / quarter of these numbers is. Recast their answers in English as necessary: *Yes, half of thirty-six is eighteen, and a quarter of thirty-six is nine.*
- Tell them to colour and write about their shape, as they did on the worksheet. Encourage them to make attractive patterns when they colour the squares.
- Arrange a display of the finished patterns.

Teaching tip

You may find it useful to use pre-printed squared paper for this activity, or to prepare a grid yourself on a photocopy master and copy it.

Song

- Ask the pupils *Can you remember the song in this unit?*
- Write what the pupils can remember on the board. Help them to remember the bits they've forgotten, then add them on the board.
- Play the song again (Listening 2.45). The pupils check that the version on the board is correct.
- Play the song again and encourage the pupils to join in.

Lesson 12

Review and self-evaluation

CB page 58

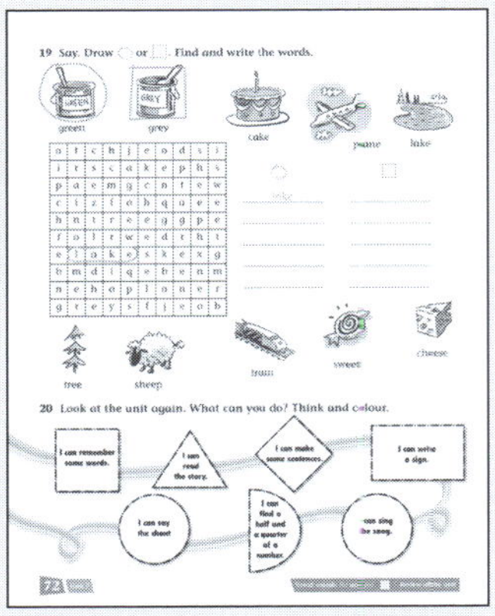

AB page 72

Objectives

- Focus on the pronunciation of vowel sounds (/iː/ and /eɪ/) with a chant
- Review the activities and the new language of the unit
- Complete a self-evaluation activity

Core language

Review of language used so far

Materials

CD 2; Rollercoaster Game poster; Character counters and game cards; Dice (one pair per class); Picture dictionary page (PMB p2) – one photocopy per pupil (optional)

CB p58 Activity 17 Listen, find and repeat.

- Point to the pictures. The pupils say the words.
- Play the CD. Pupils point and repeat.

2.49

sheep – green – sweet – tree – cheese [/iː/]
cake – train – lake – grey – plane [/eɪ/]

- Say the two vowel sounds /iː/ and /eɪ/. The pupils find the words that share the vowel sound.
- The pupils practise saying the words chorally and individually, concentrating on the pronunciation of the vowel sounds.

CB p58 Activity 18 Listen and say the chant.

- Play the chant. The pupils point to the items as they hear them.

2.50

I can see a green tree.
I can see a grey lake.
Green tree, green cheese,
Grey lake, grey cake!

I can see a grey plane.
I can see a green sweet.
Grey plane, grey train,
Green sweet, green sheep!

- Teach the chant line by line. Focus on the pronunciation points. Use choral and individual repetition to check pronunciation.
- Play the chant again and encourage the pupils to join in.

Focus on spelling

- Match the spelling with the vowel sounds.
- Highlight the spelling patterns:
  /iː/ is often spelt *ee* (*green*)
  /eɪ/ is often spelt *a*..*e* (*lake*) or *ai* (*train*)
- Show examples from the chant for each vowel sound.
- Remind the pupils that there are lots of exceptions to spelling patterns in English.

AB p72 Activity 19 Say. Draw ● or ■. Find and write the words.

- Point to each of the pictures. The pupils say the words chorally.
- Focus on the pronunciation difference between /iː/ and /eɪ/, using the words *green* and *grey*.
- Show how *green* has a circle around it and *grey* has a square round it.
- Ask the pupils to identify a word with the /iː/ sound.
- Show the pupils how to put a circle round the word.
- Repeat with the /eɪ/ sound, putting a square around the word.
- The pupils put circles and squares around the words.
- The pupils find and circle the words in the wordsearch. They copy the words into the correct columns.
- Point to the pictures at random. The pupils say the words chorally and individually. Check the pupils' pronunciation.

Answers: circle: green, sweet, tree, cheese, sheep; square: grey, cake, plane, train, lake

a	t	c	h	j	e	o	d	s	i
i	r	s	c	a	k	e	p	h	s
p	a	e	m	g	c	n	t	e	w
c	i	z	f	o	h	q	a	e	e
h	n	t	r	e	e	g	g	p	e
f	o	l	r	w	e	d	r	h	t
e	l	a	k	e	s	k	e	x	g
b	m	d	i	q	e	b	e	n	m
n	e	h	o	p	l	a	n	e	r
g	r	e	y	s	f	j	e	o	b

End-of-unit review

- Use the Rollercoaster Game poster and the Class Book to recall the main activities of the unit.
- Recall the language associated with each activity.
- Ask the pupils to let you know what they liked or didn't like, and what they found easy or difficult.

Play the Rollercoaster Game

- Divide the class into small groups. Give each group one of the character 'counters' and let them play the game as before (see p41).
- Remind them to use the poster chants when a group gets a question right or wrong.

AB p72 Activity 20 Look at the unit again. What can you do? Think and colour.

- Let the pupils do the self-evaluation activity as before (see p41).

PMB p2 Picture Dictionary (optional)

- If your pupils are making Picture Dictionaries, give out the photocopies of the template.
- Pupils continue making the dictionaries as for Unit 1 (see p42).

Lesson 12a (optional)

■ = Words ◆ = Sentences

Show what you know!

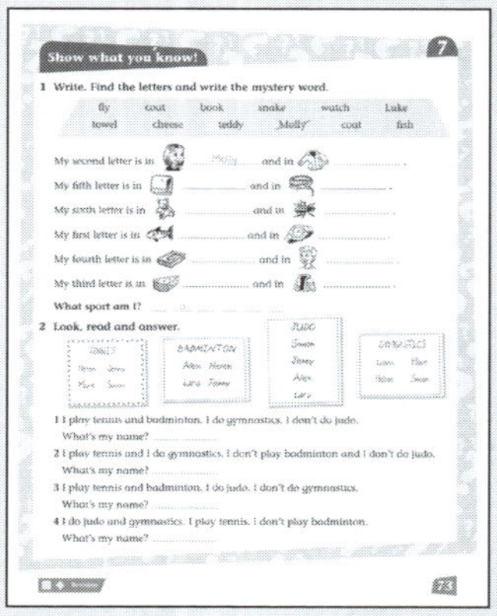

AB page 73

For suggestions on how to use *Show what you know!* see page 13.

Objectives

- Extra practice of the vocabulary of the unit
- Solve puzzles in English
- Provide extra material for homework and fast finishers

Core language

Review of language used so far

Materials

No extra materials

Review vocabulary

- Do a quick recap of ordinal numbers. Write the numbers 1 to 10 on the board in figures, and ask pupils to tell you the ordinal numbers. Get pupils to help you write the ordinals on the board, in words and figures.

AB p73 Activity 1 Write. Find the letters and write the mystery word.

- Read the words in the word pool to the pupils.
- Write six lines on the board (_ _ _ _ _ _). Say *We are going to guess the word.*
- Read the beginning of the first sentence to the pupils (*My second letter is in ...*). Ask the pupils to identify the picture (*Molly*) and write the word on the board.
- Continue with the rest of the sentence (*and in ...*). Ask the pupils to identify the next picture (*coat*) and write the word on the board.
- Ask the pupils *What letter is in Molly and in coat?* The pupils answer *o*. Ask the pupils *Where does letter 'o' go in the word?* The pupils answer *It's the second letter.* (Recast their answers if necessary.) Write the letter *o* in the second space.
- Repeat with the other sentences. The pupils copy the words on the lines in their Activity Books, and add the letters to the mystery word as they find them.

Answer: My second letter is in Molly and in coat.
My fifth letter is in towel and in snake.
My sixth letter is in teddy and in fly.
My first letter is in fish and in watch.
My fourth letter is in book and in Luke.
My third letter is in cheese and in coat.
The mystery word is *hockey*.

AB p73 Activity 2 Look, read and answer.

- Point to the lists of the sports teams. Read the names of the children. Say to the pupils *Tell me about Helen. She plays ...*
- The pupils make sentences about the sports that Helen plays (*She plays tennis and badminton. She does gymnastics*) and the sports she doesn't play (*She doesn't do judo*).
- Read the first description to the pupils. They identify the person (*Helen*).
- The pupils match the other descriptions with the people in pairs.

Answers: **1** Helen **2** Mark **3** Jenny **4** Simon

The pupils are now ready to sit the Unit 7 test. See pp194–197 for both Standard and Higher levels.

DVD VIDEO

Multimedia extension: you may now like to use the Maths 1 section of the optional DVD.

8 Uncle Bill

Lesson 1 ■ = Words

Introducing vocabulary

CB page 59

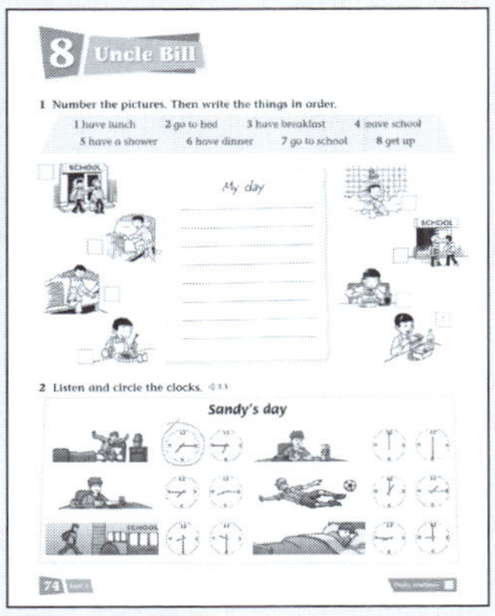

AB page 74

Objectives

- Understand the theme of the unit
- Become familiar with verbs for daily routines
- Practise listening to and asking about daily routines
- Focus on spelling

Core language

Daily routine vocabulary: *get up, have a shower, have breakfast, go to work / school, have lunch, leave work / school, have dinner, go to bed*

Other language

inventor, robot, workshop, machine

Materials

Rollercoaster Game poster; Daily routines flashcards (*get up, have a shower, have breakfast, go to school, have lunch, leave school, have dinner, go to bed*); CD 3; Pupils' bookmarks (optional) (see p28)

Unit overview

- Talk to the pupils about daily routines. Ask them what words they know for daily routines in English. Ask them what words (in their own language) they would like to learn.
- Ask the pupils to look through Unit 8 in their Class Books. Talk with them about the unit and quickly write the different topics and activities on the board, relating them to the shapes on the poster:
  - ■ Words – daily routines, electrical components
  - ▲ Story – *The Ice Cream Machine*
  - ◆ Sentences – *He works in a shop. What time does he get up?*
  - ▬ Text work – Adverts
  - ● Song – *Stop and think!* / Chant – *Noisy toys*
  - ◗ Other subjects – Science (learn to describe electrical circuits)
- Remind the pupils that they will use the poster again at the end of the unit.

Teaching tip

Please note that the flashcard set for this unit does not exactly match the vocabulary on the Class Book presentation page. The Class Book presentation includes *go to work* and *leave work* (to talk about Uncle Bill's day), whereas the flashcard set is based around the daily routine of a child, and so includes *go to school* and *leave school* instead. Teach *go to / leave school* via the flashcard presentation, and then go on to teach *go to / leave work* as preparation for the Class Book listening activity (see below).

Introduce new vocabulary *see p19*

- Use the flashcards to teach the new vocabulary. The pupils repeat the words chorally, then individually.
- Work out a gesture for each activity (for example, rubbing your eyes and stretching your arms for *get up*).
- Play *Get moving!* with the pupils. First do the gestures and ask the pupils to say the activity. Then ask individual pupils to do the gestures for the other pupils to guess.
- Put the flashcards for *go to school* and *leave school* on the board. Ask pupils where adults normally go instead of school. Recast their answers: *Yes, they go to work.* Write *go to work* and *leave work* on the board. The pupils repeat the words chorally, then individually.

CB p59 Activity 1 Look, listen and repeat.

- Look at the picture with the pupils. Ask questions such as *Who can you see? What's happening?* Recast the pupils' answers as necessary: *Yes, this man is an inventor. There are lots of machines to help him.*
- The pupils listen to the recording. They repeat each word chorally and point to the correct picture.

3.1

1 get up, **2** have a shower, **3** have breakfast, **4** go to work, **5** have lunch, **6** leave work, **7** have dinner, **8** go to bed

CB p59 Activity 2 Listen and find.

- Explain that the man is Eve's uncle, an inventor who has built lots of machines to help him at home.
- Play the dialogue.
- The pupils listen for the daily routine activities. They point to each activity as they hear it mentioned.
- Alternatively, the pupils can use their bookmarks (see p28) to focus on the pictures.

3.2

Eve:	Hi, kids. This is my Uncle Bill. He's an inventor.
Bill:	Hello, everyone!
Children:	Hello!
Bill:	Do you want to hear about my day?
All:	Yes!
Bill:	Well, I get up at half past five.
Molly:	Half past five!
Bill:	Yes. Then I have a shower. But my shower is a special shower.
Archie:	Wow!

Bill: I have breakfast at six o'clock. My robot makes my breakfast. Look – this is my robot.
Jazmin: Oh!
Bill: At half past six, I go to work.
Archie: Half past six! That's early!
Molly: Where do you work?
Bill: I work in a workshop. I invent machines. Look. This is my ice cream machine.
Luke: Wow!
Bill: I have lunch at half past one.
Jazmin: What do you have?
Bill: Sandwiches and fruit. Look.
Bill: I leave work at five. My robot makes my dinner.
Luke: What time do you have dinner?
Bill: At eight o'clock.
Luke: And after dinner?
Bill: After dinner I read a book, or watch television. I go to bed at ten o'clock.

CB p59 Activity 3 Guess the times. Ask and answer.

- Introduce the dialogue with questions such as *Do you get up at eight o'clock?*
- The pupils answer your questions with *Yes* or *No*.
- Practise the dialogue with individual pupils, using different activities and times.
- The pupils practise asking and answering the questions in pairs.

Spelling

- Ask the pupils to identify:
  1 words that are similar in their language (highlight the differences in spelling)
  2 activities with *go*, with *have*, and with *get*
  3 words with vowel + *r* (*dinner*, *work*).

AB p74 Activity 1 Number the pictures. Then write the things in order.

- Read the phrases in the word pool to the pupils. Ask the pupils to match the phrases to the pictures, and write the numbers in the boxes.
- Ask the pupils *Which activity do we do first in the morning?* The pupils say *get up*, and write this first in the list.
- The pupils write the activities in the order they do them each day.

Answers: (example) get up, have a shower, have breakfast, go to school, have lunch, leave school, have dinner, go to bed (the order may vary – for example, some pupils may have a shower in the evening instead of the morning)

Lesson 2 ■ = Words

Practising vocabulary

AB page 74

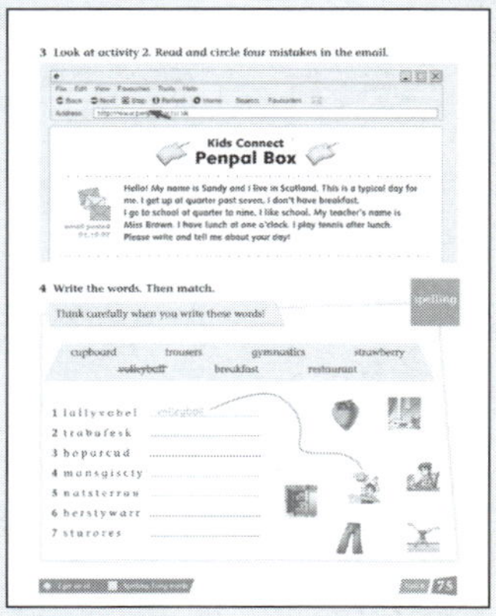

AB page 75

Objectives

- Review vocabulary for daily routines
- Practise listening and talking about daily routines
- Practise spelling long words

Core language

Review of

- daily routines
- language used so far

Materials

Daily routines flashcards (x8); Daily routines picture cards (PMB p40) – one photocopied set per pupil

Review vocabulary

- Stick the daily routines flashcards on the board like this:
  [get up] [go to bed]
  [go to school] [leave school]
  [have lunch] [have dinner] [have a shower]
- Point to the flashcards: the pupils say the words chorally and individually.
- Play *Where is it?* with the pupils: turn the flashcards face down on the board, then point to each one. The pupils say which card it is.

AB p74 Activity 2 Listen and circle the clocks.

- Ask the pupils to read the times on the clocks (*quarter past seven, quarter to seven,* etc.).
- Play the first part of the conversation, up to the pause. Ask *What time does he get up?* The pupils answer *quarter past seven* and circle the correct clock face.
- Play the rest of the conversation on the CD. During the pauses, give the pupils enough time to circle the correct time.

3.3

Adult: Hi Sandy. Where do you live?
Sandy: I live in Scotland.
Adult: Tell me about your day.
Sandy: OK. Well … I get up at quarter past seven. *[PAUSE]*
Adult. Do you have breakfast?
Sandy: Yes, of course! A big breakfast. At quarter to eight. *[PAUSE]*
Adult: And then?
Sandy: And then I go to school.
Adult: What time do you go to school?
Sandy: At half past eight.

Adult: Right. half past eight. *[PAUSE]* What time do you have lunch?
Sandy: At half past twelve. *[PAUSE]* Then I play football.
Adult: What time do you play football?
Sandy: At one o'clock.
Adult: What time do you go to bed?
Sandy: I go to bed at nine o'clock.

Answers: 1 quarter past seven **2** quarter to eight **3** half past eight **4** half past twelve **5** one o'clock **6** nine o'clock

AB p75 Activity 3 Look at activity 2. Read and circle four mistakes in the email.

- Tell the pupils they are going to look for mistakes in the letter. Ask individual pupils to read a sentence each from the letter.
- After each mistake, the pupils say what is wrong.

Answers: I don't have breakfast (he has breakfast at quarter to eight), I go to school at quarter to nine (he goes to school at half past eight), I have lunch at one o'clock (he has lunch at half past twelve), I play tennis after lunch (he plays football after lunch)

- As a follow-up, the pupils can write a letter to a penpal about their daily routine.

AB p75 Activity 4 Write the words. Then match.

- Read the words in the word pool to the pupils.
- Say *These words are difficult to spell.* Tell the pupils to concentrate on the spelling, particularly the combinations of two vowels (*cupboard*, *trousers*, etc.) and the double letters (*strawberry*, *volleyball*).
- Point to the jumbled words. Show that number 1 is *volleyball* and there is a line joining it to the volleyball picture.
- The pupils write the letters in the correct order and match the words with the pictures.

Answers: 1 volleyball **2** breakfast **3** cupboard **4** gymnastics **5** restaurant **6** strawberry **7** trousers

Spelling game

- Play *Guess the word* using daily routines vocabulary (see p20).

PMB p40 Make the picture cards

- Give out the photocopies of the daily routines picture cards. The pupils colour and cut out the picture cards.
- If your pupils are using word cards, they can prepare them now (see p30). Pupils cut them out and match them with the picture cards.
- They can use their cards to play a game, for example, *Memory (pairs)* (see p20).
- Remind the pupils to keep all the cards in a safe place.

Lesson 3 ▲ = Story

Story

CB page 60

CB page 61

Objectives

- Listen to a story
- Read a story
- Listen for words and phrases in a story
- Practise story language

Core language

He works in Middleton; What time does he leave work?

Review of language used so far

Other language

not far away, traffic jam, van, plug it in, switch it on, just right

Not too quick!; Be careful!; What's happening?

Materials

Daily routines flashcards (x8); CD of music with a strong beat; CD 3

Review vocabulary

- Put the daily routines flashcards on the board. The pupils say the words chorally and individually.
- Play *Musical flashcards* with the pupils: they say the word for the flashcard your hand is on when the music stops.

Introduce the story

- Ask the pupils to imagine they belong to the Incredible Club. What new gadgets would they like for the club? (a CD player, a games console, etc.)
- Explain that in the story the children are getting a new gadget for the club.

CB pp60–61 Activity 4 First listening with the books closed

- Tell the pupils to listen and answer this question: *What machine are they looking for?*
- The pupils listen with their books closed.

3.4

[1] At the fête …
Finn: Buy a cake!
Molly: Buy a drink!
Molly: Oh dear!

[2] Finn: Where's your Uncle Bill? We need the ice cream machine!
Eve: I know. But Bill's still at work.
Finn: Where does he work?
Eve: Not far away. He works in Middleton.

[3] Archie: What time does he leave work?
Eve: At five o'clock.
Archie: Oh good!

[4] Eve: But there's a traffic jam!
Archie: Oh dear!

[5] Half an hour later …
Eve: At last! Here's Uncle Bill.
Uncle Bill: Hi, everyone! Help me set up my machine. It's fantastic!

[6] Uncle Bill: Plug it in … and switch it on. You put the fruit in here … and the cream and milk in here.

[7] Molly: I want a strawberry ice cream, please!
Eve: I like banana.
Archie: Melon for me.
(fizzing and popping sound effects)

[8] Bill: Not too quick! Be careful … Oh no!

[9] Man: Oh, what's happening?
Child: What's that?
Woman: Let's go and look.

[10] Finn: Now that really is an incredible ice cream machine.
Archie: Just right for the Incredible Club!

- Check the answer to your question (*An ice cream machine*).

CB pp60–61 Activity 4 Second listening with the books open

- Tell the pupils to open their books and look at the story.
- Ask questions about the story such as *What ice cream does Eve want?*
- Play the recording again while the pupils follow in their books.
- Go through any vocabulary queries with the class.

CB p61 Activity 5 Read and write *true* or *false*.

- Explain that the number of each sentence refers to the number of the picture in the story.
- Ask the pupils to read the first sentence, then look at picture 1. Ask *Is that true?* The pupils answer *Yes.*
- The pupils read the sentences and write the answers (*true* or *false*) in their notebooks.

Answers: 1 true 2 false 4 false 5 true 8 false 9 false 10 true

Fun expressions

- Write these 'fun expressions' from the story on the board:
  Oh good!
  It's fantastic!
  Oh no!
- Play the story again: the pupils put up their hands when they hear one of the phrases.
- Pause the recording. The pupils repeat the phrase chorally and individually. Encourage the pupils to copy the intonation on the CD.

Lesson 4 ◆ = Sentences

Language focus 1

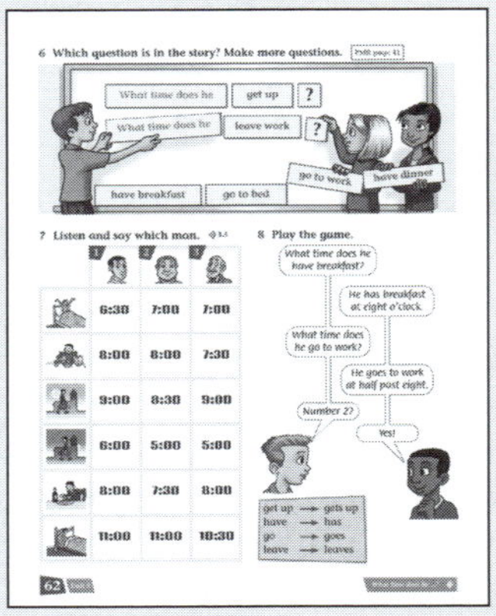

CB page 62

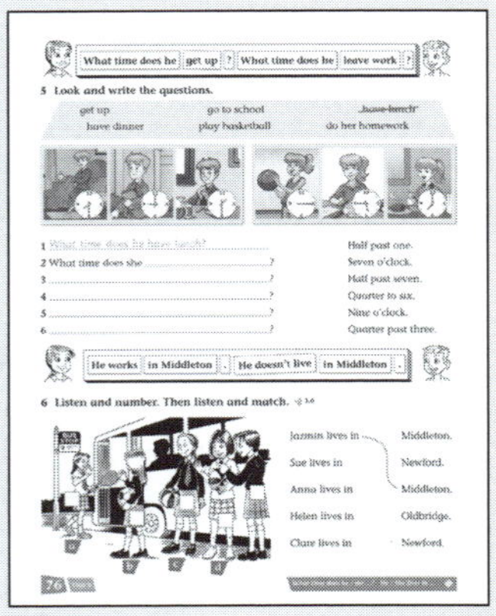

AB page 76

Objectives

- Understand the use of *What time does he …?*
- Practise using the new language

Core language

What time does he …?
Review of language used so far

Materials

CD 3; Grammar tiles (PMB p41) – one photocopy of Set 1 per pupil (optional)

Recall the story

- Ask the pupils to remember as much as they can from the story.
- Say some sentences from the story, and ask the pupils to identify who says each one, for example:
  What time does he leave work? (Archie)
  Hi, everyone! Help me set up my machine. (Uncle Bill)
  You put the fruit in here … (Uncle Bill)
  Melon for me. (Archie)
  Just right for the Incredible Club! (Archie)

PMB p41 CB p62 Activity 6 Which question is in the story? Make more questions.

- Ask the pupils to read the questions in the grammar tiles.
- Ask the pupils to say which question was in the story (*What time does he leave work?*).
- Focus on the combination of *What time* with *does*. Make sure that the pupils remember that *does* always goes with the simple form of the verb.
- The pupils say the sentences in the grammar tiles chorally and individually.
- The pupils use the remaining tiles in the picture to make questions with *What time does he …?* Choose other pupils to answer. Alternatively, give each pupil a copy of Set 1 of the grammar tiles from the PMB: the pupils cut out the tiles and arrange them in questions on their desks. Ask individual pupils to read out their questions for the class.

CB p62 Activity 7 Listen and say which man.

- Show the pupils the pictures of the daily routines. The pupils say the words.
- Ask the pupils to say the times in the table.

- Play the CD. After the first conversation, the pupils identify which man it is.
- Repeat with the other conversations.

3.5

Archie:	What time does he leave work?
Finn:	He leaves work at six o'clock.
Archie:	What time does he have dinner?
Finn:	He has dinner at eight o'clock.
Presenter:	Which man is it?
Finn:	What time does he get up?
Archie:	He gets up at seven o'clock.
Finn:	What time does he have breakfast?
Archie:	He has breakfast at half past seven.
Presenter:	Which man is it?
Archie:	What time does he go to work?
Finn:	He goes to work at half past eight.
Archie:	What time does he go to bed?
Finn:	He goes to bed at eleven o'clock.
Presenter:	Which man is it?

Answers: 1, 3, 2

CB p62 Activity 8 Play the game.

- Read the conversation to the pupils.
- Say you are thinking of one of the men. The pupils ask you questions to guess which man.
- The pupils play the game in pairs.

AB p76 Activity 5 Look and write the questions.

- Read the words in the word pool to the pupils.
- Point to the pictures in the cartoons. For each picture, ask *What's the time?*
- Read the first question and answer. Read the beginning of the second question and the answer. The pupils complete the question (... *have dinner*) and write it on the line.
- Read the answer in number 3. Ask *What's the question?* The pupils say *What time does he get up?* and write the question on the line.
- Repeat with the other questions and answers.

Answers: **1** What time does he have lunch? **2** What time does she have dinner? **3** What time does he get up? **4** What time does she do her homework? **5** What time does he go to school? **6** What time does she play basketball?

Lesson 5 ◆ = Sentences

Language focus 2

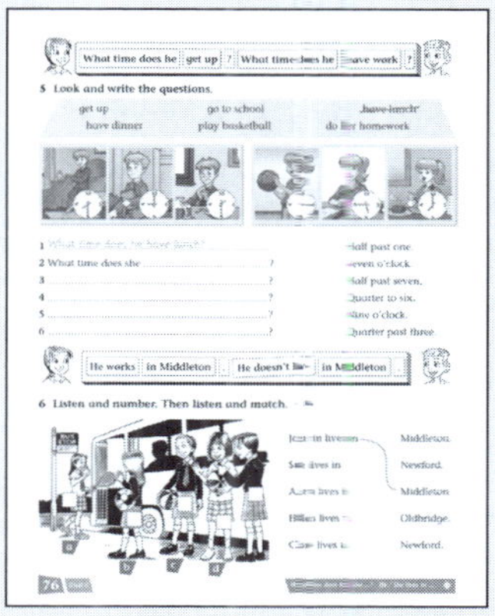

AB page 76

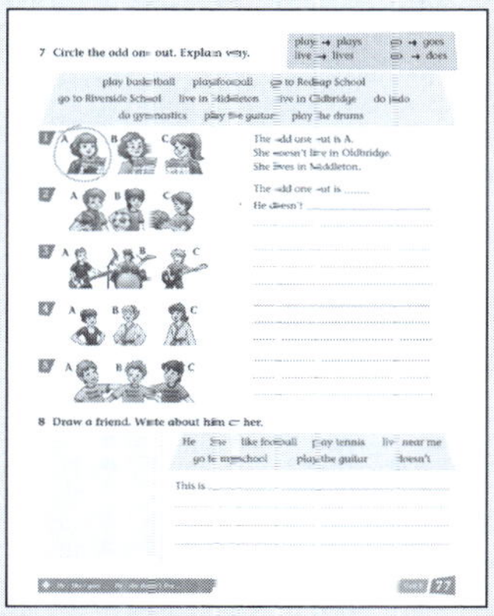

AB page 77

Objectives

- Review *He works in* ... and *What time does he ...?*
- Understand the use of *He doesn't work ...*
- Practise using the new language

Core language

He works in ...; He doesn't work in ...; What time does he ...?

Review of language used so far

Materials

Grammar tiles (PMB p41) – one photocopy of Set 2 per pupil; CD 3

PMB p41 / AB p76 Focus on language

- Read the sentences in the second set of grammar tiles to the pupils. Ask the pupils *Which sentence is in the story?* (*He works in Middleton.*)
- Point out the difference between the affirmative form (*He works ... / He lives ...*) and the negative form (*He doesn't work ... / He doesn't live ...*). Write the contraction and the long form on board *He doesn't work = He does not work.* Use a mime gesture to show how the long form 'contracts' to the short form.
- The pupils say the sentences in the grammar tiles chorally and individually.
- Give each pupil a photocopy of Set 2 of the grammar tiles from the PMB. Ask the pupils to suggest place names to put in the blank tiles (e.g. their own town, the capital city of their country, or any English towns they have heard of). Write the suggestions on the board. The pupils copy the place names in the blank tiles.
- The pupils cut out all the tiles and use them to make sentences on their desks.

AB p76 Activity 6 Listen and number. Then listen and match.

- Ask the pupils to look at the picture of Jazmin pointing at her friends.
- Play the first section of the CD. Ask *Who is it?* The pupils answer *Sue*, and write *1* in the box next to Sue.
- Repeat with the other sections of the conversation. The pupils number Jazmin's friends in the order they hear about them.

3.6

Jazmin: Hi, I'm Jazmin. I live in Middleton.

1 Jazmin: This is my friend Sue.
She plays basketball. She doesn't play tennis.
She doesn't go to school with me.
She doesn't live in Middleton. She lives in Newford.

2 Jazmin: This is my friend Anna.
She doesn't play basketball, but she plays football.
She goes to school with me. She lives in Middleton.

3 Jazmin: This is my friend Helen.
She plays basketball. She doesn't play tennis.
She goes to school with me.
She doesn't live in Middleton. She lives in Oldbridge.

4 Jazmin: This is my friend Clare.
She doesn't play basketball, but she plays tennis.
She doesn't go to school with me.
She lives in Newford.

Answers: a 4 b 2 c 3 d 1

- Tell the pupils they are going to listen again. This time, they must concentrate on where each person lives.
- Play the first section of the CD again. Show the pupils that the text *Jazmin lives in* is joined by a line to *Middleton*. Ask *Where does Sue live?* The pupils answer *Newford*, and draw a line from *Sue lives in* to *Newford*.
- Play the other sections of the CD. The pupils match the friends with the towns they live in.

Answers: Sue – Newford, Anna – Middleton, Helen – Oldbridge, Clare – Newford

AB p77 Activity 7 Circle the odd one out. Explain why.

- Read the words in the word pool to the pupils.
- Point to the grammar box and remind the pupils of the *s* form of the verb with *he* and *she* (*I play, he plays*, etc.).
- Point to the first set of pictures and ask *Which is the odd one out? Why?* The pupils say *A, she doesn't live in Oldbridge. She lives in Middleton.*
- Repeat with the second set of pictures. The pupils circle the odd one out and say (and then write) the reason.
- Repeat with the other sets of pictures.

Answers: 2 B – He doesn't play basketball. He plays football.
3 B – He doesn't play the guitar. He plays the drums.
4 A – She doesn't do judo. She does gymnastics.
5 C – He doesn't got to Redcap School. He goes to Riverside School.

AB p77 Activity 8 Draw a friend. Write about him or her.

- Read the words in the word pool to the pupils.
- Draw a picture of a friend / family member on the board. Write sentences about him / her using the phrases in the word pool, for example: *This is Rita. She doesn't live near me. She lives in .... She plays tennis. She doesn't like football. She plays the guitar.*
- The pupils draw a friend in the frame. They write sentences about their friend using the words in the word pool. While they are writing, circulate around the class and pay special attention to the correct form of the verbs.

For extra grammar practice, see AB page 104.

Activity 1 Look and write.

Answers: 2 He goes to school at half past eight. 3 What time does he have lunch? 4 She goes to bed at quarter to nine. 5 What time does he have a shower?

Lesson 6 ▲ = Story

Playscript

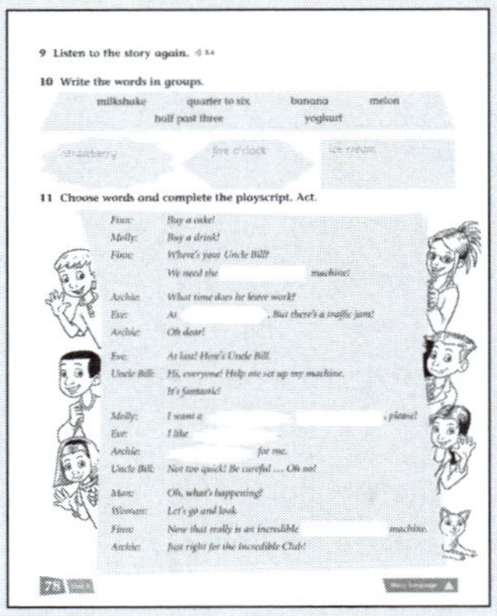
9 Listen to the story again.
10 Write the words in groups.
milkshake quarter to six banana melon half past three yoghurt
strawberry five o'clock ice cream
11 Choose words and complete the playscript. Act.
Finn: Buy a cake!
Molly: Buy a drink!
Finn: Where's your Uncle Bill? We need the ______ machine!
Archie: What time does he leave work?
Eve: At ______. But there's a traffic jam!
Archie: Oh dear!
Eve: At last! Here's Uncle Bill.
Uncle Bill: Hi, everyone! Help me set up my machine. It's fantastic!
Molly: I want a ______ ______, please!
Eve: I like ______.
Archie: ______ for me.
Uncle Bill: Not too quick! Be careful … Oh no!
Max: Oh, what's happening?
Woman: Let's go and look.
Finn: Now that really is an incredible ______ machine.
Archie: Just right for the Incredible Club!

AB page 78

Objectives

- Read and complete a playscript
- Use finger puppets to act out a playscript
- Act out the play

Core language

Review of language used so far

Materials

CD 3; Spare photocopies of the finger puppets (PMB p3)

AB p78 Activity 9 Listen to the story again.

- Tell the pupils to look at pages 60–61 in the Class Book again.
- Play the CD while the pupils listen and read.
- Alternatively, the pupils can read the story aloud in groups of eight. Each pupil should read one character.

AB p78 Activity 10 Write the words in groups.

- Read the words in the word pool to the pupils.
- Point to each of the boxes and read the word in each one. Ask the pupils to suggest words from the word pool to go in each box.
- The pupils write the words from the word pool in the correct category. Make sure they understand that in this instance fruits are grouped separately from other foods.

Answers: set 1 – strawberry, banana, melon; set 2 – five o'clock, half past three, quarter to six; set 3 – ice cream, milkshake, yoghurt

- Ask the pupils to suggest new words for each category.

AB p78 **Activity 11 Choose words and complete the playscript. Act.**

- Read the playscript to the pupils. When you come to a blank, ask *Which word was in the story?* The pupils say the words from the story.
- Read the playscript again. Ask the pupils to suggest alternative words from Activity 10 to complete the blanks.
- Divide the pupils into groups of four. In their groups, the pupils decide which words to use when they read the playscript.

Finger puppets *see p22*

- Ask the pupils *How many characters are there in the story? (seven).* The pupils identify the seven characters. (Eve, Molly, Archie, Finn, Uncle Bill, Woman, Man).
- Say *We have four pupils for seven characters. It isn't a problem. Look!* Write this table on the board:
  Pupil 1 – Eve
  Pupil 2 – Molly and Woman
  Pupil 3 – Archie and Man
  Pupil 4 – Finn and Uncle Bill
- In their groups, the pupils decide who is going to take each part.
- If the pupils have got their finger puppets with them, tell them to get out the puppet for the character they are going to play.
- Give each group three photocopies of the extra finger puppet. The pupils cut out, colour and stick the extra puppets to make the Man, Woman, and Uncle Bill puppets. If they haven't got the other puppets they need, they will have to make those too.

Practice

- Remind the pupils of the five points of successful play acting:
  1 Listen to the other actors.
  2 Wait for your turn.
  3 Speak clearly.
  4 When the puppets are speaking to each other, they should face each other.
  5 Don't move your puppets unnecessarily.
- Tell the pupils about the notes you made during the Unit 7 play acting. Encourage them to concentrate on the points you noticed. Say you will be watching them again this time.
- The pupils act out the play with their puppets. While they are doing this, circulate around the classroom. Make a note of the points the pupils should improve on next time.
- Ask one or two groups to come to the front to act out the play with their puppets.

Lesson 7 = Text work

Reading and writing

CB page 63

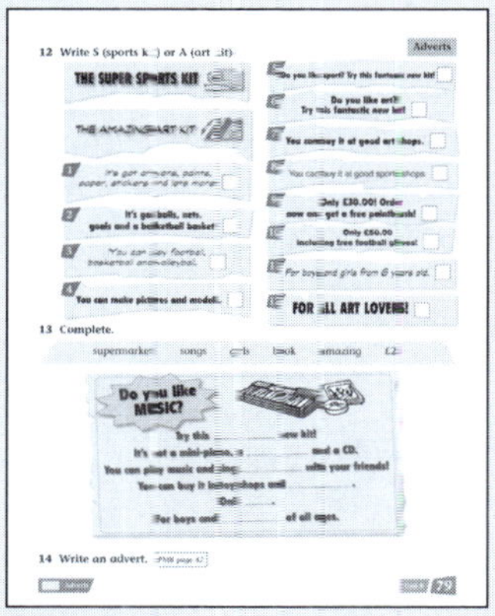

AB page 79

Objectives

- Review daily routines vocabulary
- Read and understand adverts
- Write an advert

Core language

Review of language used so far

Other language

advert, today, electronics

Materials

Daily routines flashcards (x8); Advert template (PMB p42) – one photocopy per pupil

Review vocabulary

- Write the daily routines words and phrases on the board, with the letters in a jumbled order.
- Call pupils to the front to write the letters in the correct order.
- Call other pupils to the front to put the flashcards next to the correct spellings.

CB p63 **Activity 9 Read and answer the questions about a or b.**

- Talk to the pupils about adverts. Ask questions such as *Where do you see adverts? What information do you read in adverts?*
- Ask the pupils about the adverts in the Class Book. Point to each one and ask questions such as *What is it for?* and *How much is it?*
- Tell the pupils to read the adverts. Ask the pupils to answer the questions about advert a or advert b. They write the answers in their notebooks.

Answers: advert a: **1** an ice cream machine **2** it can make hundreds of different ice creams **3** all good shops **4** £50.00 **5** all the family
advert b: **1** a robot **2** walk and talk **3** in toy shops **4** £25.00 **5** boys and girls from 6 to 10 years old

AB p79 Activity 12 Write S (sports kit) or A (art kit).

- Point to the heading *The Super Sports Kit*. Ask the pupils to suggest the items it has (*balls, bats, nets,* etc.). Ask the same question about *The Amazing Art Kit* (*paint, crayons, paintbrushes,* etc.).
- Read the text in Number 1. Ask *Which kit is it?* The pupils answer *the art kit* and write *A* in the box.
- Repeat with the other texts.

Answers: 1 A **2** S **3** S **4** A **5** S **6** A **7** A **8** S **9** A **10** S **11** S **12** A

AB p79 Activity 13 Complete.

- Read the words in the word pool to the pupils.
- Point to the advert for the music kit. The pupils complete the text with words from the word pool.

Answers: amazing, book, songs, supermarkets, £25, girls

PMB p42 / AB p79 Activity 14 Write an advert.

- Explain to the pupils that they are going to write an advert for a kit.
- Remind pupils that they have to choose work for their portfolio during the course (see p198). Point out that this piece of work would be a suitable piece to include.
- Brainstorm ideas for the kit and its contents.
- Choose some suggestions and write them on the board.
- Show the pupils how to write the advert, using the adverts in Activity 9 of the Class Book and Activity 13 of the Activity Book as a model.
- Hand out the photocopies of the writing template. Tell the pupils to choose another kit and write about it.
- The pupils write a rough copy in their notebooks for you to correct. After you have checked the rough copy, they write their final copy on the photocopied template.

Lesson 8 ● = Song / chant

Learning for life

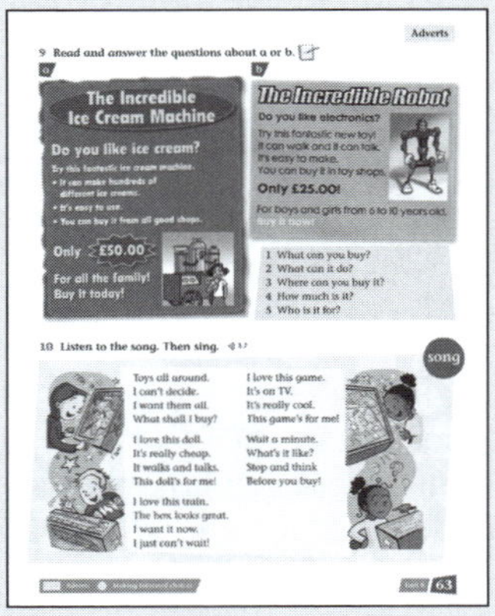

CB page 63

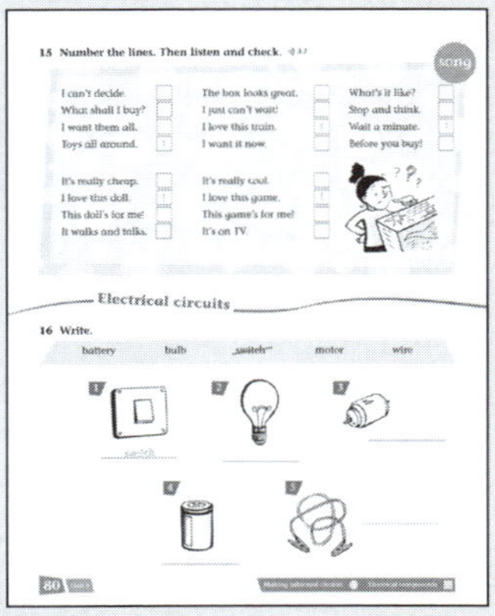

AB page 80

Objectives
- Review the unit so far
- Understand why adverts can be a bad influence
- Talk about how to respond to adverts
- Sing a song about responsible behaviour

Core language
Review of language used so far

Other language
around, decide, cheap, wait, cool

Materials
Rollercoaster Game poster; Daily routines flashcards (x8); CD 3

Unit review

- Use the Rollercoaster Game poster and the Class Book to review the unit so far. Talk with the pupils about the activities they have done.
- The pupils give examples of the language they used in each activity.

Review vocabulary (categorizing)

- Ask the pupils to tell you all the new words they remember from the unit.
- Put the daily routines flashcards on the board and ask the pupils to arrange them in these two categories: *before 12 o'clock* and *after 12 o'clock.*
- Repeat with other categories, such as: *by yourself* and *with other people.*

Introduce the topic

- Talk with the pupils about adverts. Ask questions such as: What are adverts for? Why can adverts be a bad influence?
- Encourage the pupils to talk about some or all of these ideas in their answers:
  – adverts persuade you to buy things
  – sometimes you don't need all the things you buy
  – adverts make us want things we don't need
  – adverts make us spend a lot of money
  – you don't need to spend money to have fun
- The pupils can express their ideas in their own language. If they do, recast their answers in English.

CB p63 Activity 10 Listen to the song. Then sing.

- Read the song with the pupils. Explain any new words.
- Play the song on the CD.

3.7

Girl: Toys all around,
I can't decide.
Boy: I want them all –
What shall I buy?
Girl: I love this doll,
It's really cheap.
It walks and talks –
This doll's for me!
Boy: I love this train,
The box looks great.
I want it now –
I just can't wait!
Girl: I love this game,
It's on TV.
It's really cool –
This game's for me!
Both: Wait a minute,
What's it like?
Stop and think
Before you buy!

- Work out simple mime gestures for these phrases: *This …'s for me, What shall I buy?, Stop and think.*
- Read through the song again and ask the pupils to use the mime gestures as you read.
- Play the song again and encourage the pupils to join in, singing and miming.

AB p80 Activity 15 Number the lines. Then listen and check.

- Tell the pupils to close their Class Books and open their Activity books at page 80.
- Show them the lines of the song. Ask the pupils to find the first line of the song.
- Show them how *1* is written in the box next to this line. Ask them to find the next line and to write *2* next to it.
- Repeat until they have numbered all the lines of the song.
- Play the song again; the pupils check the order they suggested.

Answers: verse 1: 2 4 3 1 verse 2: 2 1 4 3 verse 3: 2 4 1 3 verse 4: 3 1 4 2 verse 5: 2 3 1 4

- To finish the lesson, divide the pupils into four groups. Give each group a number from 1 to 4. Each group reads the corresponding line of the song chorally in the each verse.

Lesson 9 = Words = Other subjects

Learning through English

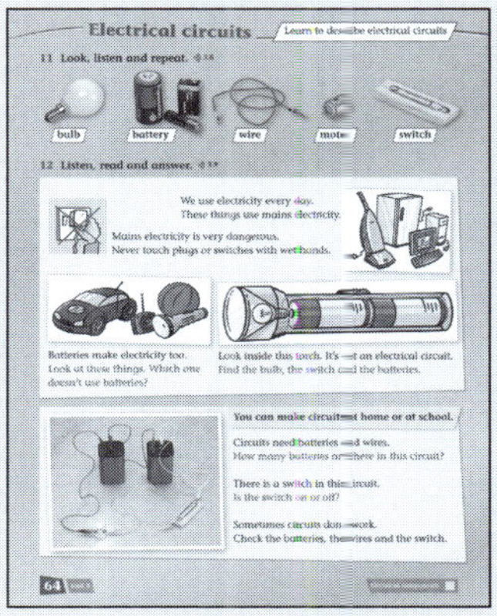

CB page 64

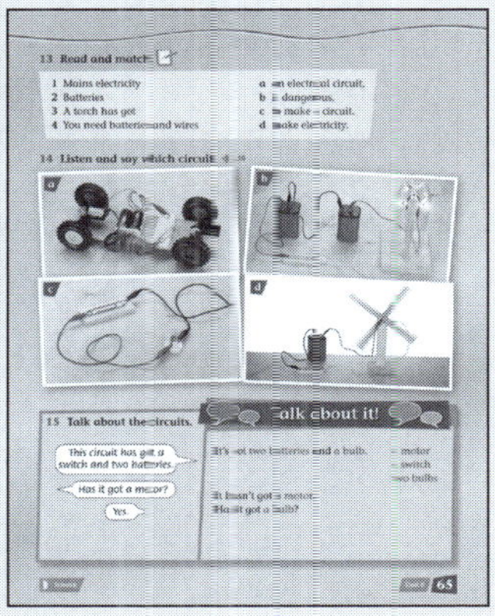

CB page 65

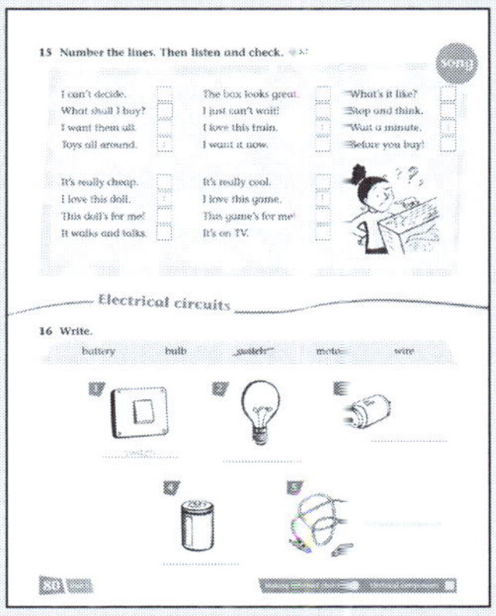

AB page 80

Objectives

- Learn some words for electrical components
- Learn about sources of electricity: batteries and mains

Core language

Electrical components vocabulary: *bulb, battery, wire, motor, switch*

Review of language used so far

Other language

plug, circuit, mains electricity, wet, sometimes

Materials

A battery torch; Electrical components flashcards (*bulb, battery, wire, motor, switch*); CD 3; Electrical components picture cards (PMB p40) – one photocopied set per pupil

Introduce the topic

- Turn on the classroom CD player. Ask pupils what is making it work (electricity).
- Ask pupils how the electricity gets to the CD player. Point out the wire and the plug going into the wall socket.
- Show the pupils the torch you have brought in. Show the bulb and turn on the torch. Ask where the electricity comes from this time (a battery). Unscrew the cap and show the pupils the battery.
- Use any other electrical items in the classroom to demonstrate and talk about electrical components, e.g. the light switch, the motor in a fan, etc.
- Tell the pupils they are going to learn about electricity.

Introduce new vocabulary *see p19*

- Use the electrical components flashcards to teach the new vocabulary. The pupils repeat the words chorally and then individually.
- Give each pupil a number between 1 and 5. Put all the flashcards on the board and give each one a number between 1 and 5.
- Play a variation of *That's my word!* with the pupils: when they hear you say their number, they point to the flashcard on the board and say the word.

CB p64 Activity 11 Look, listen and repeat.

- The pupils listen to the recording. They repeat each word chorally and point to the correct picture.

3.8

bulb – battery – wire – motor – switch

CB p64 Activity 12 Listen, read and answer.

- Look at the pictures with the pupils.
- Play the CD while the pupils listen and read.
- Pause the CD after each question for the pupils to answer. Help them to find the items in the pictures.

3.9

We use electricity every day. These things use mains electricity.
Mains electricity is very dangerous. Never touch plugs or switches with wet hands.
Batteries make electricity too.
Look at these things. Which one doesn't use batteries?

Look inside this torch. It's got an electrical circuit.
Find the bulb, the switch and the batteries.

You can make circuits at home or at school.
Circuits need batteries and wires.
How many batteries are there in this circuit?

There is a switch in this circuit.
Is the switch on or off?

Sometimes circuits don't work. Check the batteries, the wires and the switch.

Answers: the ball doesn't use electricity; the bulb is at the front, the switch is on top, and the batteries are in the middle; there are two batteries in the circuit; the switch is on

CB p65 Activity 13 Read and match.

- Read the first sentence beginning. The pupils match it with the ending (*b*).
- Repeat with the other sentence beginnings.

Answers: 1 b 2 d 3 a 4 c

AB p80 Activity 16 Write.

- Read the words in the word pool to the pupils.
- The pupils match the words with the pictures and write the words on the lines.

Answers: 1 switch 2 bulb 3 motor 4 battery 5 wire

PMB p40 Make the picture cards

- Give out the photocopies of the electrical components picture cards. The pupils colour and cut out the picture cards.
- They can use their cards to play a game, for example *That's my word!* (picture card version) (see p20).
- If your pupils are using word cards, they can prepare them now (see p30). Pupils cut them out and match them with the picture cards.
- Remind the pupils to keep all the cards in a safe place.

Lesson 10 = Words = Other subjects

Learning through English

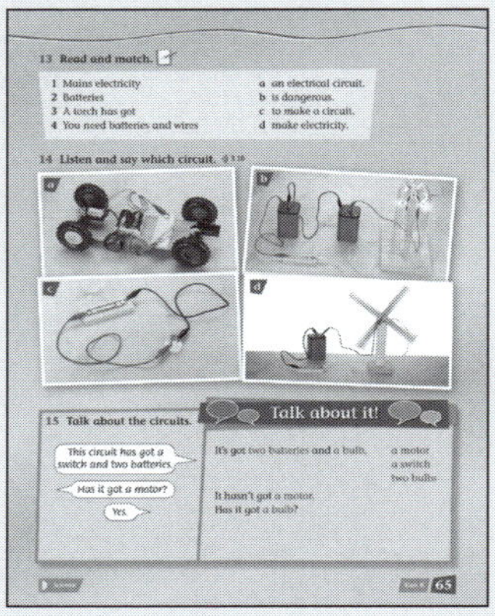

CB page 65

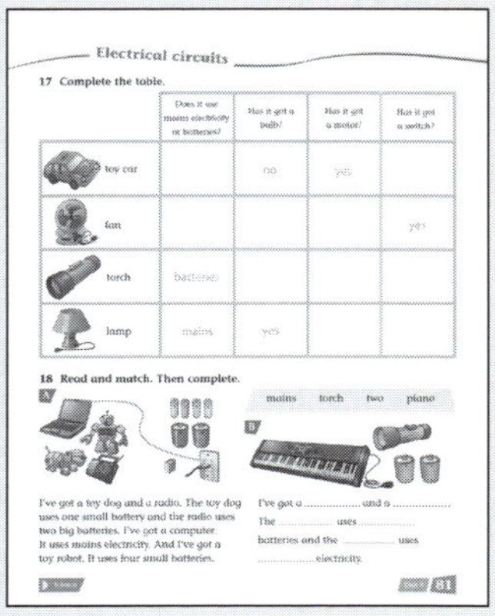

AB page 81

Objectives

- Review words for daily routines and electrical components
- Work out what electrical circuits do
- Identify electrical circuits from their components

Core language

Review of language used so far

Materials

Daily routines flashcards (x8); Electrical components flashcards (x5)

Review vocabulary

- Stick half of the daily routines flashcards and half of the electrical components flashcards on the board.
- Write up the words with jumbled letters.
- Ask pupils to come to the front to write the words and match them with the cards.
- Repeat with the other half of the flashcards.

CB p65 Activity 14 Listen and say which circuit.

- Explain that there are four different electrical circuits in the pictures.
- Ask the pupils to name the components of the circuits.
- Play the first conversation. The pupils listen and say which circuit it is.
- Repeat with the other conversations.

3.10

1 Teacher: Tell me about this circuit.
Child: It doesn't work. It's got a bulb and a switch.
Teacher: Mm, but it hasn't got a battery.
Child: Oh!

2 Teacher: Tell me about this circuit.
Child 1: It's got a motor!
Teacher: Has it got a switch?
Child 1: Yes, and it's got a battery.
Child 2: Switch it on.
(whirring sound)
Teacher: Brilliant!

3 Teacher: Tell me about this circuit.
Child 1: It's got two batteries and a motor. And a switch.
Teacher: Does it work?
Child 1: Er … oh no, it doesn't work.
Child 2: It's the switch. Switch it on.
(click)
Child 1: Oh, yes. It works now!
(sound of model car going along)

Answers: 1 c 2 d 3 a

CB p65 Activity 15 Talk about the circuits.

- Read the model conversation to the pupils.
- Point to a circuit and say *Tell me about this circuit.* Select a pupil to reply.
- Ask more questions about it, for example: *Has it got a battery?*
- Select other pupils to reply.
- The pupils talk about the circuits in pairs.
- Remind them to look at the *Talk about it!* box to help them.

AB p81 Activity 17 Complete the table.

- Look at the table with the pupils.
- Go through the questions at the top with them.
- Show the pupils how the table is partly completed for the items down the side.
- Explain that they have to complete the rest of the table.
- Look at the first item (the toy car) with the pupils. Ask *Does it use mains electricity or batteries?* Pupils answer *batteries* and write this in the table.
- Pupils complete the rest of the table by themselves, or working in pairs.

Answers: toy car – batteries, yes (switch); electric fan – mains, no (bulb), yes (motor); torch – yes (bulb), no (motor), yes (switch); lamp – no (motor), yes (switch)

AB p81 Activity 18 Read and match. Then complete.

- Read the first text. The pupils match the items with the batteries and power sources.

Answers: dog – small, square battery; radio – two big batteries; computer – plug and socket; robot – four small batteries

- Read the words in the word pool to the pupils.
- The pupils complete the second text using the words in the word pool.

Answers: torch, piano, torch, two, piano, mains

Lesson 11 = Other subjects

Learning through English (Project)

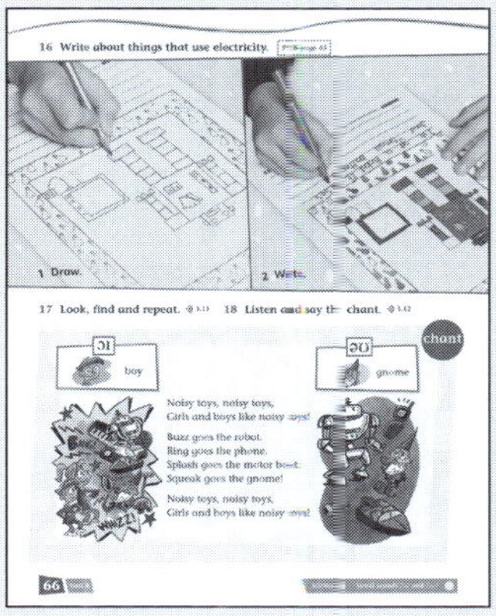

CB page 66

Objectives

- Review vocabulary for electrical components
- Draw some electrical objects from your home
- Write about the electrical objects

Core language

Review of language used so far

Materials

Electrical components flashcards (x5); 'Things that use electricity' template (PMB p43) – one photocopy per pupil

Review vocabulary

- Put the electrical components flashcards on the board. The pupils say the words chorally and individually.
- Ask the pupils what objects in their houses use electricity.
- Write their suggestions on the board.
- Call pupils to the front to write the components for each object (*switch, bulb,* etc.).

Present the project

- Tell the pupils they are going to draw some of these electrical items. They can choose which objects to draw.
- They are going to write sentences about the electrical objects.

PMB p43 / CB p66 Activity 16 Write about things that use electricity

- Give out the photocopies.
- The pupils draw rough pictures first of the electrical objects, in their notebooks or on rough paper. While they are drawing, circulate around the class. Encourage the pupils to be accurate in their drawings.
- Look at each of the rough drawings and tick each one when you think it is adequate.
- The pupils draw their electrical objects on the photocopy.
- Read the sentences from Activity Book page 81, Activity 18 again with the pupils.
- The pupils write sentences about the electrical objects. They use the sentences in the Activity Book as a model.

Display

- Display the projects in the classroom.

- Allow the pupils to move around the classroom, look at all the projects and discuss them with their friends.
- Have a feedback session in which the pupils decide on the best drawings of electrical objects and the best descriptions. Ask the pupils to give reasons for their choices.

Lesson 11a (optional)

Learning through English (Extension)

Objectives

- Review vocabulary for electrical components
- Use symbols to represent simple electrical circuits
- Experiment with electrical circuits
- Play a card game about electrical circuits

Core language

Review of

- electrical components vocabulary
- language used so far

Other language

I think the light is … dim / bright / very bright.

Materials

Electrical components flashcards (x5); Circuit-building kits – one per pair or small group (optional); Two torches – one with fresh batteries and one with batteries which are nearly dead (optional); Scissors; 'Electrical circuits' game (PMB p44) – one photocopy per pupil

Review vocabulary

- Review the electrical components vocabulary with the pupils: show the flashcards to the pupils and ask them to say the words chorally and individually.

Preparation

- Explain that electrical circuits can be represented in drawings, using simple symbols.
- Teach the symbols for wire, battery, and bulb, by drawing the following on the board:

- If possible, let the pupils make circuits using varying numbers of batteries and bulbs, so they can discover for themselves that fewer bulbs / more batteries = bright light, and more bulbs / fewer batteries = dim light.
- Teach them how to draw the circuits using the symbols (see column 2).
- Teach the words *bright*, *very bright*, and *dim*. Use the circuits to demonstrate the meaning (or you could demonstrate with two torches: one with fresh batteries, and one with batteries which are nearly dead).
- Ask pupils about their different circuits *Is it bright, very bright or dim?* (*Bright* = one battery per bulb, *Very bright* = more than one battery per bulb, *dim* = less than one battery per bulb.)
- Ask pupils to label their circuit drawings as *bright*, *very bright*, or *dim*.

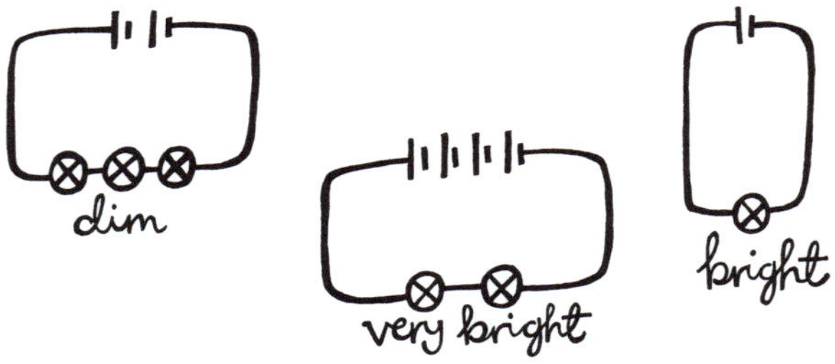

Teaching tip

If it is not possible to let the children experiment, demonstrate to the class using real circuits, or else show this with drawings on the board, letting the children guess which circuits will be bright / dim. They could say, for example: *There are two bulbs and one battery. I think the light is dim.*

PMB p44 Using the Photocopy Master

- Give each pupil a photocopy of the 'Electrical circuits' sheet and a pair of scissors.
- Pupils cut up the cards and use them to play a game in pairs.
- They combine their two sets of cards, shuffle them, and place them face-down in a pile.
- Pupils take it in turns to pick up two cards.
- If the pair of cards makes a circuit (i.e. has bulbs and batteries) the pupil keeps it.
- If the pair of cards doesn't make a circuit, the cards are put to one side.
- For each circuit they pick up, the pupils describe the light it makes: *The light is bright / dim / very bright.*
- Pupils score 1 point for *dim*, 2 points for *bright*, and 3 points for *very bright*.
- The pupil with the highest score at the end is the winner. (Pupils can either end the game when the central pile is empty, or they can re-shuffle the cards they put to one side, and play again until all the cards have been used.)

Follow-up activity

- After the game, pupils can choose three pairs of cards and stick them in their notebooks (or draw their own circuits). They write *This circuit has got two bulbs and two batteries. The light is bright*, etc.

Song

- Ask the pupils *Can you remember the song in this unit?*
- Write what the pupils can remember on the board. Help them to remember the bits they've forgotten, then add them on the board.
- Play the song again (Listening 3.7). The pupils check that the version on the board is correct.
- Play the song again and encourage the pupils to join in.

Lesson 12

Review and self-evaluation

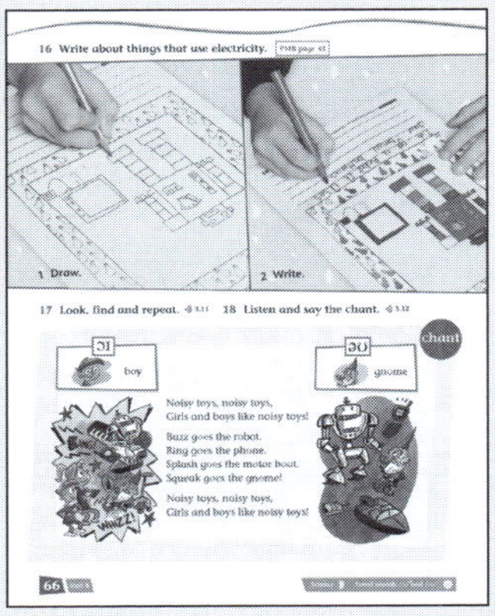

CB page 66

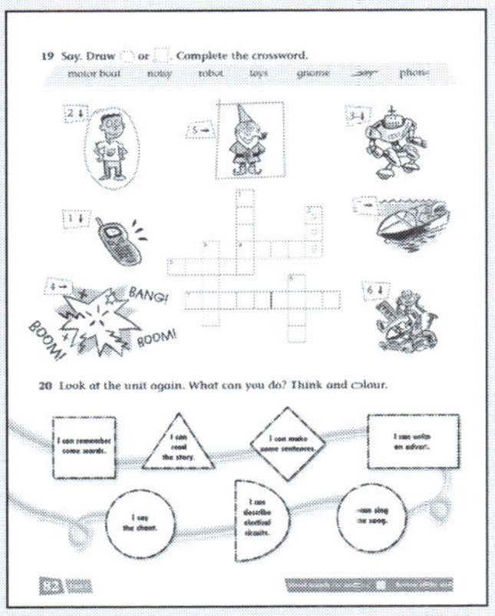

AB page 82

Objectives

- Focus on the pronunciation of vowel sounds (/ɔɪ/ and /əʊ/) with a chant
- Review the activities and the new language of the unit
- Complete a self-evaluation activity

Core language

Review of language used so far

Other language

gnome, noise, buzz, ring, splash, squeak

Materials

CD 3; Rollercoaster Game poster; Character counters and game cards; Dice (one pair per class); Picture dictionary page (PMB p2) – one photocopy per pupil (optional)

CB p66 Activity 17 Listen, find and repeat.

- Point to the pictures. The pupils say the words.
- Play the CD. Pupils point and repeat.

3.11

boy – toys – noise [/ɔɪ/]
phone – robot – gnome – motor boat [/əʊ/]

- Say the two vowel sounds /ɔɪ/ and /əʊ/. The pupils find the words that share the vowel sound.
- The pupils practise saying the words chorally and individually, concentrating on the pronunciation of the vowel sounds.

CB p66 Activity 18 Listen and say the chant.

- Play the chant. The pupils point to the items as they hear them.

3.12

Noisy toys, noisy toys,
Girls and boys like noisy toys!

Buzz goes the robot…
Ring goes the phone…
Splash goes the motor boat…
Squeak goes the gnome…

Noisy toys, noisy toys,
Girls and boys like noisy toys!

- Teach the chant line by line. Focus on the pronunciation points. Use choral and individual repetition to check pronunciation.
- Play the chant again and encourage the pupils to join in.

Focus on spelling

- Focus on the spelling patterns:
  /əʊ/ is often spelt *o…e* (*phone*)
  /ɔɪ/ is often spelt *oy* (*boy*) or *oi* (*noisy*)
- Show examples from the chant for each vowel sound.
- Remind the pupils that there are lots of exceptions to spelling patterns in English.

AB p82 Activity 19. Say. Draw ● or ■. Complete the crossword.

- Point to each of the pictures. The pupils say the words chorally.
- Focus on the pronunciation difference between /əʊ/ and /ɔɪ/, using the words *gnome* and *boy*.
- Show how *boy* has a circle around it and *gnome* has a square round it.
- Ask the pupils to identify a word with the /ɔɪ/ sound.
- Show the pupils how to put a circle round the word.
- Repeat with the /əʊ/ sound, putting a square around the word.
- The pupils put circles and squares around the words.
- Show the pupils the word *boy* in the crossword. The pupils suggest a word for 4 across (*noisy*).
- The pupils complete the crossword individually.
- Point to the pictures at random. The pupils say the words chorally and individually. Check the pupils' pronunciation.

Answers: circle: noisy, toys, boy; square: motor boat, robot, gnome, phone
1 phone **2** boy **3** robot **4** noisy **5** gnome **6** toys
7 motor boat

End-of-unit review

- Use the Rollercoaster Game poster and the Class Book to recall the main activities of the unit.
- Recall the language associated with each activity.
- Ask the pupils to let you know what they liked or didn't like, and what they found easy or difficult.

Play the Rollercoaster Game

- Divide the class into small groups. Give each group one of the character 'counters' and let them play the game as before (see p41).
- Remind them to use the poster chants when a group gets a question right or wrong.

AB p82 Activity 20 Look at the unit again. What can you do? Think and colour.

- Let the pupils do the self-evaluation activity as before (see p41).

PMB p2 Picture Dictionary (optional)

- If your pupils are making Picture Dictionaries, give out the photocopies of the template.
- Pupils continue making the dictionaries as for Unit 1 (see p42).

Lesson 12a (optional)

■ = Words ◆ = Sentences

Show what you know!

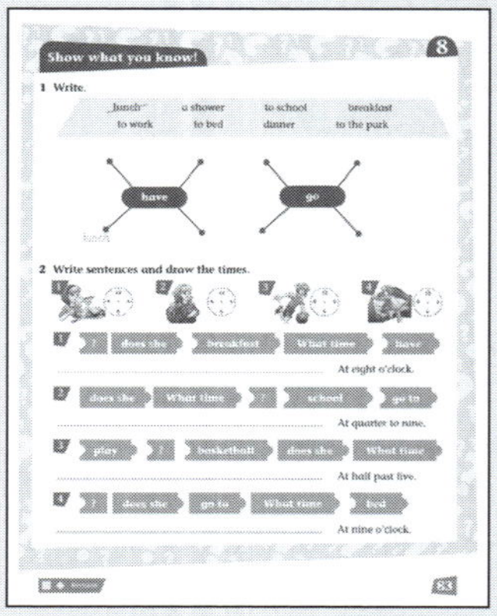

AB page 83

For suggestions on how to use *Show what you know!* see page 13.

Objectives

- Extra practice of the vocabulary of the unit
- Solve puzzles in English
- Provide extra material for homework and fast finishers

Core language

Review of language used so far

Materials

No extra materials

AB p83 Activity 1 Write.

- Read the words in the word pool to the pupils.
- Point to the word at the centre of the first spidergram (*have*). Show how *lunch* goes with *have*.
- Ask the pupils to suggest other words from the word pool to go with *have*. Write their suggestions on the board.
- Repeat with *go*.

Answers: have – lunch, a shower, breakfast, dinner; go – to school, to work, to bed, to the park

- Draw a spidergram with *play* in the centre. Call individual pupils to the front to write suitable words on the board (e.g. *a game, football, tennis, basketball, chess*).
- Repeat with the verb *do*. This time, the pupils can complete the spidergram in pairs. As well as *do judo* and *do gymnastics*, you can remind them of the phrases *do my homework* and *do a puzzle* from *Incredible English 2*.

AB p83 Activity 2 Write sentences and draw the times.

- Read the words of the first question in jumbled order to the pupils. Ask them if they can put the words in the correct order. Show them how to draw the time.
- Ask the pupils to put the words of the second question in the correct order. The pupils write the question in their books, and draw the time on the clock.
- Repeat with the other questions.

Answers: **1** What time does she have breakfast? **2** What time does she go to school? **3** What time does she play basketball? **4** What time does she go to bed?

The pupils are now ready to sit the Unit 8 test. See pp198–201 for both Standard and Higher levels.

9 The circus

Lesson 1 ■ = Words

Introducing vocabulary

CB page 67

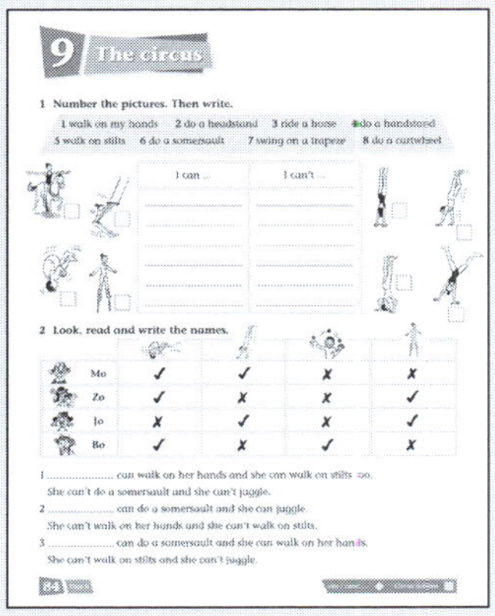

AB page 84

Objectives

- Understand the theme of the unit
- Become familiar with vocabulary for circus actions
- Practise listening to people talking about what they're doing
- Focus on spelling

Core language

Circus actions: *do a cartwheel, do a handstand, do a somersault, swing on a trapeze, walk on stilts, walk on your hands, do a headstand, ride a horse*

Review of

- circus actions: *juggle, ride a bike*
- language used so far

Materials

Rollercoaster Game poster; Circus actions flashcards (*do a cartwheel, do a handstand, do a somersault, ride a bike, swing on a trapeze, walk on stilts, walk on your hands, do a headstand, ride a horse, juggle*); CD 3; Pupils' bookmarks (optional) (see p28)

Unit overview

- Talk to the pupils about the circus. Ask them what words they know for the things people do in the circus. Ask them which words (in their own language) they would like to learn.
- Ask the pupils to look through Unit 9 in their Class Books. Talk with them about the unit and quickly write the different topics and activities on the board, relating them to the shapes on the poster:
  - ■ Words – circus actions, parts of the body
  - ▲ Story – *The circus star*
  - ◆ Sentences – *Is he riding a horse? They're swimming.*
  - ■ Text work – Posters
  - ● Song – *Everyone's a winner!* / Chant – *There's a mouse in a house*
  - ◗ Other subjects – Art (draw figures using ovals)
- Remind the pupils that they will use the poster again at the end of the unit.

Introduce new vocabulary *see p19*

- Use the circus actions flashcards to teach the new vocabulary. The pupils repeat the words chorally and then individually.
- Place the flashcards in different parts of the classroom and play *Around the class* with the pupils. First you say the words and the pupils point to the flashcards. Then you point to the flashcards and the pupils say the words.

CB p67 Activity 1 Look, listen and repeat.

- Look at the picture with the pupils. Ask questions such as *Who can you see? What are they looking at? (A circus poster.)*
- The pupils listen to the recording. They repeat each word chorally and point to the correct picture.

3.13

1 swing on a trapeze, **2** ride a horse, **3** ride a bike, **4** do a handstand, **5** juggle, **6** walk on your hands, **7** do a cartwheel, **8** do a headstand, **9** do a somersault, **10** walk on stilts

CB p67 Activity 2 Listen and find.

- Play the dialogue.
- The pupils listen for the actions and point to each one in the picture.
- Alternatively, the pupils can use their bookmarks (see p28) to focus on the pictures.

3.14

Finn:	Hey, look at the poster. There's a circus!
Woman:	Hello! We work at the circus. Look, that's me. I'm swinging on a trapeze.
Finn:	Wow! Can you do a somersault, too?
Woman:	Yes, I can.
Man:	And that's me. I'm doing a cartwheel. I'm a clown!
Jazmin:	Can you walk on your hands?
Man:	No. But I can walk on stilts!
	That's fun!
Woman:	What can you do? Can you do a headstand?
Molly:	A headstand? Yes, I can.
Jazmin:	And I can do a handstand!
Woman:	A handstand – very good!
Finn:	And I can juggle!
Woman:	Great! Can you ride a horse?
Jazmin:	No.
Finn:	No, I can't ride a horse. But I can ride a bike!
All:	*(laughing)*

CB p67 Activity 3 Ask and answer.

- Read the dialogue to the pupils.
- Say cues from the vocabulary group such as *do a handstand* or *ride a horse*. Select individual pupils to ask the questions
- Select other pupils to answer each question.
- The pupils ask and answer the questions in pairs.

Spelling

- Ask the pupils to identify:
  1 words that are similar in their language (highlight the differences in spelling)
  2 words with s+ consonant (*sw*ing, *st*ilts, hand*st*and, head*st*and)
  3 words with double letters (for example, *cartwheel*).

AB p84 Activity 1 Number the pictures. Then write.

- Read the words in the word pool to the pupils. Ask the pupils to match the words to the pictures.
- Read the categories (*I can ... / I can't ...*) to the pupils. Ask *Which activities can you do?* Select different pupils to answer.
- Pupils write the circus actions in the lists, according to whether they can or can't do them.

Lesson 2 ■ = Words

Practising vocabulary

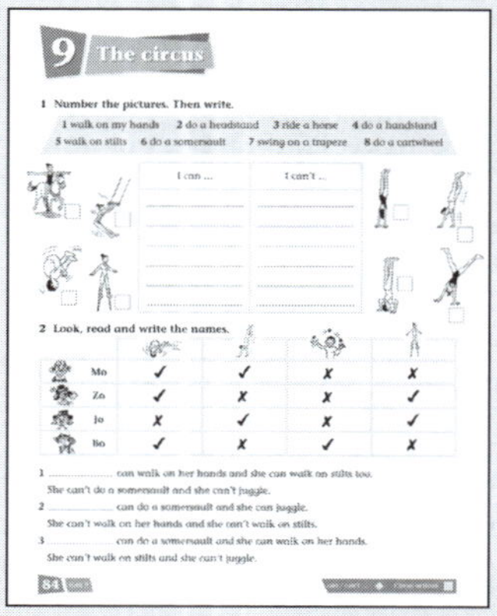
AB page 84

AB page 85

Objectives

- Review vocabulary for circus actions
- Practise asking about what people are doing
- Practise talking about what you're doing
- Practise spelling present continuous forms

Core language

Review of

- circus actions
- abilities: *can / can't*
- language used so far

Materials

Circus actions flashcards (x10); A CD of music with a strong beat (for *Musical flashcards*) Circus actions picture cards (PMB p45) – one photocopied set per pupil

Review vocabulary

- Put the circus actions flashcards on the board. The pupils say the words chorally and individually.
- Play *Musical flashcards* with the pupils: they say the word for the flashcard your hand is on when the music stops.

AB p84 Activity 2 Look, read and write the names.

- Ask questions about the clowns in the table, for example: *Can Mo do a somersault? (Yes), Can Zo juggle? (No).*
- Read the first text to the pupils and ask *Who is it?* The pupils write the name of the clown at the beginning (*Jo*).
- Repeat with the other texts.

Answers: 1 Jo 2 Bo 3 Mo

AB p85 Activity 3 Listen and number.

- Point to each picture and ask *What is he / she doing?* (*She's walking on stilts. He's doing a headstand,* etc.)
- Play the first conversation on the CD. Ask the pupils *Which picture is it?* The pupils identify the correct picture (c). Show the pupils the answer in the box.
- Repeat with the other conversations. The pupils write the numbers of the conversations in the boxes.

3.15

1	Girl 1:	Look, I'm doing a cartwheel!
2	Boy 1:	Watch me!
	Adult:	What are you doing?
	Boy 1:	I'm walking on my hands!
3	Girl 2:	Look, I'm doing a handstand!
4	Adult:	What are you doing?
	Boy 2:	I'm doing a somersault!
5	Girl 3:	Hey, look, I'm walking on stilts!
	Adult:	Well done!
6	Boy 3:	Look at me! I'm juggling!
		(sound of balls being dropped)
		Oops!
7	Boy 4:	Look, I'm doing a headstand!
8	Girl 4:	I'm riding a horse.
	Adult:	Very good!

Answers: a 5 b 2 c 1 d 4 e 6 f 3 g 8 h 7

AB p85 Activity 4 Write the words. Then match.

- Tell the pupils to look at the code on page 85 of their Activity Books. Point to the first word written in code and ask the pupils to decode it (*walk*). The pupils write the word, then match it with the picture.
- Repeat with the other code words in the two sets. The pupils can do this activity individually or in pairs.

Answers: Set 1 – walk, eat, ride, juggle, swim, run; Set 2 – eating, running, juggling, riding, walking, swimming

- The pupils match the base forms of the verbs (for example, *walk*) with the *-ing* forms (for example, *walking*) and the correct picture. Encourage the pupils to use different colours to link the items.

Spelling game

- Play *Hangman* using the circus actions vocabulary (see p20) and the correct picture. Encourage the pupils to use different colours to link the items.

PMB p45 Make the picture cards

- Give out the photocopies of the circus actions picture cards. The pupils colour and cut out the picture cards.

- They can use their cards to play a game, for example, *Who's got …?* (see p20). Ask, for example *Who's got a girl in a green jumper doing a cartwheel?*
- If your pupils are using word cards, they can prepare them now (see p30). Pupils cut them out and match them with the picture cards.
- Remind the pupils to keep all the cards in a safe place.

Lesson 3 ▲ = Story

Story

CB page 68

CB page 69

Objectives
- Listen to a story
- Read a story
- Listen for words and phrases in a story
- Practise story language

Core language
Is he / she walking on stilts?; They're juggling.
Review of language used so far

Other language
clown, acrobat, trapeze artist, best, fall

Materials
Circus actions flashcards (x10); CD 3

Review vocabulary
- Put the circus actions flashcards on the board. The pupils say the words chorally and individually.
- Play *Memory numbers* with the pupils: put all the flashcards in a line on the board, with a number from 1 to 8 under each one. Say sets of three numbers: the pupils say the corresponding words in the same order.
- Leave the flashcards on the board to give the pupils ideas for the next activity.

Introduce the story
- Ask the pupils to imagine they are going to circus. What things are they looking forward to seeing?
- Explain that in the story the children are going to visit the circus.

CB pp68–69 Activity 4 First listening with the books closed
- Tell the pupils to listen and answer this question: *Who is the star of the circus in the story?*
- The pupils listen with their books closed.

3.16

[1]	Molly:	I love circuses!
	Archie:	Me too! Come on, let's go in.
[2]	In the circus tent …	
	Luke:	I like trapeze artists best.
	Molly:	Me too. I love her dress!
[3]	Finn:	Look at the trapeze artists now. They're juggling!
	Molly:	Wow! That's amazing.
	Luke:	Oh look, there's Coco! Coco, come here!
	Jazmin:	I think she likes circuses too!
[4]	Luke:	Look at that clown.
	Molly:	He's got very long legs! Is he walking on stilts?
	Luke:	Yes. Of course he is!
[5]	Jazmin:	I like acrobats best. Look! He's doing a handstand!
	Luke:	Coco likes acrobats too – look!
	Archie:	Coco, be careful! Where are you going?
[6]	Finn:	Poor Coco!
	Molly:	Oh no! What's happening?
[7]	Luke:	She's OK. She's swinging on a trapeze.
	Archie:	She's a trapeze artist! Well done, Coco!
[8]	Jazmin:	Oh no …
	Archie:	What's happening now?
	Jazmin:	She's falling!
	Luke:	No, it's OK. She isn't falling. She's jumping!
[9]	Archie:	She's riding a horse! What a cat!
[10]	Everyone:	Fantastic! Well done!
	Molly:	Coco's a star!

- Check the answer to your questions (*Coco the cat*), and ask pupils to say what the cat does (*She swings on the trapeze and she rides the horse*). Recast the pupils' answers as necessary.

CB pp68–69 Activity 4 Second listening with the books open
- Tell the pupils to open their books and look at the story.
- Ask questions about the story such as *What does Luke like best? (Trapeze artists)*
- Play the recording again while the pupils follow in their books.
- Go through any vocabulary queries with the class.

CB p69 Activity 5 Read and find the picture.
- Explain that each sentence refers to a particular frame in the story.
- Ask the pupils to identify the frame for the first sentence.
- The pupils read each sentence and match it with a frame. This can be done as a whole-class activity or working in pairs.
- The pupils write the answers in their notebooks.

Answers: a 9 b 3 c 7 d 10 e 4 f 1 g 6

Fun expressions
- Write these 'fun expressions' from the story on the board:
  Wow! That's amazing.
  What's happening now?
  Fantastic! Well done!
- Play the story again: the pupils put up their hands when they hear one of the phrases.
- Pause the recording. The pupils repeat the phrase chorally and individually. Encourage the pupils to copy the intonation on the CD.

Lesson 4 ◆ = Sentences

Language focus 1

CB page 70

AB page 86

Objectives

- Understand the use of *Is he riding ...?*
- Practise using the new language

Core language

Is he / she riding ...?

Review of language used so far

Materials

CD 3; Grammar tiles (PMB p46) – one photocopy of Set 1 per pupil (optional)

Recall the story

- Ask the pupils to remember as much as they can from the story.
- Say sentences with key structures from the story, and ask the pupils to identify who says each one, for example:
  I love circuses! (Molly)
  Is he walking on stilts? (Molly)
  She's a trapeze artist! Well done, Coco! (Archie)
  She's riding a horse! What a cat! (Archie)
  Fantastic! Well done! (Everyone)

PMB p46 / CB p70 Activity 6 Which question is in the story? Make more questions.

- Ask the pupils to read the questions in the grammar tiles.
- Ask the pupils to say which question was in the story (*Is he walking on stilts?*).
- Write *He is walking on stilts* on the board. Under this, write *Is he walking on stilts?* Use a mime gesture to show how the order of *he* and *is* changes to make the question.
- The pupils say the questions in the grammar tiles chorally and individually. Encourage them to use your mime gesture as they say each question.
- The pupils use the remaining tiles in the picture to make questions with *Is he / she ... ing?* Choose other pupils to answer with *yes* or *no*. Alternatively, give each pupil a copy of Set 1 of the grammar tiles from the PMB: the pupils cut out the tiles and arrange them in questions on their desks. Ask individual pupils to read out their questions for the class.

CB p70 Activity 7 Listen and say which picture.

- Show the pupils the pictures. The pupils identify the actions in each picture.
- Play the first dialogue on the CD. The pupils match it with the correct picture.
- Repeat with the other dialogues.

3.17

Molly:	Is he doing a somersault?
Luke:	No.
Molly:	Is he doing a headstand?
Luke:	Yes.
Molly:	Is she walking on stilts?
Luke:	Yes.
Presenter:	Which picture is it?
Luke:	Is he riding a horse?
Molly:	No.
Molly:	Is he doing a somersault?
Molly:	Yes.
Luke:	Is she riding a horse?
Molly:	No.
Presenter:	Which picture is it?
Molly:	Is he doing a headstand?
Luke:	No.
Molly:	Is he doing a somersault?
Luke:	Yes.
Molly:	Is she walking on stilts?
Luke:	No.
Presenter:	Which picture is it?
Luke:	Is he doing a headstand?
Molly:	Yes.
Luke:	Is she doing a cartwheel?
Molly:	Yes.
Presenter:	Which picture is it?

Answers: 1 5 2 2 3 6 4 4

CB p70 Activity 8 Play the game.

- Read the conversation to the pupils.
- Say you are thinking of one of the people in the pictures. The pupils ask you questions and guess which person you are thinking of.
- The pupils play the game in pairs.

AB p86 Activity 5 Write the questions and answers. Then ask and answer.

- Read the words in the word pools to the pupils.
- Point to the first picture. Ask *What is he doing? (He's riding a horse)* and *What is she doing? (She's walking on stilts).*
- Repeat with the other pictures.
- Read the first question and answer. Read the second question. The pupils answer *No* and write the answer on the line.
- Repeat with questions 3 and 4.
- For numbers 5 to 8, the pupils suggest questions and answers. Elicit suitable questions and answers and write these on the board for the pupils to choose and copy on the lines.

Answers: **1** Yes **2** No **3** No **4** Yes **5** (example) Is he riding a horse? No. **6** (example) Is she walking on stilts? Yes. **7** (example) Is he juggling? Yes. **8** (example) Is she doing a cartwheel? No.

- Pupils can then practice the questions and answers in pairs. One pupil covers the texts with a piece of paper, and the other pupil asks the questions. They then swap and repeat.

Lesson 5 ◆ = Sentences

Language focus 2

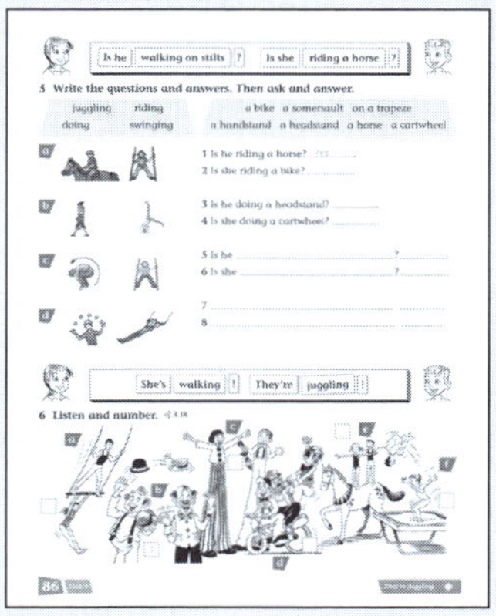

AB page 86

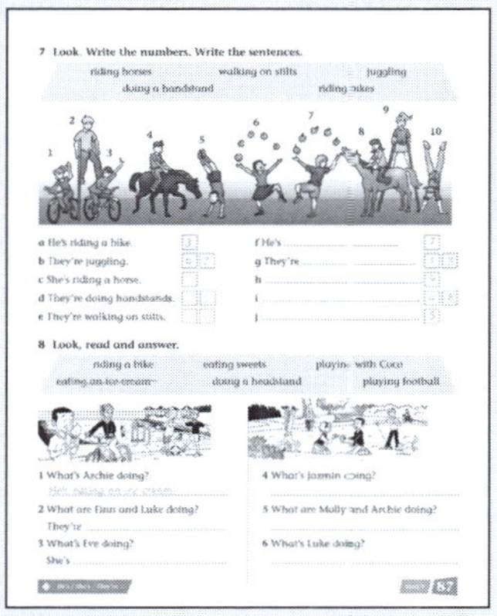

AB page 87

Objectives

- Review *Is she riding a horse …?* and *She's walking.*
- Understand the use of *They're juggling.*
- Practise listening to and talking about what people are doing

Core language

He's / She's / They're juggling.

Review of language used so far

Materials

Grammar tiles (PMB p46) – one photocopy of Set 2 per pupil; Pupils' grammar tiles (Set 1) from Lesson 4 (optional); Sports flashcards (x12); CD 3

PMB p46 AB p86 Focus on language

- Read the sentences in the second set of grammar tiles on page 86 of the Activity Book to the pupils. Ask the pupils *Which sentence is in the story?* (*They're juggling.*)
- Point out the difference between the *he / she* form with *is* and the *they* form with *are*. Write the contractions and the long forms on board: *She's walking = She is walking, They're juggling = They are juggling.* Use a mime gesture to show how the long forms 'contract' to the short forms.
- The pupils say the sentences in the grammar tiles chorally and individually.
- Give each pupil a photocopy of Set 2 of the grammar tiles from the PMB. Ask the pupils to suggest words to put in the blank tiles (*watching TV, writing, dancing,* etc.). Write the suggestions on the board. The pupils copy the words in the blank tiles.
- The pupils cut out all the tiles and use them to make sentences on their desks.
- Pupils can combine the Set 2 tiles with some of the Set 1 tiles to make more sentences, for example *He's doing a headstand. She's doing a somersault.*

Practice

- Call a pupil to the front. Show the tennis flashcard. Encourage the pupil to use a mime gesture for tennis.
- Select a pupil and ask *What is he doing?* The pupil says *He's playing tennis.*
- Call another pupil to the front – there are now two pupils at the front. Encourage them to use a mime gesture for tennis and show the tennis flashcard again.
- Select a pupil and ask *What are they doing?* The pupil says *They're playing tennis.*
- Repeat with other pupils at the front, with other flashcards. Use individuals and groups at the front so that the pupils have to use *he / she* and *they.*

AB p86 Activity 6 Listen and number.

- Point to each of the groups of circus people in the picture and ask *What are they doing?* (*They're swinging on a trapeze, They're juggling,* etc.).
- Play the first conversation on the CD. Ask *Which group of people is it?* The pupils answer *b*. Show the pupils that group b has *1* in the box.
- Repeat with the other conversations. The pupils write the numbers of the conversations in the correct boxes.

3.18

1 Child 1: Hey, look at the clowns. I love clowns.
Child 2: What are they doing?
Child 1: They're juggling.
Child 2: Oh, yes! They're juggling with their hats!

2 Child 2: Look at the acrobats on the trampoline!
Child 1: What are they doing?
Child 2: They're doing somersaults.
Child 1: Wow!

3 Child 1: Look. More clowns.
Child 2: What are they doing?
Child 1: They're riding a bike!
Child 2: Three clowns on one bike!

4 Child 2: Look – children.
Child 1: What are they doing?
Child 2: They're walking on stilts.
Child 1: Oh, I can do that too.

5 Child 1: Look at the trapeze artists.
Child 2: What are they doing?
Child 1: They're swinging on a trapeze. Wow!

6 Child 2: Ooh, look. More children.
Child 1: What are they doing?
Child 2: They're riding a horse.
Child 1: They're standing up!

Answers: a 5 b 1 c 4 d 3 e 6 f 2

AB p87 Activity 7 Look. Write the numbers. Write the sentences.

- Point to the picture and ask *What is number 1 doing? (She's riding a bike).* Repeat with other people in the picture.
- Read the first sentence and ask *Who is it?* The pupils say *Number 3.* Show the pupils that the box next to the sentence has *3* in it.
- Read the next sentence. The pupils identify the two people (6 and 7) Show them the example answers in the boxes again.
- Repeat with sentences c, d, and e. The pupils identify the people and write the numbers in the boxes.
- Point to the *7* in the box of sentence f. Ask the pupils to suggest a sentence. The pupils say *He's juggling* and write the sentence on the line.
- Repeat with the rest of the sentences.

Answers: a 3 b 6, 7 c 8 d 5, 10 e 2, 9 f He's juggling. g They're riding bikes. h She's walking on stilts. i They're riding horses. j He's doing a handstand.

AB p87 Activity 8 Look, read and answer.

- Read the words in the word pool to the pupils.
- Read the first question and answer to the pupils.
- Read the second question. The pupils answer *They're playing football* and write the answer on the line.
- Repeat with the other questions.

Answers: 1 He's eating an ice cream. 2 They're playing football. 3 She's riding a bike. 4 She's doing a headstand. 5 They're eating sweets. 6 He's playing with Coco.

For extra grammar practice, see AB page 104.

Activity 2 Write the words in order. Then answer.

Answers: 1 riding a bike? riding a 2 Is he doing a cartwheel? He's doing a 3 Is she doing a headstand? She's doing a 4 Is she walking on stilts? She's

Lesson 6 ▲ = Story

Playscript

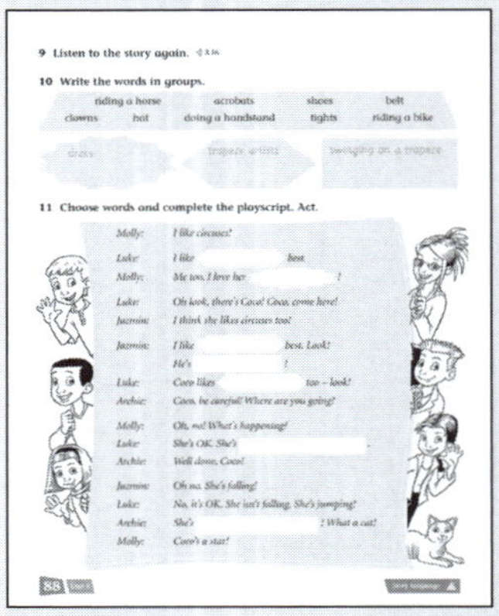
9 Listen to the story again.

10 Write the words in groups.

riding a horse acrobats shoes belt clowns hat doing a handstand tights riding a bike

dress | trapeze artists | swinging on a trapeze

11 Choose words and complete the playscript. Act.

Molly: I like circuses!
Luke: I like ______ best.
Molly: Me too. I love her ______!
Luke: Oh look, there's Coco! Coco, come here!
Jazmin: I think she likes circuses too!
Jazmin: I like ______ best. Look!
He's ______!
Luke: Coco likes ______ too – look!
Archie: Coco, be careful! Where are you going?
Molly: Oh, no! What's happening!
Luke: She's OK. She's ______.
Archie: Well done, Coco!
Jazmin: Oh no. She's falling!
Luke: No, it's OK. She isn't falling. She's jumping!
Archie: She's ______! What a cat!
Molly: Coco's a star!

88

AB page 88

Objectives

- Read and complete a playscript
- Use finger puppets to act out a playscript
- Act out the play

Core language

Review of language used so far

Materials

CD 3; Spare photocopies of the finger puppets (PMB p3)

AB p88 Activity 9 Listen to the story again.

- Tell the pupils to look at pages 68–69 in the Class Book again.
- Play the CD while the pupils listen and read.
- Alternatively, the pupils can read the story aloud in groups of four. Each pupil should read one character.

AB p88 Activity 10 Write the words in groups.

- Read the words in the word pool to the pupils.
- Point to each of the boxes and read the word in each one. Ask the pupils to suggest words from the word pool to go in each box.
- The pupils write the words from the word pool in the correct category.

Answers: set 1 – dress, hat, shoes, tights, belt; set 2 – trapeze artists, clowns, acrobats; set 3 – swinging on a trapeze, riding a horse, riding a bike, doing a handstand

- Ask the pupils to suggest new words for each category.

AB p88 Activity 11 Choose words and complete the playscript. Act.

- Read the playscript to the pupils. When you come to a blank, ask *Which word was in the story?* The pupils say the words from the story.
- Read the playscript again. Ask the pupils to suggest alternative words from Activity 10 to complete the blanks.
- Divide the pupils into groups of four. In their groups, the pupils decide which words to use when they read the playscript.

Finger puppets *see p22*

- Ask the pupils *How many characters are there in the story? (four, plus the cat)*. The pupils identify the four characters. (Molly, Archie, Jazmin, and Luke).
- In their groups, the pupils decide who is going to take each part. One pupil can also take the part of Coco the cat.
- If the pupils have got their finger puppets with them, tell them to get out the puppet for the character they are going to play.
- If the pupils haven't got their finger puppets, they will have to make them now. Give each pupil a photocopy of the finger puppets. The pupils cut out, colour and stick the photocopy of the character they are going to play.

Practice

- Remind the pupils of the five points of successful play acting:
  1 Listen to the other actors.
  2 Wait for your turn.
  3 Speak clearly.
  4 When the puppets are speaking to each other, they should face each other.
  5 Don't move your puppets unnecessarily.
- Tell the pupils about the notes you made during the Unit 8 play acting. Encourage them to concentrate on the points you noticed. Say you will be watching them again this time.
- The pupils act out the play with their puppets. While they are doing this, circulate around the classroom. Make a note of the points the pupils should improve on next time.
- Ask one or two groups to come to the front to act out the play with their puppets.

Lesson 7 = Text work

Reading and writing

CB page 71

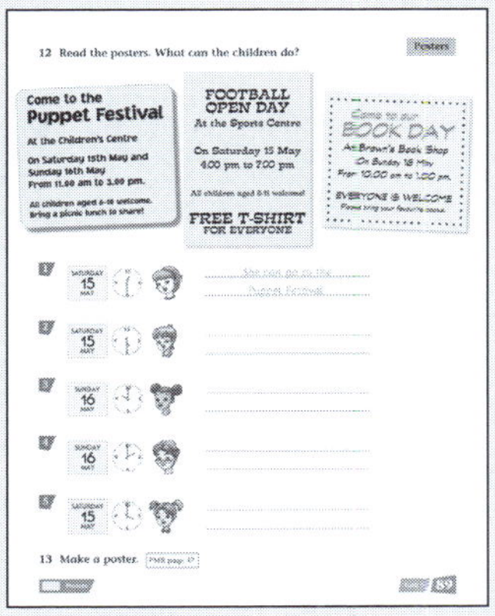

AB page 89

Objectives

- Review circus actions vocabulary
- Read and understand posters about events
- Write a poster

Core language

Review of language used so far

Other language

poster, sports day, laugh, races

Materials

Circus actions flashcards (x10); Poster template (PMB p47) – one photocopy per pupil

Review vocabulary

- Put the circus actions flashcard on the board. The pupils say the words chorally and individually.
- Play *Bingo* with the pupils (see p21): they choose four of the actions and write them in their notebooks to use as their Bingo cards.

CB p71 Activity 9 Read and answer the questions.

- Talk with the pupils about posters they see in the street. Ask *What are these posters for? What sort of events are they for?*
- Ask the pupils about the posters in the Class Book. Point to each one and ask questions such as *What is it for?* and *How much is it?*
- Tell the pupils to read the posters. Ask the pupils the first question. The pupils answer *Greenhill Park.*
- The pupils answer the rest of the questions in their notebooks.

Answers: 1 It's in Greenhill Park. **2** It's on Saturday 8th April and Sunday 9th April. **3** All the family / Adults and children can come to the circus. **4** It's at Middleton School. **5** It's on Wednesday 9th June. **6** Parents and children can come to Sports Day.

AB p89 Activity 12 Read the posters. What can the children do?

- Read each of the posters to the pupils. Say sentences about each event such as *It's from 11.00 am to 3.00 pm, It's at the Sports Centre, It's for children from 6 to 10, It's for people who like books,* etc. The pupils identify the poster for each sentence.
- Point to the first girl. Ask *What time is it? (half past twelve)* and *What day is it? (Saturday 15th May).*
- Ask *What can she do?* The pupils find a suitable activity for her (*the puppet festival*). Show the pupils the example answer *She can go to the Puppet Festival.*
- Repeat with the other boys and girls. In each case, the pupils write a sentence about what the boy or girl can do.

Answers: 2 She can go to the Puppet Festival. **2** He can go to the Football Open Day. **3** She can go to the Book Day. **4** He can go to the Puppet Festival. **5** She can go to the Football Open Day.

Teaching tip

Ask pupils to notice how capital letters are often used in posters for emphasis, e.g. Puppet Festival, FOOTBALL OPEN DAY, BOOK DAY, etc.

PMB p47 AB p89 Activity 13 Make a poster.

- Explain to the pupils that they are going to write a poster for an event.
- Remind pupils that they have to choose work for their portfolio during the course (see p198). Point out that this piece of work would be a suitable piece to include.
- Brainstorm ideas for events, times, dates, age groups, and other information to put on the poster.
- Choose some suggestions and write them on the board.
- Show the pupils how to write the posters, using the posters in Activity 12 as a model.
- Hand out the photocopies of the writing template. Tell the pupils to choose another event and write about it.
- The pupils write a rough copy in their notebooks for you to correct. After you have checked the rough copy, they write their final copy on the photocopied template.

Lesson 8 ● = Song / chant

Learning for life

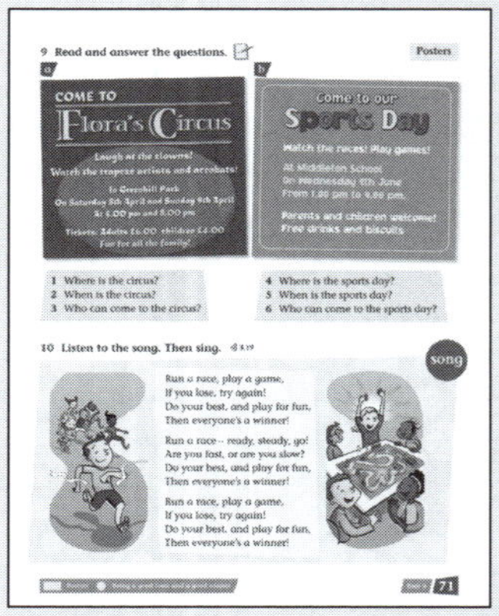

CB page 71

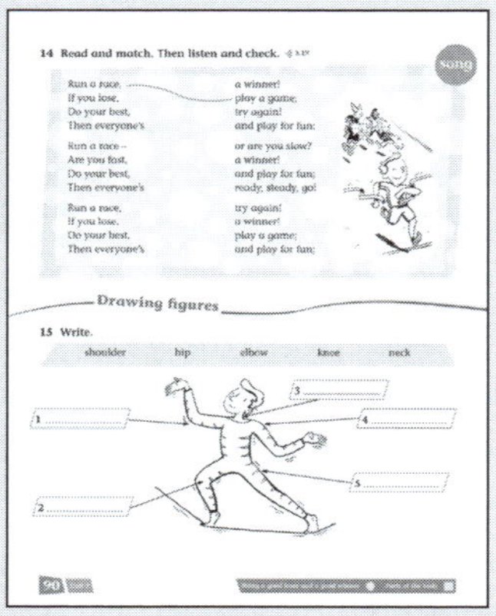

AB page 90

Objectives

- Review the unit so far
- Understand the idea of a good winner and a good loser
- Talk about what makes a good winner and a good loser
- Sing a song about winning and losing

Core language

Review of language used so far

Other language

lose, try again, winner, fun

Materials

Rollercoaster Game poster; Circus actions flashcards (x10); CD 3

Unit review

- Use the Rollercoaster Game poster and the Class Book to review the unit so far. Talk with the pupils about the activities they have done.
- The pupils give examples of the language they used in each activity.

Review vocabulary (categorizing)

- Ask the pupils to tell you all the new words they remember from the unit.
- Put the circus actions flashcards on the board and ask the pupils to arrange them in these two categories: *activities I can do* and *activities I can't do.*
- Repeat with other categories, such as:
  activities with extra equipment / activities without extra equipment
  easy activities / difficult activities.

Introduce the topic

- Talk with the pupils about winning and losing. Ask questions such as: How do you feel when you win? How do you feel when you lose? Are there any problems with winning?
- Encourage the pupils to talk about some or all of these ideas in their answers:
  – you feel excited and happy when you win
  – you feel disappointed when you lose
  – other people can be envious when you win
  – you don't want to try again when you lose
  – the way to get better is to keep on trying
- The pupils can express their ideas in their own language. If they do, recast their answers in English.

CB p71 Activity 10 Listen to the song. Then sing.

- Read the song with the pupils. Explain any new words.
- Play the song on the CD.

3.19

Run a race, play a game,
If you lose, try again!
Do your best, and play for fun,
Then everyone's a winner!

Run a race – ready, steady, go!
Are you fast, or are you slow?
Do your best, and play for fun,
Then everyone's a winner!

Run a race, play a game,
If you lose, try again!
Do your best, and play for fun,
Then everyone's a winner!

- Work out a simple mime gestures for the verbs in the song (*run, play, lose, try again*).
- Work out a mime gesture for *Then everyone's a winner!*
- Read through the song again and ask the pupils to use the mime gestures as you read.
- Play the song again and encourage the pupils to join in, singing and miming.

AB p90 Activity 14 Read and match. Then listen and check.

- Tell the pupils to close their Class Books and open their Activity Books at page 90.
- Read the first part of the first line of the song to the pupils. Ask the pupils to match it with the rest of the line. Write their suggestions on the board.
- Repeat with the other lines of the song.
- Play the song again; the pupils check their suggestions.
- Make any necessary corrections to the lines on the board. The pupils correct their answers in their Activity Books.
- To finish the lesson, tell the pupils to close their books. Help them to say the whole song again, chorally, from memory.

Answers: (see song lyrics above)

Lesson 9 = Words = Other subjects

Learning through English

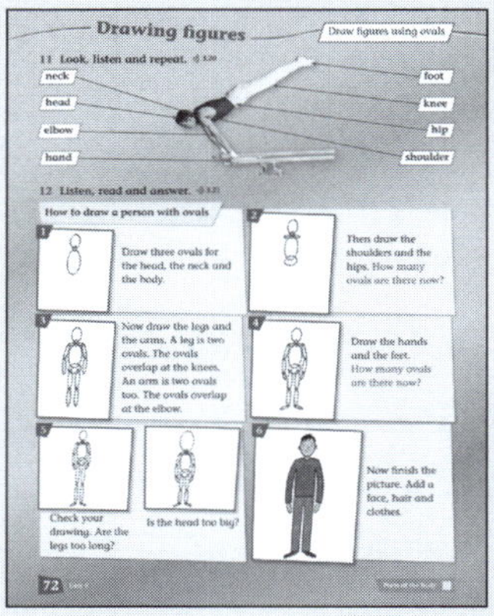

CB page 72

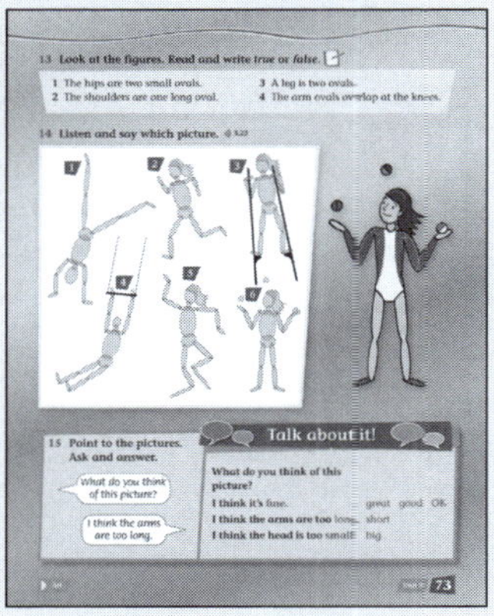

CB page 73

AB page 90

Objectives

- Learn some words for parts of the body
- Learn how to draw figures using ovals

Core language

Parts of the body vocabulary: *shoulder, hip, elbow, knee, neck, foot*

Review of

- body vocabulary: *head, hand*
- language used so far

Other language

oval, overlap

Materials

CD 3; Parts of the body flashcards (*shoulder, hip, elbow, knee, neck, head, hand, foot*); Parts of the body picture cards (PMB p45) – one photocopied set per pupil

Introduce the topic

- Talk with the pupils about how they draw people. Encourage the pupils to talk about these points:
  - the easiest part of the body to draw
  - the most difficult part of the body to draw
  - tricks to draw well
- Recast the pupils' answers if necessary.

Introduce new vocabulary *see p19*

- Use the parts of the body flashcards to teach the new vocabulary. The pupils repeat the words chorally and then individually.
- Play *Memory words* with the pupils. Say sequences of three parts of the body (for example, *shoulders, elbow, foot*); the pupils repeat the words in the same sequence and touch the correct parts of their bodies at the same time.

CB p72 Activity 11 Look, listen and repeat

- Talk about the picture with the pupils. Ask the pupils what they can see.
- The pupils listen to the recording. They repeat each word chorally and point to the correct picture.

3.20

neck – head – elbow – hand – foot – knee – hip – shoulder

CB p72 Activity 12 Listen, read and answer.

- Show the pupils the picture of the figure in frame 6. Explain to the pupils how it is drawn with oval shapes.
- Play the CD while the pupils listen and read.
- Pause the CD after each question for the pupils to answer.

3.21

How to draw a person with ovals.

1 Draw three ovals for the head, the neck and the body.

2 Then draw the shoulders and the hips. How many ovals are there now?

3 Now draw the legs and the arms. A leg is two ovals. The ovals overlap at the knee. An arm is two ovals too. The ovals overlap at the elbow.

4 Draw the hands and the feet. How many ovals are there now?

5 Check your drawing. Are the legs too long? Is the head too big?

6 Now finish the picture. Add a face, hair and clothes.

Answers: five, seventeen

CB p73 Activity 13 Look at the figures. Read and write *true* or *false*.

- Read the first sentence to the pupils. Ask *Is that true or false?* The pupils answer *false* and write *false* in their notebooks.
- Repeat with the other sentences.

Answers: 1 false 2 true 3 true 4 false

AB p90 Activity 15 Write.

- Read the words in the word pool to the pupils.
- The pupils write the words on the correct writing lines.

Answers: 1 elbow 2 knee 3 neck 4 shoulder 5 hip

PMB p45 Make the picture cards

- Give out the photocopies of the parts of the body picture cards. The pupils colour and cut out the picture cards.
- They can use their cards to play a game, for example, *What's missing?* (picture cards version) (see p19).
- If your pupils are using word cards, they can prepare them now (see p30). Pupils cut them out and match them with the picture cards.
- Remind the pupils to keep all the cards in a safe place.

Lesson 10 ■ = Words ◗ = Other subjects

Learning through English

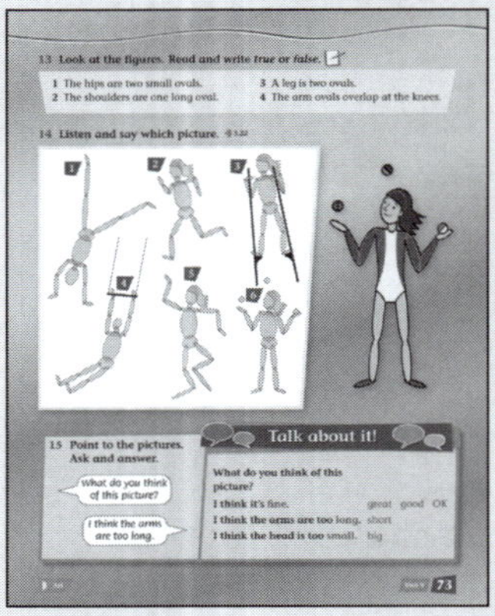

CB page 73

AB page 91

Objectives

- Review words for circus actions and parts of the body
- Discuss drawings of people

Core language

Review of language used so far

Other language

leotard

Materials

Circus actions flashcards (x10); Parts of the body flashcards (x8)

Review vocabulary

- Stick half of the circus actions flashcards and half of the parts of the body flashcards on the board.
- Write up the words with jumbled letters.
- Ask pupils to come to the front to write the words and match them with the flashcards.
- Repeat with the other half of the flashcards.

CB p73 Activity 14 Listen and say which picture.

- Show the pictures to the pupils.
- Ask the pupils to identify the pictures that are badly drawn. Show the pupils how the problem is because the ovals are the wrong size.
- Play the first conversation to the pupils. They identify which picture it is.
- Repeat with the other conversations.

3.22

Child 1: What do you think of this picture?
Child 2: I think the feet are too big.
Child 1: Me too.

Child 2: What do you think of this picture?
Child 1: I think the head is too small.
Child 2: Yes, I think you're right.

Child 1: What do you think of this picture?
Child 2: Mmm ... I think it's fine.
Child 1: Me too. She's juggling!

Child 2: What do you think of this picture?
Child 1: I think the arms are too short.
Child 2: Yes, you're right.

Child 2: What do you think of this picture?
Child 1: I think the legs are too long.
Child 2: Me too.

Child 2: What do you think of this picture?
Child 1: I think it's fine.
Child 2: Me too. She's walking on stilts!

Answers: 5, 4, 6, 2, 1, 3

CB p73 Activity 15 Point to the pictures. Ask and answer.

- Read the conversation to the pupils.
- Read the opinions and alternative adjectives in the *Talk about it!* box.
- Point to one of the pictures and ask *What do you think of this picture?*
- The pupils give their opinion.
- Ask other pupils to ask about other pictures.
- The pupils practise asking for and giving opinions in pairs.

AB p91 Activity 16 Read and match.

- Point to the pictures and say *There are mistakes in all these pictures.*
- Read the first sentence. The pupils identify the picture (2). Show the pupils that the number 2 is written in the box.
- Repeat with the other sentences. The pupils write the picture numbers in the boxes.

Answers: a 2 b 6 c 4 d 1 e 5 f 3

AB p91 Activity 17 Read and colour pictures 1 and 2. Then colour picture 3 and write.

- Read the first text to the pupils. The pupils colour the acrobat according to the text. Teach the word *leotard.*
- Repeat with the second text.
- Point the picture in number 3. Say *Colour the picture.* After the pupils have coloured the picture, they write a description of it, using numbers 1 and 2 as models.

Lesson 11 = Other subjects

Learning through English (Project)

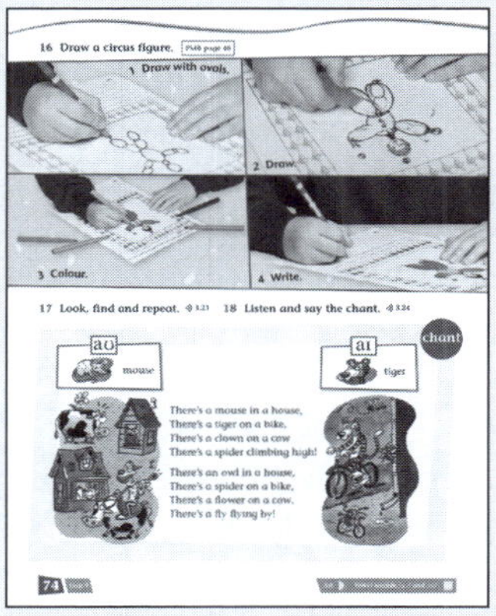

CB page 74

Objectives
- Review vocabulary for parts of the body
- Draw a figure
- Write about the figure

Core language
Review of language used so far

Materials
Parts of the body flashcards (x8); 'Draw a circus figure' template (PMB p48) – one photocopy per pupil

Review vocabulary
- Put the parts of the body flashcards on the board. The pupils say the words chorally and individually.
- Place the flashcards in different parts of the classroom and play *Around the class* with the pupils. First you say the words and the pupils point to the flashcards. Then you point to the flashcards and the pupils say the words.

Present the project
- Tell the pupils they are going to draw a circus figure. They can draw the figure doing any circus action.
- They are going to write sentences about the figure.

PMB p48 / CB p74 Activity 16 Draw a circus figure.
- Give out photocopies of the circus figure template
- Elicit ideas for what the figure is doing and wearing.
- The pupils draw rough pictures first, using ovals, in their notebooks or on rough paper. While they are drawing, circulate around the class. Encourage the pupils to think of how the figure will look doing the action.
- Look at each of the rough figures and tick each one when you think it is adequate.
- The pupils copy their rough figures on the photocopy, then add the details of clothes and hair.
- Read the sentences from Activity Book page 91, Activity 17 again with the pupils.
- The pupils write sentences about their figure. They use the sentences in Activity 17 as a model.

Display
- Display the circus figures in the classroom.

- Allow the pupils to move around the classroom, look at all the figures and discuss them with their friends.
- Have a feedback session in which the pupils decide on the best figure and the best description. Ask the pupils to give reasons for their choices.

Lesson 11a (optional)

Learning through English (Extension)

PMB page 49

Objectives
- Practise the vocabulary for parts of the body
- Make moving pictures
- Practise describing circus actions

Core language
Review of
- parts of the body
- language used so far

Materials
'Moving pictures' template (PMB p49) – one photocopy per pupil; A completed picture strip from the PMB to demonstrate the activity; Scissors; Glue; Paper (optional)

Review vocabulary
- Review vocabulary for parts of the body with the pupils; point to your knee, elbow, hand, etc. and ask the pupils to say the word in English.
- Ask individual pupils to do the same, and other pupils to reply.

Preparation
- Tell the pupils that in this lesson they are going to make a moving picture of a figure.
- Demonstrate your moving picture to the pupils (see below for further details of how to make the picture work).
- Ask pupils to tell you what they can see, for example *He's juggling.*
- You can tell pupils that this is a very simple demonstration of how cartoons are made – individual pictures are shown very quickly, with a slight change in each picture to give the appearance of movement.

PMB p49 Using the Photocopy Master
- Give each pupil a photocopy of the 'Moving pictures' template.
- The pupils colour and cut out each picture pair. Explain that for each pair, the figure's clothes and hair should be coloured the same in both pictures.

- Ask the pupils to choose one of their picture pairs, and show them how to make the moving pictures:
  1 Fold the long piece of paper in half, so the picture is on the front.

  2 Stick the second picture on the inside.

  3 Roll the top picture strip tightly around a pencil.

  4 Holding the strip down on the table, quickly move the pencil up and down so that the pictures appear to move.

- Pupils can make moving pictures with their other picture pairs.
- They can also use blank paper to make more moving pictures, using what they have learnt about drawing figures (for example someone swinging on a trapeze, someone doing a handstand, etc.).
- Ask pupils to demonstrate their moving pictures to each other in pairs. They should say what their partner's figure is doing, for example *Look, she's jumping!*

Extra activity (optional)

- Show the pupils how the addition of motion lines (see below) can make a picture more interesting.
- The pupils add motion lines to the hands and / or feet on their second picture.

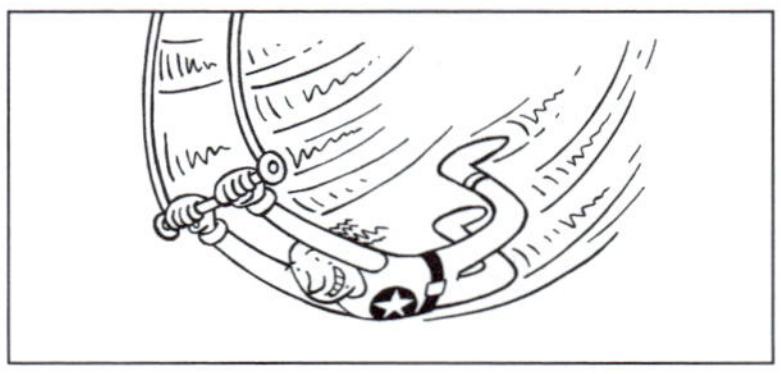

Display

- Arrange a display of each pupil's favourite moving picture. Allow the pupils to move around the classroom and try out all the pictures.
- Arrange a feedback session. Ask the pupils *Which is the best moving picture?* Encourage the pupils to give reasons for their choices. Recast their language if necessary.
- Arrange a vote in the class for the best moving pictures and congratulate the winners.

Play a game

- Play a memory game with the pupils. Say lists of three, four, or five parts of the body, for example *neck, hand, hips, foot, elbow*.
- Say *Now show me the same parts of the body, in the same order.*
- The pupils touch the correct parts of their bodies in the same order as you said.

Song

- Ask the pupils *Can you remember the song in this unit?*
- Write what the pupils can remember on the board. Help them to remember the bits they've forgotten, then add them on the board.
- Play the song again (Listening 3.19). The pupils check that the version on the board is correct.
- Play the song again and encourage the pupils to join in.

Lesson 12

Review and self-evaluation

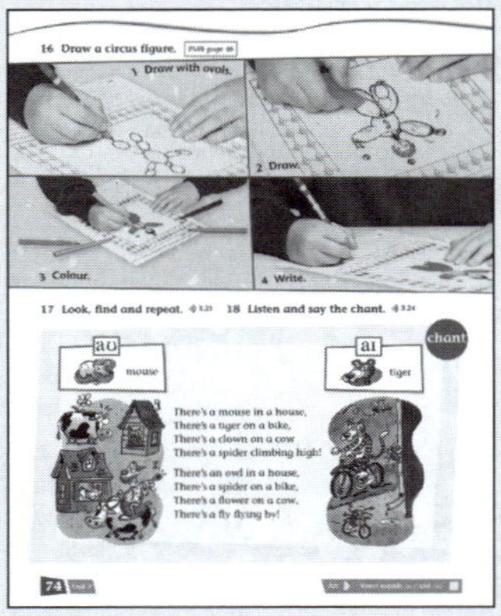

CB page 74

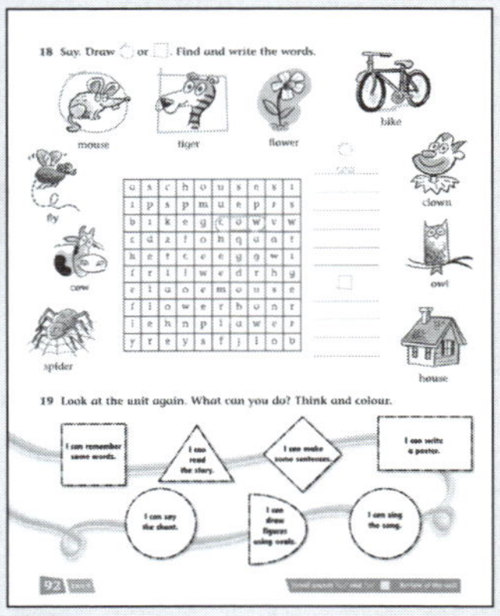

AB page 92

Objectives

- Focus on the pronunciation of vowel sounds (/aʊ/ and /aɪ/) with a chant
- Review the activities and the new language of the unit
- Complete a self-evaluation activity

Core language

Review of language used so far

Materials

CD 3; Rollercoaster Game poster; Character counters and game cards; Dice (one pair per class); Picture dictionary page (PMB p2) – one photocopy per pupil (optional)

CB p74 Activity 17 Listen, find and repeat.

- Point to the pictures. The pupils say the words.
- Play the CD. Pupils point and repeat.

3.23

owl – flower – mouse – cow – clown – house [/aʊ/]
tiger – bike – spider – fly [/aɪ/]

- Say the two vowel sounds /aʊ/ and /aɪ/. The pupils find the words that share the vowel sound.
- The pupils practise saying the words chorally and individually, concentrating on the pronunciation of the vowel sounds.

CB p74 Activity 18 Listen and say the chant.

- Play the chant. The pupils point to the items as they hear them.

3.24

There's a mouse in a house,
There's a tiger on a bike,
There's a clown on a cow,
There's a spider climbing high!

There's an owl in a house,
There's a spider on a bike,
There's a flower on a cow,
There's a fly flying by!

- Teach the chant line by line. Focus on the pronunciation points. Use choral and individual repetition to check pronunciation.
- Play the chant again and encourage the pupils to join in.

Focus on spelling

- Match the spelling with the vowel sounds.
- Focus on the spelling patterns:
  /aʊ/ is often spelt *ou* (*mouse*), or *ow* (*flower*)
  /aɪ/ is often spelt *i* (*high*), *y* (*fly*), or *i…e* (*bike*)
- Show examples from the chant for each vowel sound.
- Remind the pupils that there are lots of exceptions to spelling patterns in English.

AB p92 Activity 18. Say. Draw ● or ■. Find and write the words.

- Point to each of the pictures. The pupils say the words chorally.
- Focus on the pronunciation difference between /aʊ/ and /aɪ/, using the words *mouse* and *tiger*.
- Show how *mouse* has a circle around it and *tiger* has a square round it.
- Ask the pupils to identify a word with the /aʊ/ sound.
- Show the pupils how to put a circle round the word.
- Repeat with the /aɪ/ sound, putting a square around the word.
- The pupils put circles and squares around the words.
- The pupils find and circle the words in the wordsearch. They copy the words into the correct columns.
- Point to the pictures at random. The pupils say the words chorally and individually. Check the pupils' pronunciation.

Answers: circle: mouse, flower, clown, house, owl, cow;
square: tiger, bike, spider, fly

a	s	c	h	o	u	s	e	s	i
i	p	s	p	m	u	e	p	r	s
b	i	k	e	g	c	o	w	v	w
c	d	z	f	o	h	q	a	a	t
h	e	t	c	e	e	g	g	w	i
f	r	l	l	w	e	d	r	h	g
e	l	a	o	e	m	o	u	s	e
f	l	o	w	e	r	b	o	n	r
l	e	h	n	p	l	a	w	e	r
y	r	e	y	s	f	j	l	o	b

End-of-unit review

- Use the Rollercoaster Game poster and the Class Book to recall the main activities of the unit.
- Recall the language associated with each activity
- Ask the pupils to let you know what they liked or didn't like, and what they found easy or difficult.

Play the Rollercoaster Game

- Divide the class into small groups. Give each group one of the character 'counters' and let them play the game as before (see p41).
- Remind them to use the poster chants when a group gets a question right or wrong.

AB p92 Activity 19 Look at the unit again. What can you do? Think and colour.

- Let the pupils do the self-evaluation activity as before (see p41).

PMB p2 Picture Dictionary (optional)

- If your pupils are making Picture Dictionaries, give out the photocopies of the template.
- Pupils continue making the dictionaries as for Unit 1 (see p42).

Lesson 12a (optional)

■ = Words ◆ = Sentences

Show what you know!

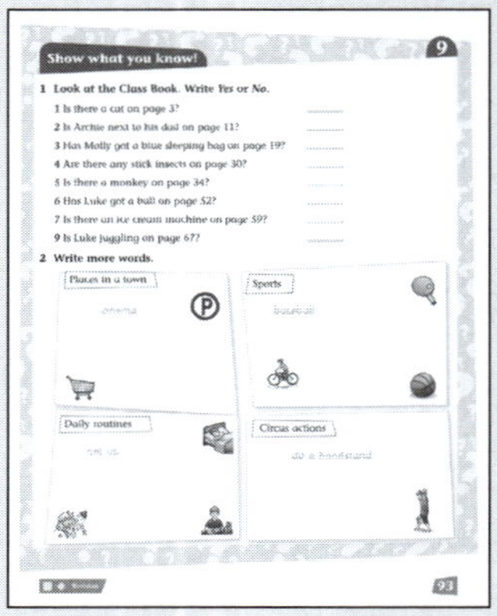

AB page 93

For suggestions on how to use *Show what you know!* see page 13.

Objectives

- Extra practice of the vocabulary of the unit
- Solve puzzles in English
- Provide extra material for homework and fast finishers

Core language

Review of language used so far

Materials

No extra materials

AB p93 Activity 1 Look at the Class Book. Write *Yes* or *No*.

- Tell the pupils to open their Class Books. Read the first question. The pupils look on page 3 of their Class Books to find the answer and write it on the line.
- The pupils answer the rest of the questions in pairs.

Answers: **1** Yes **2** Yes **3** Yes **4** No **5** Yes **6** Yes **7** Yes **8** No

AB p93 Activity 2 Write more words.

- Point to the first box (*Places in a town*). Read the word in the box (*cinema*) and ask the pupils *Can you think of some more words for this box?* Write suitable suggestions on the board.
- The pupils copy the words from the board into the boxes.
- Repeat with the other boxes. Alternatively, the pupils can work in pairs or groups to complete the boxes.

Answers:

Places in a town – cinema, bus station, swimming pool, shopping centre, car park, restaurant, supermarket, library, post office, park, school

Sports – baseball, tennis, basketball, table tennis, hockey, badminton, chess, judo, gymnastics, volleyball, football

Daily routines – get up, have breakfast, go to school, go to work, have lunch, leave school, leave work, have dinner, go to bed, have a shower

Circus actions – do a handstand, ride a horse, swing on a trapeze, do a somersault, walk on stilts, walk on your hands, do a cartwheel, do a headstand, juggle, ride a bike

The pupils are now ready to sit the Unit 9 test. See pp202–205 for both Standard and Higher levels. They are also ready to sit the Term 3 test on pp210–211 and p214.

The pupils are now ready to do the culture lessons on 'Sport in my country' (see p164).

DVD VIDEO

Multimedia extension: you may now like to use the Art section of the optional DVD, if you haven't already used it in Unit 2.

Festivals

Christmas

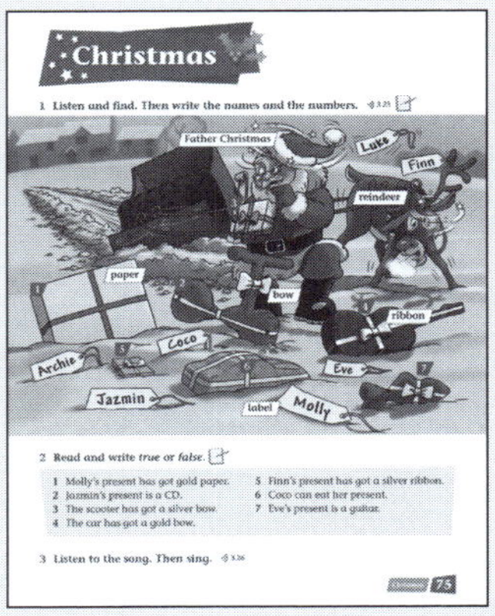

CB page 75

Objectives

- Become aware of some words associated with Christmas
- Talk about different aspects of the Christmas celebration
- Compare Christmas traditions from different countries
- Make a gift box and use it to send a Christmas message in class
- Sing a Christmas song

Language

Christmas vocabulary: *Father Christmas, reindeer, paper, ribbon, bow, label*

Review of language used so far

Materials

Christmas objects (Father Christmas figure, reindeer figure, wrapping paper, ribbon, bow, label) (optional); CD 3; Christmas gift box template (PMB p50) – one photocopy per pupil; Scissors; Glue; Several sheets of white paper

Teaching tip: Christmas facts and figures

Over the Christmas period in England:
– 3 million tonnes of extra rubbish are produced
– 150 million Christmas cards are sent
– 10 million turkeys and twenty five million Christmas puddings are eaten
– £20 billion (that's twenty thousand million pounds, or £20,000,000,000,) / $38 billion dollars / 30 billion euros are spent on food, drinks, decorations and presents

Introduce the topic

- Ask when Christmas is, then discuss with the pupils how they celebrate Christmas in their families. Recast the pupils' answers as necessary.
- Talk with the pupils about what Christmas means for them. Ask them questions such as:
  – What's the best thing about Christmas for you?
  – Is Christmas important in your family?
  – Do people behave differently at Christmas?
- Encourage the pupils to share what they know about Christmas in other countries and cultures. Ask them questions such as: *Do you know any Christmas traditions from other countries?*
- Recast the pupils' answers as necessary.

Introduce the vocabulary

- If you have brought the Christmas objects suggested above (*Father Christmas, reindeer, paper, bow, ribbon, label*) to class, use them to present the vocabulary. Alternatively, point to each of the items in the picture for Activity 1.
- Say the words clearly. The pupils repeat the words chorally and individually.

CB p75 Activity 1 Listen and find. Then write the names and the numbers.

- Explain the situation to the pupils: Father Christmas has crashed in his sleigh and all the presents are mixed up. Now he's trying to work out who each present is for.
- Point to present number 1 and ask the pupils to describe it (*It's big, it's got gold paper, it's got a red ribbon*). Encourage the pupils to guess what the present is. Repeat with the other presents.
- Play the first conversation. Ask the pupils *Which present is it? (3)*. Write the number on the board. Repeat with the other conversations and write the other numbers in a column on the board.

3.25

Father Christmas: Oh no! All the labels have come off the presents!
Now let me think …
This present's got silver paper and a green bow. It's a book. It's for Eve.
Now, where's the label?
Ah! There it is!

This present's got gold paper and red ribbon. It's a game. It's for Luke
Now, where's the label?
Ah! There it is!

This present's got red paper and a silver bow. It's a scooter. It's for Finn.
Now, where's the label?
Ah! There it is!

This present's got green paper and gold ribbon. It's a car. It's for Archie.
Now, where's the label?
Ah! There it is!

This present's got blue paper and a silver bow. It's a guitar. It's for Jazmin.
Now, where's the label?
Ah! There it is!

This present's got green paper and a silver bow. It's a CD. It's for Molly.
Now, where's the label?
Ah! There it is!

This present's got red paper and a gold bow. It's a fish. It's for Coco.
Now, where's the label?
Ah! There it is!

Answers: 3, 1, 2, 6, 4, 5, 7

- Play the first conversation again. Ask *Who is it for? (Eve)*. Write the name next to the number on the board (*3 – Eve*). The pupils copy this into their notebooks.
- Play the other conversations. The pupils write the number of each present, and the person it is for, in their notebooks.

Answers: 3 Eve 1 Luke 2 Finn 6 Archie 4 Jazmin 5 Molly 7 Coco

CB p75 Activity 2 Read and write *true* or *false*.

- Ask *Can you remember what the presents are?* Point to each of the presents and ask *What is it?* The pupils say what the present is. If they have problems remembering, play the appropriate conversation to check. Add each present to the columns on the board, for example *1 – Luke – game*.
- Read the first sentence to the pupils. Ask *Is that true or false? (false)*. Pupils write the answers to the questions in their notebooks.

Answers: 1 false 2 false 3 true 4 false 5 true 6 true 7 false

PMB p50 Make a gift box

- Give each pupil a photocopy of the Christmas Photocopy Master. Explain that the pupils are going to make the box, write a message to put in it, and give it to another pupil.
- The pupils cut out, colour, and assemble the gift box.
- Ask each pupil to write a Christmas message on a piece of paper and put it in the box.
- Elicit ideas for the message from the pupils, and write their suggestions on the board, for example: *Happy Christmas!, Merry Christmas!, Peace at Christmas.* (If you prefer, pupils can write longer messages in their own language.)
- Write each pupil's name on a piece of paper and put them in a box. Without looking, take the first name and say, for example, *Ana, you are going to give your box to ...* Take out the second name and say it, for example, *Tom*. Then say *Tom, you are going to give your box to ...* Take another name out of the box and read it. Repeat until every pupil knows who he / she is going to give the box to.
- If you like, include yourself in the Christmas gift box exchange. This will make two pupils – the one who receives a gift box from you, and the one who gives a gift box to you – feel very special. You could even secretly choose who those two pupils are, to give extra motivation to the pupils in your class who need it most.

Teaching tip

It isn't a good idea to let the pupils decide who to give their box to: if they do that, then some pupils might receive several boxes and some pupils might not receive any.

- The pupils complete the tag with their own name and the name of the person they are giving it to.
- Practise a suitable dialogue for giving the gift boxes, for example:
  Happy Christmas, Tom! This is for you!
  Thank you, Ana. Happy Christmas!
- The pupils give their gift boxes to each other.

CB p75 Activity 3 Sing the song.

- Copy the lyrics for the song onto the board.
- Read the song with the pupils. Explain any new words. Note that *jingle* is the sound a bell makes.
- Play the song on the CD.

3.26

Jingle bells, jingle bells,
Jingle all the way.
Oh, what fun it is to ride
In a one horse open sleigh!

Oh, jingle bells, jingle bells,
Jingle all the way.
Oh, what fun it is to ride
In a one horse open sleigh!

- With the pupils, work out a simple mime gesture of ringing a bell for these lines in the song: *Jingle bells, Jingle bells, Jingle all the way!* (Or pupils could use their pencil cases / boxes as percussion instruments, by shaking them.)
- Read through the song again and ask the pupils to use the mime gestures as you read.
- Play the song again and encourage the pupils to join in, singing and miming.
- Optional activity: pupils can copy the lyrics into their notebooks or onto a blank piece of paper, and draw a picture to illustrate the song.

Valentine's Day

CB page 76

Objectives

- Become aware of some of the traditions around Valentine's Day
- Become aware of different interpretations of Valentine's Day in different countries
- Become aware of words associated with Valentine's Day

Language

coupon, promise

Review of language used so far

Materials

Valentine's Day coupons template (PMB p51) – one photocopy per pupil; CD 3; Scissors

---

Teaching tip

Make sure your pupils realize that, more and more, Valentine's Day is becoming associated with friendship in addition to romantic love. In several South American countries, for example, it is called 'Love and friendship day'.

Introduce the topic

- Ask the pupils when Valentine's Day is (February 14th).
- Discuss with the pupils how Valentine's Day is celebrated. Talk with them about how Valentine's Day is associated with friendship in many countries.
- Talk with the pupils about special things they can do with their friends on Valentine's Day.
- Recast the pupils' answers as necessary.
- Read the information box with pupils, and check they understand the vocabulary, e.g. *coupon* and *promise*.

CB p76 Activity 1 Read and listen. Write the names and numbers.

- Point to each of the people and ask *Who is it?* The pupils say the names.
- Ask questions such as *Who is Molly's Mum?* The pupils point to the correct picture.
- Point to coupon 1 and read it to the pupils. Use mime gestures and the picture on the coupon to make sure the pupils understand the idea of making breakfast.
- Explain that the people in Molly and Luke's family are going to give these coupons to each other on Valentine's Day. Ask the pupils to guess who is going to give coupon 1, and who he / she is going to give it to.
- Ask individual pupils to read the other coupons. After each one, ask other pupils to explain what activity the coupon is for. Recast the pupils' answers as necessary.
- Explain that it's Valentine's Day and the family are giving the coupons to each other. Play the first conversation on the CD. Ask *Who is the coupon for? (for Molly)* and *Which coupon is it? (6)*.
- Write *Molly – coupon 6* on the board. The pupils copy this in their notebooks.
- Play the rest of the conversations. The pupils write the people and their coupons in their notebooks.

3.27

Dad:	Hello, Molly. Happy Valentine's Day. This is for you.
Molly:	Oh, thank you! Excellent! A coupon for having a special pizza! Thank you, Dad!
Luke:	Hello, Grandpa. Happy Valentine's Day! This is for you.
Grandpa:	Really?! Oh very nice! A coupon for doing the shopping. That's lovely!
Molly:	Hello, Grandma. Happy Valentine's Day. This is for you.
Grandma:	For me?!
Molly:	Yes.
Grandma:	Oh, very nice! A coupon for helping in the kitchen! Thank you!
Mum:	Hello, Luke. Happy Valentine's Day. This is for you.
Luke:	Ooh! What is it?
Mum:	Open it and look.
Luke:	Oh great! A coupon for watching a special film! Oh thanks, Mum!
Molly:	Hello, Dad. It's Valentine's Day. This is for you.
Dad:	Wow! What is it?
Molly:	Have a look!
Dad:	Oh, what a good idea! A coupon for washing the car. Fantastic!
Luke:	Hello, Mum. Happy Valentine's Day. This is for you.
Mum:	Oh, thank you. What is it?
Luke:	Open it and see.
Mum:	Oh great! A coupon for making breakfast! Brilliant.

Answers: Molly – coupon 6, Grandpa – coupon 2, Grandma – coupon 3, Luke – coupon 5, Dad – coupon 4, Mum – coupon 1

PMB p51 Make coupons

- Give each pupil a photocopy of the Valentine's Day Photocopy Master. Ask the pupils to suggest people to give the coupons to (*Mum, Dad, sister, brother, friends*). Write their suggestions on the board.
- Ask the pupils to suggest ideas for the coupons (*doing the washing up, tidying the living room*, etc.) Write their suggestions on the board.
- The pupils write their coupons, cut them out and colour them.
- Ask individual pupils to show their coupons to the class and explain them.
- The pupils take their coupons home. Make a note to ask your pupils in a week's time if they have done the things they promised on their coupons.

Environment Day

CB page 77

Objectives

- Become aware of World Environment Day
- Become aware of some words associated with the environment and recycling
- Discuss the importance of recycling

Language

wrapping paper, plastic bag, pass on, use, less, reuse, recycle, reduce

Review of language used so far

Materials

Environment Day recycling chart (PMB p52) – one photocopy for each pupil; CD 3

Teaching tip

Visit the United Kingdom Environment Agency's web page at www.environment-agency.gov.uk/wed/ to find out more about World Environment Day. The *make a promise* link is very relevant to the activities in this lesson.

Introduce the topic

- Ask the pupils if they know when World Environment Day is. (5th June)
- Discuss with the pupils the sort of thing we should think about on World Environment Day. Ask them questions such as:
  - What environmental problems do we have in our city / our country / the world?
  - What can we do about these problems?
  - Can we make a difference?
- Recast the pupils' answers as necessary.

CB p77 Activity 1 Read the sentences and find the pictures.

- Read each of the sentences to the pupils. Encourage the pupils to guess the meaning of unfamiliar words, using the pictures in Activity 2 for reference.
- For example, read the sentence *Save old wrapping paper!* Ask *Who can show me wrapping paper in the pictures?* and point to the pictures in Activity 2.
- The pupils point to the first picture. Say *That's right!* If some students are unsure of the meaning, say the word in their own language.
- Ask *What does 'save' mean?* The pupils reply with the word in their own language. Say *That's right! Save old wrapping paper!*

Teaching tip

Here we are using the pupils' own language to help them understand *save* and *wrapping paper*. However, avoid translating the whole sentence into their own language if possible. We are using their own language to explain the meaning of words, but we should not encourage the pupils to translate everything.

- Pupils match the sentences with the pictures.
- Point to pictures in Activity 2 and ask individual pupils to read the corresponding sentence aloud.

Answers: 1 Save old wrapping paper! **2** Pass on your clothes! **3** Use less water! **4** Use plastic bags again! **5** Put glass in the glass bin! **6** Put plastic in the plastic bin!

CB p77 Activity 2 Listen and write the numbers. Then say *recycle*, *reuse* or *reduce* for each picture.

- Play the first conversation to the pupils. Ask *Which picture is it? (6)*. The pupils write the number of the picture in their notebooks.
- Repeat with the other conversations.

3.28

Mum:	Put this in the bin.
Luke:	Which bin?
Mum:	The one over there. That's the plastics bin.
Luke:	OK.
Mum:	Go and have a shower.
Luke:	I want a bath.
Mum:	No a shower is better. You use less water.
Luke:	OK.
Mum:	A quick shower!
Molly:	Dad! Have you got some wrapping paper?
Dad:	Yes, here you are. What colour do you want?
Molly:	Red, please.
Shop assistant:	Take a bag.
Dad:	No, thanks. I've got one here.
Shop assistant:	Oh, OK.
Molly:	Can I put the bottles in?
Mum:	OK. Be careful.
	(sound of bottle smashing)
Mum:	What about this jumper?
Luke:	It's too small.
Mum:	And this T-shirt?
Luke:	Too small.
Mum:	All for little cousin Sam then!

Answers: 6, 3, 1, 4, 5, 2

- Explain the words *recycle*, *reuse* and *reduce*:
  recycle – when we put the object in a recycling bin, and it's taken to be processed and made into something else. Example: plastic milk bottles are made into fleece jackets.
  reuse – when we use something a second time instead of throwing it away. Example: we keep wrapping paper from a present and use it to wrap another present.
  reduce – when we use less of something. Example: we can reduce the amount of water we use by having showers instead of baths.

- Point to picture 1. Ask the pupils to choose from *recycle, reuse, reduce (reuse).*
- Repeat with the other pictures.

Answers: 1 reuse **2** reuse **3** reduce **4** reuse **5** recyle **6** recycle

PMB p52 Make a recycling chart

- Give each pupil a photocopy of the Environment Day Photocopy Master. Read the heading and ask *What can we recycle?* Point to the squares in the left column and ask *What pictures can we draw here?* Write the pupils' suggestions (*paper, glass, tins*, etc.) on the board.
- Point to the list and say *Choose six of these and draw them.* Point to the squares on the Photocopy Master to show the pupils where to draw them. The pupils then draw the pictures on their photocopies.
- Show the pupils one of the completed photocopies. Point to each picture and ask *What is it*? Explain that they can take these sheets home and stick them on the fridge in the kitchen. Every time they recycle something, they can put a tick in the box.
- Arrange a date (in two or three weeks) for the pupils to bring their recycling charts back to the class. On that day, display the charts around the class. The pupils can decide who is the best recycler.

Children around the world

(To be taught after Unit 3.)

My country (1)

CB page 78

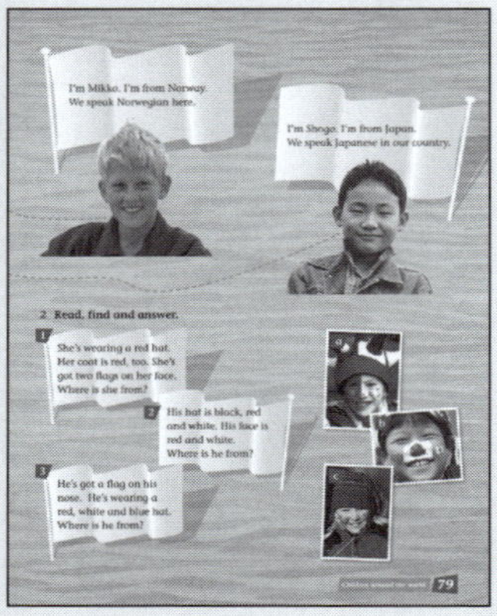

CB page 79

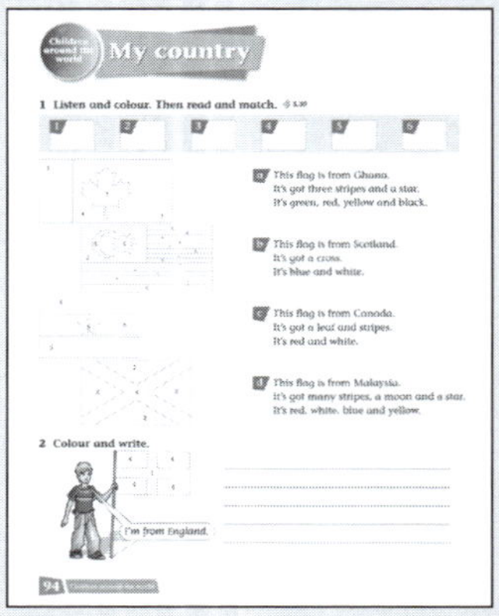

AB page 94

Objectives

- Get to know about children from four countries (Morocco, Wales, Norway, Japan)
- Learn about flags and national colours
- Describe flags

Language

Countries: *Morocco, Wales, Norway, Japan*
Languages: *Arabic, Welsh, Norwegian, Japanese*
stripe, cross, dragon, moon
Review of language from Units 1–3

Materials

World map or globe; CD 3; An object with stripes (e.g. a striped shirt, or a notebook with stripes on the cover); Coloured chalks / board pens

Introduce the topic

- Show the pupils a world map or globe. Point to the countries which the pupils have seen in previous levels and ask *What country is it?* The pupils say the countries; if they have problems remembering the names, prompt them with the first sounds of the word, for example, for *Canada say C ... Ca ... Can ...*, etc.
- Write the names of the countries they are going to see in Level 3 on the board. Ask the pupils if they know where these countries are. Call individual pupils up to the front to find them.

Cultural note

Many people think that *England* and the *United Kingdom* are the same place. In fact, *England* is just one of four countries that make up the *United Kingdom* or *UK*. The other countries are *Wales*, *Scotland*, and *Northern Ireland*.
A person from *England* can say he / she is *English* (= from England) or *British* (= from the United Kingdom).
A person from *Wales* can say he / she is *Welsh* (= from Wales) or *British*. People from *Wales* do not like to be called *English*!

CB pp78–79 Activity 1 Read. Then listen and find.

- Point to the pictures of the four children. Say their names and the country they are from.
- Point to the countries on the map / globe.
- Read the sentences about Khadija. Ask the pupils *What's her name?* (*Khadija*), *Where is she from?* (*Morocco*) and *What language does she speak?* (*Arabic*). Repeat with the sentences about the other children.
- Point to the shapes on the flags at the bottom of the map. For each one, ask *What is it?* (*dragon, star, cross,* and *circle*). Write the words on the board and say them again. The pupils repeat the words chorally and individually.
- Describe one of the flags with *It's got ...* (for example, *It's got a blue and white cross*). Ask the pupils to describe the other flags.
- Play the first conversation on the CD. Ask *Who is it? (Khadija)* and *Which flag is it?* (the pupils point to the flag with the green star). Ask *Which country is it?* (the pupils point to Morocco on the map).
- Repeat with the other conversations.

3.29

Khadija:	I live in a big country in Africa. Our flag is red. It's got a green star on it. Can you find my country?
Shogo:	I live in a small country in Asia. Our flag is white. It's got a red circle. Can you find my country?
Mikko:	I live in a big country in Europe. Our flag is red. It's red and has got a blue and white cross on it. Can you find my country?
Bethan:	I live in Europe, too. Our flag is green and white. It's got a red dragon on it! Can you find my country?

Answers: Khadija – flag 2, Shogo – flag 4, Mikko – flag 3, Bethan – flag 1

AB p94 Activity 1 Listen and colour. Then read and match.

- Point to the numbered boxes at the top of the page. Say *Each number is a colour. Listen and colour the boxes.*
- Play the first sentence on the CD. Ask *What colour is it? (red)* The pupils colour the first box red.
- Repeat with the other sentences. The pupils colour all the boxes.

3.30

Presenter: Number one is red.
Number two is blue.
Number three is green.
Number four is white.
Number five is yellow.
Number six is black.

Answers: 1 red 2 blue 3 green 4 white 5 yellow 6 black

- Point to areas labelled '1' on the first flag. Ask *What colour is it? (red).* Ask *What other flags have number 1?* (the second and third flags). The pupils colour all the areas marked 1 with a red crayon, then continue with the other colours.
- Read the first description to the pupils. Use the striped object you brought to the class to teach or revise the meaning of *stripe.* Ask *Which flag is it?* (the third flag). The pupils draw a line from text *a* to the third flag.
- Repeat with the other descriptions and flag. (Teach the word *moon* if pupils do not know it already.)

Answers: **a** the third flag **b** the fourth flag **c** the first flag **d** the second flag

Design a class flag or school flag

- Say *We're going to design a flag.* The pupils can decide if the flag is for the class, the school, or for something else like a football team. When they have decided, write a title on the board, for example *A flag for our class.*
- Arrange the pupils in groups of four or five. Draw an outline of a flag on the board for each group. Ask the pupils to suggest what can be put on the flag (stripes, stars, a circle, a cross, a picture, etc.) Write the words on the board.
- Show the pupils the coloured chalks / board pens and say *You can use these colours.* Ask the pupils to name the colours of the chalk / pens, and write the colours on the board.
- Tell the pupils they have five minutes to decide in their groups on a design for their flag.
- After five minutes, call one pupil from each group to draw their designs on the board with the coloured chalk / pens. When they have finished, point to each flag and say *Describe this flag.* The pupils describe the flag with the colours (for example, *It's yellow and blue*) and the shapes (for example, *It's got red stripes*).
- Arrange a vote in the class to decide which design is the best.

My country (2)

(See mini pages for Lesson 1)

Objectives

- Read and write descriptions of flags
- Draw the national flag and write a description of it

Language

Review of language from Units 1–3

Materials

'My flag' (PMB p53) – one photocopy per pupil; A picture of the Union Jack flag (optional)

Cultural note

The four countries of the United Kingdom (England, Scotland, Wales, and Northern Ireland) each have their own flag. The flags of England, Scotland, and Northern Ireland were combined to make the Union Jack, which is the flag of the United Kingdom.
Visit www.crwflags.com/fotw/flags/gb.html to find out more about these flags.

Recall the topic

- Point to the pictures of the children on page 78 of the Class Book and ask *Who is it?, Where is he / she from?,* and *What language does he / she speak?*
- Point to the flags and ask the children to describe the objects in them (*circle, cross, star,* and *dragon*). Ask the pupils to describe each flag with *It's got ...*

CB p79 Activity 2 Read, find and answer.

- Point to the pictures of the children. Ask the pupils to describe the flags they can see.
- Read the first description to the pupils. Point to the three pictures and ask *Which picture is it?* and *Where is she from?*
- Repeat with the other descriptions.

Answers: 1 c (Norway) 2 a (Wales) 3 b (Japan)

AB p94 Activity 2 Colour and write.

- Ask the pupils what famous flag they associate with England. The pupils will probably not know the name (the Union Jack), but they may know the colours (blue, red, and white). Show them a picture of the Union Jack if possible.
- Explain that the Union Jack is the flag of the United Kingdom. England, however, has a special flag of its own, the St. George's cross. Say *Listen. The flag of England is white. It's got a red cross.*
- The pupils colour the flag in their Activity Books. They can look at the key in Activity 1 to help them.
- Read the description of flag b in Activity 1 again (Scotland). Tell the pupils they are now going to write about the flag for England.
- Guide the pupils to writing a text about the flag. Cue the beginning of each sentence (*This flag ..* , etc). After they say each sentence, write it on the board.
- The pupils copy the description into their Activity Books.

Answer: This flag is from England. It's got a cross. It's red and white.

PMB p53 My flag

- Give each pupil a photocopy of the Photocopy Master. Show the pupils the flag, then ask them to describe the flag of their country (for example, *It's got a yellow star. It's got red and white stripes*).
- The pupils draw and colour inside the flag outline to make it into their country's flag. (If you have pupils in your class who are from a different country of origin, allow them to choose which country's flag they will draw – their country of birth, or their new country.)
- The pupils draw their face on the figure holding the flag. They then complete the description of the flag in the speech bubble.

(To be taught after Unit 6.)

My town (1)

CB page 80

CB page 81

AB page 95

Objectives

- Learn more about the children and the towns they are from
- Describe places in towns
- Draw a perfect town and write about it

Language

market, castle, square, building

Review of language from Units 4–6

Materials

CD 3; 'My perfect town' (PMB p54) – one photocopy per pupil

Recall

- Point to the pictures of the children on Class Book page 80. Ask the pupils *Who is it?* The pupils say the names.
- Ask the pupils other questions about the children: *Where is he / she from? What language does he / she speak?*

CB pp80–81 Activity 1 Read. Then listen and find.

- Point to the pictures of Marrakech. Say the name of the place. Ask the pupils to describe the pictures, for example, *There's a ..., There are some ...*
- Repeat with the other pictures.
- Use the pictures to teach the new vocabulary (*market, castle, square,* and *building*). Say the words and get pupils to repeat them chorally and individually.
- Play the first conversation to the pupils. Ask *Who is it?* (*Bethan*). Ask the pupils to identify the place (*Conwy*).
- Repeat with the other conversations.

3.31

Interviewer: Hello, Bethan. Where do you live?
Bethan: I live in a small town in Wales.
Interviewer: Are there tall buildings there?
Bethan: No, nothing like that. There is a very, very small house there! It's very old, too.
Interviewer: Hmm ... Are there any castles there?
Bethan: Yes! We've got a very old, very big castle. And there is a big bridge next to the castle. They are both beautiful.
Interviewer: What's the name of your town? *[pause]*
Bethan: Conwy.

Interviewer: Hello, Shogo. Where do you live?
Shogo: I live in a big city in Japan.
Interviewer: Oh, are there big buildings there?
Shogo: Yes! There are lots of very tall buildings there.
Interviewer: Are they old or new?
Shogo: They're new. But we've got old places, too.
Interviewer: Tell me about them.
Shogo: We've got some beautiful castles. Osaka castle is fantastic!
Interviewer: What's the name of your city? *[pause]*
Shogo: Osaka!

Interviewer: Hello, Khadija. Where do you live?
Khadija: I live in a city in Morocco.
Interviewer: Is there a shopping centre or market there?
Khadija: Oh yes! There's a fantastic market there. You can buy scarves, baskets, rugs ...everything!
Interviewer: What else?
Khadija: There is also a big square next to the market. I go there with my family in the evenings.
Interviewer: Tell me about the square.
Khadija: There are snake charmers – I love it!
Interviewer: What's the name of your city? *[pause]*
Khadija: Marrakech.

Interviewer: Hello, Mikko. Where do you live?
Mikko: I live in a big town in Norway.
Interviewer: Is there a market there?
Mikko: Yes, there is a big fish market there. I go to the market with my dad. We like fish!
Interviewer: Anything else?
Mikko: Oh yes – the cable car!
Interviewer: What's that?
Mikko: I go up the mountain in the cable car. I can see my whole town. It's brilliant!
Interviewer: What's the name of your town? *[pause]*
Mikko: Bergen.

Answers: 1 Bethan, Conwy **2** Shogo, Osaka **3** Khadija, Marrakech **4** Mikko, Bergen

- Ask the pupils to describe interesting places in their town. Recast their answers as necessary.

AB p95 **Activity 1 Read and write A or B.**

- Point to picture A. Say *Tell me about the picture.* The pupils describe the picture with *There is ... / There's ...* and *There are ...* Then point to picture B and ask the pupils to describe it in the same way.
- Read the first sentence to the pupils. Ask *Picture A or Picture B?* (*A*). The pupils write *A* in the box.
- Repeat with the other pictures.

Answers: 1 A **2** A **3** B **4** B **5** A **6** A

PMB p54 **My perfect town**

- Give each pupil a photocopy of the Photocopy Master. Ask the pupils to suggest places in their perfect town. They will probably want to suggest places which they don't know the words for in English, so be prepared to recast their answers. Write a list of their suggestions on the board.
- Copy the thought bubble from the Photocopy Master on the board, and begin to draw your idea of a perfect town. Talk about what you are drawing (*There's a big park, and in the park there's a very nice café,* etc.).
- The pupils draw their perfect towns in the thought bubbles on the photocopies. As they are drawing, circulate around the class and encourage them to use their imagination.
- Next to your picture of a perfect town on the board, begin to write a description of it, using the beginning provided on the Photocopy Master (*In my perfect town there is ...*).
- The pupils write a description of their towns.
- Pupils can add features to the figure with the thought bubble to make it look like themselves.
- Arrange a display of the completed pictures and descriptions in the class. Encourage the pupils to look at the pictures and talk about them. After this, arrange a feedback session in which the pupils talk about their favourite features and ideas.

My town (2)

(See mini pages for Lesson 1)

Objectives

- Read descriptions of towns
- Listen to a description of a town
- Write about a place in your town

Language

Review of language from Units 4–6

Materials

CD 3

Recall

- Point to the picture of Marrakech on Class Book page 80. Ask the pupils *What do you know about Marrakech?* The pupils recall all the information they learnt about Marrakech in the previous lesson.
- Repeat with the pictures of the other towns.

CB p81 **Activity 2 Read, find and answer *true* or *false*.**

- Read the first sentence to the pupils. Point to the picture of Conwy and ask *Is there a very old castle in Conwy? (Yes).* The pupils write the answer in their notebooks.
- Repeat with the other sentences. The pupils write the answers (*Yes* or *No*) to each question in their notebooks.

Answers: 1 true **2** false **3** false **4** true **5** true **6** false **7** true **8** false

AB p95 **Activity 2 Listen and draw.**

- Say *You're going to listen to a description of a town.* Ask *What places do you think the person will describe?* The pupils suggest places in the town, for example *school, shops,* etc. Encourage the pupils to suggest all the places and things in the listening script (*church, school, park, trees, slide, swings, swimming pool, bridge, river, train station*). Write all their suggestions on the board.
- Play the CD. Ask the pupils *Which places did you hear?* The pupils say all the places on the list (see above). As they say each place, point to the word on the board.
- Say *Now listen again. Draw the town.* Play the CD again. Pause after each sentence to give the pupils time to draw what they have just heard.
- After they have listened, the pupils can compare their pictures with their partners' pictures.

3.32

Child: I live in a small town in Europe. There is a church in the centre of the town. My school is next to the church. It's a small school. Next to my school, there is a big park. It's got lots of trees, a slide and swings. There's a swimming pool, too. I go swimming there in the summer. There's a very old bridge across the river. On the other side of the river, there is a train station. Sometimes I take the train to visit my Grandma. She lives in the next town.

Writing about a place in the town

- Say *I'm going to talk about a place in this town. Listen. Where is it?* Think of a part of the town the pupils know and describe it with *There is ...* and *There are ...* For example:
  There are lots of people. There are some shops. There are lots of trains. The pupils try to guess the place (= *the train station*).
- Tell the pupils to think of a place in the town and write sentences about it. The pupils write the sentences in their notebooks. While they are writing, circulate around the class and help them with vocabulary, grammar, and suggestions. Encourage faster pupils to write a description of a second place.
- Choose one of the faster pupils to read one of his / her descriptions. The pupils guess where it is. Repeat with the other pupils who have written two descriptions.
- In pairs, the pupils read their own descriptions and listen to their partners' descriptions.

(To be taught after Unit 9.)

Sport in my country (1)

CB page 82

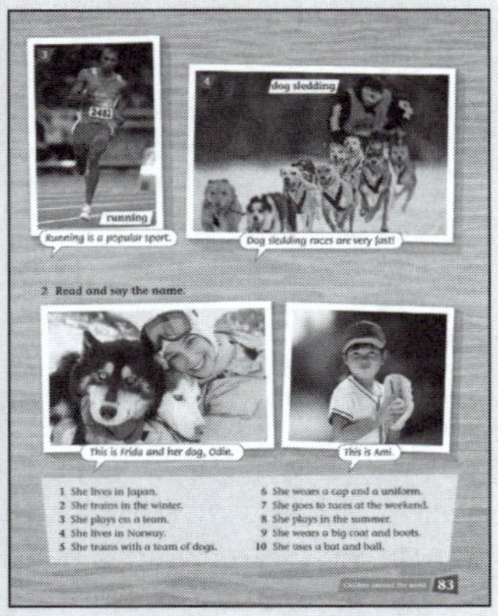

CB page 83

AB page 96

Objectives

- Learn more about the four children and their countries
- Learn about sports in these countries
- Listen to conversations about sports
- Write about sports

Language

rugby, baseball, running, dog sledding
player, stadium, snow, winter, sled, race
Review of language from Units 7–9

Materials

CD 3; Cut-outs from magazines etc. of sportspeople doing / playing different sports

Recall

- Point to the pictures of the children on Class Book page 82. Ask the pupils *Who is it?* The pupils say the names.
- Ask the pupils other questions about the children: *Which country is he / she from? Which town is he / she from? What language does he / she speak?*

CB p82 Activity 1 Read. Then listen and find.

- Point to each of the sports pictures. Say the name of the sport (*rugby, baseball, running, dog sledding*).
- Read the first sentence to the pupils (*There are fifteen players in a rugby team*). Explain any new words. Repeat with the other sentences.
- Play the first conversation on the CD. The pupils identify the picture. Repeat with the other conversations.

3.33

Adult: I like this photo. Where is it?
Khadija: It's in a stadium in Morocco.
Adult: What is he doing?
Khadija: He's running a race.
Adult: Do you like running?
Khadija: Yes, I love it!

Adult: Wow – look at the snow! Where is this?
Mikko: It's in Norway – in winter!
Adult: What are they doing?
Mikko: They're dog sledding.
Adult: Tell me about it.
Mikko: The dogs are pulling the sled and the man is riding on the sled. They're going very fast! They are in a race!
Adult: Do you go to races?
Mikko: Yes, my friend Frida is a dog-sledding champion!

Bethan: Look at this photo. It's in Wales.
Adult: What are they doing?
Bethan: They're playing rugby. Can you see the ball?
Adult: Oh yes. Where are they playing?
Bethan: They're playing in a stadium.
Adult: Do you like rugby?
Bethan: I love rugby – and the Welsh rugby team is fantastic!

Adult: This is a good photo. Where is it?
Shogo: It's in Japan.
Adult: What are they doing?
Shogo: They're playing baseball. They're wearing baseball caps and uniforms.
Adult: Are they playing in a stadium?
Shogo: Yes.
Adult: Do you play baseball?
Shogo: Yes! I play on a team with my sister Ami. We play at weekends. It's my favourite sport.

Answers: 3, 4, 1, 2

AB p96 Activity 1 Read and complete.

- Read the list of words to the pupils. Explain any new words.
- Point to the picture of the first girl. Read the first sentence beginning (*She does* ...). The pupils suggest a suitable answer (*gymnastics*).
- The pupils complete the rest of the answers individually in their Activity Books. Explain that they will not need to use all the words from the word pool at this point.

Answers: She does gymnastics. She goes to a sports club. She can do a handstand. He plays basketball. He wears shorts and trainers. He throws a ball.

- Point to the verbs in the activity (*does, wears, plays, throws*). Focus on the *–s* or *–es* with *he* and *she*. Also point out that *can* doesn't change, and the verb with *can* (in this case, *do*) is always in the base form.

Talking about sports and sports people

- Show the pupils your magazine cut-outs of people playing sports. For each picture, ask *What sport is it?* Write the pupils' answers as a list on the board.
- Stick all the cut-outs on the board and write a number next to each one. Say a sentence about one of the pictures with *plays / does / wears* or an action verb (*jump, throw, run*, etc.), for example *She wears blue shorts and white trainers* or *He plays basketball* or *They*

run at a sports centre. The pupils guess which picture it is and say the number.

- Ask individual pupils to say a sentence about a picture. The other pupils guess which picture it is.
- The pupils say sentences and guess in pairs. Alternatively, they can write descriptions with three or four sentences of one of the pictures and then read them to their partners or to the whole class.

Sport in my country (2)

(See mini pages for Lesson 1)

Objectives

- Read and write about people and sports
- Draw a picture of a favourite sport and write about it

Language

train (v)

Review of language from Units 7–9

Materials

'Sport in my country' (PMB p55) – one photocopy per pupil

Recall

- Point to each of the sports pictures on Class Book pages 82 and 83. Ask *What sport is it? (rugby, baseball, running, dog sledding).*

CB p83 Activity 2 Read and say the name.

- Point to the first picture and read the sentence under it. Ask *What's her name? (Frida)* and *Where is she from? (Norway)*. Repeat with the second picture (*Ami – Japan*).
- Read sentence number 1 (*She lives in Japan*). Ask *Who is it?* (*Ami*). Repeat with the other sentences.

Answers: 1 Ami **2** Frida **3** Ami **4** Frida **5** Frida **6** Ami **7** Frida **8** Ami **9** Frida **10** Ami

AB p96 Activity 2 Look and write.

- Point to the picture of the girl. Read the first sentence beginning (*I do* ...) and ask the pupils to complete it (*ballet*). Show the pupils the word *ballet* in the word pool for Activity 1. The pupils complete the sentence in their Activity Books.
- The pupils complete the rest of the sentences, using words and phrases from the Activity 1 word pool.

Answers: I do ballet. I wear a skirt and tights. I go to class on Saturday.

- Focus on the verb forms with *I* (*do, wear, go*) and contrast them with the verb forms with *he* and *she* in Activity 1 (*does, wears, plays, throws*).

PMB p55 Sport in my country

- Quickly review the days of the week with the pupils.
- Give each pupil a photocopy of the Photocopy Master. Read the title of the page (*My favourite sport*).
- Ask the pupils to suggest favourite sports (*football, volleyball*, etc.) Write their suggestions on the board.
- Point to the sentence beginnings in the speech bubble. Read them and ask individual pupils *What sport do you play? What do you wear? When do you go? Where do you go?* Help them with new vocabulary and write the new words on the board.
- Quickly copy the Photocopy Master on the board and draw a picture of yourself doing your favourite sport. Complete the sentences for yourself, for example:
  I play tennis.
  I wear a T-shirt, shorts and tennis shoes.
  I go to the tennis club on Saturday.
- The pupils draw a picture of the favourite sport they play and complete the sentences.
- Arrange a display of the completed Photocopy Masters around the class. Let the pupils move around and see all the Photocopy Masters. After this, arrange a class discussion and vote to decide on the best one.

Test transcripts / answers

(All listenings are provided at the end of CD 3.)

Unit tests

Two levels of tests are provided for each unit test (see page 8 for an explanation).

Unit 1 Standard Test

1 Look and write.

Answers: **1** bike **2** glasses **3** bag **4** magazine **5** cat **6** rollerblades **7** sweets **8** umbrella **9** football **10** watch **11** yo-yo

2 Listen and colour.

3.34 Transcript / Answers

Adult: Would you like to colour the picture?
Child: Oh, yes, please.
1 Adult: Can you see the parrot behind the box?
Child: Yes, I can.
Adult OK, now colour it red.
Child: Pardon?
Adult: Colour the parrot behind the box. Colour it red.
2 Adult: Now find the parrot in front of the cushion. Can you colour it green?
Child: OK, I'm colouring it green.
3 Adult: Can you see the parrot next to the box?
Child: Yes, it's hopping!
Adult: Oh yes! Colour it blue.
4 Adult: Look at the parrot behind the bag.
Child: Where?
Adult: Behind the bag. Colour it yellow.
5 Adult: Can you see the parrot next to the hat?
Child: Look! He's eating!
Adult: Colour it orange.
Child: OK, orange.
Adult: Look at the picture now. It's great!

3 Read and write *true* or *false*.

Answers: **1** false **2** true **3** false **4** false **5** false **6** true

Unit 1 Higher Test

1 Listen and colour.

See Unit 1 Standard Test for transcript and answers.

2 Write about the picture.

Answers: **2** The yellow parrot's / is behind the bag. **3** The blue parrot's / is next to the box. **4** The orange parrot's / is next to the hat. **5** The green parrot's / is in front of the cushion. **6** The red parrot's / is behind the box.

3 Look and write.

Answers: **2** glasses **3** bag **4** magazine **5** rollerblades **6** sweets **7** umbrella **8** football **9** watch

4 Read and write.

Answers: **1** It's on the bed. **2** They're on the table. **3** It's in front of the bed. **4** They're on the bed. **5** It's behind the bed.

5 Look and write.

Answers: **2** It's half past five. **3** It's quarter past seven. **4** It's quarter to two.

Unit 2 Standard Test

1 Read and write the numbers.

Answers: **1** 4 **2** 3 **3** 2 **4** 2 **5** 4 **6** 3 **7** 1 **8** 4 **9** 1 **10** 2

2 Listen and colour.

3.35 Transcript / Answers

Adult: Look at the brother and sister. Can you colour them?
Child: What colour is her dress?
Adult: Her dress is red. Colour her dress red.
Child: What colour are her tights?
Adult: Blue.
Child: OK, I'm colouring her tights blue. What colour are her shoes?
Adult: Black. Her shoes are black.
Child: What about her brother? What colour is his tracksuit?
Adult: It's green. Colour his tracksuit green.
Child: And his cap? What colour's his cap?
Adult: His cap's orange.
Child: Orange?
Adult: Yes.
Child: Wow! They look great now!

3 Find and circle. Write.

Answers: **1** He's happy. **2** He's angry. **3** She's serious. **4** They're sad. **5** She's rich.

Unit 2 Higher Test

1 Listen and colour.

See Unit 2 Standard Test for transcript and answers.

2 Write about the picture.

Answers: **1** It's red. **2** It's green. **3** They're black. **4** What colour's his cap? **5** What colour are her tights?

3 Look and write.

Answers: **2** This is Dan's scarf. **3** This is Dan's coat. **4** These are Dan's gloves. **5** These are Lucy's trainers. **6** These are Dan's shoes.

4 Look and write.

Answers: **1** He's happy. **2** He's angry. **3** She's serious. **4** They're sad. **5** She's rich.

Unit 3 Standard Test

1 Look and write.

Answers: **1** pyjamas **2** sleeping bag **3** blanket **4** torch **5** mat **6** pillow **7** comb **8** toothbrush **9** towel **10** sunglasses

2 Read and write *yes* or *no*.

Answers: **1** No. **2** No. **3** No. **4** No. **5** Yes.

3 Listen and write.

3.36 Transcript

1 *(Low music by a double bass)*
2 *(Slow music by a flute)*
3 *(Loud music by drums)*
4 *(Quiet music by a harp)*
5 *(Fast music by a violin)*

Answers: **1** It's low. **2** It's slow. **3** It's loud. **4** It's quiet. **5** It's fast.

Unit 3 Higher Test

1 Look and write.

Answers: **1** I've got my pillow. **2** I haven't got my toothbrush. **3** I've got my towel. **4** I've got my sleeping bag. **5** I haven't got my sunglasses. **6** I've got my torch. **7** I've got my blanket. **8** I haven't got my comb. **9** I've got my mat. **10** I've got my pyjamas.

2 Write the questions and answers.

Answers: **1** Have you got any gloves? No. **2** Have you got a cap? Yes. **3** Have you got any trainers? No. **4** Have you got a comb? No. **5** Have you got a sleeping bag? Yes.

3 Listen and write.

See Unit 3 Standard Test for transcript.

Answers: **1** It's low. **2** It's slow. **3** They're loud. **4** It's quiet. **5** It's fast.

Unit 4 Standard Test

1 Read and number.

Answers: Boy's list (from the top): [rabbit] **3** [snail] **6** [canary] **7** [butterfly] **9** [tortoise] **5**; Girl's list (from the top): **4** [stick insect] **4** [lizard] **8** [guinea pig] **1** [fish] **10** [ant] **2**

2 Listen and circle.

3.37 Transcript

1 Adult: Has he got a guinea pig?
Child: No, he hasn't got a guinea pig. He's got a rabbit.
2 Adult: Has she got a fish?
Child: No, she hasn't got a fish. She's got a stick insect.
3 Adult: Has he got a lizard?
Child: Yes, he's got a lizard.
Adult: Has he got a stick insect?
Child: No, he hasn't got a stick insect.
4 Adult: Has she got a tortoise?
Child: No, she hasn't got a tortoise. She's got a parrot.
5 Adult: Has he got a butterfly?
Child: Yes, he's got a butterfly.
Adult: Has he got a canary?
Child: Yes, he has.
Adult: Has he got a guinea pig?
Child: No, he hasn't.

Answers: **1** first picture (rabbit) **2** first picture (stick insect) **3** first picture (lizard only) **4** second picture (parrot) **5** second picture (butterfly and canary)

3 Read and write *true* or *false*.

Answers: **1** false **2** false **3** true **4** true **5** true **6** true

Unit 4 Higher Test

1 Look and write.

Answers: **1** He's got a rabbit. **2** She's got a stick insect. **3** He's got a snail. **4** She hasn't got a lizard. **5** He hasn't got a canary. **6** She's got a guinea pig. **7** He's got a butterfly. **8** She hasn't got a fish. **9** He hasn't got a tortoise. **10** She's got an ant.

2 Listen and circle.

See Unit 4 Standard Test for transcript.

Answers: 1 a 2 a 3 a 4 b 5 b

3 Write about the pictures.

Answers: **1** Has he got a rabbit? Yes. **2** Has she got a fish? No. **3** Has he got a lizard? Yes. **4** Has she got a parrot? Yes. **5** Has he got a guinea pig? No.

4 Look and write.

Answers: **1** He's got an ant, a grasshopper and a ladybird. **2** He hasn't got a fly, a bee, or a dragonfly.

Unit 5 Standard Test

1 Look and write.

Answers: **3–6** (in any order) He likes coconuts. He doesn't like flour. He likes biscuits. He doesn't like broccoli. **7–12** (in any order) She likes strawberries. She doesn't like sugar. She doesn't like asparagus. She likes cocoa. She doesn't like butter. She likes spinach.

2 Read and write *true* or *false*.

Answers: **1** true **2** false **3** false **4** true **5** false

3 Listen and write the numbers.

3.38 Transcript

This is a tomato plant.
Number 1 is the root.
Number 2 is the leaf.
Number 3 is the flower.
Number 4 is the stem.
Number 5 is the seed.

Answers:

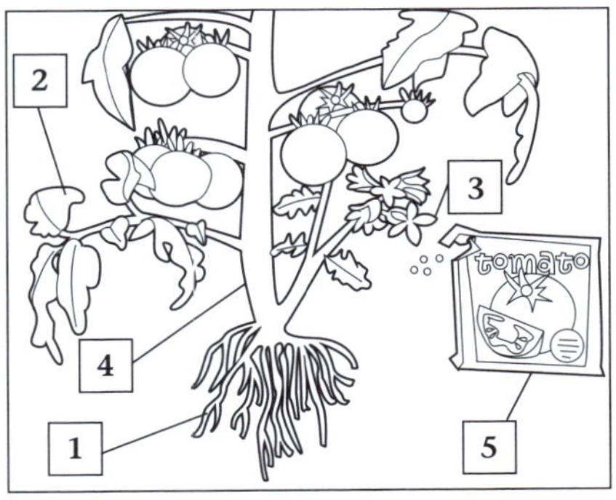

Unit 5 Higher Test

1 Look and write.

Answers: **1–6** (in any order) He doesn't like flour. He likes coconut. He doesn't like cheese. He doesn't like broccoli. He likes eggs. He likes biscuits. **7–12** (in any order) She likes spinach. She likes strawberries. She likes cocoa. She doesn't like asparagus. She doesn't like butter. She doesn't like sugar.

2 Write the questions.

Answers: **1** Does he like spinach and asparagus? **2** Does she like strawberries? **3** Does he like asparagus and coconut? **4** Does she like cheese and eggs?

3 Listen and write numbers. Then label.

See Unit 5 Standard Test for transcript and answers.

Unit 6 Standard Test

1 Read and number.

Answers: **1** e (park) **2** i (swimming pool) **3** a (bus station) **4** b (car park) **5** d (cinema) **6** j (shopping centre) **7** h (library) **8** g (post office) **9** c (supermarket) **10** f (restaurant)

2 Write.

Answers: **3–4** There's a swimming pool. There's a cinema. **6–8** (in any order) There's a restaurant. There are two swimming pools. There are two cinemas.

3 Listen and colour.

3.39 Transcript

1 Adult: Can you see the path?
Child: Yes. Look, there's a butterfly on the path!
Adult: Yes, colour it yellow.
Child: OK, the butterfly on the path. Colour it yellow.

2 Adult: Find the butterfly in the river.
Child: Sorry? The butterfly in the river?!
Adult: Yes! Colour it blue.
Child: OK. There's a blue butterfly in the river.

3 Adult: Look at the butterfly under the bridge.
Child: OK. Can I colour it?
Adult: Yes, colour it yellow.
Child: OK. Colour the butterfly under the bridge yellow.

4 Adult: Now find the wood.
Child: Yes.
Adult: There's a butterfly in it. Colour it orange.
Child: OK. There's an orange butterfly in the wood.

5 Adult: Look at the picnic area.
Child: It's got a butterfly in front of it!
Adult: Yes. Colour it purple.
Child: Good. I like purple!

Unit 6 Higher Test

1 Look and write.

Answers: **1** There's a bus station. **2** There's a post office. **3** There's a library. **4** There's a car park. **5** There's a supermarket. **6** There's a swimming pool. **7** There's a park. **8** There's a cinema. **9** There's a shopping centre. **10** There's a restaurant.

2 Look and write

Answers: **1–4** (in any order) There are two supermarkets. There are two cinemas. There are two swimming pools. There's a restaurant.

3 Listen and colour.

See Unit 6 Standard Test for transcript and answers.

4 Write about the picture.

Answers: **1** Is there a picnic area? Yes. **2** Is there a wood? Yes. **3** Is there a beach? No. **4** Are there any butterflies? Yes. **5** Are there any shops? No. **6** Is there a bridge? Yes.

Unit 7 Standard Test

1 Read and write *true* or *false*.

Answers: **1** false **2** true **3** true **4** false **5** true **6** true **7** true **8** true **9** false **10** false

2 Look and write.

Answers: Do you do judo? Do you play chess? Yes, I play chess. Do you do gymnastics? No, I don't do gymnastics.

3 Listen and write the numbers.

3.40 Transcript

1 He's got a wig.
2 He's got a drum.
3 She's got a flag.
4 She's got a hat.
5 He's got a scarf.

Answers: 1 b 2 d 3 e 4 c 5 a

Unit 7 Higher Test

1 Look and write.

Answers: **1** I do judo. **2** I don't play baseball. **3** I play table tennis. **4** I play tennis. **5** I don't play volleyball. **6** I play badminton. **7** I play basketball. **8** I don't play hockey. **9** I play chess. **10** I don't do gymnastics.

2 Look and write.

Answers: (in any order) Do you play tennis? Yes. Do you play chess? Yes. Do you play hockey? Yes. Do you do judo? No. Do you do gymnastics? No.

3 Listen and write the numbers.

See Unit 7 Standard Test for transcript.

Answers: 1 b 2 d 3 e 4 c 5 a

Unit 8 Standard Test

1 Read and number.

Answers: 1 g 2 h 3 b 4 c 5 a 6 e 7 d 8 f 9 j 10 i

2 Listen and match.

3.41 Transcript

1 Adult: What time does Millie get up?
Child: She gets up at 7 o'clock.
2 Adult: What time does Millie have dinner?
Child: She has dinner at 6 o'clock.
3 Adult: What time does Ben go to school?
Child: He goes to school at 8 o'clock.
4 Adult: What time does Dad play basketball?
Child: He plays basketball at 8 o'clock.
5 Adult: What time does Mum get up?
Child: She gets up at 6 o'clock.
6 Adult: What time does Ben have lunch?
Child: Ben has lunch at 12 o'clock.

Answers: top left picture (a) – 8.00, top middle picture (b) – 6.00, top right picture (c) – 7.00, bottom left picture (d) – 6.00, bottom middle picture – (e) 8.00, bottom right picture (f) – 12.00

3 Look and write the words.

Answers: 1 bulb 2 battery 3 wire 4 motor 5 switch

Unit 8 Higher Test

1 Listen and match.

See Unit 8 Standard Test for transcript.

Answers: **a** 8.00 **b** 6.00 **d** 6.00 **e** 8.00 **f** 12.00

2 Write questions about the pictures.

Answers: **a** What time does he / Dad play basketball? **b** What time does she / Millie have dinner? **d** What time does she / Mum get up? **e** What time does he / Ben go to school? **f** What time does he / Ben have lunch?

3 Look and write.

Answers: 1 **b** She has a shower 2 **a** She doesn't have breakfast **b** She has breakfast 3 **a** She doesn't leave school. **b** She leaves school 4 **a** She doesn't play football **b** She plays football 5 **a** She doesn't go to bed **b** She goes to bed

4 Look and write.

Answers: 1 It's a switch. 2 It's a battery. 3 It's a wire. 4 It's a motor. 5 It's a bulb.

Unit 9 Standard Test

1 Read and write *yes* or *no*.

Answers: 1 yes 2 yes 3 no 4 yes 5 no 6 no 7 yes 8 no 9 yes 10 yes

2 Listen and write the numbers.

3.42 Transcript

1 She's walking on stilts.
2 He's juggling.
3 He's doing a handstand.
4 She's riding a horse.
5 She's doing a cartwheel.
6 He's doing a headstand.

Answers: 1 d 2 b 3 f 4 a 5 e 6 c

3 Look and write.

Answers: 1 shoulder 2 elbow 3 foot 4 neck 5 knee

Unit 9 Higher Test

1 Look and write.

Answers: 1 He's walking 2 He's doing 3 juggling. 4 He's walking 5 He's riding 6 doing 7 She's doing 8 He's doing 9 They're riding 10 He's swinging

2 Listen and write the numbers.

See Unit 9 Standard Test for transcript.

Answers: 1 d 2 b 3 f 4 a 5 e 6 c

3 Write questions about the pictures.

Answers: **a** Is she riding **b** Is he juggling? **c** Is he doing **d** Is she walking **e** Is he doing **f** Is he doing

4 Look and write.

Answers: 1 It's a shoulder. 2 It's an elbow. 3 It's a foot. 4 It's a neck. 5 It's a knee.

Term tests

Two parallel tests are provided for the reading and writing component of each term test (see p8 for an explanation of how to use the parallel tests A and B). One listening test is provided for each term.

Term 1 Test A

1 Look and write.

Answers: 1 This is a cap. 2 This is a pillow. 3 This is a magazine. 4 This is a belt. 5 This is a sleeping bag. 6 This is a scarf.

2 Look and read. Write *true* or *false*.

Answers: 1 false 2 true 3 true 4 false 5 true 6 false

Term 1 Test B

1 Look and write.

Answers: 1 This is a tracksuit. 2 This is a dress. 3 This is a football. 4 This is a shirt. 5 This is a toothbrush. 6 This is a teddy.

2 Look and read. Write *true* or *false*.

Answers: 1 false 2 true 3 true 4 false 5 true 6 false

Term 2 Test A

1 Look and write.

Answers: 1 fish 2 strawberries 3 fly 4 car park 5 biscuits 6 restaurant

2 Look and read. Write *true* or *false*.

Answers: 1 true 2 true 3 false 4 true 5 false 6 true

Term 2 Test B

1 Look and write.

Answers: 1 snake 2 cheese 3 snail 4 cinema 5 eggs 6 school

2 Look and read. Write *true* or *false*.

Answers: 1 true 2 true 3 false 4 true 5 false 6 false

Term 3 Test A

1 Look and write.

Answers: 1 stilts 2 judo 3 school 4 basketball 5 tennis 6 trapeze

2 Look and read. Write *true* or *false*.

Answers: 1 false 2 false 3 true 4 false 5 false 6 true

Term 3 Test B

1 Look and write.

Answers: 1 juggling 2 gymnastics 3 hockey 4 chess 5 badminton 6 horse

2 Look and read. Write *yes* or *no*.

Answers: 1 no 2 no 3 no 4 no 5 no 6 yes

Term 1 Listening Test

Listen and tick (✓) the box.

3.43 Transcript

1 Adult: What's the matter, Jo?
Girl: I've lost my glasses.
Adult: Are they on your pillow?
Girl: No.
Adult: Are they behind your cap?
Girl: No.
Adult: Look. There they are. They're next to your cap.
Girl: Oh, yes, thank you.
2 Adult: Have you got any brothers, Sam?
Boy: No.
Adult: Have you got any sisters?
Boy: No, I haven't got any sisters either. I've just got a mum, a dad and a cat!
3 Adult: What time is it?
Child: It's quarter to seven.
Adult: Are you sure?
Child: Oh, no, sorry, I'm sorry, it's quarter to eight.
Adult: Oh no, I'm late!
4 Adult: Tom, have you got a torch?
Boy: Yes, I've got a torch. And I've got a sleeping bag.
Adult: Have you got a pillow?
Boy: Oh dear! No, I haven't got a pillow.
5 Child: Mum, where are my trainers?
Adult: Are they behind your shoes?
Child: No.
Adult: Are they next to your coat?
Child: No.
Adult: Are they in your bedroom?
Child: Oh, yes, they're next to my rollerblades.
6 Adult: What's in your bag, Sid?
Child: Look, this is my towel. These are my trainers. And this is my blanket.

Answers: 1 B 2 A 3 B 4 C 5 A 6 B

Term 2 Listening Test

Listen and tick (✓) the box.

3.44 Transcript

1 Adult: There's a great wood near my house.
Child: Really? Are there any paths?
Adult: Yes, there's one path.
Child: Is there a river?
Adult: Yes, and there are two bridges.

2 Child: Ben's town is great – there are two cinemas!
Adult: Is there a library?
Child: No, but there's a shopping centre.

3 Adult: Does Jo like broccoli?
Child: No, but she likes asparagus and spinach.
Adult: Does she like strawberries?
Child: Yes, she likes strawberries.

4 Adult: Has Tom got a stick insect?
Child: No, he hasn't got a stick insect.
Adult: Has he got a guinea pig?
Child: No, he doesn't like guinea pigs.
Adult: Does he like tortoises?
Child: Yes, he likes tortoises. He's got a tortoise.

5 Adult: Oh, look, that's Jill's bag.
Child: She's got butter, cheese and broccoli.
Adult: Has she got any strawberries?
Child: No, she hasn't got any strawberries – she doesn't like strawberries.

6 Adult: Is there a post office in your town, Nick?
Boy: No, there isn't. There are two supermarkets, a car park, a school and a shopping centre.

Answers: 1 C 2 B 3 C 4 C 5 C 6 C

Term 3 Listening Test

Listen and tick (✓) the box.

3.45 Transcript

1 Adult: Do you play basketball, Bill?
Boy: No, I don't play basketball or hockey, but I play tennis.

2 Adult: Emma, what time does your dad get up?
Child: He gets up at 7 o'clock.
Adult: What time does he have breakfast?
Child: Half past seven. And he leaves for work at 8 o'clock.

3 Adult: Is Tom doing a somersault?
Child: No!
Adult: Is he doing a cartwheel?
Child: No! Look, there he is. He's doing a headstand!
Adult: Oh, yes!

4 Adult: What time does Sid get up?
Child: He gets up at half past seven.
Adult: What time does he have breakfast?
Child: At eight o'clock. And he goes to school at half past eight.

5 Adult: What are the clowns doing? Are they juggling?
Child: No.
Adult: Are they walking on their hands?
Child: No. Look, they're swinging on a trapeze!

6 Child: Is Beth swimming?
Adult: No.
Child: Is she playing football?
Adult: No, look, she's walking on stilts!
Child: Wow!

Answers: 1 A 2 C 3 B 4 C 5 B 6 A

1 Test

Standard

1 Look and write. 10 marks

yo-yo umbrella bag watch cat ~~bike~~ football sweets
rollerblades glasses magazine

1 bike ______
2 ______
3 ______
4 ______
5 ______
6 ______
7 ______
8 ______
9 ______
10 ______
11 ______

2 Listen and colour. 3.34 5 marks

3 Read and write true or false. 5 marks

1 It's quarter past four.

false

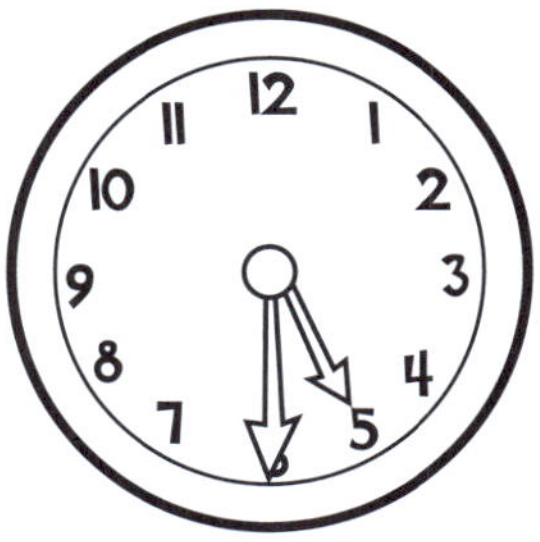

2 It's half past five.

______

3 It's quarter past three.

______

4 It's quarter to seven.

______

5 It's half past six.

______

6 It's quarter to two.

______

1 Test

Higher

1 Listen and colour. 3.34 5 marks

2 Write about the picture. 5 marks

1 The box is on the table ______

2 The yellow parrot ______

3 The blue parrot ______

4 The orange parrot ______

5 The green parrot ______

6 The red parrot ______

3 Look and write. 8 marks

umbrella
bag
watch
~~bike~~
football
sweets
rollerblades
glasses
magazine

1 bike ______ 4 ______ 7 ______
2 ______ 5 ______ 8 ______
3 ______ 6 ______ 9 ______

4 Read and write. 4 marks

1 Where's the cat? It's on the bed.
2 Where are the glasses? They're ______
3 Where's the football? ______
4 Where are the sweets? ______
5 Where's the bike? ______

5 Look and write. 3 marks

1 It's half past two.

3 ______

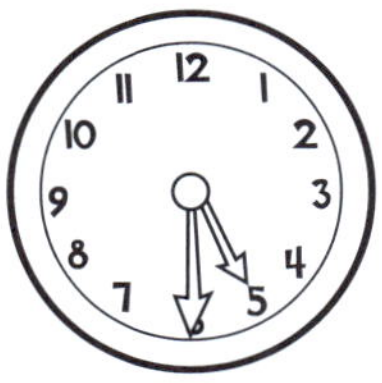

2 ______

4 ______

2 Test

Standard

1 Read and write the numbers. 10 marks

1 He's wearing a coat.	☐	6 She's wearing trainers.	☐
2 She's wearing a tracksuit.	☐	7 She's wearing tights.	☐
3 He's wearing a belt.	☐	8 He's wearing gloves.	☐
4 He's wearing a cap.	☐	9 She's wearing a dress.	☐
5 He's wearing a scarf.	☐	10 He's wearing a shirt.	☐

Standard

2 Listen and colour. 3.35 5 marks

3 Find and circle. Write. 5 marks

a	y	k	m	i	b	p
r	i	c	h	a	h	t
k	u	s	b	n	a	c
l	s	a	z	g	p	m
o	x	d	t	r	p	n
e	j	e	v	y	y	s
s	e	r	i	o	u	s

1 He's ____________

2 ____________

3 ____________

4 ____________

5 ____________

2 Test

Higher

1 Listen and colour. 3.35 5 marks

2 Write about the picture. 5 marks

1 What colour's her dress? It's ___

2 What colour's his tracksuit? ___

3 What colour are her shoes? ___

4 What colour ___ It's orange.

5 ___ They're blue.

3 Look and write. 10 marks

coat gloves scarf shoes ~~tracksuit~~ trainers

1 This is Lucy's tracksuit.
2 ______
3 ______
4 ______
5 ______
6 ______

4 Look and write. 5 marks

1 He isn't angry.
He's ______

2 He isn't sad.
______

3 She isn't happy.
______

4 They aren't rich.
______

5 She isn't serious.
______

3 Test

Standard

1 Look and write. 10 marks

pillow pyjamas comb toothbrush sleeping bag towel
blanket sunglasses mat torch

1 ______________________ 6 ______________________

2 ______________________ 7 ______________________

3 ______________________ 8 ______________________

4 ______________________ 9 ______________________

5 ______________________ 10 ______________________

2 Read and write *yes* or *no*. 5 marks

1 Have you got any gloves?

______

2 Have you got any trainers?

______

3 Have you got a comb?

______

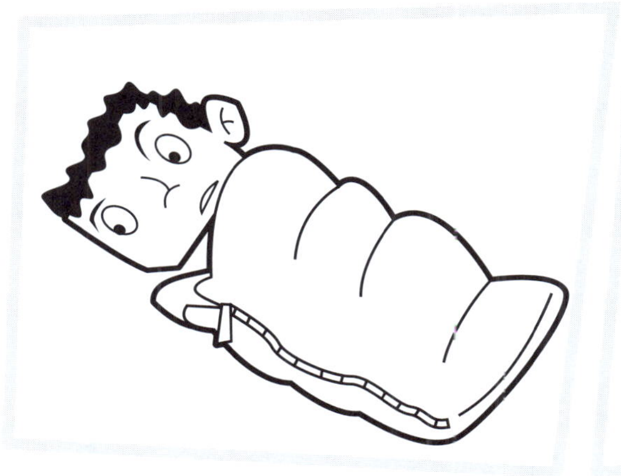

4 Have you got a pillow?

______

5 Have you got a cap?

______

3 Listen and write. 3.36 5 marks

	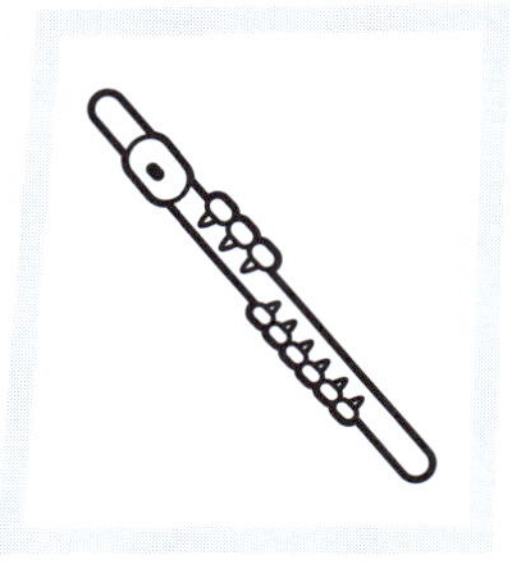		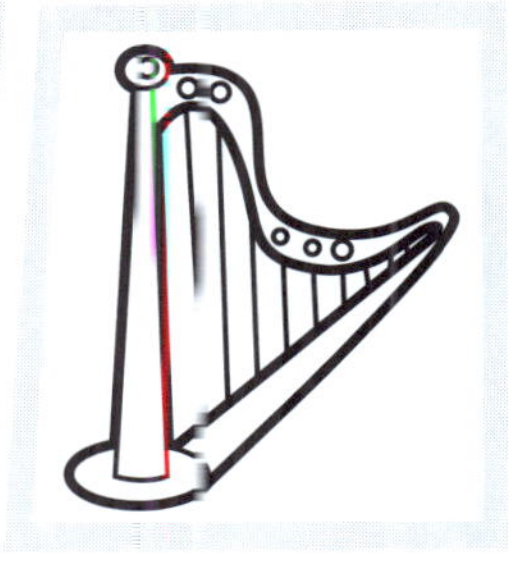	
wol	losw	udol	tieuq	tsaf
1 It's ______	2 ______	3 ______	4 ______	5 ______

3 Test

Higher

1 Look and write. 10 marks

pillow pyjamas comb toothbrush sleeping bag towel
blanket sunglasses mat torch

1 I've got my ____________

2 I haven't got my ____________

3 ____________

4 ____________

5 ____________

6 ____________

7 ____________

8 ____________

9 ____________

10 ____________

Higher

2 Write the questions and answers. 10 marks

1

gloves?

2

cap?

3

trainers?

4

comb?

5

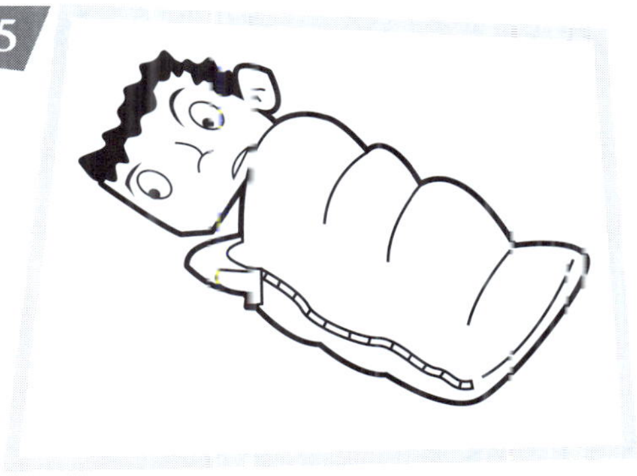

sleeping bag?

1 Have you got ______________________ ______________________

2 ______________________ ______________________

3 ______________________ ______________________

4 ______________________ ______________________

5 ______________________ ______________________

3 Listen and write. 3.36 5 marks

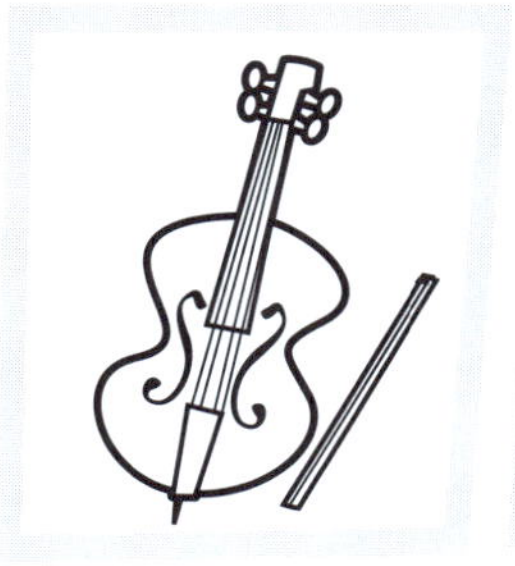

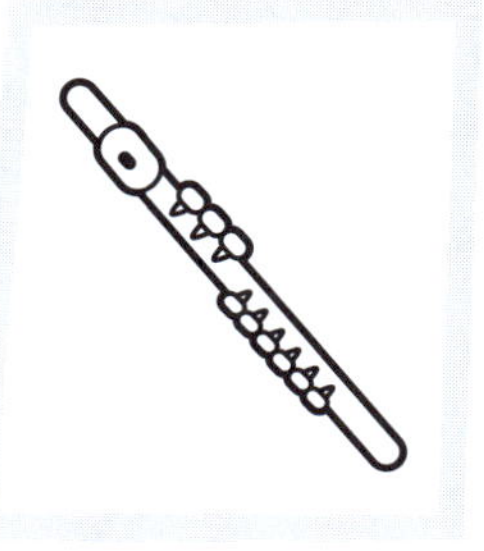

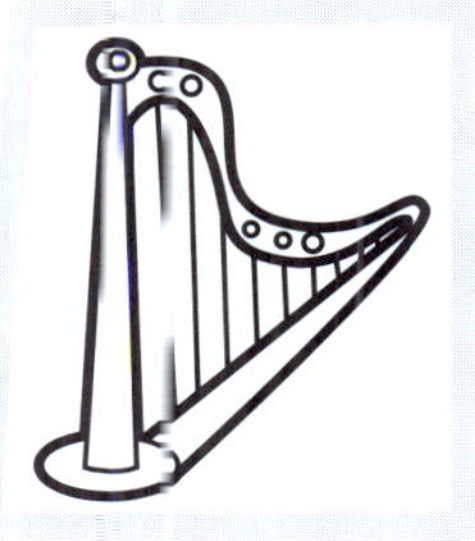

1 It isn't low. It's low ______

2 It isn't fast. ______

3 They aren't quiet. ______

4 It isn't loud. ______

5 It isn't slow. ______

4 Test

Standard

1 Read and number. 10 marks

1 She's got a guinea pig.
2 She's got a ant.
3 He's got a rabbit.
4 She's got a stick insect.
5 He's got a tortoise.
6 He's got a snail.
7 He's got a canary.
8 She's got a lizard.
9 He's got a butterfly.
10 She's got a fish.

2 Listen and circle. 3.37 5 marks

3 Read and write *true* or *false*. 5 marks

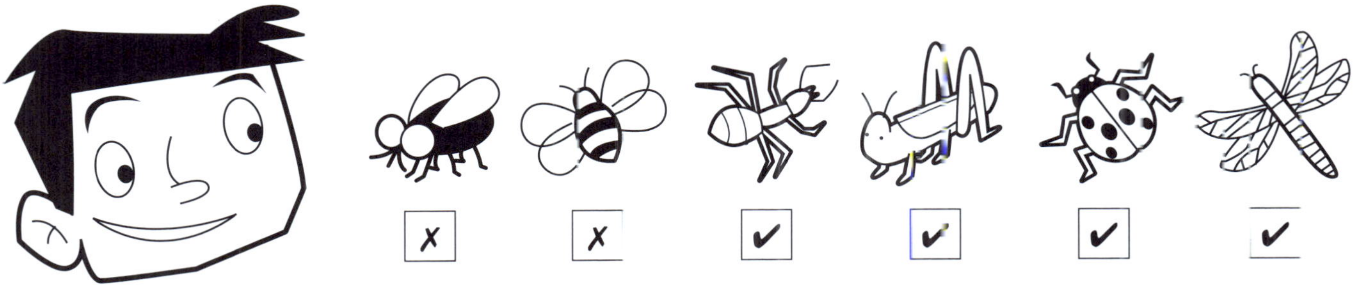

1 He's got a bee. false

2 He's got a fly. ____________

3 He's got a dragonfly. ____________

4 He's got a grasshopper. ____________

5 He's got a ladybird. ____________

6 He's got an ant. ____________

4 Test

Higher

1 Look and write. 10 marks

ant butterfly canary fish guinea pig lizard rabbit
snail stick insect tortoise

1 *He's got* ______________________

2 ______________________

3 ______________________

4 ______________________

5 ______________________

6 ______________________

7 ______________________

8 ______________________

9 ______________________

10 ______________________

2 Listen and circle. 3.37 5 marks

3 Write about the pictures. 5 marks

1 Has ______________________ a rabbit?

____

2 ______________________ a fish?

____

3 ______________________ a lizard?

____

4 ______________________ a parrot?

____

5 ______________________ a guinea pig?

____

4 Look and write. 5 marks

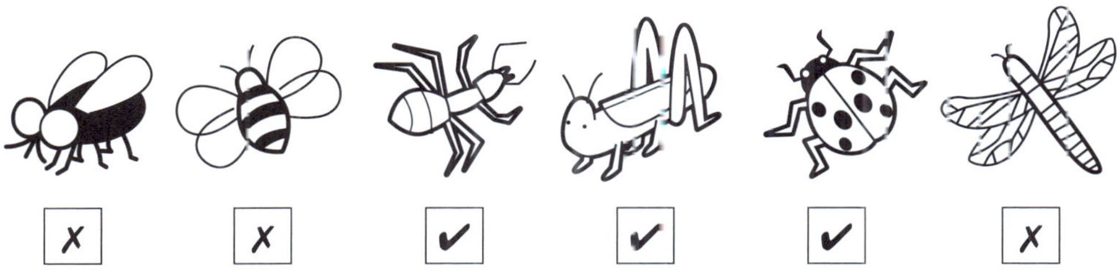

1 He's got an ant, ______________ and ______________

2 He hasn't got ______________, ______________ or ______________

5 Test

Standard

1 Look and write. 10 marks

strawberries sugar asparagus cocoa butter spinach
coconut flour ~~eggs~~ ~~cheese~~ biscuits broccoli

1 He doesn't like cheese.

2 He likes eggs.

3 ____________________

4 ____________________

5 ____________________

6 ____________________

7 ____________________

8 ____________________

9 ____________________

10 ____________________

11 ____________________

12 ____________________

2 Read and write *true* or *false*. 5 marks

1 She likes spinach and asparagus.
She doesn't like strawberries. ____________

2 She likes strawberries.
She doesn't like asparagus. ____________

3 She likes strawberries and asparagus.
She doesn't like coconuts. ____________

4 She likes cheese and eggs.
She doesn't like broccoli. ____________

5 She likes broccoli and cheese.
She doesn't like eggs. ____________

3 Listen and write numbers. 3.38 5 marks

5 Test

Higher

1 Look and write. 12 marks

strawberries sugar asparagus cocoa butter spinach
coconut flour eggs cheese biscuits broccoli

2 Write the questions. 3 marks

1 

Does he like spinach and asparagus?

Yes.

2 

____

No.

3 

____

Yes.

4 

____

Yes.

3 Listen and write numbers. Then label. 3.38 10 marks

flower leaf root seed stem

6 Test

Standard

1 Read and number. 10 marks

1 There's a park.

2 There's a swimming pool.

3 There's a bus station.

4 There's a car park.

5 There's a cinema.

6 There's a shopping centre.

7 There's a library.

8 There's a post office.

9 There's a supermarket.

10 There's a restaurant.

2 Write. 5 marks

1 There's a supermarket.
2 There are two restaurants.
3
4
5 There are two supermarkets.
6
7
8

3 Listen and colour. 3.39 5 marks

6 Test

Higher

1 Look and write. 10 marks

bus station car park cinema library park
post office restaurant shopping centre supermarket swimming pool

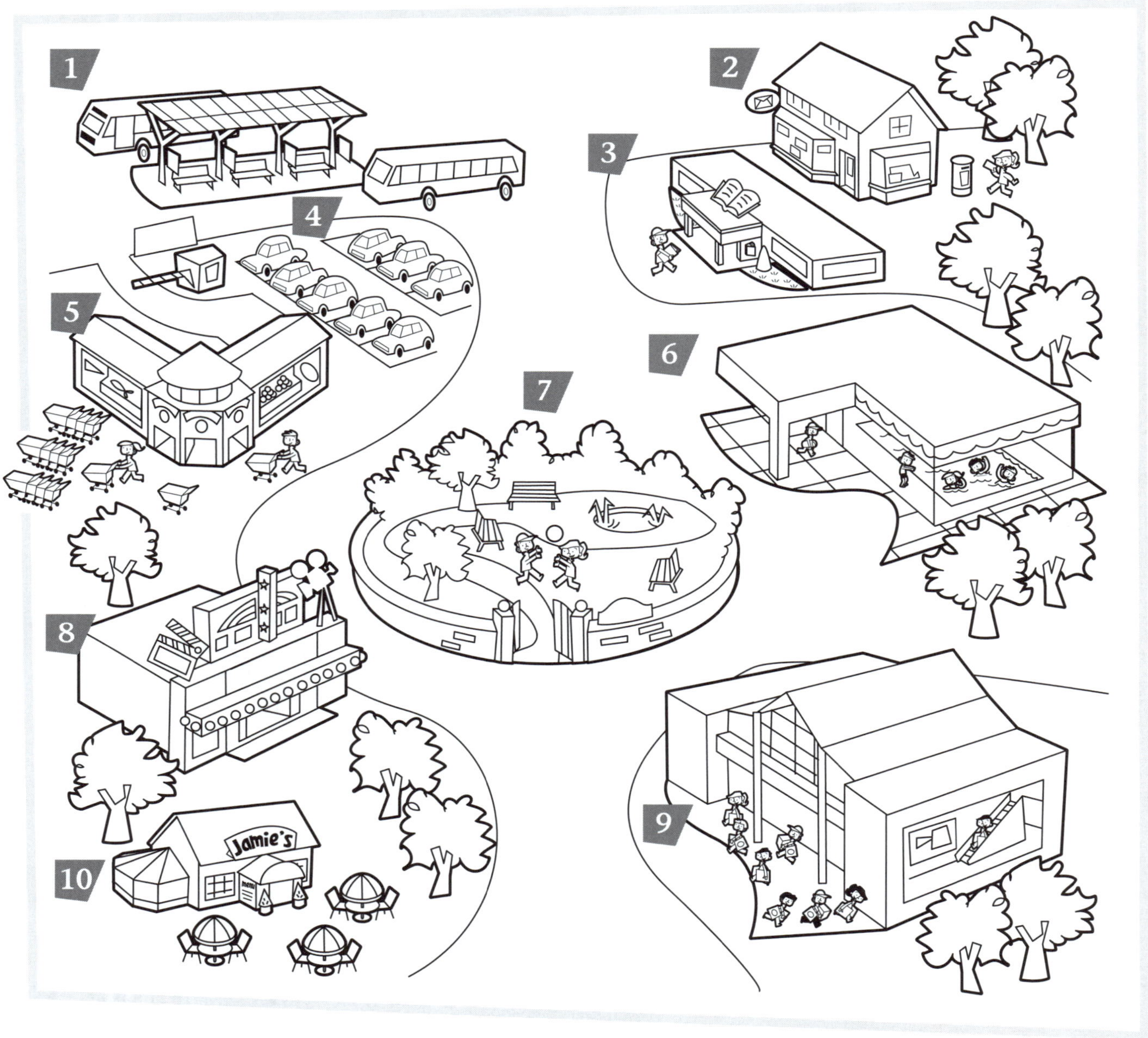

1 There's a ______
2 ______
3 ______
4 ______
5 ______
6 ______
7 ______
8 ______
9 ______
10 ______

Higher

2 Look and write. 4 marks

1 There are two ______________________

2 ______________________

3 ______________________

4 ______________________

3 Listen and colour. 3.39 5 marks

4 Write about the picture. 6 marks

1 Is there a ______ picnic area? ______________

2 ______________________ wood? ______________

3 ______________________ beach? ______________

4 Are ______________________ butterflies? ______________

5 ______________________ shops? ______________

6 ______________________ bridge? ______________

7 Test

Standard

1 Read and write *true* or *false*. 10 marks

SPORTS CENTRE A

Monday	
Tuesday	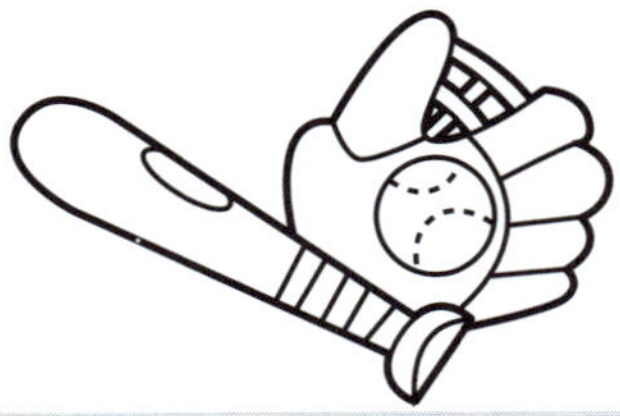
Wednesday	
Thursday	
Friday	

SPORTS CENTRE B

Monday	
Tuesday	
Wednesday	
Thursday	
Friday	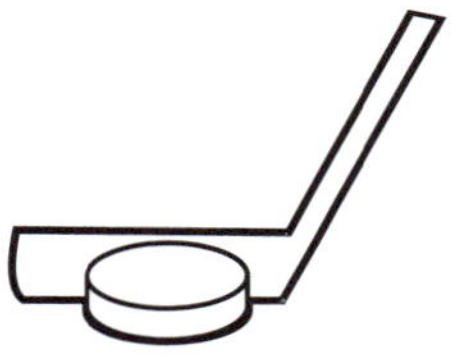

1 There's a hockey class on Friday. ____

2 There's a volleyball class on Wednesday. ____

3 There's a table tennis class on Friday. ____

4 There's a chess class on Wednesday. ____

5 There's a badminton class on Monday. ____

6 There's a gymnastics class on Thursday. ____

7 There's a basketball class on Tuesday. ____

8 There's a judo class on Monday. ____

9 There's a baseball class on Tuesday. ____

10 There's a tennis class on Thursday. ____

2 Look and write. 5 marks

3 Listen and write the numbers. 3.40 5 marks

a

b

c

d

e

Higher

1 Look and write. 10 marks

badminton baseball basketball chess gymnastics
hockey judo table tennis tennis volleyball

2 Look and write. 10 marks

3 Listen and write the numbers. 3.40 5 marks

8 Test

Standard

1 Read and number. 10 marks

1 get up
2 go to bed
3 go to school
4 play basketball
5 have breakfast
6 have dinner
7 have lunch
8 leave school
9 play football
10 have a shower

2 Listen and match. 3.41 5 marks

a

b

c

d

e

f

3 Look and write the words. 5 marks

1

lbub

____

2

ttreaby

____

3

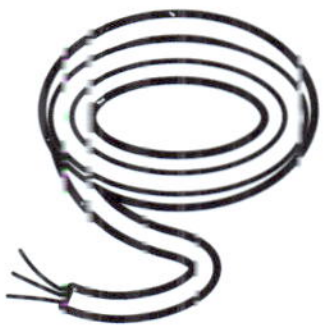

riwe

____

4

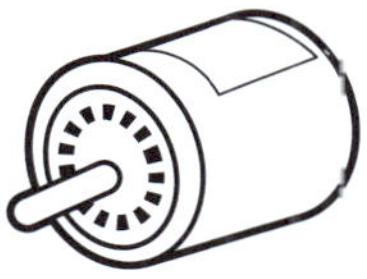

tomor

____

5

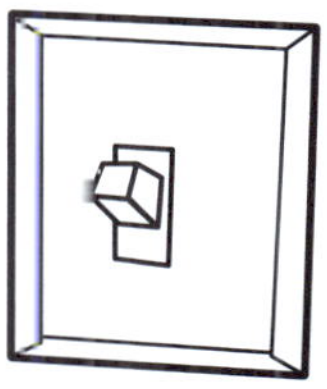

wstihc

____

8 Test

Higher

1 Listen and match. 3.41 5 marks

2 Write questions about the pictures. 5 marks

get up go to school have lunch play basketball have dinner

a ______________________________

b ______________________________

c *What time does she get up?*

d ______________________________

e ______________________________

f ______________________________

3 Look and write. Draw the times. 10 marks

1

✗ ✓

have → has a shower

a She doesn't have a shower at 6 o'clock.

b ______ at 7 o'clock.

2

✗ ✓

have → has breakfast

a ______ at 7 o'clock.

b ______ at 8 o'clock.

3

✗ ✓

leave → leaves school

a ______ at 4 o'clock.

b ______ at 3 o'clock.

4

✗ ✓

play → plays football

a ______ at 6 o'clock.

b ______ at 5 o'clock.

5

✗ ✓

go → goes to bed

a ______ at 8 o'clock.

b ______ at 9 o'clock.

4 Look and write. 5 marks

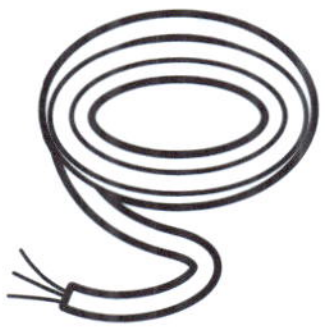

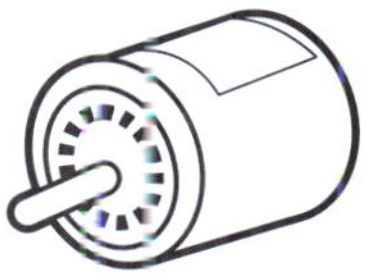

1 It isn't a battery. **2** It isn't a motor. **3** It isn't a bulb. **4** It isn't a switch. **5** It isn't a wire.

It's a ______ ______ ______ ______ ______

9 Test

Standard

1 Read and write *yes* or *no*. 10 marks

1 Is he walking on stilts? ______

2 Is he doing a somersault? ______

3 Are they doing handstands? ______

4 Is he walking on his hands? ______

5 Is he doing a cartwheel? ______

6 Is she riding a horse? ______

7 Is she doing a headstand? ______

8 Are they juggling? ______

9 Are they riding bikes? ______

10 Is he swinging on a trapeze? ______

2 Listen and write the numbers. 3.42 5 marks

3 Look and write. 5 marks

1 _ _ _ _ _ _ _ _ _ _

2 _ _ _ _ _ _

3 _ _ _ _

4 _ _ _ _

5 _ _ _ _

9 Test

Higher

1 Look and write. 10 marks

doing juggling riding swinging walking

1 He's ______ ______ on stilts.		6 She's ______ ______ a cartwheel.	
2 ______ ______ a somersault.		7 ______ ______ a headstand.	
3 They're ______ .		8 ______ ______ a handstand.	
4 ______ ______ on his hands.		9 ______ ______ bikes.	
5 ______ ______ a horse.		10 ______ ______ on a trapeze.	

2 Listen and write the numbers. 3.42 5 marks

3 Write questions about the pictures. 5 marks

a ______________________ a horse? Yes.

b ______________________? Yes.

c ______________________ a handstand? No, he's doing a headstand.

d ______________________ on stilts? Yes.

e ______________________ a somersault? No, she's doing a cartwheel.

f ______________________ a handstand? Yes.

4 Look and write. 5 marks

1 It's a _ _ _ _ _ _ _ _ _ _

2 It's an _ _ _ _ _ _

3 It's a _ _ _ _

4 It's a _ _ _ _

5 It's a _ _ _ _

Term 1 Test A

1 Look and write. 5 marks

magazine belt ~~cap~~ pillow sleeping bag scarf

1 This is a _cap_ ________.

2 This is a ____________.

3 This ____________.

4 ____________.

5 ____________.

6 ____________.

2 Look and read. Write *true* or *false*. 5 marks

1 Jo's wearing a coat. _false_

2 She's wearing a cap and sunglasses. ________

3 The sweets are in front of the pyjamas. ________

4 The gloves are next to the comb. ________

5 The comb is next to the pyjamas. ________

6 Jo's angry. ________

Term 1 Test B

1 Look and write. 5 marks

football dress ~~tracksuit~~ toothbrush teddy shirt

1 This is a tracksuit.
2 This is a ______.
3 This ______.
4 ______.
5 ______.
6 ______.

2 Look and read. Write *true* or *false*. 5 marks

1 Jon's wearing a shirt. false
2 He's wearing a tracksuit and trainers. ______
3 The glasses are in front of the watch. ______
4 The pyjamas are next to the torch. ______
5 The towel is next to the watch. ______
6 Jon's sad. ______

Term 2 Test A

1 Look and write. 5 marks

1

ishf

fish

2

srrwbestriae

______

3

yfl

______

4

acr rapk

______

5

sisutbci

______

6

suratenart

______

2 Look and read. Write *true* or *false*. 5 marks

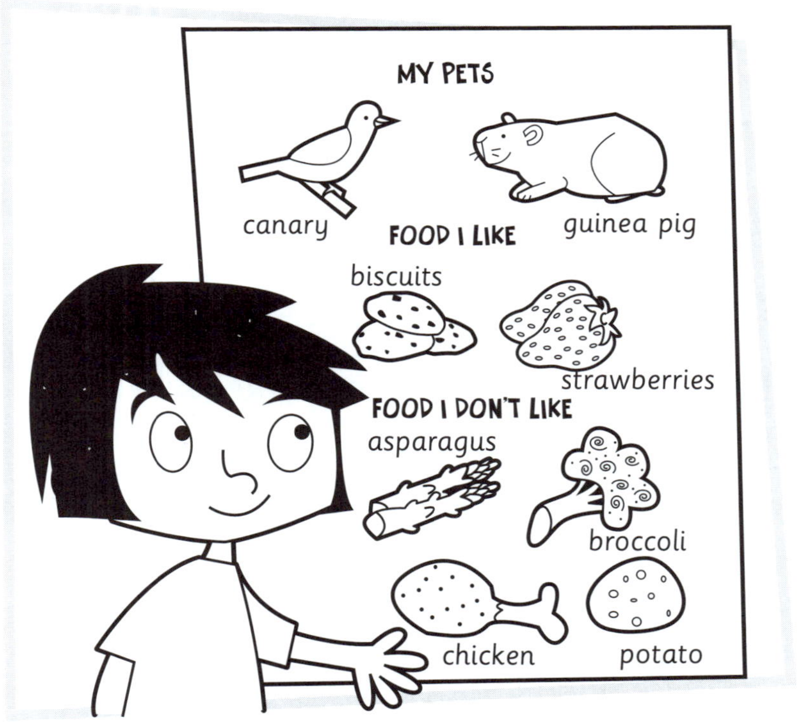

1 She likes biscuits. true

2 She hasn't got a tortoise. ______

3 She likes broccoli. ______

4 She likes strawberries. ______

5 She's got a lizard. ______

6 She's got a guinea pig. ______

Term 2 Test B

1 Look and write. 5 marks

1

ksane

snake

2
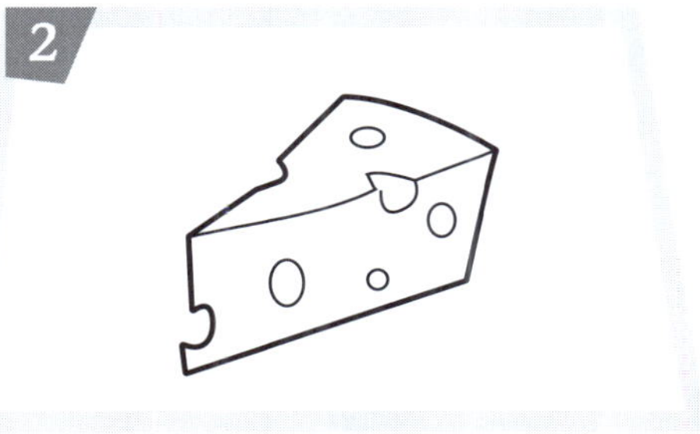

escehe

______

3

ilnas

______

4
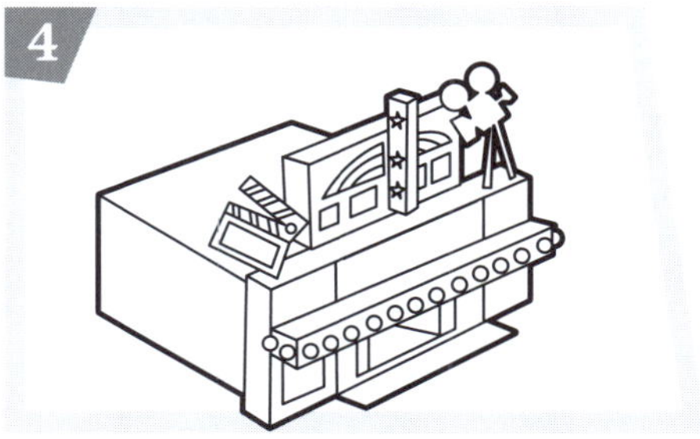

mecnia

______

5
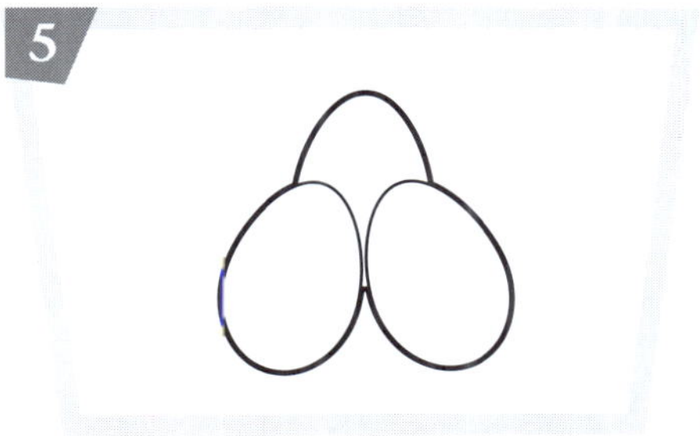

gesg

______

6

olhcos

______

2 Look and read. Write true or false. 5 marks

1 He likes spinach. true

2 He hasn't got a guinea pig. ______

3 He likes cheese. ______

4 He likes asparagus. ______

5 He's got a stick insect. ______

6 He's got a tortoise. ______

Term 3 Test A

1 Look and write. 5 marks

babtsalkel holcos zetepar netnsi duoj ~~tsilst~~

1 They're walking on stilts.
2 They're doing ________.
3 They're going to ________.
4 They're playing ________.
5 They're playing ________.
6 They're swinging on a ________.

2 Look and read. Write *true* or *false*. 5 marks

1 They're walking on stilts. false
2 He has breakfast at 7 o'clock. ________
3 She's doing a somersault. ________
4 They're playing hockey. ________
5 He goes to work at 6 o'clock. ________
6 They're playing chess. ________

Term 3 Test B

1 Look and write. 5 marks

cehoky sehcs herso mondatinb snytsgimac ~~gijugnl~~

1 They're juggling.

2 They're doing ________.

3 They're playing ________.

4 They're playing ________.

5 They're playing ________.

6 They're riding a ________.

2 Look and read. Write *yes* or *no*. 5 marks

1 They're swinging on a trapeze. no

2 She goes to work at 9 o'clock. ________

3 Is he doing a somersault? ________

4 They're playing hockey. ________

5 She goes to school at 6 o'clock. ________

6 They're playing football. ________

Term 1 Listening Test

Listen and tick (✔) the box. 3.43 **5 marks**

1 Where are Jo's glasses?

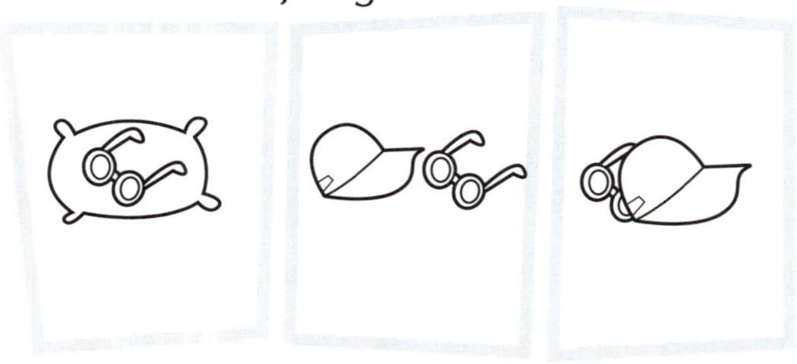

A ☐ B ☑ C ☐

2 Which is Sam's family?

A ☐ B ☐ C ☐

3 What time is it?

A ☐ B ☐ C ☐

4 What's in Tom's bag?

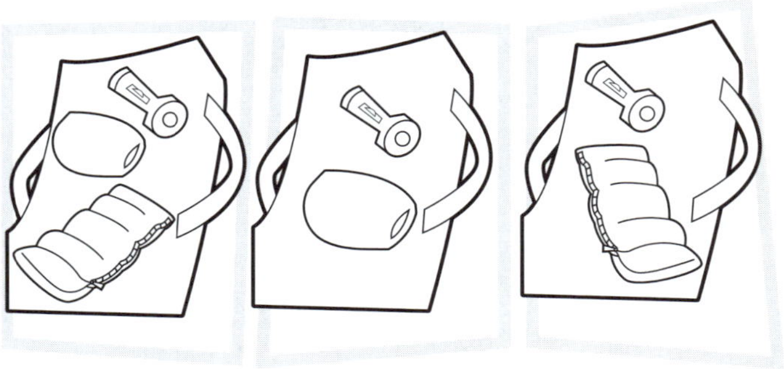

A ☐ B ☐ C ☐

5 Where are Ben's trainers?

A ☐ B ☐ C ☐

6 What's Sid got in his bag?

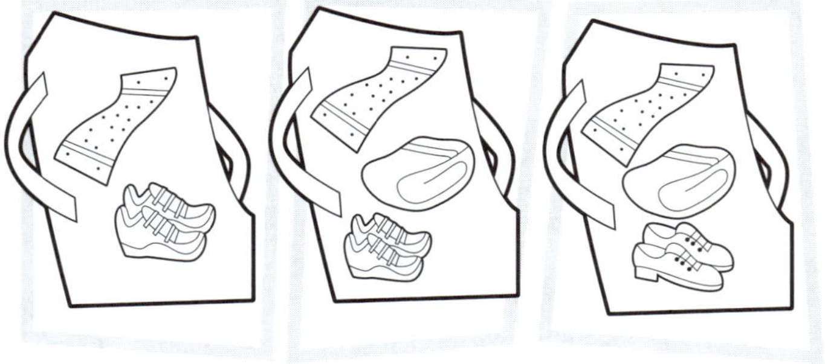

A ☐ B ☐ C ☐

Term 2 Listening Test

Listen and tick (✔) the box. 3.44 **5 marks**

1 What's in the wood?

A ☐ B ☐ C ✔

2 What's in Ben's town?

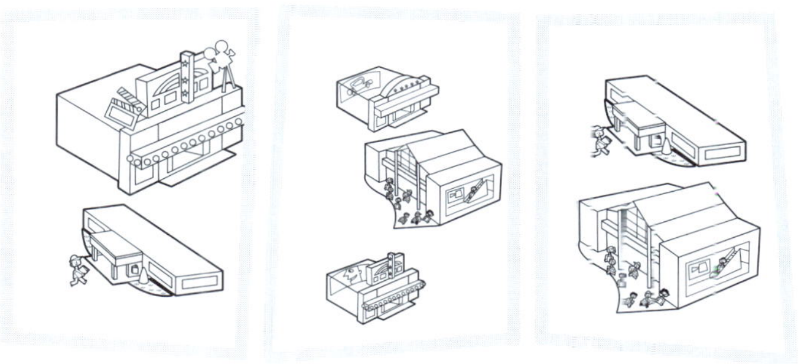

A ☐ B ☐ C ☐

3 Which is Jo's shopping?

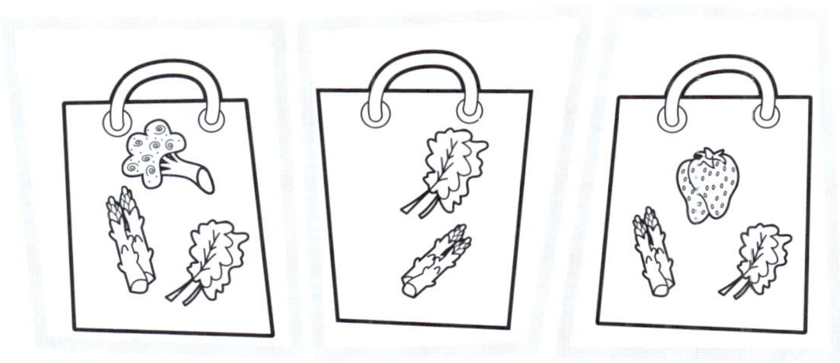

A ☐ B ☐ C ☐

4 Which is Tom's pet?

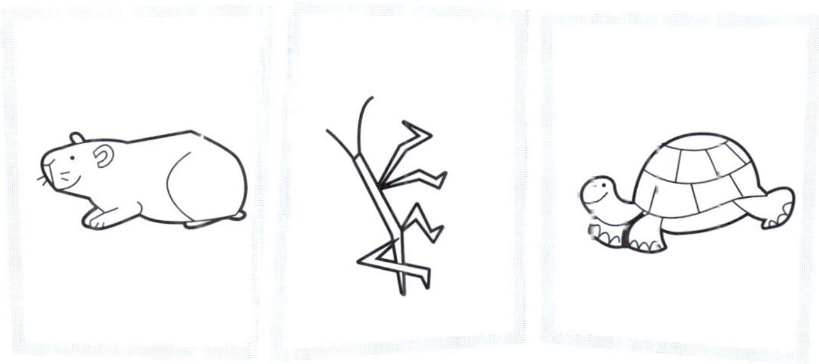

A ☐ B ☐ C ☐

5 Which is Jill's bag?

A ☐ B ☐ C ☐

6 Which is Nick's town?

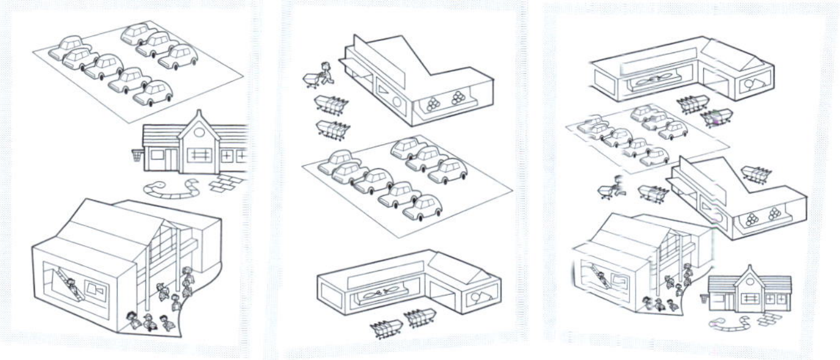

A ☐ B ☐ C ☐

Term 3 Listening Test

Listen and tick (✔) the box. 3.45 **5 marks**

1 What does Bill play?

A ✔ B ☐ C ☐

2 Which is Emma's dad?

A ☐ B ☐ C ☐

3 What's Tom doing?

A ☐ B ☐ C ☐

4 When does Sid go to school?

A ☐ B ☐ C ☐

5 What are the clowns doing?

A ☐ B ☐ C ☐

6 What's Beth doing?

A ☐ B ☐ C ☐

Record card: Linguistic objectives (Units 1–9)

Name of pupil: ....

	Needs a lot of help	Needs some help	Target achieved	Test score
Unit 1				
Unit 2				
Unit 3				
Term 1 test				
Unit 4				
Unit 5				
Unit 6				
Term 2 test				
Unit 7				
Unit 8				
Unit 9				
Term 3 test				

Tick the relevant column for the pupil's level of achievement in each unit. In addition, you may like to use the following key to indicate in which areas the pupil still needs help:

V = vocabulary   L = listening   S = speaking   R = reading   W = writing

Use the 'Test score' column to keep a record of each pupil's scores for the unit tests and term tests.

Portfolio

What is a language portfolio?

The aim of creating a language portfolio with your pupils is to promote the learning of languages in general, and to record and validate all their linguistic abilities and language learning experiences (including those from outside the classroom).

The European Language Portfolio

The Council of Europe is promoting the use of the 'European Language Portfolio', a three-part portfolio which has the aim of encouraging lifelong language learning, providing a record of linguistic skills that is internationally recognized, and promoting tolerance and cultural awareness through learning other languages. The intention is that each student has their own personal Portfolio that will accompany them throughout their learning experience. The European Language Portfolio is divided into the following sections:

Passport

The Passport section provides an overview of each student's ability in a language or languages. It includes self-evaluation and teacher assessment as well as any certificates a student may have received or records of courses they have completed.

Biography

The Biography section allows the student to reflect upon and assess his or her progress. It encourages the student to think about what he / she can do in the language.

Dossier

The Dossier contains selected pieces of work which illustrate the student's achievements, abilities, and experiences, as recorded in the Biography or Passport.

What is the *Incredible English* Portfolio?

The idea of the *Incredible English* Portfolio is to raise awareness of the existence of the European Language Portfolio and to prepare children to use future portfolios in the secondary education system. It is a useful tool for teachers in future years as it allows them to see what each child has studied so far. It is also extremely motivating as it gives children the opportunity to be responsible for their own learning as they indicate what they can do in English and decide autonomously what work to include in their Portfolio.

The *Incredible English* Portfolio does not aim to exactly match the structure of the European Language Portfolio, but instead takes the elements from it which are most relevant for children of this age.

Each child's personalized *Incredible English* Portfolio might consist of a selection of the following, stored together in a designated file, folder, or box:

Passport / Biography section:

- Photocopies of pages 219–221 (*My English*), completed at the end of each term
- A photocopy of the certificate for Level 3 (p222)
- Completed unit and term tests
- Certificates of any external exams pupils have sat, e.g. UCLES 'Starters / Movers' exam

Dossier section:

- Posters, projects, displays, etc. which the pupils have done throughout the course (e.g. the Lesson 11 'Learning through English' mini projects)
- Photocopies of completed pages from the Activity Book and / or the Photocopy Masters Book
- Cassette or video recordings of pupils singing songs or acting out stories, e.g. performing the Lesson 6 playscripts
- Other (see 'Further ideas' below)

The *Incredible English* Portfolio can be included in the classroom routine as much or as little as you choose. A good point to start working on the Portfolio would be towards the end of the first term, when you can explain to the pupils what a language portfolio is, let them make the cover pages and complete the first *My English* page (see below), and tell them that they will be responsible for choosing which pieces of work they would like to include in the Dossier section (they can choose the pieces of work which they are most proud of, which they have most enjoyed doing, or which they think would be most interesting to other people).

Parents should be encouraged to support their children's language learning by helping them collect items for their Portfolio or making suggestions about what pieces of work to include in the Dossier section.

The *Incredible English* Portfolio for Level 3 contains the following material:

Portfolio cover

This can be found on page 218. Pupils fill this in and stick it on the cover of the file, folder, or box that they are going to use for their *Incredible English* Portfolio. They can also stick on a photo or a drawing of themselves.

My English pages

These can be found on pages 219–221 (one page for every three units). These summary / self-evaluation pages are intended to be completed at the end of each term, and are divided into three sections: *My words*, *My sentences*, and *My work*.

My words

Pupils tick the boxes and colour the pictures to indicate which vocabulary sets they have studied, and then complete the self-evaluation line to say how many of the words they can remember (go through the language with them for this first).

My sentences

Pupils tick the boxes to indicate which language functions they are able to perform. Go through the 'I can' statements with the pupils first to make sure they understand them, and help them as necessary by reminding them of the language from the relevant units and writing examples on the board.

My work

Pupils tick the boxes to say which items they have made. The blank line can be used to write any additional items or projects that they have completed (e.g. any of the optional extra 'Learning through English' worksheets from the PMB, or any of the festivals projects from PMB pp50–52). If pupils have chosen to include any of these items in the Dossier section of their Portfolio, they can draw or stick a star next to the item to indicate this. (It will be very motivating for pupils if you can provide them with gold star stickers to use for this section.)

The items listed are taken from the following sections of the course:

(Units 1–3)

Picture / word cards (Units 1–3, PMB pp4–5, 10, 15)
A leaflet (Unit 1, PMB p7)
A clock (Unit 1, PMB p8)
A menu (Unit 2, PMB p12)
A portrait (Unit 2, PMB p13)
A certificate (Unit 3, PMB p17)
Animal music (Unit 3, PMB p18)
Children around the world (*My flag*, PMB p53)

(Units 4–6)

Picture / word cards (Units 4–6, PMB pp4, 20, 25, 30)
A postcard (Unit 4, PMB p22)
An insect (Unit 4, PMB p23)
A recipe (Unit 5, PMB p27)
A food mini-book (Unit 5, PMB p28)
A web page (Unit 6, PMB p32)
An island map / leaflet (Unit 6, PMB p33)
Children around the world (*My perfect town*, PMB p54)

(Units 7–9)

Picture / word cards (Units 7–9, PMB pp35, 40, 45)
A sign (Unit 7, PMB p37)
A picture of football fans (Unit 7, PMB p38)
An advertisement (Unit 8, PMB p42)
A project on electricity (Unit 8, PMB p43)
A poster (Unit 9, PMB p47)
A circus figure (Unit 9, PMB p48)
Children around the world (*Sport in my country*, PMB p55)

Certificate

This can be found on page 222. At the end of the year, the teacher signs the certificate to say the pupil has completed the level. Each pupil then ticks the box for their favourite unit, and signs the certificate.

What does the Dossier contain?

It is important that pupils understand that they make the choice of which pieces of work to include in their personal Dossier. They can choose the pieces of work which they are most proud of, which they have most enjoyed doing, or which they think would be most interesting to other people. In addition to the *My work* items suggested on the *My English* pages, pupils may like to include photocopies of their favourite pages from the Activity Book (e.g. the *Show what you know!* pages from each unit, or any other writing or drawing activities), and video or cassette recordings of themselves singing songs or doing role-plays from the course (e.g. acting out the Lesson 6 playscripts).

Further ideas

English language learning is not restricted to the classroom, and as part of the Portfolio's aim to foster positive attitudes towards other cultures, pupils should be encouraged to notice any examples of English language and culture around them. Pupils can collect (or photocopy) comics, food packaging, CD and DVD covers, stamps, tickets, postcards, song lyrics, etc. and keep them in their Portfolio folder or box. Alternatively, you could create an 'English corner' in the classroom where such objects could be displayed for the whole class to see.

Pupils can also write (in L1) about their experiences with English, e.g. listing any projects they have done, performances of plays, courses attended (including after-school classes and summer schools), details of trips to English-speaking countries, communication with / exchanges with pen pals, and simply a list of English-speaking people they know. They can illustrate their work with pictures of their experiences.

Encourage pupils to take pride in their Portfolios, and to regularly go through the Dossier section, tidying and organizing it, and adding work as necessary to keep it updated. Encourage them to show their Portfolios to friends, family, and other teachers in the school, and remind them that is a valuable record of their achievements in English. Fostering early pride and motivation in this way will encourage pupils to continue learning and using English (and other languages) throughout their lives.

INCREDIBLE ENGLISH 3

My English Language Portfolio

Stick your photo here

Name ______________________

Age ______________________

Class ______________________

School ______________________

Teacher ______________________

My English (Units 1–3)

My words

I can say words for:

 My things ☐

 Time words ☐

 Clothes ☐

 Describing people ☐

 Camping things ☐

 Describing music ☐

I can remember: some of the words. ☐ ★

most of the words. ☐ ★ ★

all of the words. ☐ ★ ★ ★

My sentences

I can …

ask where things are ☐
Where are my glasses?

say where things are ☐
The glasses are next to the bag.

tell the time ☐
It's half past two.

say who things belong to ☐
This is Luke's CD.

ask what colour things are ☐
What colour are her shoes?

ask what someone has got ☐
Have you got a torch?

say what I haven't got ☐
I haven't got any pyjamas.

My work

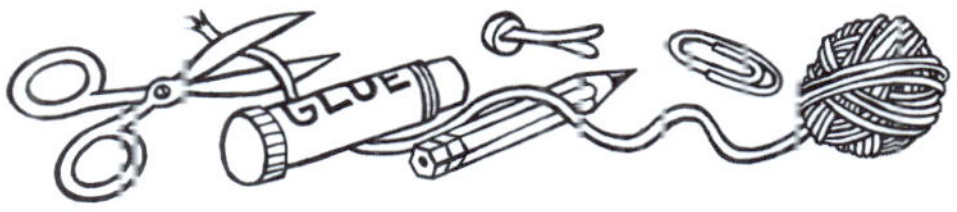

I have made:

Picture / word cards ☐

A leaflet ☐

A clock ☐

A menu ☐

A portrait ☐

A certificate ☐

Animal music ☐

Children around the world *(My flag)* ☐

______________________ ☐

★ = **my best work (look in my dossier)**

My English (Units 4–6)

My words

I can say words for:

 Animals ☐

 Insects ☐

 Food ☐

 Parts of a plant ☐

 Places in a town ☐

 Places in the countryside ☐

I can remember: some of the words. ☐ ★

most of the words. ☐ ★★

all of the words. ☐ ★★★

My sentences

I can …

ask what pets someone has got ☐
Has he got a guinea pig?

say what pets someone has / hasn't got ☐
She hasn't got a lizard.

ask what someone likes ☐
Does he like marbles?

say what someone likes ☐
He likes strawberries.

say what someone doesn't like ☐
She doesn't like cocoa.

describe a place ☐
There's a … / There are …

ask about a place ☐
Is there an airport?

My work

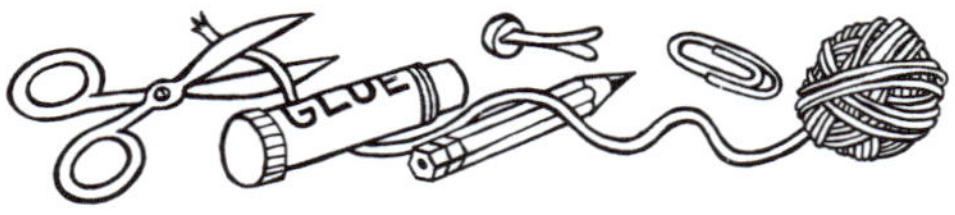

I have made:

A postcard ☐

An insect ☐

A recipe ☐

A food mini-book ☐

A web page ☐

An island map / leaflet ☐

Children around the world ☐
(My perfect town)

______________________ ☐

★ = **my best work (look in my dossier)**

My English (Units 7–9)

My words

I can say words for:

 Sports and activities ☐

 Things for football fans ☐

 Daily routines ☐

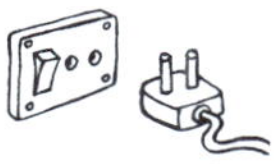 Electrical components ☐

 Circus actions ☐

 Parts of the body ☐

I can remember:

some of the words. ☐ ★

most of the words. ☐ ★★

all of the words. ☐ ★★★

My sentences

I can ...

ask what activities someone does ☐
Do you play chess?

say what activities I do ☐
I play tennis. / I don't do judo.

talk about someone's day ☐
He gets up at seven o'clock.

ask about someone's day ☐
What time does he leave work?

ask what someone is doing ☐
Is she walking on stilts?

say what is happening ☐
We're walking. / They're swimming.

My work

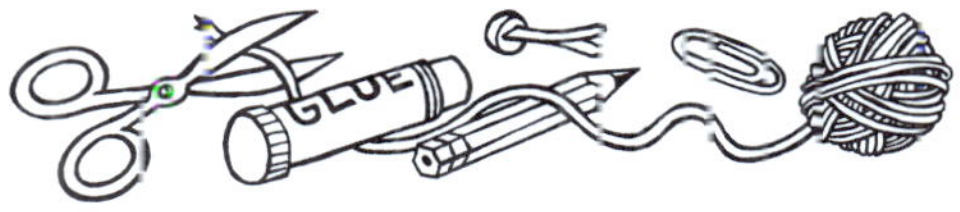

I have made:

Picture / word cards ☐

A sign ☐

A picture of football fans ☐

An advertisement ☐

A project on electricity ☐

A poster ☐

A circus figure ☐

Children around the world ☐
(Sport in my country)

____________________ ☐

★ = **my best work (look in my dossier)**

INCREDIBLE ENGLISH 3

This is to certify that

____

has completed the
***Incredible English* course (Level 3)**

Signed (teacher) ______________________________

My favourite unit was ...

Unit 1 ☐
Hello, kids!

Unit 2 ☐
Saturday morning

Unit 3 ☐
Camping

Unit 4 ☐
Looking at animals

Unit 5 ☐
At the supermarket

Unit 6 ☐
Our town

Unit 7 ☐
At the sports centre

Unit 8 ☐
Uncle Bill

Unit 9 ☐
The circus

Signed (pupil) ______________________________

Wordlist

This wordlist shows the core language items in **bold** and other language items (e.g. from songs and stories) in non-bold, and gives the unit where the word or phrase is first used. 'C' indicates the 'Children around the world' sections and 'F' indicates the Festivals sections.

a quarter of 7
abdomen 4
abstract 2
acrobat 9
address 4
adult 6
adventure 6
advert 8
afternoon 1
amazing 2
angry 2
ant 4
antennae 4
Are there any ...? 6
Are they ...? 1
around 8
asparagus 5
at school 1
autograph 2

badminton 7
bag 1
banana skin 6
baseball 7
basketball 7
battery 8
Be careful! 8
beach 6
bean 5
bear 3
beautiful 4
bee 4
belt 2
best 9
big hand / small hand (on a clock) 1
bin 6
birthday 5
biscuits 5
blanket 3
board game 1
book 3
boring 4
bottom half 2
bow F
bowl 5
breakfast 5
bridge 6
broccoli 5
building C
bulb 8
bus station 6
butter 5
butterfly 4
buy 5
buzz 8

Can I help you? 7
Can you spell that, please? 1
canary 4
cap 2
car park 6
cards 1
carry 1
castle C
cat 1
certificate 3
chameleon 4
change colour 4
cheap 8
cheese 5
chess 7
chop 5
cinema 6
circuit 8
class 7
clock 1
clown 9
clubhouse 3
coat 2
cocoa 5
coconut 5
coffee 2
comb 3
Come on! 7
congratulations 3
cool 8
coupon F
crawl 4
cross (v) 6
cross (n) C

decide 8
delicious 5
digital 1
do a cartwheel 9
do a handstand 9
do a headstand 9
do a somersault 9
Do you play /do ...? 7
Does he / she like ...? 5
dog sledding C
Don't forget ... 3
dragon C
dragonfly 4
drawing 2
dress 2
drink (n) 1
drive 6
drop 6
drum 7

eggs 5
elbow 9
electronics 8
energy 2
enormous 6
evening 1
everyone 1
everything 3
Excuse me? 6

face (on a clock) 1
fall 9
farm 7
fast 3
Father Christmas F
field 4
fish 4
flag 7
flour 5
flower 5
fly (n) 4
foot 9
football (object) 1
football (game) 7
fork 5
free 7
frog 1
fruit 5

get up 8
glass 5
glasses 1
gloves 2
gnome 8
Go away! 1
go to bed 8
go to school / work 8
grass 4
grasshopper 4
guinea pig 4
gymnastics 7

half of 7
half past (six) 1
hand 9
happy 2
Happy Birthday! 5
Has he / she got ...? 4
hat 7
have a shower 8
have breakfast 8
have dinner 8
have fun 1
have lunch 8
Have you got a / any ...? 3

He / she has / hasn't got ... 4
He / she likes / doesn't like ... 5
head 9
hedge 7
her 2
Here are you. 2
high 3
hip 9
his 2
hockey 7
hold 4
hole 7
hook 3
hour 1
Hurry up! 4

I haven't got a / my / any ... 3
I play / don't play ... 7
in 1
in bed 1
inventor 8
Is there a ...? 6
island 6
It's on the (twenty-third of October). 0

Japan C
Japanese C
jar 5
join 1
judo 7
juggle 9
jungle 4
just right 8

key (to map) 6
knee 9

label F
ladder 7
ladybird 4
lamp 4
late 6
laugh 9
lay eggs 4
leaf 5
leaflet 2
leave school / work 8
less F
Let me see. 7
library 6
lizard 4
Look out! 5